CLARENDON ANCIENT HISTORY SERIES

The aim of the CLARENDON ANCIENT HISTORY SERIES is to provide authoritative translations, introductions, and commentaries to a wide range of Greek and Latin texts studied by ancient historians. The books will be of interest to scholars, graduate students, and advanced undergraduates.

DIDYMOS
on Demosthenes

Introduction, Text, Translation,
and Commentary
by

Phillip Harding

CLARENDON PRESS · OXFORD

OXFORD
UNIVERSITY PRESS

Great Clarendon Street, Oxford OX2 6DP

Oxford University Press is a department of the University of Oxford.
It furthers the University's objective of excellence in research, scholarship,
and education by publishing worldwide in

Oxford New York

Auckland Cape Town Dar es Salaam Hong Kong Karachi
Kuala Lumpur Madrid Melbourne Mexico City Nairobi
New Delhi Shanghai Taipei Toronto

With offices in

Argentina Austria Brazil Chile Czech Republic France Greece
Guatemala Hungary Italy Japan South Korea Poland Portugal
Singapore Switzerland Thailand Turkey Ukraine Vietnam

Published in the United States
by Oxford University Press Inc., New York

British Library Cataloguing in Publication Data

Data available

Library of Congress Cataloging-in-Publication Data

Data available

Typeset by Regent Typesetting, London
Printed in Great Britain
on acid-free paper by
Biddles Ltd., King's Lynn

ISBN 0–19–815043–1   978–0–19–815043–5
ISBN 0–19–928359–1 (Pbk.)   978–0–19–928359–0 (Pbk.)

1 3 5 7 9 10 8 6 4 2

PREFACE

Work on this book began almost a decade ago. The original plan was to produce a volume consistent with others in the Clarendon Ancient History Series: a translation, with introduction and commentary, of the fragmentary papyrus that contained Didymos' work *On Demosthenes*. At the time there was no translation of the entire papyrus, though I had rendered some parts in *From the End of the Peloponnesian War to the Battle of Ipsus* (Cambridge, 1985) and *Androtion and the* Atthis (Oxford, 1994), and there never had been an attempt at a complete commentary, either of the text or its historical context. Furthermore, although there was a fairly recent new edition of the text by Pearson and Stephens (Stuttgart, 1983), sufficient dissatisfaction had been found with it—especially by Wankel (1987)—to warrant a fresh new look at the papyrus. The idea was to include any resultant text as an appendix at the end of the book. Then, as so often happens in academic life, administrative responsibilities intervened.

But the resultant delay has a positive side. In the meantime several studies of individual topics related to the papyrus and its contents have appeared, by which my own thoughts were either confirmed or challenged. In particular, Craig Gibson's study of the ancient commentators on Demosthenes, *Interpreting a Classic* (Berkeley, Los Angeles, and London, 2002), forced me to rethink many issues. My work has been able to benefit from the insights and contributions of all these scholars. Nevertheless, in both focus and scope it is distinctive.

First, it provides a new text, which now accompanies the translation in a face-to-face format. Such a combination is unavailable elsewhere. This text is based upon my own study of the papyrus. Whilst I would not claim any greater expertise in palaeography than the great scholars who have preceded me, I felt there was value in taking a fresh look with new eyes. As I did so, I found myself not infrequently unable to substantiate the readings of the most recent editors and quite unwilling to accept many of their very speculative restorations. In fact, those who compare my text with earlier editions will find that it is closer to that of Diels and Schubart and more conservative than Pearson and Stephens'.

Next, the translation sets out to replicate the state of the text, using square and round brackets to indicate restored or partially restored words. This may be less attractive to read than one that conceals the textual difficulties, but it is hoped that it will be more useful to serious students of ancient history who lack Greek in that it will not mislead them into thinking that there is more certainty about what can be read than is the case. The facing text will enable readers with Greek to check the translation for themselves.

Finally, the commentary is both textual and historical, much as would be expected for an epigraphic publication. In the case of the text, I have tried to discuss most serious attempts at recreating or restoring what Didymos wrote, in essence translating and interpreting the apparatus criticus, even when I had to guess what motivated a given scholar to put forward the proposal he made. The discussion of the historical context of Didymos' comments is as complete as I could make it. No doubt some will find something missing, but I hope that will not be the case too often.

I owe an apology to the editors of the Oxford University Press for the long delay in finishing this work and many thanks for their patience. The careful work of the staff at OUP, particularly Enid Barker and Susan Milligan, has helped bring some consistency to a difficult text. I feel an especial debt to Brian Bosworth, who took time from his own busy schedule to read the whole typescript and to offer many useful suggestions for improvement. But the greatest gratitude is to my wife, who has stood by my side throughout my whole academic career. She alone knows what that has meant. *Nunc pede libero pulsanda tellus.*

Vancouver, 2004   P. H.

CONTENTS

ILLUSTRATIONS

ABBREVIATIONS

Jacoby, *Notes*	F. Jacoby, *Die Fragmente der griechischen Historiker*, vol. 3b Suppl. 2 (Leiden, 1954)
Kirchner, *PA*	J. Kirchner, *Prosopographia Attica* (Berlin, 1901–3)
LGPN	M. J. Osborne and S. G. Byrne (eds.), *A Lexicon of Greek Personal Names*, vol. ii, *Attica* (Oxford, 1994)
LSJ	*A Greek–English Lexicon*, compiled by H. G. Liddell and R. Scott, revised by H. S. Jones (Oxford, 1968)
OCD	S. Hornblower and A. Spawforth (eds.), *The Oxford Classical Dictionary*, 3rd edn. (Oxford and New York, 1996)
Osborne	K. T. Osborne, *The* Peri Demosthenous *of Didymos Grammatikos*, doctoral dissertation, University of Washington (Seattle, 1990)
PCG	R. Kassel and C. Austin (eds.), *Poetae Comici Graeci* (Berlin, 1983–)
P-S	L. Pearson and S. Stephens (eds.), *Didymi in Demosthenem Commenta* (Stuttgart, 1983)
RE	*Real-Encyclopädie der klassischen Altertumswissenschaft*, eds. Pauly, Wissowa, Kroll (Mittelhaus, 1893–)
SEG	*Supplementum Epigraphicum Graecum*
SIG[3]	W. Dittenberger (ed.), *Sylloge Inscriptionum Graecarum*, 3rd edn. (Leipzig, 1915–21)
Souda	A. Adler (ed.), *Suidae Lexicon*, 4 vols. (Leipzig, 1928–35)
Tod	M. N. Tod, *A Selection of Greek Inscriptions*, vol. 2 (Oxford, 1948)

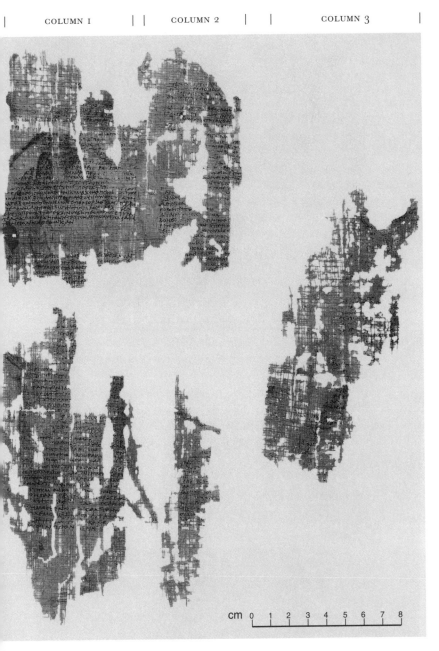

Fig. 1. The Papyrus: cols 1–3

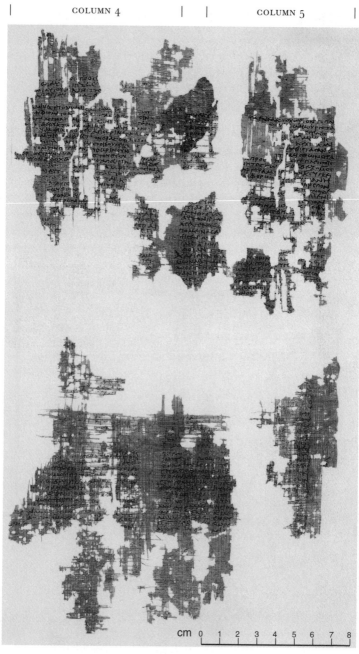

Fig. 2. The Papyrus: cols 4–5

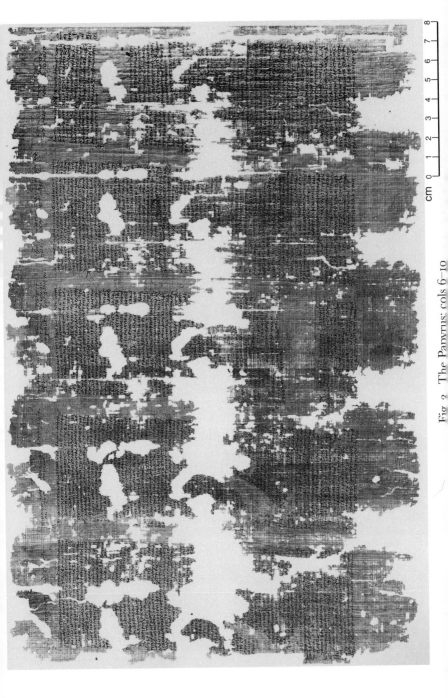

Fig. 2 The Papyrus: cols 6–10

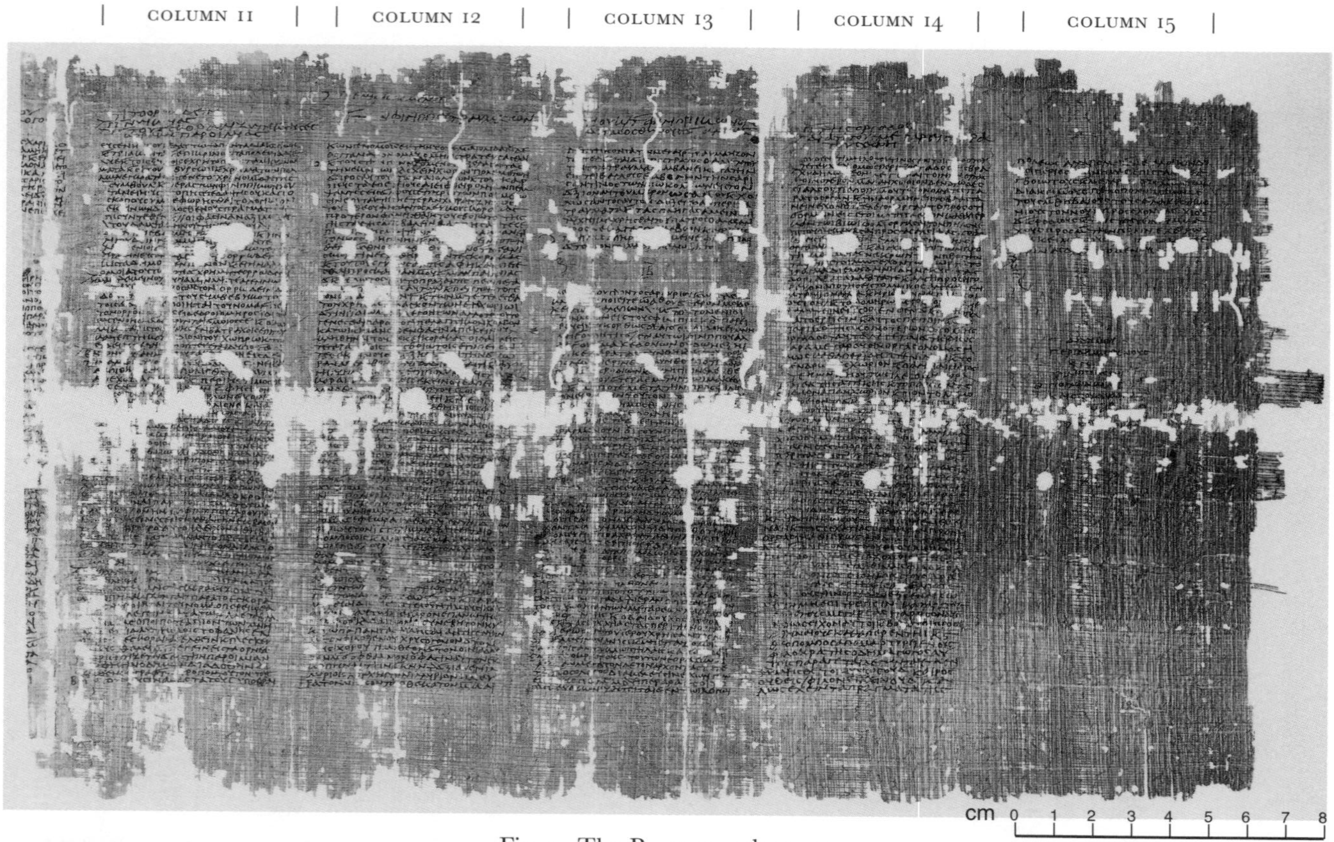

Fig. 4. The Papyrus: cols. 11–15

INTRODUCTION

I. DIDYMOS

That Didymos was the author of the papyrus text to which this volume is devoted is stated unequivocally in the subscript at its conclusion, where it is called Didymos' *On Demosthenes*. About this Didymos we know a great deal, not all of it complimentary. The uncontroversial testimony comes from the *Souda* (s.v. Didymos). There we learn that he was the son of Didymos, a salt-fish merchant; that he was an Alexandrian scholar, who followed in the tradition of Aristarchos, the scholar librarian of the second century BC (on whom see Pfeiffer (1968) 210ff.); that he flourished in the time of Antony and Cicero (i.e. in the second half of the first century BC) until the time of Augustus (i.e. at least into the first century after Christ); that he was nicknamed Khalkenteros ('he of brazen guts') for his tolerance of books, whether because of his indefatigable appetite for reading or his inexhaustible energy for writing them; finally that he was reputed to have composed 3,500 volumes.

Additional information is provided by other entries in the *Souda*, as well as by other sources. The *Souda* identifies the later scholars, Apion and Herakleides Pontikos, as students and assistants of Didymos, in entries under their names. It also (s.v. Iobas) reaffirms his date by making him the contemporary of Juba, the historian king of Mauretania, who died in 23 AD, and indicates that they had some scholarly disagreements. Athenaios confirms the number of his publications (*Deipnosophistai* 4.139c) and reveals another nickname—Bibliolathas ('book forgetter'), for which he cites the authority of the obscure Demetrios of Troizen. Quintilian (*Institutio Oratoria* 1.8.20) provides a probable context. The report was that once he was caught condemning a story as false that he had already included in an earlier publication. In other words his production was so great that he could not remember what he had written from one book to the next. This would not be surprising, if he really produced 3,500 volumes, and even less so, if the number was closer to 4,000, as was claimed by Seneca, the philosopher (*Ep.* 88.37).

The prodigious output attributed to Didymos is not impossible, but would have required his writing about a hundred volumes, like the one represented by our papyrus, each year of a thirty-five to forty year career (i.e. based on the completely unverifiable assumption that he began writing at age thirty and did not live beyond seventy). That works out at about two books a week. In doing this, Didymos surely worked largely from memory, but he will also have used notes, culled from his extensive reading. Like anyone else's notes, his will sometimes have included verbatim quotations from his sources, sometimes a reference to a specific passage, and on other occasions the barest indication that someone had said something somewhere. It was, no doubt, left to his students to track down these references, since while Didymos was a veritable fountain house of learning, he could not have achieved all this by himself. A host of students, of whom Apion and Herakleides were but two, would have been needed to check references and proofread, whilst others were busy copying what he dictated (see Foucart (1909): 31–6). In short, Didymos was the very epitome of the sort of scholar modern university administrations seem to desire, both for his productivity and for the number of graduate students he supported.

But there are, as everyone knows, those who disapprove of this sort of scholarship and the nicknames that were attached to Didymos make it quite clear that not all his contemporaries were impressed by his methods (see Seneca, *Ep.* 88. 37), and for good reason. As has already been mentioned, Didymos himself could make mistakes and it stands to reason that his students could also. It is probably the case, given his incredible rate of production, that he had little or no chance to review a volume, after it had left his study. In fact, this was an inevitable consequence of publication in antiquity (Potter (1999): 29–35). So it depended upon the diligence of his students whether his citations were accurate or not or even, in some cases, whether they were found at all (West (1970): 293–4). Examples of such defects and deficiencies in Didymos' scholarship will be found throughout our papyrus.

Despite this, later grammarians had the greatest respect for Didymos. Macrobius, for example, called him 'the most learned of all scholars' (*Saturnalia* 5.18.9) and 'the most instructive of all scholars past or present' (5.22.10), whilst the *Souda* refers to him as 'the great' (s.v. Apion) or 'the greatest in Alexandria' (s.v. Herakleides Pontikos). Nowhere is the ambivalence towards him shown better than in Harpokration's *Lexikon of the Ten Orators*. Numerous references show that Harpokration made great use of Didymos' work and yet he disagreed with his ideas or criticized his judgement frequently (see Cohn, *RE* 5 [1903] s.v. Didymos: 458–60; Gibson: 43–4).

The extent of Didymos' energy was matched only by the breadth of his interests. We have more than fifty titles (Schmidt (1854): 11–14), many of which will, of course, have been multi-volumed. The *On Demosthenes*, for example, may have been twenty-eight books long (on this problem, see below). His works can be arranged in a variety of ways, but the sample of titles given under the following four headings should suffice as a demonstration.

1. *Syngrammata,* monographs on particular topics: *On Aristarchos' Rescension of Homer; On the Lyric Poets; On Proverbs; On Orthography; On the Axones of Solon.*

2. *Hypomnemata,* running commentaries on marked texts of specific authors: the list here is huge and includes all the best known, and many of the less well known, authors of Greek literature in verse, e.g. Homer, Hesiod, Pindar, Bakkhylides, Aiskhylos, Sophokles, Euripides, Aristophanes, and Menander—and prose, e.g. Thucydides and most of the Attic orators.

3. Lexicographical works: especially his *Lexeis tragikai* ('tragic terms') and *Lexeis komikai* ('comic terms').

4. Finally, there are assorted works of no particular category, like the *Symmikta symposiaka (Miscellany of Party-pieces)*.

In short, Didymos' works ranged over a vast field from grammar and lexicography through literary and historical criticism to textual studies, antiquities, proverbs, and anecdotes. His influence on the later scholarly tradition was considerable. Many of the scholia on Homer, Pindar, Sophokles, and Aristophanes go back to him; his lexicographical books were much used by later lexicographers and his *On Proverbs* was a primary source for the collections of proverbs. By contrast, the scholia on the orators show few signs of his influence, largely because the interest in rhetorical terms and techniques overwhelmed the earlier interest in history and philology that he represented.

Despite his huge output, however, no complete or even near complete work by Didymos survived from antiquity and we were compelled to judge him through the citations in these later sources. The general opinion that was held of him, before the discovery of our papyrus, was of an unoriginal scholar, who compiled the works of his predecessors. It was felt that he was to be applauded for preserving and passing on to us a great deal of Alexandrian scholarship that would otherwise have been lost, but that, whenever he expressed his own opinion, it was either wrong, uncritical, or just plain silly (Cohn, *RE* 5 [1903] s.v. Didymos: 446). The discovery of the papyrus *On Demosthenes* at the beginning of this century was, consequently, greeted with considerable excitement, since it provided an opportunity to examine these assumptions.

2. THE PAPYRUS

The papyrus that contains Didymos' *On Demosthenes* was purchased from an antiquities dealer in Cairo in 1901. The purchaser was able to ascertain that it came from the ruins of a house on the site of ancient Hermoupolis (el-Ashmunein), which is located approximately 250 km up the Nile from Cairo; no further information was forthcoming. It was brought to Berlin, where it is presently preserved in the Bode Museum as *P. Berol.* 9780; in fact the best preserved part of it (cols. 6–15) was on display in the papyrus exhibit there when I visited in 1995.

The papyrus was, of course, rolled up; as a result the outer layers had suffered damage. When unrolled, it was found that there was writing on both sides (the term for such a text is opisthographic). On the recto, the inside (with the fibres of papyrus running horizontally), the roll contained Didymos' *On Demosthenes*; on the verso, the outside (with the fibres running vertically), was the *Elements of Ethics* of the Stoic philosopher, Hierokles, who flourished in the time of the emperor Hadrian (*OCD* s.v. Hierokles). The *On Demosthenes* and the *Elements* were written in opposite directions to one another. Thus, when the outer layers of the roll were damaged, it was the beginning of the *On Demosthenes* that suffered, whilst the end of Hierokles' treatise was lost. The publication of the text of the philosophical work was entrusted to H. von Arnim and appeared as *Berliner Klassikertexte* 4, 1906. Herman Diels and Wilhelm Schubart took charge of the *On Demosthenes* and published two versions of it, both in 1904. The first to appear was the more detailed edition, number 1 in the *Berliner Klassikertexte*. Subsequently, they produced a shorter version (sometimes referred to as the *editio minor*) in the Teubner series. These will be referred to respectively as D-S[1] and D-S[2] throughout this volume.

The remains of the papyrus roll measure 30 cm from top to bottom, and its length is *c.*134 cm. The text of Didymos is inscribed in fifteen columns, of which the first five are in a very fragmentary state (see above), while columns 6 to 15 (about 90 cm of papyrus) are more or less readable. In the early columns there were seventy or more lines of writing, but this decreased to little more than sixty near the end. Also, the early columns have more letters to the line, often forty or even more, while the number of letters to the line in the later columns ranges between twenty-five and thirty-five. Some columns also show a decrease in the length of line from top to bottom. Column 15 is only partially inscribed, but concludes with the important summation of the contents of the roll, the author's name and the title of the work that has already been referred to.

Most of the columns have a heading at the top that indicates the topic(s) that Didymos discussed in each. In fact, of those columns with a preserved top only cols. 5 and 15 do not, and in each case the reason is obvious: no new issue is raised in either. Column 5 continues the excursus on Hermias of Atarneus that begins in column 4 and runs over into column 6. Column 15 merely concludes a topic that had been raised in column 14. The handwriting of the headings is of a more sloppy appearance than the body of the text and is in a somewhat more pronounced cursive style. Whether they were written by the same hand in haste or by someone else is unfortunately a matter of subjective opinion. I incline to the belief that the differences do not preclude the possibility that they were by the same hand. This is not the case, however, with the instruction to the scribe that someone wrote above the heading to column 12. This is preceded by a sign like a backwards semicircle (*antisigma*), which reappears beside line 3 of the text, indicating the point where the correction is to be made. The instruction itself is fully cursive and was surely by a different hand. All these details are pertinent to a consideration of the questions, 'Who produced this text, for whom, why and when?' These will be discussed below.

The handwriting of the main text is not very elegant, though usually not difficult to read. The impression of inelegance is created by a number of factors: the irregularity of the letters in size and shape; the inconsistency in the slope of the letters, sometimes forward, sometimes back; the combination of capital letter forms of the 'school hand' (on which see Turner (1968): 89) with cursive shapes (particularly alpha, epsilon, and xi), while kappa, upsilon, and phi alternate between the capital and the cursive; the presence of the occasional ligature (especially epsilon and iota). In addition, the scribe employs a great number and variety of abbreviations (see the list in front of the Greek text), though unpredictably he will give the unabbreviated form on occasion. This habit can make restoration an even less precise endeavour than usual.

Equally inconsistent is his use of punctuation. A pair of dots, like the diaeresis, is frequently placed over an iota, though on no clear principle. Sometimes it is over a final iota (the deictic iota), sometimes over an initial one, sometimes over an iota in the middle of a word. It does not seem to matter whether the iota is aspirated or not, nor whether it is surrounded by vowels or consonants. He knows the colon, but is quite erratic in using it, sometimes not putting it where he should, on at least one occasion putting it where he should not (col. 6.13). He usually indicates a *lemma* from the text of Demosthenes with the *diple* (a marginal sign like a sideways V, i.e. >, on which see Turner (1968): 117), but sometimes forgets, and his intention to use the paragraphos (—) to mark off the beginning and end of a quotation from a secondary source is not always realized. The commentary is, however, quite consistently inset a letter space or two from the left-hand margin in relation to the *lemmata*. Finally, the iota subscript is normally written on the line and only missed a few times. There are no breathings or accents.

It may not be surprising to learn, then, that the whole text is marred by numerous errors. Some of these clearly resulted from carelessness on the part of the scribe and he corrected many of them himself. Several are attributable to iotacism, particularly the confusion of epsilon and iota for iota and vice versa. On about a dozen occasions he inserts a gratuitous epsilon before an iota (e.g. col. 6.5 *ANTIΠ[E]IΠTONTΩN*; col. 11.22 *[E]IΔEΔPOI*; col.11.26 *[E]IΔIEI*; col. 11.28, 33 *N[E]IKAIA*), on others he leaves out an epsilon from the diphthong epsilon iota (e.g. col. 13.52 *ΛAKPAT⟨E⟩IΔHΣ*). Sometimes he adds an unnecessary iota after another vowel (i.e. eta or alpha). There may also be another instance of iotacism in the instruction to the scribe above the heading of column 12 referred to earlier (Gibson (2000): 148). All these peculiarities of the text can be seen from the still invaluable transcription provided by Diels and Schubart on the left-hand pages of the *Berliner Klassikertexte* (D-S[1]). Other errors are more serious and obviously existed in the original, from which the scribe was copying, and may even be traced back to Didymos himself. This issue will be treated elsewhere and especially where appropriate in the Commentary.

One final point needs to be mentioned about the physical appearance of the text. The system of abbreviations used for writing numerals in this text is the one that was standard for Hellenistic scholars, namely the alphabetic system, in which A = 1, I = 10,

IA = 11, K = 20 and so on. It can be found laid out in any Greek grammar book (e.g. Smyth, pp. 102–4b). Our author, or the scribe, was in the habit of putting a bar over his numerals, as was commonly done. In one place, however, he failed to do so. This was over the numeral 28 in the subscript in column 15. Since this is a crucial numeral for deciding not only the length but also the form of the work we are dealing with, there has been a great deal of controversy about the absence of the bar over this numeral. The question of the length and form of Didymos' work will be dealt with separately, but I will go on record here as saying that the absence of the bar has no significance to it and must be an error (cf. P-S, p. vi). The only significance it could have is to distinguish between cardinal and ordinal numerals, but this distinction is not observed at any other point in the papyrus. In other words, throughout the text the bar is placed over cardinal and ordinal numerals alike without discrimination. Whilst it is an important issue whether the number 28 is a cardinal or an ordinal, a solution must be based upon other criteria

3. THE SCRIBE AND HIS WORK

Regarding the identity of the scribe who wrote this papyrus, we can say with confidence that he was clearly not Didymos himself. That is to say this is not the original that emanated from the scholar's workshop. Quite apart from the evidence for the date provided by the handwriting, which will be discussed below, there is material proof from the content. The scribe was able to correct his own scribal errors by reference to some other text, i.e. the one he was copying from. Whether that version was Didymos' original is not so easily answered. There are passages in our papyrus whose incoherence cannot be explained by scribal error (e.g. the text of Aristotle's paian to Hermias). The scribe found these corruptions in his exemplar. At one point (col. 8.54f.) a space of ten lines is left uninscribed, after a sentence that appears to be introducing a quotation. The text resumes with a new *lemma* from Demosthenes. The scribe had made no attempt to copy any part of the missing quotation. The logical conclusion is that there was no quotation for him to copy, i.e. it was missing from his exemplar. It is possible that these corruptions and omissions crept into the exemplar through the process of transmission over time, but it is equally likely, given Didymos' productivity, that they were there from the beginning (see West (1970):

293ff.). In that case, the exemplar could have been the original. On the whole, though, I find this hard to accept, in light of the evidence for the date (see below). I suspect that a combination of factors is at work: the missing passage may well go back to Didymos' original publication, but the other corruptions are the result of errors in transmission over a considerable period of time. In any case, it is safe to conclude that there was only one copy of the *On Demosthenes* available for the scribe to use and check his work against, since he could not look elsewhere to solve his problems with the corrupt passages.

It is also manifest that the scribe of the papyrus was not a professional. The lack of quality of his product shows that. So, it is most unlikely that the purpose of his copy was for selling; it was surely intended for private use. That being the case, we have to ask who wanted it. After all, while it is reasonable to expect educated Greeks, isolated at Oxyrhynchos or Hermoupolis, to have in their libraries original texts such as Homer or Plato or even Aristotle's *Constitution of the Athenians* or the *Hellenika Oxyrhynchia*, it is quite another thing to keep a scholarly monograph on one of those texts. Only a teacher or a student would need such a thing. So, it is reasonable to conclude that it was at some educational establishment that the papyrus was found. The teacher himself is hardly likely to have made this copy, both because of the poor quality of the writing and because he is probably the person who wrote the correction at the top of column 12. He might, however, have been dictating it, if this is when the instances of iotacism (an aural error) occurred. A student or a slave was presumably the scribe. Whether he did so for his own use or for his teacher's, we cannot tell, but I think we can rule out the possibility that it was simply an exercise in writing with no commitment to the content (see Turner (1968): 88–96). Another possibility, that the writer was excerpting entries from Didymos' original for his own purposes and according to his own interests (Gibson: 51–69), will be discussed below.

It remains to establish the date at which the Didymos text was written. In their initial study Diels and Schubart concluded that the appearance of the handwriting, combined with the other peculiarities of orthography, was consistent with a date in the first half of the second century after Christ; thus, about one hundred years after Didymos' time. The text of Hierokles' *Elements of Ethics* could not have been written at the same time, they felt, given his own dates, and probably belonged in the second half of that century (D-S[1],

p. xii). Later, in his publication of a selection of Greek papyri from Berlin, Schubart dated it somewhat earlier, at the end of the first or beginning of the second century after Christ (Schubart (1911): p. xviii). Only seven years after that, however, he had radically revised his opinion and now dated it to the end of the second or beginning of the third century, about two hundred years after Didymos (Schubart (1918): 163). He had also come to believe that it had been written at the same time as the text of Hierokles, but by a different hand (Schubart (1918): 147). That was still his opinion several years later in *Palaeographie* (Schubart (1925): 133–4), though the date was now definitely third century and he was prepared to entertain the possibility that both the Didymos and the Hierokles had been written by the same person ('mag hier ein Student oder Gelehrter von vornherein beide Schriften auf einer Rolle vereinigt haben?'). He based his opinion on the similarity that he saw in the orthography and system of abbreviations used in both texts.

But comparison of the two documents makes the last idea implausible. Whilst the features mentioned may be similar, the fact remains that the handwriting of the Hierokles is much neater in appearance and was surely the work of a more careful scribe. Anyone interested can now confirm this impression for themselves from the illustration in R. Seider's *Paläographie der Griechischen Papyri* (vol. ii, Plate XIX), where a page from each of the two is set side by side. Seider himself dates the Didymos to the beginning of the third century after Christ and the Hierokles to the middle of the same century (Seider (1970): 104–7). Only Pearson and Stephens in their edition of the text assign this work once again to the first part of the second century and the Hierokles to the end (P-S, p. iv; and see Wankel (1987): 214), but they offer no justification for these dates. Judging from the advanced cursive forms, I incline towards the higher date of late-second or even third century after Christ.

4. CONTENT

I think it might be useful at this point, following a suggestion by Rusten (Rusten (1987): 266), to present an outline of the content of the papyrus as it stands, *lemma* by *lemma*.

Speech 9 (*Third Philippic*)

1. 9.57? Column 1.1–25. This is the last entry on this speech and is very poorly preserved. The precise reference in the speech that is being commented on is not agreed upon, nor is the exact focus of Didymos' discussion clear. Most of what we have left, however, concerns the Athenian expeditions to Oreus and Eretria in Euboia in 342/1 and 341/0. In support of his argument (whatever it was) Didymos cites a passage from Demosthenes' speech *Against Ktesiphon /On the Crown* (18.79) and two passages from the *Atthis* of Philokhoros.

Speech 10 (*Fourth Philippic*)

2. 10.1. Column 1.25–col. 2? Where exactly this entry ends cannot be defined, because of the sorry state of columns 2 and 3, but it certainly continued on into column 2. It is clear, however, that the point of this note is to establish the date of the speech. In the course of his discussion Didymos refers to another passage in the same speech (10.17) and cites one or more passages from the *Atthis* of Philokhoros.

3. The Heading to column 2 lists four topics for that column. Three of these must have been completed within the column, the fourth surely carried over into column 3. It has proven difficult to identify the passages involved (see Commentary). They, and any other passages that Didymos commented on in column 3 (heading lost), must have preceded 10.32, the treatment of which begins at the latest at column 4.47. In the course of his discussion of the fourth topic Didymos cited a decree of the Amphiktyonic Council (*SIG*[3], no. 224)

4. 10.32. Column 4.47?–6.62. This is the longest entry in the text. It involves Hermias of Atarneus, especially the assessment of him by his contemporaries. In this section Didymos either cites or makes reference to works by Theopompos, Hermippos, Kallisthenes, Aristotle, Bryon, Theokritos of Khios, and Anaximenes.

5. 10.33–4. Column 6.63–8.32. Didymos' purpose in this long analysis is to clarify Demosthenes' references to past and recent benefactions of the Great King to Athens. His source here is Philokhoros, but he also makes reference to the Atthidographer Androtion and to Anaximenes.

6. 10.35. Column 8.32–44. Here Didymos raises the topic of the effect of the Theoric Fund on Athenian preparedness for war, but, rather than discussing the Fund itself, combines this entry with the next two to create an extended treatment of the decline and revival of the Athenian financial situation in the fourth century.

7. 10.37. Column 8.44–54? As part of the above-mentioned discussion Didymos tries to establish the time when Athens' revenues dropped to 130 talents. He intended to substantiate his argument with a concluding quotation from a secondary source. Unfortunately, he fails to name this source and the quotation is missing. In its place we have an uninscribed space of ten lines.

8. 10.38. Column 8.55–9.9. Didymos attempts to substantiate Demosthenes' statement that Athens' revenues increased to 400 talents from 130 with a quotation from the fourth-century Athenian politician Aristophon of Azenia which he found in Theopompos' *Philippika*.

9. 10.44. Column 9.9–37. Didymos struggles to comprehend Demosthenes' explanation of the discontent of the wealthy with corruption in the administration of Athens' finances. No secondary source is referred to.

10. 10.70. Column 9.38–10.11. Demosthenes' mention of a person called Aristomedes calls forth this note on two men of that name. In support of his argument Didymos produces citations from the orator Deinarkhos, and the comedians Philemon and Timokles. He also refers to Philip's letter to the Athenians, to Theopompos, and Anaximenes, but only by name.

Speech 11 (*Reply to Philip's Letter*)

11. 11.1. Column 10.13–11.14. Didymos is concerned to date speech 11 (*The Reply to Philip's Letter*) and to question its authenticity. During the course of this entry he cites passages from Philip's letter, from Demosthenes' reply, and from Philokhoros. He also mentions Theopompos and Anaximenes by name.

12. 11.2. Column 11.14–26. Didymos discusses the charge that a word (*orrodein*) is too vulgar to be Demosthenic. He proceeds to explain the etymology of the word, citing Homer and Aristophanes in the process.

13. 11.4. Column 11.26–52. This note is prompted by Demosthenes' reference to Theban unhappiness with Philip for his retention of Nikaia. Didymos quotes from *On Harbours* by Timosthenes to establish the precise location of the place. He elucidates the historical issue by a quotation from the *Atthis* of Philokhoros.

14. 11.11. Column 11.53–12.33. Didymos attempts to explain the etymology of the word *skorakizein*. He cites a brief piece from Aristophanes' *Birds* (line 28) and a long excerpt from Demon's *On Proverbs*.

15. 11.16. Column 12.33–7. Didymos refers to his own work on the speech *On the Crown* for a demonstration of the fact that the Macedonians had once paid tribute to Athens.

16. 11. 22. Column 12.37–13.12. A discussion of when and where Philip sustained his wounds. The sources Didymos refers to in this section are Theopompos of Khios, Marsyas the Macedonian, and Douris of Samos.

Speech 13 [12 for Didymos] (*On Organization*)

17. 13.1. Column 13.13–40. Didymos argues against those who include this speech amongst the *Philippics*. He cites a passage from the speech itself (13.7) in support of his case, but no other sources are used.

18. 13.1. Column 13.40–14.2. Whilst he does not consider this speech to be one of the *Philippics*, Didymos still attempts to establish the date when it was written. This leads him into a discussion of the dispute between Athens and Megara over the *Sacred Orgas*, on which he quotes from Philokhoros once again.

19. 13.1. Column 14.2–14.35. Didymos tries his hand at etymology again, this time to explain the meaning of the word *Orgas*. In this context he introduces short quotations from Sophokles, Aiskhylos, Homer, and Kallimakhos.

20. 13.1. Column 14.35–49. Here Didymos concludes this lengthy digression by returning to the topic of the dispute between Athens and Megara. This time he quotes from the Atthidographer Androtion.

21. 13.32. Column 14.49–15.10. The final entry on the papyrus offers an explanation of Demosthenes' reference to the Megarians

as 'accursed'. His source here is book 26 of Theopompos' *Philippika*,
where he found a reproduction of a speech supposedly made by the
contemporary politician Philokrates.

5. COMMENTARY OR MONOGRAPH?

I have regularly been referring to this work as Didymos' *On Demosthenes*. This is the title given to it in the subscript to the text on column fifteen, which runs as follows: **Didymos' On Demosthenes
28** (or twenty-eighth) **Of the Philippics 3** (or third). The subscript
then proceeds to list speeches 9, 10, 11 and 12 (modern 13) with
their opening lines. But, while the words are clearly legible, their
precise meaning has been in contention since the first publication.
The disagreement involves interpretation of both the title and the
numerals in the subscript. I think it important to review the history
of this debate, since the outcome has important consequences for
our understanding of Didymos' purpose and his place in the history
of scholarship (*pace* P-S, p. vii).

Diels and Schubart devoted a large part of their introduction
to the *Berliner Klassikertexte* to this topic (D-S[1], pp. xv–xxix). They
based their analysis on the assumption that this work was part of
a commentary (*hypomnema*) of Didymos on the works of Demosthenes, known to us from Harpokration's *Lexikon* under the entry
for *ENΘPYΠTA*. It says: 'Demosthenes (uses the word) in the
(speech) *For Ktesiphon* (18.260). Didymos, the scholar, in his commentary (*hypomnema*) on the speech says that *ENΘPYΠTA* . . .'
Consequently, they designated both their editions of the text as
Didymos' *Commentary* on Demosthenes. As for the numerals in the
subscript, they took the view that 28 had to be different from the
other numerals around it, because of the absence of the bar; that the
other numerals had to be ordinals; and that as a result 28 had to be a
cardinal number, whilst the 3 was ordinal. Illogically, they thought
that the word to be understood with each numeral was different,
hypomnemata (commentaries) with the 28, books with the 3. Thus, the
subscript was made to read: **28 (*hypomnemata*) of Didymos'
On Demosthenes: Of the *Philippics*, the third (book).**

Proceeding from this basis they developed far-reaching theories
about the papyrus. They took it to be part of a collection of twenty-
eight *hypomnemata*, each of which was presumed to be on an individual speech of Demosthenes. Since this volume covered four

speeches, they hypothesized that each roll did. Thus there were
seven rolls, the first three of which had been devoted to the speeches
classified as *Philippics*, which were, therefore, shown to have been
twelve in number (i.e. *Olynthiacs* I–III, *Philippics* I–IV, *On the Peace,
On Halonnesos, On the Chersonese, Reply to Philip's Letter, On Organization*). On the view that the number of genuine speeches attributed
to Demosthenes by Alexandrian scholarship was sixty, they were
forced to hypothesize another part to the scholar's work, this containing the remaining thirty-two speeches in eight rolls of four
speeches each. The first seven rolls contained the public speeches,
the last eight the private. The division into groups of four (tetrads)
was shown to be a feature of the first-century BC scholar Tyrannion
of Amnisos. The whole theory seemed exquisitely neat and it was
then pressed, by rather circuitous argument, into service to address
the more important issue of the tradition of Demosthenes' speeches
from the fourth century to the Alexandrian period and the corpus
of Demosthenes that Didymos had to work with.

It should come as no surprise that this elaborate scheme was
criticized by reviewers. Friedrich Blass rejected it as 'too subtle'
and argued convincingly against all the key points of the theory
(Blass (1906): 285). He was particularly critical of the interpretation of the number 28. Whilst he accepted the view that it was a
cardinal numeral (and claimed the support of Ulrich Wilcken for
this: 285 n. 1), he showed the difficulty of understanding the word
'commentaries' with it and pointed out how much easier and more
natural it was to assume the word 'books' with both the numerals.
On this more reasonable approach the work was seen to be twenty-
eight books long and could be presumed to be a commentary on all
the works of Demosthenes. So, the idea of fifteen scrolls containing
sixty commentaries on the same number of speeches, all arranged
by fours, went by the wayside, and Blass concluded that we could
infer little about the corpus of Demosthenes available to Didymos
from this papyrus. Even the position of the *Philippics* within the work
was questioned. Since the commentary on the speech *On the Crown*
had to precede them (col. 12.36), they could not have come first as
Diels and Schubart presumed.

A far more radical challenge was offered by F. Leo in his review
of the edition (Leo (1960 [1904]): 387–94). He put forward a very different interpretation of the numerals in the subscript and of certain
features of the papyrus that had bothered Diels and Schubart. They
had been disappointed by the apparent brevity, inconsistency, and,

at times, shoddiness of the commentary and by the absence from it of any notes on some words, from the speeches concerned, that Didymos had almost certainly written (e.g. Harpokration, *Lexikon*, s.v. *ΑΝΤΡΩΝΕΣ, ΜΟΡΑΝ, ΠΡΟΠΥΛΑΙΑ*). In an attempt to explain these defects and omissions they had suggested that the text of the papyrus was only an epitome or an abbreviated version of the original, partly attributable to the exemplar, partly to the scribe himself, who out of tiredness or boredom had cut his text down. Leo, by contrast, suggested that these defects were the fault of the genre to which the work belonged, not of the scribe.

He pointed out that the title in the subscript did not claim to be a 'Commentary (*hypomnema*) on the speeches of Demosthenes', but a work 'about' or 'on' Demosthenes. He proceeded to argue that this difference in title was the feature that distinguished a commentary from a monograph on a specific topic (a *syngramma*). His clarification of this point has, until recently, had considerable effect upon the study of Hellenistic scholarship (see Pfeiffer (1968): 278 and n. 2). Leo also argued that Didymos knew and observed the difference between a *hypomnema* and a *syngramma*. On this basis he concluded that the work contained by the papyrus is not the same as that referred to in Harpokration, but a separate monograph, *On Demosthenes*, in twenty-eight books. Finally, he proposed that the numeral 28 is, in fact, an ordinal that indicates that this is the twenty-eighth book of the work. The next part of the subscript tells us that this roll is also at the same time the third book of the *Philippics*, which thus comes at the very end of the work. How the other speeches of Demosthenes were distributed over the remaining twenty-five books could only be guessed, he felt, but like Blass he totally rejected the theories of Diels and Schubart. Even Wilcken came out in support of this understanding of the numerals (Wilcken (1920): 324–5).

Leo's interpretation held the field for more than sixty years (see e.g. Turner (1968): 114). Old habits were, however, hard to shake and scholars continued to call the work Didymos' *Commentary* (e.g. Lossau (1964): *passim*). The obvious reason for this was that it bears many of the hallmarks of a *hypomnema*. For example, it introduces passages from the text under discussion (*lemmata*) and attempts to interpret or elucidate some point about them, just as a commentary does. The fact that the *diple* is used to signpost the *lemmata*, and the practice of indenting the accompanying notes on the quotation are also both characteristics of a commentary (see Turner (1968:

112–18). Though there is no evidence of an edition of the text of Demosthenes marked at the appropriate places by the same critical signs, as would be the case for a commentary, it is not so easy to see this work as a special monograph *On Demosthenes*, because there seems no unifying theme (but see Turner (1968): 114). So, it was almost inevitable that a sober second look be taken at the problem. This was the contribution of S. West in her article 'Chalcenteric Negligence' (West (1970): 288–96).

One of the consequences of Leo's interpretation appeared to be that Didymos had written two large works on Demosthenes: one, this monograph that was at least twenty-eight books long, the other, the commentary referred to by Harpokration. West challenged the plausibility of this idea. There is only reference to one title in our tradition, namely the commentary. Furthermore, it is difficult, as I noted above, to see what criteria Didymos could have used to decide what material should go into which work. To get around this Leo had hypothesized that the commentary contained material of an exclusively grammatical nature, whilst the monograph emphasized the historical. It is true that the papyrus does contain a substantial quantity of historical comment, but it also discusses issues involving etymology, literary criticism, and paroemiography, as can be seen from the outline of its contents. There really is not much left to put into a separate work. As for those entries in Harpokration that dealt with words that belonged to the speeches covered by the papyrus and supposedly derived from Didymos but were not in our text, she put forward good reasons for the absence of each (West (1970): 290).

West also maintained that the distinction between *hypomnema* and *syngramma* in the scholarly tradition was not as rigid as Leo believed and concluded that this work was the one Harpokration knew as a commentary. Further, she suggested that, if the work was disappointing and defective, this was not the result of transmission and scribal error, as Diels and Schubart had believed, nor the fault of the genre, as Leo claimed, but rather must be attributed to Didymos himself. Even the missing ten lines in column 8 must go back to the original text, as Foucart had suggested long before (Foucart (1909): 37). Consequently, the text had been published in an incomplete state, much in the manner outlined in the first section of this introduction. West's image of Didymos is remarkably similar to that which was current before the papyrus was discovered: of a man who wrote with 'haste, inaccuracy, and superficiality' and who produced 'potted scholarship, hurried compilation rather than intelligent re-interpretation' (West (1970): 296). This seems to be the current evaluation of Didymos as a scholar (cf. Harris (1989): 36–44), though it has not gone unchallenged (see Osborne: *passim*; Gibson: 54–62). It is perhaps rather harsh. To be sure Didymos must have produced his prolific output at speed (see Introduction under Didymos), but hasty production does not necessarily imply unoriginal research. This issue will be reconsidered in a later section on Didymos and his sources. We are concerned here with identifying the type of work Didymos wrote, and that remains unresolved.

It is true that other studies besides West's have challenged Leo's sharp distinction between *hypomnemata* and *syngrammata* (e.g. Arrighetti (1977): 49–67) and revealed the large range of meaning the word *hypomnema* was capable of (Bömer (1953): 215 ff.). It could refer to nothing more than a student's note or excerpt from a source as an aid to memory, whilst at the other extreme it could denote a finished commentary. It has even been maintained that, if it differed from a *syngramma* at all, it may only be that the latter was considered the term for a more polished product (Gibson: 53, n. 9). Whatever the difference, both eventually were reduced to scholia or *lexika* through the process of excerption (Naoumides (1969): 181–202; Arrighetti (1977): 49–67). In fact, the demonstration that ancient scholars were constantly excerpting from their predecessors has led the most recent study of this papyrus to revert to a modified version of Diels and Schubart's original suggestion that this work was not by Didymus but by someone who was excerpting Didymus' original for his own purposes (Gibson: 13–25, 51–69).

This suggestion has some superficial appeal, but, as the author himself admits, it is open to the criticisms set forth in West's article and the arguments adduced are all circumstantial. In the first place, the main argument in support of excerption, namely that we do not know the mind of ancient scholars and should not hold them to our standards or expect them to be necessarily interested in what interests us (an argument which I strongly endorse), serves just as well to justify the attribution to Didymos and to explain his choice of passages for comment. And the conclusion, that the excerptor was specifically interested in historical issues, expressed in the vision of an 'Hermoupolite historian, an active researcher into fourth-century history or at least the historical circumstances of Demosthenes' orations . . . combing through Didymus's commentaries and excerpting material to use toward [his] own interests' (Gibson:

69), fails to account for the large amount of non-historical material in the text. Finally, perhaps the most persuasive argument, in my mind, against the excerptor theory is the space in the text of column 8 previously referred to. It is difficult to conceive of an excerptor who excerpted an uninscribed space.

Furthermore, whilst the studies mentioned above have success-fully demonstrated that the terms *hypomnema* and *syngramma* might not have been considered by everyone in antiquity as denoting such distinct genres as Leo claimed, and have even shown that a later author, like Galen, could use them as synonyms (West (1970): 291 n. 2), they have not invalidated Leo's point (Leo (1960 [1904]): 392–3) that Didymos, at least, did treat the *syngramma* as something different from the *hypomnema*, and, incidentally, set higher store by the *syngramma*. In this context his title, and we have no reason to suspect that it is not his (*pace* Osborne: 14; Gibson: 53–4), tells us that he thought he was writing a work that was in some way superior to a commentary, even though the difference may not be apparent to us. And, indeed, in support of this view, it should be noted that the quotations from Demosthenes (the *lemmata*) are rather substantial, if they were intended to refer back to a marked text, as they would if this were a commentary, and the absence of the *hoti* formula (on which see Turner (1968): 114–15) is unusual. Furthermore, Leo's suggestion that Didymos wrote two studies of the complete works of Demosthenes, one a monograph, the other a commentary, the sug-gestion that West was at such pains to refute, is not actually required by the evidence. The only commentary by Didymos on a work of Demosthenes (as distinct from a *hypomnema* on 'the orators' referred to in a work ascribed to Ammonius) that Harpokration (or anyone else) refers to is one on the *For Ktesiphon* (s.v. *ENΘΡΥΠΤΑ*). It is not inherently impossible that this was the only *hypomnema* Didymos actually wrote and that the other entries that Harpokration derived from Didymos came from the monograph *On Demosthenes*. This pos-sibility might seem to receive some measure of support from the fact that the only one of his works on Demosthenes that Didymos cross-references in our papyrus is a work *On the Crown* (col. 12.36). This is usually taken to be a reference to an earlier part of the papyrus, but could just as well refer to a separate study, namely the commentary on the *For Ktesiphon*, mentioned in Harpokration. Unfortunately, there are some problems with this reference (Bliquez (1972): 356–7), and it might be unsafe to base any theory upon it (though see Gibson: 59–60).

There is, indeed, a further indication that Didymos did not conceive of this work as a simple commentary. In contrast to the impression of haste and shoddiness that West and others have emphasized, not all of which can in any case be blamed upon the author (see Introduction under The Papyrus and The Scribe and his Work), there are signs that Didymos had literary ambitions for his publication. As Diels and Schubart noted in their introduction (D-S[1], pp. xxvii–xxviii), the style of writing, especially of the formulaic expressions, is rather fulsome and leaves the impression of an attempt at literary composition ('Unser Interpret fühlt sich als Schriftsteller', D-S[1], p. xxviii). This would accord well with Gibson's distinction that '*syngrammata* seem to have been regarded as more polished literary efforts intended for public distribution, while *hypomnemata* were more spare, perhaps simply in the form of "notes"' (Gibson: 53 n. 9).

In conclusion, because of the many peculiarities about the format and appearance of this work, I do not feel that the question whether it is the same as or different from a commentary by Didymos on the whole corpus of Demosthenes can be resolved as confidently as others, following West, believe (e.g. Osborne: 11–16; Pearson and Stephens use the title *Commenta* without discussion), especially since we cannot be sure that Didymos wrote such a commentary. For my part, I incline towards accepting the indication of the author that this is somehow different from a commentary, and will continue to refer to the work in the way he did, as Didymos' *On Demosthenes*. On the other hand, I am quite prepared to accept, as others do, that this is Didymos' main study of the speeches of Demosthenes, though we reach that conclusion from opposite positions.

Of course, this discussion should have been rendered quite unnecessary by the fact that the scribe took the trouble to tell us what he thought he was doing and wrote it down in the extant subscript to his text. But, as is obvious, that enigmatic reference has caused more problems than it has solved. Not the least of these, as has been indicated in several places, concerns the numerals 28 and 3. The nature of the problem has already been outlined and I have stated my conviction that the absence of a bar over this numeral has no significance (see Introduction under The Papyrus). Both could be ordinals or cardinals, or one could be one, the other another. Any permutation is possible. The answer to the question can only be derived from the context. The different theories have been outlined in the discussion above. None is entirely satisfactory. Some

consensus appears to be growing around the view that the text is
trying to say that this is book three of the *Philippics* from Didymos'
On Demosthenes (which was) on 28 (speeches) (Sealey (1993): 228; Gibson: 51–4, 101, 136). This does, however, involve understanding a
different noun with each numeral and some may still prefer Blass's
strictly rational suggestion that the subscript means that this is *book*
three of the section on the *Philippics* from Didymos' twenty-eight-*book* study of the whole corpus of Demosthenes. In either case, we
should accept, I think, that speech 18 (*On the Crown*) was not included, but received separate treatment.

6. SOURCES

One of the most notable features of Didymos' work *On Demosthenes* is
the presence of a large number of verbatim quotations from ancient
authors, many of whom have only been preserved in fragmentary
form. This was the feature that caused the most surprise and excitement when the papyrus was first published, and, it is fair to say, this
is still the reason why most scholars study this text. Whilst some of
these sources are well known and need no introduction, i.e. Homer,
Sophokles, Aiskhylos, or Aristophanes, many of them are quite unfamiliar and even obscure. This section is designed to provide a
brief introduction to these authors.

Anaximenes

Anaximenes, son of Aristoteles, was born in Lampsakos in the
Troad round about the year 380. He lived for approximately sixty
years. In antiquity, it was believed that he was in his prime in 329/8
BC (*FGrHist* 72 T5). The *Souda* (s.v. Anaximenes) claims that he was
trained by Diogenes the Cynic and Zoilos of Amphipolis, the so-called 'Scourge of Homer' for his harsh criticism of his credibility.
Since Zoilos himself was schooled in the Cynic tradition, it is not
likely that Anaximenes studied with both master and pupil, but
surely we are to accept that he was of the Cynic persuasion. This is
consistent with his known works, which show a sharp and critical
mind. He was famous both as a rhetorician and as a historian.

As a rhetorician he can best be appreciated through the *Rhetorike
pros Alexandron*, a letter outlining the theory of the art of persuasion.
This is generally accepted as the work of Anaximenes (Quintilian,

Institutio Oratoria 3.4.9) and is of great importance to students of rhetoric, since it is the only extant study of the technique that pre-dates Aristotle. As a historian he was known to have written three major works: a *Hellenika*, outlining Greek history from the birth of the gods to the battle of Mantineia (362 BC) in twelve books (Diod. Sic. 15.89.3); a *Philippika*, in at least eight books (Pausanias 6.18.2; Harpokration, s.v. *KABYΛH*), and a monograph on Alexander, that was probably called the *Deeds of Alexander* (Diogenes Laertios 2.3; Pausanias 6.18.2) or something like it. It is unfortunately well nigh impossible to evaluate the capabilities of this important intel-lectual on the basis of the forty or so fragments that remain, which are collected in *FGrHist* 2a, no. 72. An indication, however, of his wit, and also of his relationship to one of his contemporaries, Theo-pompos, is his polemic *Trikaranos* ('The Three-headed Monster'). This attack on political leadership in Athens, Sparta, and Thebes was maliciously published and circulated under the name of Theopompos and only increased that historian's unpopularity in Greece (Pausanias 6.18.5). On Anaximenes' historical works still valuable are Wendland (1904) and (1905).

Androtion

Androtion, son of Andron, of Gargettos (*c.*410–post 344/3), was an Athenian politician and author of an *Atthis* (*Local Chronicle of Attika*). After studying under the rhetorician Isokrates, he entered politics some time before 385/4 BC, and thereafter served the state in a variety of capacities for more than forty years. He is said to have ended his life (some time after 344/3) in exile in Megara, where he wrote his *Atthis*. This work was eight books in length, twice as long as the *Atthis* of Kleidemos that preceded it. Whilst many of the local historians of Attika concentrated their energies on the mythi-cal period of Athenian 'history,' Androtion (like Philokhoros after him) was more interested in the history of his own time. So, five of his eight books cover the period from 403/2 onward. His work was clearly respected, since it was used by Aristotle, in the writing of his *Athenaion Politeia,* and exploited extensively by Philokhoros, the last and most respected of the Atthidographers (Harding (1994): 13–52). Sixty-eight fragments of Androtion's *Atthis* are extant. The Greek text can be found in *FGrHist* 3b, no. 324. There is a translation in Harding (1994: 53–77). Both Jacoby (*Text*: 85–171 and *Notes*: 77–156) and Harding (1994: 78–197) provide a commentary.

Bryon

No author of this name is otherwise known. To add to the problem Diogenes Laertios (5.1.11), citing the same passage, calls him Ambryon. But Didymos is likely to be right here. Bryon is not a common Greek name, but is attested for Khios, where a person of that name was an ambassador to Athens at the time of the treaty of 384/3 BC (*IG* II² 34). The suggestion of Laqueur (*RE* 5A:2, col. 2025) that it was this man's grandson who collected the witticisms of his countryman Theokritos into a book is attractive and has been accepted (see e.g. Wormell (1935): 74 n. 32). Dusanic (1999: 6–7) goes even further in tracing the relationship between the two families back to 384/3, by restoring the name [Θεοκ]ριτος as the third ambassador from Khios in that year and associating them both with Isokrates and Konon.

Deinarkhos

Deinarkhos, son of Sostratos, of Corinth was considered in antiquity as the last of the canon of ten Attic orators, even though he was never granted Athenian citizenship and remained a metic (resident alien) all his life. He was probably born *c*.361, moved to Athens some time after 340, studied for a while under Theophrastos and Demetrios of Phaleron, and finally began his career as a speechwriter (logographer) about 336/5. He was decidedly antidemocratic. So, he became a friend of Antipater and his son Kassander, and in the years after Alexander's death this friendship greatly helped his career. An anecdote from Plutarch's *Life of Demosthenes* (31) illustrates this relationship: It was Deinarkhos who accused Demades of treachery (*prodosia*), for having referred to Antipater in a letter to Perdikkas as 'an old and rotten thread' (cf. Arrian, *FGrHist* 156 F9; Harding (1985), no. 125B). This famous incident became a notorious *topos* in antiquity and even appears in a fragmentary papyrus (*P. Berol.* 13045 in Kunz (1923): 13–31) in the form of a fictitious debate on the issue between the two orators (I owe this reference to Professor Bosworth). But in 307/6, when Demetrios Poliorketes arrived in Athens and a change of government took place, Deinarkhos fled from prosecution in Athens and made his home in Khalkis on Euboia. In 292/1, after another change of government, he was able to return to Athens. When, where, and how he died are unknown. Ancient scholars recognized somewhat over sixty speeches as authentically by Deinarkhos. Of these only three have survived, all involved in the prosecution of those who were charged in the Harpalos affair, the most famous of whom was Demosthenes. The text can be found in N. C. Conomis, *Deinarchi Orationes* (Leipzig, 1975). There is a new commentary by I. Worthington, entitled *A Historical Commentary on Dinarchus* (Ann Arbor, 1992), and a translation of the speeches (by the same author) in *Dinarchus, Hyperides, and Lycurgus*, trans. I. Worthington, C. Cooper, and E. Harris (Austin, Tex., 2001).

Demon

This author is known to us by his works alone. We do not know his patronymic nor his deme name. We do not even know that he was Athenian. We assume that he was, from the one and only reference to him, which is in the *Souda*, s.v. Philokhoros. This tells us that Philokhoros wrote a work entitled *In Response to the Atthis of Demon*. The attribution to him of an *Atthis* is the basis of the assumption (inconclusive, to be sure) that he was an Athenian. That Philokhoros bothered to comment on his work suggests that it was fairly recent (i.e. that it was the immediately preceding *Atthis*, belonging in the late-fourth or early-third century) and not of the highest quality. Three fragments of his *Atthis* have come down to us, which suffice to confirm the fact that he was an Atthidographer and to suggest that Philokhoros was justified in his criticism. The small number of quotations implies that his *Atthis* was not a respected source (or, at least, had not survived Philokhoros' critique) and the content, all related to the mythical period, confirms the view that he was not a historian of the first calibre. But this was perhaps not his chief interest. He also wrote a monograph *On Sacrifice*, from which only one fragment has survived, and, more importantly, a major work *On Proverbs*. The popularity of this study, proven by the fact that it was cited sixteen times, suggests that this was Demon's forte. The Greek text of Demon's fragments can be found in *FGrHist* 3b, no. 327. Still the best commentary on this author is by Felix Jacoby (*Text*: 201–19; *Notes*: 168–71). See also Harding (1994: 31–2).

Douris of Samos

Douris of Samos is an interesting and controversial figure. He lived from about 330 to approximately 260, i.e. he was a little younger than Philokhoros. He was possibly born in Sicily, when the Samians were in exile, following Timotheos' capture of their island for Athens in 366/5. His father, named Kaios, was a victor at boxing in the Olympic Games some time during the period of exile (336/5–322/1 BC). After the return Kaios became tyrant of Samos, a position which Douris inherited later in his life, not long after 300 BC. Before that, perhaps between 307/6 and 301/0, Douris and his brother Lynkeus had been at Athens, studying at the Lyceum under Theophrastos. After the battle of Corrupedium in 281 Samos fell under the control of Ptolemy II and Douris probably lost his position in Samian politics. Perhaps it was after that that he turned to writing. For the above details see Kebric (1977: 2–9). In the manner of the Hellenistic scholar he wrote on a variety of subjects, for example monographs *On Tragedy*, *On Euripides*, *On Sophocles*, *On Homeric Problems*, *On Engraving*, *On Contests*, and *On Customs*. But his most important works were a *Chronicle of Samos*, a biography of Agathokles of Syracuse and a *Macedonian History*. This last work was twenty-three books long and was his most famous product. As a historian he had a reputation for introducing tragic techniques to the writing of history; that is, the embellishment of the facts to incite the emotions. His originality and significance in this respect are in question. See especially Walbank (1960: 216–34) and Fornara (1983: 124ff.). The fragments of his works can be found in *FGrHist* 2a, no. 76.

Hermippos

This third-century Alexandrian scholar (originally from Smyrna) is of fundamental importance to the biographical tradition. He was known in antiquity as a follower of Kallimakhos and as a Peripatetic (Athenaeus, *Deipnosophistai* 2.58f; 5.213f; 15.696d; Wehrli (1974): 11, fr. 1; Bollansée (1999*b*): T5). This is exemplified by his rather paradoxical concern for chronological and factual accuracy (for which he was careful to cite his sources), combined with his fondness for anecdote and gossip; the first was likely based upon Kallimakhos' *Pinakes*, the second followed the style of the Peripatos (Cooper (1992): 202–11). He wrote many biographies of Greek literary and philosophical stars, like Pythagoras, Aristotle, Isokrates, and Demosthenes, and of schools (i.e. *On the Students of Isokrates*). In the field of biography he was highly respected in antiquity and became a source for later scholars, like Dionysios of Halikarnassos, Diogenes Laertios, Pliny, and Plutarch. Nowadays, however, he is considered a scandalmonger, of questionable reliability. On this basis, he is often identified as the source of otherwise unattributed information, especially if it is of a sensational character. This is probably rather unfair. For the fragments of Hermippos (with commentary) see Wehrli (1974): *passim*. He is evaluated as 'Less conscientious (sc. than Kallimakhos), even sensational' by Pfeiffer (1968: 129). A more positive assessment can be found in Cooper (1992: 202ff.). There is now an excellent new study by Jan Bollansée (1999), who has also re-edited the fragments with Commentary as *FGrHist* 1026.

Kallimakhos

It is clearly impossible to describe this important scholar poet in the brief compass allowed for these introductory notes. A succinct appraisal will have to suffice. Born in Cyrene of a good family, he moved to Alexandria and worked there under the favour of Ptolemy II and Ptolemy III, i.e. for most of the third century. As a creative artist he propounded strong opinions about the writing of poetry that had great influence over later generations of poets, both Greek and Roman. In particular, he was averse to large works ('a big book is a big nuisance' fr. 465) and believed in erudite inspiration ('none of my poems is unresearched' fr. 612). His wit was sharp. Unfortunately, of his huge output (reputed to be 800 books) little has survived. We have six of his *Hymns*, updated versions modelled upon the Homeric Hymns; fragments of the *Aitia* ('Sources'), poems that set out to explain the origins (often mythical) of cities, festivals, or cults, and pieces of his *Iambi* and *Hekale*. All these exhibit the same qualities of succinct wit and learning. And, indeed, despite his creative works, for one of which he is cited by Didymos, it is his scholarship and learning that has left the strongest legacy.

As a scholar Kallimakhos was as broad in his interests as any other Hellenistic intellectual, writing on topics that ranged from 'nymphs' to *nomoi* (customs), i.e. from myth to anthropology, with literature taken in along the way. But, there is no doubt that his most important contribution to the history of scholarship (and therefore of this study) was his catalogue of the contents of the library at Alexandria. His *Pinakes*, 'Tables of all those who were eminent in any kind of literature and of their writings in 120 books' (the *Souda*, s.v. Kallimakhos; Pfeiffer (1968): 128), was a catalogue of all texts in the library arranged by genre. To each author was attached a brief biography and a list of works that were accepted as authentic. The influence of this catalogue on the scholarly tradition, particularly the genre of biography, is inestimable (see Pfeiffer (1968): 128–34; Cooper (1992): *passim*, esp. 202ff.). See under Hermippos.

Kallisthenes

Kallisthenes of Olynthos was a nephew and student of Aristotle. Though reputed later in life as both a rhetorician and a philosopher (see Plutarch, *Alexander* 52–5; Arrian, *Anabasis* 4.10–14), his known publications are almost all historical. He worked on chronology and helped Aristotle in organizing the victor list for the Pythian Games at Delphi. They were both honoured for this in a partially preserved inscription (*SIG*³ 275; Harding (1985): no. 104). He wrote a study of the Third Sacred War (356–346 BC) and a *Hellenika* in ten books, covering the period 386–356 BC. In 334 BC he joined Alexander's expedition as its self-proclaimed historian, 'not for the sake of his own fame, but to make Alexander's' (Arrian, *Anabasis* 4.10). The result was his *Deeds of Alexander*. This work seems to have been frankly flattering to the king and to have cast him in the mould of a Homeric hero. It may well have been designed as propaganda for the Greeks back home. In 327 he fell out of favour with Alexander by opposing the institution of *proskynesis*, was subsequently found guilty of involvement in a conspiracy to assassinate Alexander (the so-called Conspiracy of the Pages; Arrian, *Anabasis* 4.13–14; Plutarch, *Alexander* 55) and put to death. At some time he also composed the *Enkomion to Hermias of Atarneus* that is quoted by Didymos. His fragments are collected in *FGrHist* 2b, no. 124. A useful introduction to his work can be found in Pearson (1960): 22–49.

Marsyas the Macedonian

There are two Macedonian historians named Marsyas known to us. One was from Pella, the other from Philippi. Their fragments are collected together by Jacoby in *FGrHist* 2b, nos. 135/6. It is almost certain, however, that the Marsyas referred to here is the one from Pella (Heckel (1980): 454–8). If so, we know a little about him. On the basis of the *Souda* (s.v. Marsyas) it can be established that he was the son of a man called Periander, was half-brother of Antigonos the One-eyed, that he was raised together with Alexander the Great and, consequently, was born about 356 BC. Diodoros (20.50.4) identifies him as commander of part of the Antigonid fleet at the battle of

Salamis in 306 BC. It follows that he was still alive at this point, and a date after 294 BC has been suggested for his death (see on all this Heckel (1980): 444–8). So, he was from the Macedonian elite, and well positioned to know details about court life and politics. According to the *Souda*, 'He wrote a *History of Macedonian Affairs* (*Makedonika*) in ten books, beginning from the first kings up to the time of Alexander's setting out into Syria, after the foundation of Alexandria' (i.e. 331 BC). The most recent study of his fragments suggests that he was a serious historian of political and military affairs, who concentrated his efforts (at least books three through eight) largely upon the life and times of Philip II of Macedon, a period with which he was intimately familiar (Heckel (1980): 444–62).

Philemon

Philemon was a writer of New Comedies. Born either in Syracuse in Sicily (*Souda* s.v. Philemon) or in Soli in Cilicia (Strabo 14.5.8 C671) in the early 360s, he moved to Athens and became a citizen there before 307/6 (*IG* ii² 3073, where he is referred to as son of Damon, of the deme Diomeia). He lived about a hundred years and died at the time of the Chremonidean War (Aelian, fr. 11), on which see Habicht (1999: 142–9) and under Philokhoros below. During his long life he produced ninety-seven plays, the names of many of which are known. He was very popular in his own day, competing successfully against the likes of Menander on several occasions. None of his works has, however, survived and fewer than 200 fragments of his huge output remain. These can now be found in *PCG* vii. 221–317.

Philokhoros

Philokhoros, son of Kyknos, was an Athenian of many talents. His birth date is unrecorded, but was probably close to 340 BC. We know more about his death. According to the *Souda* (s.v. Philokhoros) he was arrested and put to death on the orders of Antigonos (Gonatas) for having been a supporter of Ptolemy (Philadelphos). The occasion must have been the Chremonidean War (268/7–262/1), the last war in which Athens fought for the freedom of the Greeks (*IG* ii² 687). So, Philokhoros was a patriot and a nationalist. He was also a prophet and a diviner, in other words an expert in religious affairs. But he is best known as a scholar and historian. His interests ranged over a wide field of subjects, including local history, cult, chronography, and literature. His most famous work was his *Atthis*, which was seventeen books long. His *Atthis* was the last and most respected in the genre. It was quoted frequently by later sources, not least by Didymos, who used it as one of his two main historical authorities. We have possibly 170 fragments of this work. They can be consulted in *FGrHist* 3b, no. 328. Jacoby discusses the fragments in detail in *Text* (pp. 220–595) and *Notes* (pp. 171–486).

Theokritos of Khios

Theokritos of Khios was a student of Metrodoros, who was himself a student of Isokrates (the *Souda*, s.v. Theokritos). He was a contemporary and political opponent of Theopompos (Strabo 14.1.35 C645), who wrote disparagingly of him to Alexander the Great (*FGrHist* 115 F252). But, in the dealing out of abuse, Theokritos was no sluggard. Besides the attack on Aristotle contained in this papyrus, he assaulted Anaximenes (on whom see above) for being dressed in an uncultured way (Hermippos in Athenaeus, *Deipnosophistai* 1.21c), a metaphor for 'having an uneducated style of oratory', and said of his speech that 'the words come out in a torrent, but contain only a trickle of thought' (Stobaeus, *Florilegium* 36.20). He also earned the hostility of Alexander, when he referred to the king's institution of a poll tax to pay for ceremonial crimson robes as a 'crimson death' (Plutarch, *On the Education of Children* 11b). Eventually, however, his mouth led to his demise, when he referred to Antigonos the One-eyed as a Cyclops (Plutarch, *On the Education of Children* 11c; Macrobius, *Saturnalia* 7.3.12).

Theopompos

Tradition (notably the *Souda*, s.v. Theopompos and Photios, *Bibliotheka* 176 p. 120b.19) knew Theopompos as a younger contemporary of Ephoros. He was probably born about 380 BC. Both were believed to have been students of Isokrates, the Athenian rhetorician, though they were very different in character. Ephoros needed the goad, Theopompos the rein. Theopompos was involved in the politics of his home state, Khios. At least, according to Photios, he and his father were exiled from Khios for showing pro-Spartan sympathies. Photios also records that none other than Alexander the Great personally secured Theopompos' return by a letter. This event, if true, would belong to the period 334/3–332 (Harding (1985), no. 107). After Alexander's death Theopompos is said to have fled to Egypt, where Ptolemy was only narrowly persuaded from putting him to death. Amongst his works were two historical monographs, the *Hellenika* (Greek Affairs) in twelve books that continued Thucydides' history down to the battle of Knidos (394 BC) and the *Philippika*, a giant study of Philip II of Macedon in fifty-eight books that digressed far and wide from its professed topic. Of the former we have very few fragments, of the latter over 200. The Greek text of these fragments can be found in *FGrHist* 2b, no. 115. They have been translated by Shrimpton (1991: 196–274).

Theopompos was also known as an orator, and a reading of his fragments reveals that he did not know where to draw the line between rhetoric and history. All too often his evaluation of individuals (almost always negative) is based upon rhetorical simplifications of moral prejudices. So, for example, his unusually favourable evaluation of Lysander (F20) praises him for his 'temperance and control over pleasures. At any rate, though he became master of almost all Greece, it will be clear that in none of the cities did he give himself over to sexual pleasures or indulge inappropriately in drinking and carousing.' By contrast, his condemnation of Philip ('a man the likes of whom Europe has not produced before this' T19) contains all the graphic descriptions of moral depravity one finds in the *Philippics* of Demosthenes. The impression one gains from the chance-preserved fragments of his works is fully corroborated by the judgement of Polybios (8.9.1–10.1). In short, Theopompos was one of those historians who could write neither without bias (*sine studio*) nor emotion (*sine ira*). See further Lane Fox (1986) and Flower (1994).

Timokles

The *Souda*, s.v. Timokles, identifies two writers of comedies of the same name, both Athenian, and assigns different plays to each. It is more likely that they are one and the same, as they are treated in *PCG* vii 754–81, where the forty-two fragments of his works can be consulted. He was a fourth-century poet, who lived at least until the time of Demetrios of Phaleron's governance of Athens, as is shown by the reference to the *gynaikonomoi* in fr. 34. He was victorious at the Lenaia at least once (*IG* ii² 2325.158). His style is characteristic of the earlier period of New Comedy (often called Middle Comedy), in which personal attack, like that familiar from Old Comedy, can still be found.

Timosthenes

Timosthenes of Rhodes is a rather neglected representative of Hellenistic scholarship. One will find no mention of him in Pfeiffer's study, nor in the most recent book about Hellenistic Rhodes (Berthold (1984)), and yet he is important to both. In fact, one is hard put to find any reference to him, and the best analysis of his significance remains the article by Gisinger in *RE* 6A: 2, col.1310–22. This may partly be explained by the fact that little is known about him, except that he was the commander of the fleet of Ptolemy II Philadelphos (see e.g. Strabo 9.3.10. C421; Pliny, *NH* 6.183). But this detail alone marks him out as a person of significance in third-century history, and demonstrates the primacy of Rhodians in naval affairs at this time. More important, however, was his contribution to the study of geography. His work *On Harbours* in ten books was a main source for Eratosthenes' *Geography*, and through him for Pliny and Strabo. Starting from Egypt, his description moved anti-clockwise up the coast of Asia to the Pontos and thence to Thrace. That Greece was treated in the fifth book is shown from this fragment in Didymos; another fragment from book six (scholion to Aiskhylos' *Persians* 303) is on Salamis and suggests that Timosthenes worked down the coast from north to south. He also covered north Africa. Overall, his study appears to reflect his experience and concentrates mainly on the eastern Mediterranean. He probably made Rhodes the central point of his compass, which was based upon twelve wind positions (Dilke (1985): 31) and it may be as a result of his influence that Alexandrian scholars came to use the parallel of latitude that passed through Rhodes as the zero meridian and the basic grid reference in nautical and geographic studies (Schneider (1967–9): i.398).

Others

In addition to these named sources Didymos frequently refers to less clearly defined authors by such titles as *ENIOI* ('some people'), or *TINEΣ* ('certain persons'), or quite simply, 'there are those who say'. These individuals (the plurals are merely rhetorical generalization) are surely other scholars, either predecessors or contemporaries. He refers to them for opinions only; he never cites them as the source of a quotation. Furthermore, their opinions are introduced either to be refuted or dismissed. Through these citations we acquire some idea of what issues had been addressed by Didymos' predecessors and what had not.

It is worth noting, in conclusion, a source that Didymos does not mention, namely the κοιναὶ ἱστορίαι used by his contemporary Dionysios of Halikarnassos as one of his sources for the dates of Demosthenes and Aristotle in his *Letter to Ammaeus* (*Ad Ammaeum* 1.3). This (or these) work(s) was (were) said by Dionysios to have been put together by men who had written the lives of Demosthenes and Aristotle. It (they) is (are) often ascribed to Hermippos (for want of a better candidate). A recent study of Dionysios' dates (Lane Fox (1997): 167–203) reveals several discrepancies between Dionysios and Didymos and makes it all but certain that Didymos did not use this source.

7. DIDYMOS THE SCHOLAR

The number and variety of sources Didymos used in his attempt to explicate the text of Demosthenes is most impressive, especially in the space of somewhat less than twelve columns of readable material. Even more impressive is the substantial size of many of these verbatim quotations. As I indicated above (Introduction under Sources), scholars have not failed to acknowledge this. From the first editors onward it has been standard to celebrate with some excitement the fact that Didymos has preserved for us so many fragments from works that were otherwise lost. One might have expected that this excitement would have translated into a more positive evaluation of Didymos as a scholar. Surprisingly, it has not. The opinion that is held of him today, with few exceptions (i.e. Osborne: *passim*; Sealey (1993): 228; Gibson: 54–69), is much the same as the one that existed before the discovery of the papyrus (see Introduction under Didymos). So, it remains common to diminish Didymos' scholarly contribution, by maintaining that he did not consult his sources at first hand, but through the works of intermediaries, who had done all the legwork for him . He was, it is often stated, only a compiler of other people's efforts (e.g. D-S[1] xxxii–xliii; Pfeiffer (1968): 276;

West (1970): 296; Smith (1995): 76). Even in that function he is also deemed a failure, who misinterpreted or misunderstood what he read in his sources, and sadly lacked in critical judgement (West (1970): 288–96; Harris (1989): 36–44; Yunis (1997): 1049–55).

The quality of Didymos' critical abilities can best be examined in the course of an analysis of his text. This issue will, consequently, be addressed in the Commentary, where it will be a matter of primary concern. It should, however, be pointed out right away that it is unfair to apply standards of modern scholarship to this work, as one suspects has often been the case, not least with West. In this instance, Didymos should be compared with his own kind; that is, scholars who wrote explications of *prose* works of *historical* significance in antiquity. But that comparison is not possible, since no other work exactly like this has survived. The Didymos papyrus is rightly celebrated because it stands virtually alone. The surviving commentaries that we have are almost exclusively on poetic texts and much later (e.g. Servius' commentary on Vergil's *Aeneid* of the fourth century after Christ and Eustathios' on the *Iliad* and *Odyssey* in the twelfth), and it should be obvious that analysis of poetic texts, which was the main focus of ancient scholarship from the Alexandrian period onward, is a quite different business. Nevertheless, our text does not compare unfavourably in most respects with these, and in the matter of documentation of references is superior (see Osborne: 14–16).

As far as scholarly works that involved historical criticism are concerned, it is the opinion of one eminent scholar that, in comparison with what else we have, Didymos' analysis 'shines like gold' (Turner (1968): 120). His comparison is with papyri that contain commentaries on Thucydides (e.g. *P. Oxy.* 853). But some remains of commentaries on Demosthenes have survived. All of these have recently been discussed by Craig Gibson in an excellent study, in which he provides text, translation, and commentary (Gibson: 157–99). Even in their case Didymos fares well. For example, we have a very small part of a commentary on Demosthenes' speech *Against Androtion* (22.13–21), often referred to as the Strasbourg Papyrus (it is no. 84 in the collection there), or, in the more fanciful style of the first editor (Keil (1902): *passim*), the *Anonymus Argentinensis*. It is a mere fragment of papyrus from the first century after Christ, containing the right-hand portion of some twenty-six lines of writing, and probably less than half the original width at that. But in that space as many as eight passages are commented upon. The text is quite controversial. See Gibson: 178, who, however, follows the very problematic reconstruction of Wade-Gery and Meritt (1957: 164). For a variety of different restorations (translated) see Fornara (1982), no. 94.

It is a very different sort of work from Didymos'. In the first place it has eliminated the *lemmata* or, rather, incorporated them into the comment in paraphrase. Next, the comments are all introduced by the word *hoti* ('that' or 'because'), much as they are in marginal scholia to our manuscripts. This may be an abbreviation for the formula 'the sign is placed because', which is usually associated with a mark in the margin of the text next to the word or words being commented upon (Turner (1968): 114–15) or indicate a paraphrased *lemma* with a meaning something like '(where Demosthenes says) that . . .' (Gibson: 176). To give an example, the comment on the passage, 'You know that recently you sent help to the Euboeans within three days' (Dem. 22. 14) runs as follows: '(The sign is placed) because/ (where Demosthenes says) that: in three days they sent help [to the Euboeans]: the Athenians [came to their support] as they were being attacked in war, [and with this help they gained the victory] over the The[b]ans [and] with a trireme *freely contributed* by the orator.'

As can be seen, the explication is brief and basic, so compressed it is almost garbled, and includes no references to other sources nor any quotations. On the other hand, the author of this text has selected for comment as many passages from a small portion of a speech as Didymos did for a whole speech. This particular format is unique (Turner (1968): 115) and obviously better suited to marginal scholia than a commentary on a separate text. Current opinion holds that it is, in fact, an example of the way a commentary was reduced through excerption by the authors of *lexika* (see now Gibson: 13–20). Nevertheless, it may be more like the average ancient *hypomnema* than we think, and this fact may help to explain why Didymos decided to title his study as though it were a *syngramma*.

Quite different is the mutilated fragment of a commentary on Demosthenes *Against Aristokrates* (speech 23). This papyrus (*P. Berol.* 5008) was first published by F. Blass in *Hermes* 17 (1882). Blass dates it to the fourth or fifth century after Christ. It was certainly composed after Didymos, because at one point it cites him as a source. It is from a work that arranged its entries alphabetically, like the *lexikon* of Harpokration. The extant portion contains the entries for *ΜΙΛΤΟΚΥΘΗΣ, ΜΟΡΑΝ, ΟΔΟΣ, Ο ΚΑΤΩΘΕΝ ΝΟΜΟΣ*, and

ΟΤΙ ΘΕΜΙΣΤΟΚΛΗΣ ΩΣΤΡΑΚΙΣΘΗ. The commentary on each entry is quite detailed, about twenty lines, much longer than in the papyrus discussed above, somewhat longer than the average article in Harpokration, but less fulsome than most of Didymos' explications. The notes do contain references to other sources and provide some direct quotations from them. Many of the sources used are similar to those cited by Didymos, i.e. Anaximenes, Aristotle, Philokhoros, and Theopompos, and the additional ones, Xenophon and Ephoros, were surely known to him. These similarities, and the fact that Didymos is the only scholar referred to, suggests that this work is derived from his (Hubbell (1957): 191). This view is reinforced by the fact that the information provided in the papyrus on the second, third, and fourth of the entries is found in identical but abbreviated form in Harpokration, who also used Didymos. The derivation appears to be more direct than is the case with the earlier (that is, if Blass's date for the papyrus is correct) borrowings of Harpokration (2nd century after Christ) and suggests a common source, rather than direct borrowing one from the other (Gibson (1997): 375–81).

There are a few other fragments of commentaries on Demosthenes' *Aristokrates* and *Meidias*, the most important of which is *P. Rain.* inv. 7 (part of a *lexikon* to Demosthenes 21), for which see Gibson: 190–9. Others are rhetorical in emphasis and belong to a different scholarly tradition (see Hubbell (1957): 181–93; Lossau (1964): 111–23, 129–40). They are not interested in historical issues and do not cite any of the sources used in our papyrus. A not unreasonable conclusion of this review of the material available for comparison with Didymos' *On Demosthenes* would be that Didymos was responsible for the introduction of detailed citations from original sources, including verbatim quotations, into the *exegesis* of the text of Demosthenes. Unfortunately, this has not been the prevalent opinion. In fact, from Diels and Schubart onward there has been a strong body of scholarly opinion that holds that Didymos derived his material, quotations and all, from some intermediary sources. The arguments in favour of this view are threefold: 1. Dionysios of Halikarnassos (*Ad Ammaeum* 1.11) and Didymos (col. 1.67f. and col. 11.37f.) use the same passages of the *Atthis* of Philokhoros; since they had no contact with each other, they must have used a common source (D-S¹, p. xxxiv). 2. At another point (col. 11.7–14) Didymos cites the opinion of 'some people' to the effect that speech 11 (*The Reply to Philip's Letter*) had been written by Anaximenes of Lampsakos and had been inserted almost verbatim in the seventh book of his *Philip-pika*; Didymos does not express an opinion on this one way or the other, and yet surely if he had done his own research he should have confirmed or denied this assertion (D-S[1], pp. xxxiv–xxxv). 3. In the long excursus on Hermias of Atarneus Didymos cites the earlier scholar, Hermippos of Smyrna (col. 6.51–3); this biographer is the most likely person to have collected together all these quotations on Hermias and must, therefore, have been Didymos' ultimate source, though *via* the intermediation of some one (or others) else, i.e. the unnamed scholars he often refers to (D-S[1], pp. xxxvi–xliii; Wormell (1935): *passim*).

The first argument is not well founded and prompted an early reaction from Foucart (1909: 43–4). It was definitively rejected by Felix Jacoby (*Text*: 329–31). Dionysios and Didymos cite the passages from Philokhoros in different form, one omitting one section and including another, the other likewise. This is because each had a different purpose in view, Dionysios to show that Demosthenes composed his speeches without the aid of Aristotle's *Rhetorike*, Didymos to explicate certain points of historical interest as they occurred. Indeed, the fact that each adapted his quotation from Philokhoros to his needs is clear evidence that each consulted Philokhoros independently, rather than through a common source.

At first sight the second argument appears more impressive, until one realizes that it may be based upon a misunderstanding of Didymos' scholarly method. Lossau was the first to point this out (1964: 108), and he has been followed by Osborne: 20–2. The passage is a difficult one that is corrupt at several points, but the outline of the argument is clear enough. Didymos began his treatment of this speech in column 10 by discussing the questions of its date and the circumstances that motivated it. He concluded that section with a summary statement (col. 11.5–7). Then he proceeded to the issue of authenticity, about which there was some disagreement. He began by expressing his own suggestion (at least that is the most natural way to interpret the potential optative used impersonally, i.e. 'one would not be off target . . .', *pace* Lossau (1964): 93–5; see Osborne: 31–3, 43–4 and Gibson: 30–5) that the speech was a pastiche of passages from earlier Demosthenic speeches. Whether Demosthenes was responsible or not he does not state explicitly, but the tone of the preceding discussion of the date and circumstances leaves the impression that Didymos thought he was.

After that he mentions two other opinions about the authenticity,

but without comment. The first ('there are those who say') was that
the author of the speech was Anaximenes and that it could be found
almost verbatim in the seventh book of his *Philippika*; the second
was the view of 'some people' that the vocabulary was not Demosthenic, and so, presumably, that the speech was not authentic for
that reason. We may feel disappointed that Didymos did not elaborate upon these theories, but we have to accept that it was a common
practice of ancient scholars to refer to divergent opinions in this
oblique way, just to show that they knew they existed (see the good
discussion in Gibson: 30–5). The scholia exemplify this feature at
every point, but it may be more useful to cite a more accessible
work like the *Constitution of the Athenians* by Aristotle. Like Didymos,
the author of this study frequently refers to the conflicting views of
'some people', 'certain people', or 'others'. Sometimes he disagrees,
as, for example, in 9.2: 'some people think that he (Solon) made the
laws unclear on purpose . . . This is not likely . . .'. But at other points
he leaves the discrepancy unresolved, as, for example, in 14.4, where
he reports about Phye, the girl who was dressed up as Athena to
escort Peisistratos into Athens, that Herodotos said she came from
the deme Paiania, but 'some people' said she was from Kollytos.

There is no reason to assume that this author had not personally consulted the works he was referring to, nor need we do so in
Didymos' case. It was not relevant to his argument to refute these
other views. In fact, in this case we can see Didymos' method quite
clearly. Having put forward his own opinion on the question of
authenticity, he dismissed two contrary theories, only to pass on
to a discussion of the etymology of the word *orrodein*, though not
in an attempt to demonstrate whether the word was Demosthenic
or not. Lossau has well shown (1964: 99–106) that there were two
etymologies put forward by scholars in Alexandria for this word
and that the one advanced here was the one used by Didymos in his
lexikon of *Comic Terms*; it is, in fact, specifically attributed to him in
a scholion to Aristophanes' *Frogs,* line 223. So, we find the learned
scholar rushing over questions of interest to us in order to show off
his own etymological knowledge, even though he cannot apply it
to the issue at hand. We may not be very impressed with his judgement, but on the matter at stake in this discussion, namely whether
Didymos did his own research or derived his material from an intermediary source, the answer is clear. His approach is so idiosyncratic
that it must be his own (see on this now Gibson: 30–5).

The results of the investigation of Didymos' relationship to his sources so far makes it somewhat redundant to address the third question, which author or authors served as his intermediary (-ies). But some additional points are worth making on this issue. The idea that the Hellenistic biographer Hermippos of Smyrna was the ultimate source of the passages cited by Didymos, filtered through the commentaries of the unnamed scholars, was first advanced by Diels and Schubart, expanded by Wormell, and is in part subscribed to by Lossau who, while he rejects Hermippos (1964: 107–9), still holds that Didymos was compiling the works of previous generations of Alexandrian scholars, who he believes had commented extensively on Demosthenes' speeches (1964: 68–95). Fundamental to this whole line of reasoning is the basic prejudice that Didymos was not an original scholar, but derived his opinions and arguments from others (cf. Smith (1995): 76).

I shall begin with Hermippos. The view that Hermippos was Didymos' main source derived from the fact that he was cited, along with a number of other authors, in the long excursus on Hermias of Atarneus. In column 6, lines 51–3, Didymos cites book two of Hermippos' *On Aristotle* for the view that Hermias died in prison. The nature of the citation should have been enough to deter anyone from concluding that Hermippos was Didymos' source for the whole excursus on Hermias. The precise reference to author, work, and book is one of the outstanding characteristics of this papyrus, but, more importantly, it puts the reference to Hermippos on a par with all the other authors cited in this section. To be sure, Hermippos is known to have written biographies of the philosophers, but there is no evidence that Hermias was one of them, and for an excursus this long on Hermias to have been contained in a biography on Aristotle is most unlikely. The fact is that we know very little about the methods of this biographer and this makes him a convenient scapegoat for theories of this kind. More specifically, as Jacoby has pointed out (*Text*, 329), there is no evidence that Hermippos ever introduced long verbatim quotations from his sources, nor that he was in the habit of citing his sources by chapter and verse. One thing we can say, however, is that, as a biographer, his aims and method must have been quite different from those of a person writing an explication of the text of the speeches of Demosthenes (or anyone else for that matter). In sum, the only fair conclusion to arrive at is that Hermippos was consulted by Didymos for the specific piece of information attributed to him and nothing more. This is also the conclusion reached by other recent studies by Osborne

(17–45), Milns (1994: 80–1), Yunis (1997: 1052), and Gibson (107). Somewhat different is the seemingly illogical position of Bollansée (2001: 83–97) that Didymos took the summary review of Hermias' death (col. 6.50–9) entirely from Hermippos, but used a different source for the rest of the Hermias episode (or maybe even was himself responsible for it).

The same argument holds good against the anonymous Alexandrian scholars, who had supposedly composed such detailed commentaries on the speeches of Demosthenes that there was nothing left for Didymos to do but compile and compress their studies and transmit them to subsequent generations. There is no doubt that some sort of scholarship on Demosthenes existed before Didymos. His oblique references to its authors shows this. But that it was complete and left nothing to be added cannot be shown (Douglas (1966): 191). Again, there is no evidence whatsoever that that scholarship was the source of the long verbatim citations from earlier authors that are such a important feature of this papyrus. In fact, it will become apparent throughout the commentary on this text that Didymos' verbatim quotations are not associated with his references to the opinions of others, but always in support of his own (however idiosyncratic) views. This only confirms the conclusion that Didymos did his own research and collected his own quotations for his own purposes (Jacoby, *Text*: 329; Sealey (1993): 228; Osborne: 18–35).

Ironically, this conclusion was staring Diels and Schubart in the face, if they had not allowed themselves to be led astray by the long-established prejudice regarding Didymos' scholarship. Early in their Introduction (p. xiii) they pointed out that the presence of so many quotations from the local historians of Attika (the Atthidographers) in the text of the papyrus removed any objections to accepting Didymos' authorship of the commentary from which our scholia on Sophokles' *Oidipous at Kolonos* were derived; they, too, show a keen interest in and acquaintance with the works of the Atthidographers. Even though Didymos' name was frequently mentioned in them, many scholars had been unprepared to accept that a scholar in the Aristarchan tradition was interested in factual and historical details. The papyrus proved them wrong.

The obvious conclusion to draw from this was that Didymos' use of these authors was a distinctive and original feature of his scholarship, but instead, as we know, Diels and Schubart went on to argue that he had derived all this information from an intermediary. It is time to put that idea to rest and to accept that Didymos engaged in original scholarship. In fact, it is interesting to note that the other scholar known to have introduced substantial quotations from the Atthidographers in support of his arguments, especially when he was trying to establish a date, was Dionysios of Halikarnassos, a contemporary of Didymos. The suggestion (Osborne: 47–8) that this was an original contribution of this generation of scholars is a felicitous one and refutes the view that they were merely compiling the works of their great predecessors, though one should note in passing a similar abundance of substantial quotations from source material (including the Atthidographer Philokhoros) in Philodemos' *Academica* (*P. Herculanensis* 1021 and 164) that was composed a generation or two earlier.

8. DIDYMOS AND THE TEXT OF DEMOSTHENES

Quite apart from the places where Didymos discusses the question of the authenticity of a particular speech, which will be examined as appropriate in the commentary, the papyrus has relevance to the textual tradition of Demosthenes in two specific ways. The first concerns the speech, which is number 12 in current editions of Demosthenes: *The Letter of Philip to the Athenians*. This letter is found in only two of our main manuscripts, F and Y. The other two, A and S, do not have it. It obviously does not legitimately belong in the corpus of Demosthenes and so it is appropriate that Didymos does not write any notes on it. This does not necessarily mean, however, that a letter from Philip was not included in the text of Demosthenes that Didymos consulted. For he clearly knew of the existence of the text of such a letter , since at column 10.24–30 he quotes its conclusion. It is also the case that he, like the scholar who compiled the text from which F and Y derived, considered that the letter he had was none other than the letter of Philip to which Demosthenes' speech 11 (*To the Letter of Philip*) was a reply. This is not the prevailing view of modern scholarship, however (see e.g. Sealey (1993): 239–40), which, while accepting the authenticity of Dem. 12 (Griffith (1979): 714–16; Sealey (1993): 240), argues that the chronological references in it are prior to those in Dem. 11 by some weeks and that Dem. 11 is replying to some other letter of Philip that has not survived (Griffith (1979): 567; *contra* Bliquez (1969): 18; Osborne: 186).

The situation is further complicated by the fact that Didymos' version of the conclusion of the letter, whilst in essence the same as in our extant text of Dem. 12, is quite different in some important respects of wording (these will be discussed in the commentary). Furthermore, in column 9.43 Didymos makes another reference to a letter of Philip, in the context of a discussion of the name Aristomedes. He claims that an Aristomedes of Pherai was complained about by Philip in his letter to the Athenians. No such reference exists in the text of our speech 12. So, it appears that Didymos had a different text of Philip's letter available to him, but one that was too similar to have been a separate letter. Which of the two, if either, is to be preferred will be examined in the commentary. It is sufficient for this discussion of the textual tradition of the corpus of Demosthenes to note that there existed in Didymos' time a version of Philip's letter that was quite different from the one that has survived in our manuscript tradition.

Second, since Didymos quoted extensive sections from his text of Demosthenes, the Didymos papyrus might be expected to have made a contribution to the textual criticism of Demosthenes on the question of the relationship of our main manuscripts (SFAY) to each other, in particular the contention over the superiority of S (Parisinus Graecus 2934). Unfortunately, although the papyrus shows a tendency to side with S (and, to a lesser extent, A), the text of the passages cited by Didymos shows no definitive preference in favour of any one manuscript tradition. In fact, this testimony is quite consistent with the impression given by the numerous other fragments of works of Demosthenes that have been found on papyrus, namely that the Alexandrian text (or texts) of Demosthenes did not bear any clear relationship to the stemma (confused as it is) of the Byzantine manuscripts. Specific places where Didymos' text agrees with one manuscript or another will be noted in the commentary. Anyone who wishes to pursue this issue further should consult Hausmann ([1921], 1978) and Pack (1965) for the papyrological material, and Irmer (1961, 1968, and 1972: *passim*) for the manuscript tradition. Cf. also Wankel (1976, i. 63–82), Lewis (1997: 230–51), and, for a brief summary, Sealey (1993: 222–3).

9. CONCLUSION

P. Berol. 9780 is, in my opinion, a copy (most likely not a direct one) of an original work by Didymos that was entitled *On Demosthenes*. It was probably made by a student (under supervision) in an establishment in Hermoupolis in Egypt some time late in the second century after Christ. The excessive presence of errors of iotacism (an aural not a visual phenomenon) may indicate that he was taking dictation, although these errors are more likely to have been embedded in his copy from previous editions, if the peculiar error he made at column 1.9 is rightly interpreted as a visual one. The *On Demosthenes* represents all the comments that Didymos saw fit to make on the four speeches from Demosthenes that it covers and, at the same time, provides a glimpse at the work of his predecessors. As such, it gives us a valuable insight into the interests and working methods of a Hellenistic scholar. If these seem to us to be idiosyncratic and less than satisfactory, that may well be because we have different expectations and standards. It is unhelpful to judge Didymos' by our own, and it closes our minds to the real lessons to be learned from this text. In any case, whilst his critical judgement may not always be sound (in our opinion), he addressed issues that are still of concern today (e.g. dating and authenticity) and quotes (with appropriate reference) substantial passages from ancient sources, culled from his own reading and research, to support his arguments. This last feature may, in fact, be a hallmark of his scholarship. He attracted students, some of whom made a name for themselves later (e.g. Apion and Herakleides), and succeeding generations of scholars consulted his work with respect (Sealey (1993): 228; Gibson: 34–5). No doubt he was no better than other scholars in his tradition, but there is no reason to believe he was worse (Lewis (1997): 244–6). He made an important contribution to the ancient discussion on the orations of Demosthenes and to our understanding of it.

TEXT AND TRANSLATION

TEXT

This text is provided as an aid to those who can read Greek, so that they can check the translation whenever they need. It is the product of personal examination of the papyrus in Berlin and consultation at home in Vancouver of excellent photographs produced by the staff at the Bode Museum. It has also benefitted from the careful work of the previous editors, Diels and Schubart and Pearson and Stephens. Serious students of the text will need to refer to their editions in disputed passages. Comparison will show that my text is closer to that of Diels-Schubart than to the version of Pearson-Stephens, many of whose readings I could not confirm. I have also been deliberately conservative with restorations, except in the case of passages for which we have parallel versions; for those I have printed a composite text. I have not provided an apparatus criticus, in the belief that such a thing would be meaningless to a Greekless reader. Anyway, it was often opaque even to me how to interpret some of the suggested supplements. Instead, I have discussed the more important elements of the apparatus in the Commentary in a manner that I hope will be helpful.

EDITORIAL CONVENTIONS

The editorial practices and symbols used by the scribe are discussed in the Introduction under The Papyrus.

MODERN EDITORIAL SYMBOLS

( )	indicate an explanatory addition to the text or letters left out by abbreviation in the original
[ ]	enclose letters or words that are no longer extant, but have been restored by modern scholars
{ }	indicate letters excised by modern editors

⟨ ⟩	indicate letters or words thought to have been omitted from the papyrus by accident
⌞ ⌟	indicate letters or words supplied from a parallel text
. . . .	indicate missing letters; each dot is intended to indicate one letter in places where the number of missing letters is almost certain
[±14], [c.18]	indicates places where the number of missing letters can be calculated less precisely
α, β, γ . . .	indicates a letter whose identification is not certain
|	indicates the end of a line on the papyrus
/	indicates the end of a line of verse
(lacuna)	indicates that a portion of the text is deemed to be missing

ABBREVIATIONS USED IN THE PAPYRUS AS REPRESENTED IN THE TEXT

ὰ	α(να)
γ́	γ(αρ)
δ́	δ(ε)
δ̀	δ(ια), δ(ας)
έ	ε(πι)
κ́	κ(αι)
κ̀	κ(ατα)
μ́	μ(εν)
μ̀	μ(ετα)
ό	ο(υν)
οἱ	οι(ον)
π̀	π(αρα)
π́	π(ερι)
ċ	σ(υν)
τό	το(υς)
δ́, λ́, ν́, ρ́, τ́, φ́	δ(ων), λ(ων), ν(ων), ρ(ων), τ(ων), φ(ων)

$\overset{\scriptscriptstyle\backprime}{\lambda}, \overset{\scriptscriptstyle\backprime}{\nu}, \overset{\scriptscriptstyle\backprime}{\tau}, \overset{\scriptscriptstyle\backprime}{\chi}$ $\lambda(\eta\nu), \nu(\eta\nu), \tau(\eta\nu)/\ \tau(\alpha s), \chi(\eta\nu)$

$\lambda', \nu', \rho', \tau'$ $\lambda(\eta s), \nu(\eta s), \nu(\alpha s), \rho(\alpha s), \tau(\eta s)$

/ $\dot{\epsilon}\sigma\tau\dot{\iota}(\nu)$

\ $\hat{\epsilon}\hat{\iota}\nu\alpha\iota$

// $\epsilon\dot{\iota}\sigma\dot{\iota}(\nu)$

There are also some other abbreviations for whole words, which involve letters written superscript above letters, e.g. an upsilon over an omicron stands for $o\ddot{v}\tau\omega$, an upsilon over a nu equals $\nu\hat{v}\nu$ and a nu over an omicron is shorthand for $-o\nu\tau os$. For the other less common examples of this practice see D-S[1] (p. 3), D-S[2] (p. 2), and P-S (p. xx).

EDITORIAL CONVENTIONS USED IN THE TRANSLATION

These are the same as those used in the text with the following exceptions:

[...]   is used to indicate all gaps in the text, without regard to the number of letters missing. Sometimes, where a reasonable restoration has been accepted, the restored words will be enclosed within square brackets, but part of a word will only be so indicated in the case of restored names, e.g. Philo[kho]ros

(45)   numerals enclosed in round brackets indicate every fifth line of the text

italics   *italics* have been used to indicate places where only part of a word (excluding names) is extant on the papyrus, e.g. in *this man's* archonship

/   divides two alternative translations

TEXT AND TRANSLATION

[ΔΙΔΥΜΟΥ ΦΙΛΙΠΠΙΚΩΝ Θ–ĪΒ]

COLUMN ONE

Heading: Lost

1

[c.31   ]αγνο̣[.]εγε[......]
[c.24   ]μ[....]σιν κ(αὶ) [±12   ]
[c.21   ]αν[....] Ἐρετρίας π[......]
[c.22   ]αυ[..] στρατείας [±9   ]
[c.31   ]τεχ[±11   ]   5
[c.34   ]συμμαχικα
[c.17   ]ωντος [±11   ]οιλογο[......]
[c.10   Φι]λίππου δ(ια)[........]—"Κ(αὶ) πρι̣ῶτον μ(ὲν) τι̣ὴν εἰς
⟨Πελοπόννησον πρεσβείαν ἔγραψα, ὅτε πρῶτον ἐκεῖνος εἰς⟩
ι̣Πελοπόννηι̣σον ι̣π̣αρει̣δ̣ι̣ύετο, ι̣εῖ̣τα τὴν ι̣εἰς Εὔβι̣οιαν
ι̣ή̣ι̣νι̣κ᾽ Εὔβι̣οιαι̣ς ἥ̣ι̣πτετ᾽, εἶτα τὴν εἰς Ὠρει̣ο̣ι̣ν ι̣ἔξι̣οδον,   10
ι̣ο̣ὐκέτι̣ι̣ πι̣ρεσβεί̣ι̣αν, κ(αὶ) τὴν εἰς ι̣Ἐρι̣έτριαν, ι̣ἐπειδὴ κε̣ι̣ι̂
ι̣νο̣ι̣ς ι̣τυράνι̣νο̣υς ἐν ταύταις ται̣ῖ̣ς̣ πι̣ο̣ι̣λε̣σι κ̣ατέ̣ι̣σ̣ι̣τ̣η̣σ̣ε̣ν."
[..........Φιλο]χόρωι μαρτυρεῖ· περὶ μ(ὲν) γ(ὰρ) τῆ̣ς πρὸ̣ς
[Ὠρεὸν ἐξελθ]ού̣σης βοηθείας προθεὶς ἄρχοντα Σωσ[ι̣]γέ-
[νη φησὶ ταῦ]τα· "Κ(αὶ) σ(υμ)μαχίαν Ἀθηναῖοι πρὸς Χαλκιδ-   15
εῖς ἐποι-
[ήσαντο κ(αὶ)] ἠλευθέρωσαν ['Ω]ρ⟨ε⟩ίτας μ(ετὰ) Χαλκιδ⟨έ⟩ων
μηνὸς
[Σκιροφο]ριῶνος, Κηφισοφῶντος στρατηγοῦ[ντο]ς, κ(αὶ) Φι-
[λιστίδ]ης ὁ τύραννος ἐτελεύτησε." περὶ δ(ὲ) τ(ῆς) εἰς Ἐρέτριαν
[πάλιν ὁ αὐ]τὸς προθεὶς ἄρχοντα Νικόμαχόν φησιν οὕ(τως).
"Ἐπὶ τού-
[του οἱ Ἀθ]ηναῖοι διέβησαν εἰς Ἐρέτριαν, Φωκίωνος στρατη-   20
[γο(ῦν)τος, κ(αὶ)] κατάξοντος (-ντος, pap. -ντες, D-S, P-S) τὸν
δῆμον ἐπολιόρκο(υν) Κλείταρχον,
[ὃς πρό]τερον μ(ὲν) ἀντιστασιώτης ἦν Πλουτάρχου κ(αὶ) δ[ι]ε-
[πολι]τεύετο πρὸς αὐτόν, ἐκείνου δ᾽ (ἐ)κπεσόντος ἐτυράν-
[νησε· τ]ότε δ᾽ ἐκπολιορκήσαντες αὐτὸν Ἀθηναῖοι τῶι δή-
[μωι] τὴν πόλιν ἀπέδωκαν."   25

[DIDYMOS' *PHILIPPICS* 9-12]

COLUMN ONE

Heading: Lost

[. . .]*tyrant became* [. . .] | [. . .] | [. . .] of Eretria [. . .] |
[. . .] campaigns [. . .] | (5) [. . .] | [. . .] matters related to alliance |
[. . .] of [. . .]phon [. . .] | [. . .] of [Phi]lip [. . .]. 'And first the
embassy to the Peloponnese was my proposal, at the time when
that man (sc. Philip) was making his initial attempt to sneak into the
Peloponnese, then (I proposed) the embassy to Euboea, (10) when
he was laying hold of Euboea, next (I proposed) the expedition—no
longer an embassy—to Oreus and the one to Eretria, after that man
had established tyrants in those cities.' [. . . in Philo]khoros testifies.
For regarding the aid [that went out] to [Oreus], after the heading 'the archon (was) Sos[i]ge[nes]', (15) [he says] *this* : 'And (the)
Athenians *made* an alliance with (the) Khalkidians and in conjunction with (the) Khalkidians liberated the [O]reitans in the month
of [Skiropho]rion; Kephisophon was the general; and Phi[listid]es
the tyrant died.' And regarding the (aid that went out) to Eretria
[again] *the same man* (i.e. Philokhoros) says as follows, after the heading 'the archon (was) Nikomakhos': 'In *this man's* (20) *archonship* [the
Ath]enians went across (to Euboea) against Eretria with Phokion as
their general and, with the intention of restoring the People, began
to besiege Kleitarkhos, (a man) [who] *previously* was a factional rival
of Ploutarkhos and *used to conduct politics* in opposition to him, but
(who) became tyrant after that man (i.e. Ploutarkhos) had been
expelled. On this occasion the Athenians, after overcoming him
(i.e. Kleitarkhos) by siege, (25) restored the city to the *People*.'

Ī

"⌊Κ(αὶ) σπου⌋δαῖα νομίζ(ων), ὦ (ἄνδρες) Ἀθ(ηναῖοι), περὶ ὧν
β⌊ο⌋υλ⌊ε⌋ύεσθε, κ(αὶ) ἀναγ-
⌊καῖα τῆι⌋ πόλει, πειράσομαι π(ερὶ) αὐτ(ῶν) εἰπεῖ⌊ν ἃ⌋
νομίζω σ(υμ)φέ-
⌊ρειν⌋." [τοὺς κ]αιρ[οὺ]ς τοῦ λόγου τάχ᾽ ἄν τ[ις σ]υν[ίδοι......]

[±14 ἄρ]χοντα Νικόμαχ[ον ±12]			30
[±15]η[.....]ην προ[±16]			
[c.20]οι γεγρα[±14]			
[c.42]			
[c.42]			
[c.42]			35
[c.42]			
[c.20]η[c.20]			
[c.22]σ[c.19]			
[c.18]νενων[c.18]			
[c.17]νωνειτ[c.17]			40
[c.18]ησθε[c.18]			
[c.17]νοιησα[c.18]			
[c.17]ιερωμεν[c.17]			
[c.17]σκουσα[c.18]			
[.....]μετ[±9]ραιαν[c.19]			45
[.......]σου βου[λόμ(εν)]ος οὐδὲ [c.19]			
[±12]Ὠρ⟨ε⟩ίτου ἐπὶ Σω[σιγένους ±9]			
[±10]ον δ(ὲ) τοῦ Ἐρετριέ[ως ἐπὶ Νικομ]άχο[υ]			
[±10] κ(αὶ) ταῦτα πιστώ[σεται Φιλόχ]ορος [.]			
[±9] ἐπὶ [τ]έλει τ(ῆς) Νικ[ομάχου ἀρχῆ]ς αρ[.]			50
[±10]ογος. οὐκο(ῦν) ὅτι μ[(ὲν) πρότερον γέγ]ραπτ[αι]			
[±9] σης ἀρχῆς ὁ λόγ[ος[±8]α Νικ[ο]			
[μαχ.....ἱ]κανῶς ἑώρατα[ι ±9] προθε[ὶς]			
[±14]Νικομα[χ ±10 δ]ειξειν			
[±15]ύ[π]ὲρ τῆς πρὸς Φίλιππον			55
[c.17]κ(αὶ) ἡ περὶ τῶν σ(υν)θ[η]κ(ῶν) στή-			
[λη ±7]ρη[...]ἐπὶ Θεοφράστου ἄρχο[ντ]ος ε-			
[±9]ο[....]ηνεσατ[.]τε[..]υθε[..]ωτ[.]			
[±9]ν[....]τε πάντηι τε κ(αὶ) πάν[τω]ς πρ[.]			
[±15]αι· σαφὴς δ(ὲ) μάρτυς, [ὡ]ς ἐγὼ ἀ-			60
[.......Δη]μοσθέ[ν]ης ταυτὶ λέγων· "Ταῦ⌊τα νῦ⌊ν⌋			

⌊ἕκαστον εἰ⌋δότα ⌊κ(αὶ)⌋ γ⌊ι⌋γνώσκον⌊τ⌋α παρ᾽ αὐτῶ⌊ι δ⌋εῖ μὰ
⌊Δ⌋ί᾽ οὐ γράψαι κε⌊λεύ⌊ει⌋ν πόλεμον τὸν τὰ βέλ⌊τ⌋ιστ᾽

(Speech) 10

'And because I consider, men of Athens, (that) the matters, about which you are deliberating, (are) serious and crucial for the city, I shall attempt to put into words concerning them what I think is beneficial.' One could perhaps *glimpse* [the] *circumstances* of the speech [. . .] (30) [. . .] *the archon* was Nikomakh[os . . .] **Too little remains of lines 31–45 for intelligible translation.** (46) [. . .] neither *wishing* nor [. . . Phi] | [listides the] Oreitan [. . .] in the archonship of So[sigenes], | and [Kleitarkh]os the Eretri[an in the archonship of Nikom]akho[s] | [. . .]. These things also [Philokh]oros *will confirm* [.] (50) [. . .] at the end of Nik[omakhos' magistrac]y [. . .] | [. . .]*speech.* Well then, that the *speech has been written* [before] | [. . .] of magistracy [. . .] Nik[o] | [makhos . . .] has been seen. [. . .] *under the heading* | [. . .] Nikoma[khos . . .]*will show* (55) [. . .] *concerning* the [peace] with Philip | [. . .]and the *stele* regarding the treaty | [. . .] in the archonship of Theophrastos | **Nothing intelligible can be recovered from line 58.** [. . .] both in every way and completely [. . .] (60) [. . .]. And a clear witness, *as/that* I [.] | [. . .] (is) Demosthe[n]es, when he says the following: 'So, because each one (of you) knows these facts and recognizes them for himself, he should not, by Zeus, bid the man who always gives the best counsel for all just reasons to make a proposal for war. That is

⌞ἐπὶ πᾶσι δικαίοι⌟ς σ(υμ)βουλεύοντα· τοῦτο μ(ὲν) γ(ὰρ) ∟(ἐστι)
    λ⌟αβεῖν
⌞ὅτωι πολεμή⌟σετε βουλομ(έν)ων, οὐχ ἃ τῆι πόλει ⌞σ⌟(υμ)φέρε⌞ι⌟   65
⌞πράττειν.⌟" [ο]ὐ γ(ὰρ) ἄν δήπου ταῦτ' ἔλεγε[ν], εἰ λελυκ[ό]
[τες τὴν εἰ]ρήν(ην) ἐτύγχανον Ἀθην[αῖο]ι. ὅτι μ(ὲν) [ο(ὖν)]
[ἐπὶ Θεοφράστο]υ τοῦ μ(ετὰ) Νικόμαχον ἄ[ρ]ξαντος
[αἱ σ(υν)θῆκαι ἐλύ]θησαν, ἀρκέσει Φιλ[ό]χορος ἐκ-
[φανῶς διὰ τῆς] ἔκτης γράφ(ων) οὕ(τως)· "Ὁ δ(ὲ) δῆμος ἀκού-   70
⌞σας τῆς ἐπιστολῆς⌟, Δημοσθένους π(αρα)καλέσαντο⌞ς⌟
⌞αὐτὸν πρὸς τὸν π⌟όλεμον κ(αὶ) ψήφισμα γράψαν-
⌞τος, ἐχειροτόνησ⌟αν τὴν μ(ὲν) στήλ(ην) καθελ⌞εῖν⌟
⌞τὴν περὶ τῆς π⌟ρὸς Φίλιππον ⌞ε⌟ἰρήν(ης) κ⌞(αὶ) συ⌟μ-

COLUMN TWO

Heading: Τίνες οἱ περὶ [c.20   ]
       Π(ερὶ) τὴν ὑπόνοια[ν   ±12   ]
       Θηβαίο(υ)ς συμμα[±12   ]
       Ὅτι δυσνόως ἐχε[..]ο[±9   ]

μαχ⌞ί⌟ας σταθεῖσαν, ναῦ⌞ς δ(ὲ) πληροῦν κ(αὶ) ἐνερ-⌟
γε⌞ῖ⌟ν τὰ ⌞το⌟ῦ π⌞ο⌟λέ⌞μ⌟ου." ἔνιοι δ[(ὲ) φασι τὸν λόγον ἐπὶ Σω-]

[σ)ιγ[έ]νους συντετάχθαι· [±16   ]
τον[±7]ους· ειδ[..]τ[±16   ]
μαλ[±7]νη[...]μ[±18   ]   5
[±9]ρεις κ(αὶ) ημ[.]σ[±15   ]
[±11]ειδιο[...]η[±13   ]
[±10]τα περὶ αὐτο[±13   ]
[±10] ὅτι πολιο[±14   ]
[±12]κ(αὶ) εἰ[ς Μ]ακεδ[ον ±11   ]   10
[±13]ιδ[..]κη[±14   ]
[±13]στρατου[±13   ]
[±11]τερωι κ(αὶ) γεν[±13   ]
[......μνημ]ονεύει λόγωι· κ(αὶ) [±11   ]
[±11]ειν τουσανει[±11   ]   15
[±12]γέγονε τ[±14   ]
ανα[±13   ]υ[c.16   ]
φων[±11   ]γν[c.17   ]

the act of those, (65) who want to find someone for you to make war against, not of one who wants to act in the city's interest.' For he would surely *not* speak this way, if (the) Athen[ian]s had just *broken* [the] *peace*. [Now] as to the fact that (it was) in the archonship of [Theophrasto]s, the archon after Nikomakhos, [that the treaty] *was broken*, it will *clearly* suffice (70) (to quote) Phil[o]khoros, who writes as follows [in his] sixth (book): 'When [the] People had heard [the letter], after Demosthenes had exhorted [them to] war and had proposed the motion, they *voted* to destroy the stele, [the one that] had been set up [regarding the] peace

COLUMN TWO

Heading: Who are the supporters [. . .]
Concerning the suspicion [. . .]
Thebans *alliance* [. . .]
That ill-disposed [. . .]

and *alliance* with Philip, [to man] a fleet [and] *to put in motion preparations for war.' But* some [say the speech] was composed [in the time] of [Sos]ig[e]nes.

Insufficient remains are extant in either column 2 or column 3 for intelligible translation.

ἀθροισαν[c.25   ]
ροδησειτω[....]ηρ[c.20   ]   20
αταισ[....]Σκυ[θ]ῶν μ[c.19   ]
βοηθησαντ[..] ἐπανῆγε π[±14   πε-]
ρὶ τὸ Βυζ[άντ]ιον· κ(αὶ) περὶ μ(ὲν) [c.16   ]

———

σειν[±7]νω· συμβου[c.16   ]
  σ[±7]ς αὐτοῖς πολ[±15   ]   25
  [±8] μ(ὲν) κιν[δύ]ευο̣ν̣[±14   ]
  [±7]αζομ(έν)ους; τὰ γ(ὰρ) ι̣[±15   ]
  [......]βασιλέα τὸν μέγ[αν   ±12   ]
  [.....λ]εγ[ό]ντας ἃ σύνη[θες   ±12   ]
  [±9 κ]οινὸς ἐχ[θρὸς   ±12   )   30
  [±8 Ἑλ]λάδα [c.19   ]

Lines 32–54 are completely lost.

  [c.30   ]μου   55
  [c.29   ]ασιν
  [......]του[c.24   ]
  [±8]αστα[c.23   ]
  [±11]εο[c.20   ]
  [±14   ]ψ[.]ωι[±15   ]   60

Lines 61–3 are completely lost.

  [±12   ]τινο[±12]σεκ
  [±10   ]ων εγν[c.18   ]   65
  [±7]Μακεδ[c.21   ]
  [......]ετασσ[c.22   ]
  [±7 ο]υ(νν)τες [c.22   ]
  [±8]μ[c.24   ]
  [±8]ὑπὲρ τουτ[c.17   ]   70
  [±7]περ[c.23   ]
  [±7]κ(αὶ) διὰ το[ύ]του [±15   ]
  [±7]στο[ν] αὐτὸν [c.17   ]
  [±7]υντο Ἑλλη[ν   c.17   ]
  [......τ]ῆι ἕκτηι [c.19   ]   75
  [±8]ουμ(εν)ω[c.21   ]
επ[......]αφεινα[ι   c.22   ]
νο[.....]εγγ[c.24   ]

COLUMN THREE

Lines 1–18 are completely lost.

```
[         c.23         ]ο̣σ̣[ ±10  ]
[      c.20      ]ιασ[ ±10  ]                        20
[  ±11  ]μ̣[ ±8  ]αστ[    ±12   ]
[  ±11  ]αυτ̣[       c.21        ]
[  ±11  ]περ[        c.22       ]
[  ±11  ]λλον[..]μ(ἐν) μο̣[     ±15    ]
[   ±14   ]τ[.]ισνικο[  ±13  ]                        25
[   ±14   ]μ(ἐν) τὸν ε̣σ̣τ̣[   ±14   ]
[   ±14   ]μ̣[..]εκ[    c.16   ]
[      c.20      ]κ[   ±14  ]
[   ±14   ]ε[      c.20      ]
[   ±14   ]λ[     c.20      ]                         30
[             c.35             ]
[  ±8  ] γ(ὰρ) [         c.26        ]
[             c.35             ]
[             c.35             ]
[  ±8  ] ἵνα μὴ ν[     c.21        ]                  35
[......] ἀρκέσει δε[....]ρ[   ±14   ]
[  ±7  ]σ̣τ̣ε̣[ ±8  ]υα[   ±15   ]
[......]ιδοσ[ ±8  ]αβ[   ±15   ]
[.....]σ ἐπολιορκ[....]επι̣[    ±14   ]
[.....]α[ ±7  ]σταλ[.]φει[   ±14   ]                  40
[....]α̣γγ[...]τ[.....]πολ[   c.16   ]
[  ±7  ]τ[.] κ(αὶ) παρὰ τῶν [    c.18    ]
[  ±10  ] πρόφ[α]σιν [    c.17    ]
[  ±11  ]αι[.]ε[    c.20    ]
[             c.35             ]                      45
[..]ιτυ[.....]ε[      c.24      ]
[..]εθωτο[        c.28        ]
[...]μ(ἐν) [.]υν̣[        c.28        ]
[.....]ε̣ν[     c.28     ]
[......]αι[      c.27      ]                           50
[......]ατη[     c.26     ]
[...]τ̣αθη[      c.28      ]
[...]δ(ιὰ) προ[        c.28        ]
[..]απαντα[       c.27       ]
[..]ο(υν)[..]μ[          c.29          ]              55
```

παρα[...]νε[*c.*26   ]
τουσ[.]α[*c.*29   ]
τὴν τ(ῆς) [*c.*31   ]
ς οὔ(τως) [*c.*32   ]
τα[.]τ[*c.*31   ]   60
ν[*c.*34   ]
θ[*c.*34   ]

Lines 63–75 are completely lost.

COLUMN FOUR

Heading: [±9   ]ạ[..]εις πρὸς β[±15   ]
     [..]ν ἐπ᾽ αὐτ[ὸ]ν π(αρα)σκευ[ὰς.]μη[.....]
     [Π(ερὶ) Ἐρ]μίου τοῦ Ἀταρνείτο[υ Τί λ]εγο[υσιν;]
     [οἱ] τὰ περὶ αὐτὸν ἀνα[γράψα]ν̣[τε]ς

[τῶν Ἀ]μφικτυόνων κ(αὶ) μ(ετα)σχῶσι τ(ῆς) [Ἀμφικ]τυο[νε]ίας
[...] ψήφισμα τόδ(ε)· "[Ἔ]δοξε τοῖς Ἀμφικτύ[ο]σιν· ἐπει-
[δὴ] Μεγαλοπολῖται κ(αὶ) Μεσσήνιοι ἠξ[ί]ωσαν ε[ὐέ]ρ-
[γέτ]αι [τ]ο[ῦ] θεοῦ κ(αὶ) τῶν Ἀμφικτυ[ό]ν(ων)
     ἀ(να)γραφῆνα[ι] κ(αὶ)
[......]αι Ἀμφικτύονες, ἀποκρίνασθαι αὐτοῖς   5
[ὅτι πε]ρὶ μ(ὲν) τῆς Ἀμφικτυονείας ἐπανενεγ-
[κόντες] εἰς τ(ὰς) πόλεις ἕκαστοι βουλεύσονται κ(αὶ) εἰ[ς]
[τὴν ἐρ]χομ(έν)ην πυλαίαν ἀποκρινοῦνται [αὐτ]οῖς
ὑπὲρ τούτων· εὐεργέτας δ(ὲ) τοῦ θεοῦ κ(αὶ) [τ]ῶν Ἀμ-
φικτυόν(ων) δ(ε)δόχθαι ⟨εἶναι⟩ αὐτούς. ἀποκρίνασθαι δὲ   10
[±7   ]οις ὅτι [δο]κεῖ τοῖς Ἀμφικτύοσιν ἀ-
[ναγραφῆν]αι αὐτοὺ[ς] εὐε[ργ]έτας τοῦ θεοῦ κ(αὶ) [τ]ῶν
[Ἀμφικ]τυόν(ων) καθάπερ [αἰτ]οῦνται." κ(αὶ) [......]
[±7   ]τα Ἀριστο[τέλης ἐν τ]ῆι τρίτη[ι   ±7   ]
[±7   ]τ̣(ῶν) Σκυθῶν ἔθ[..ἐ]στί, φη[σ]ὶ̣ [±8   ]   15
[......]τ̣ο[..]ρον μεικρα[.....]δε[±10   ]
[±9   ]του προσαγορ[ε]υθῆναι [ὑπὸ τ]ῶν βαρ-
[βάρων.....]δ[..]ι̣ν τῆς δρα[±7   ]ασαρι
[±11   ] (εἶναι) θ[...]ελλ[±9   ]ουσευ
[±7   ]ηνη[*c.*18   ]ασπαι   20
[±8   ]ευσ̣[*c.*19   ]δεπι
[±9   ]σ̣σ[*c.*20   ]ου κ(αὶ)

COLUMN FOUR

Heading: [. . .] to [. . .]
    [. . .] *preparations* against *him* [. . .]
    [. Her]mias the Atarneita[n . . .]
    [. . .] the things concerning him [. . .]

[of the A]mphiktyons and [having] a share in the [Amphik]tyo[n]y
[. . .] following decree: 'Resolved by the Amphikty[o]ns: *since* (the)
Megalopolitans and (the) Messenians requested (that they) be
registered (as) *benefactors* of the god and of the Amphikty[o]ns and
(5) [. . .] Amphiktyons, answer shall be made to them [that] they
(i.e. the Amphiktyons) will *refer* the matter of the Amphiktyony to the
cities individually for consideration and will reply to *them* regarding
these matters *at* [the] *next* Pylaia. But (that) they ⟨are⟩ benefactors of
the god and of *the* (10) Amphiktyons, let it be resolved. And answer
shall be made [. . .] *that it seems good* to the Amphiktyons (that) they
be registered as benefactors of the god and of *the* [Amphikty]ons, just
as they are *requesting*.' And [. . .] Aristo[tle in] *the* third (book) [. . .]
(15) [. . .] of the Scythians [. . .] *is, says* [. . .] | **Nothing intelligible
remains of lines 16–58.**

[*c.*32   ]ο[.]
[*c.*32   ]δε
[*c.*31   ]ρμο   25
[*c.*32   ]ευ
[*c.*33   ]μ(ετα)
[*c.*31   ] μ(ὲν) αυ

Lines 29–46 are completely lost.

[*c.*21   ]ελημφθ[±8]
[±15   ]ο̣φυ[..]ν ἐξαπατ̣[±8]
[±15   ]ου κ(αὶ) [*c.*16   ]

Lines 50–8 are completely lost.

[*c.*26   ] ἐπεὶ δ' εἰς
[μεγίστην διαφ]ο̣ρὰν ἤκο̣υσιν ο[ἰ] τὰ περὶ τὸν   60
[Ἑρμίαν π(αρα)δεδω]κότες, τῆς φιληκοίας ἕ-
[νεκα τῶν κ(αὶ) νῦν π]ολυπραγμονούντ(ων) τὰ τοιαῦ-
[τα ἐπὶ πλέον] δ[ο]κῶ μοι περὶ τούτων [εἰ]πεῖν. αὐ-
[τίκα γὰρ οἱ μ(ὲν) ἐ]πὶ τῶι βελτίστωι μνημ[ο]νεύου-
[σι τἀνδρός], οἱ δ(ὲ) πάλιν ἐπὶ τῶι φαυλο̣τάτωι·   65
[ἐν οἷς ἄλλοι τ]ε κ(αὶ) Θεόπομπος ἐν τῆι ἕκτηι
[κ(αὶ) ......]ακοστῆι τῶν Περὶ [Φίλι]ππον·
[οὑτωσὶ γ(ὰρ) γρ]άφει· "Ὥρμησε δ(ὲ) [Ἑρ]μ̣[ία]ς ἐπὶ
[ταύτην τ(ὴν)] ὁδόν, εὐνοῦχος ὢ[ν κ](αὶ) [Β]ιθυ[ν]ος
[±8   ]ρα τρίτον δεσπ̣ο̣[..]ασ̣[...]ομ(εν)ος   70
[....]ωνος[...]ελαβε[±11   ]σον

COLUMN FIVE

τὸν ἐκειν[.....] Ἀταρνέα κ(αὶ) τὸ χωρίον τὸ πλη-
σίον· ἁπάν[τ(ων) γ(ὰρ) οὗτος ὠμό]τατα κ(αὶ) κακουργότα-
τα κ(αὶ) τοῖς [πολίταις κ(αὶ) τοῖς] ἄλλοις διετέλεσε
προσφερό[μενος πᾶσι, τὸν μ(ὲν) γ]ὰρ φαρμάκοις
τὸν δ(ὲ) [βρό]χ[ωι διεχρήσατο. κ(αὶ) τ(ῆς)] χώρ(ας) ἧς   5
          Χῖοι κ(αὶ) Μι-
τυληνα[ῖοι   ±15   ] καθΐστασαν ἐ-
κεῖν[ο]ν π[±14   ] (εἶναι) τ(ῶν) ἀμίσθων στρα-
τ[ε]υμάτ(ων) π[±8   ] κ(αὶ) προεπηλάκισε πλείστους
Ἰώνων· [ἀργυρώ]νητος γ(ὰρ) ὢν κ(αὶ) καθεζόμ(εν)ος
ἐπὶ τρά[πεζαν] ἀργυραμοιβικήν, κ(αὶ) συγκει-   10

[. . .] And since (60) there has arisen [a very great] *difference of opinion* amongst those who *have handed down a report* about [Hermias], *because* of the fondness for listening to/of [those who even now] busy themselves with such matters, I think it appropriate for me to discourse [more extensively] on these topics. *For example,* [you see, some] put the best interpretation on *the memory* (65) [of the man], while others, by contrast, interpret (it) for the worst. [This is particularly the case with] Theopompos in the [. . .]-sixth (book) of his <u>Concerning [Phili]p</u>. For, he *writes* [as follows]: 'And [Her]m[ia]s set out upon [this] path, *though he was* a eunuch [and B]ithy[n]ian by (70) [birth . . .]. And/but third [. . .] | [. . .] *he seized* [. . . As]sos | [. . .]

COLUMN FIVE

that *man's* [. . .] Atarneus and the nearby territory. [For of] *all men* [this one] always *behaved* most [cruel]ly and most basely both to the [citizens and the] *others* [all of them]. *For* [one] by means of poisons, (5) another [by the noose he did away with. And of the] territory, over which the Khians and Mytilen[ians . . .] established him [. . .] to be of the unpaid soldiery/campaigns, [. . .] and he treated very many of the Ionia[ns] with abuse. For, being a *bought slave* and one who sat (10) at the money changers' *table* and *composed* [. . .] of

[μένων ..... σ]υμφορῶν, οὐχ ἡσυχίαν ἦ-
[γεν   c.16   ] ἄμ[α τ]ὸ πρέπον
[±14   ]δ[....]σ[..]ε· πολλῶν δὲ
[±13   ]ν[...]πεχ[....]ε π(αρ)' ἐνί-
[ου]ς δ(ὲ) συνε[.....]γας τὰς ὑπα[ρχο]ύσ(ας) πολι-   15
τείας κ(ατα)[λῦσαι]. οὐ μὴν ἀθῶιός γε διέφυ-
γεν οὐδ(ὲ) κ(ατὰ) [πάντ' ἔλ]αθ[ε]ν ἀσεβῆ κ(αὶ) π[ο]νηρὸν
αὐτὸν π(αρα)σχ[ών, ἀλ]λὰ ἀνάσπαστ[ο]ς ὡς βασ[ι]
λέα γενόμ(εν)ο[ς πολλ]ὰ[ς] τῶι σώ[μ]ατι λύμ[ας ὑ-]
πομείνας ἀ(να)[σταυρω]θεὶ[ς] τ[ὸν βί]ο̣ν̣ [ἐτελε]ύ̣-   20
τησεν." ὁ δ' α[ὐτὸς ἐν τῆι πρ]ὸς Φί[λιππον ἐπισ]το-

λῆι κ(αὶ) ἦν π[αρεσκεύαστο π]αρ[ὰ τοῖς] Ἕλλησι
δόξαν ἱστορ[εῖ· "   c.19   ] δὲ

χαρίεις κ(αὶ) φιλ[όκαλ]ος γε[γον]ώς, κ(αὶ) [βάρβ]αρος
μ(ὲν) ὢν μ(ετὰ) τῶν Π[λατω]νείων [φ]ιλο[σο]φεῖ, δοῦ-   25
λος δ(ὲ) γενόμ(εν)ος ἀ[δ]ηφάγοις ζεύγεσιν ἐν ταῖς
πανηγύρεσ[ι]ν ἀγωνίζεται. σκοπέλους δὲ
[κ](αὶ) μικρ[ὰ χωρία] κεκτημ(έν)ος, ἔτυ[χε] μ(ὲν) τῆς
[.....]ει[....τὴ]ν δ(ὲ) πόλιν τ(ὴν) Ἡλ(ε)ίων ἐπ[αγγέλλ]ειν
[πρὸς αὐτὸν τὴν] ἐκεχειρία[ν] ἔ[π]εισ[εν....]   30
[±9   ἐκ]είνου γ(ὰρ) ἑορτ[±11   ]
[c.20   ]ων[.]δ(ε)[±8   ]
[c.18   ]δ̣(ια)λογ[..]λ[......]
[c.22   ]ο[...]μ(ὲν)[......]

Lines 35–44 are completely lost.

[c.32   ] γ(ὰρ)   45
[c.32   ] μ(ετα)
[c.30   ]λλο
[c.32   ]σ
[c.25   κ](αὶ) μετ[..] μ(ὲν) [.]
[c.29   ]ησεν   50
[c.20   ]κα[..]εω[..]ηκοτα
τὴ[ν] πλατ[c.16   ]ε̣ι̣ς τ[(ὴν)] πέριξ
σ̣τ̣ρατηγει[c.19   ]κ[..] κ(αὶ) Ἔ-
ραστον κ(αὶ) Ἀριστοτ[έλην   ±11   ], διὸ κ(αὶ)
πάντ[ες οὗ]τοι π(αρ)[±14   ]ν, ὕστε-   55
ρον [δ' ἄλλων] ἡκό[ντων, χωρίον τ]ι ἔδωκεν

----

misfortunes/[. . .] *beset* by calamities, he did not rest [. . .] at the same time propriety [. . .]. And of many [. . .], but amongst (15) some [. . .] *to dissolve* the *existing* constitutions. And yet he did not escape scot-free nor [did it go totally] *unnoticed* (that) he was behaving like an impious and base man, *but* after he had been dragged up-country to the King, (and) after he had endured *many* bodily outrages (20), he *ended his life by crucifixion.*'

And the *same* (author, i.e. Theopompos) also records [in his] *letter to* Phi[lip] the reputation which he (i.e. Hermias) *had made for himself amongst* [the] Hellenes: '[. . .], yet [. . .] being refined and *fond of honour/culture*, and though he is not *of Greek origin*, (25) he *studies* in the company of the P[lato]nists, and though born a slave, he competes in the international festivals with expensive (racing) teams. And though possessing (only) rocky crags *and little* [lands], he got the [. . .], and he *persuaded* [the] city of (the) Eleians to (30) *proclaim* [the] (Olympic) truce [for him] [. . .] | (31) [. . .] for when that man *was celebrating the festival* [. . .] **Nothing intelligible remains between lines 31 and 51.**

(52) the *of* Plat[o] [. . .] into the (country) roundabout (53) he used to lead his army [. . .] and Erastos and Aristot[le . . .], for which reason, indeed, (55) *all these men* [. . .], [and] later, [when others] *had come*, he gave *them* [some territory] *as a gift*. [. . .]. And [. . .] the

αὐτ[οῖς δ]ωρεά[ν   *c*.17   ]ες δ(ὲ) τ[ὴν]

———

τυραν[νίδ]α με[.]εστη[±7   π]ρ[αο]τ[έ]ραν δυ-
ναστείαν. διὸ κ(αὶ) πάσ[ης τῆς σύ]νε[γγ]υς ἐπῆρ-
ξεν ἕως Ἀσσοῦ, ὅτε δ[±9   ]θε[.]ς τοῖς εἰ-   60
ρημ(έν)οις φιλοσόφοις ἁ[±8   ] τὴν Ἀσσίων
πόλιν. μάλιστα δ᾽ αὐτ[ῶν ἀποδεξ]άμ(εν)ος Ἀρι-
στοτέλην οἰκειότατα [διέκειτο πρ]ὸς τοῦτον."

———

ἀλλὰ γ(ὰρ) κ(αὶ) Καλλισθέν[ης   ±8   ] τι συν-
τάξας περὶ αὐτοῦ π[ολλά τε λέγει ἄλ]λα κ(αὶ) [ταυ-]   65
τί· "οὐ μόνον τοι[οῦτος   ±9   ] κιν-

———

δύνων, ἀλλὰ κ(αὶ) πλησίον κ[αταστὰς ... ὅ]μοιος
ὢν διετέλει, κ(αὶ) μεγί[στην τότε πίστι]ν ἔ-
δωκε τῆς ἀρετῆς ἐν αὐτ[ῶι τῶι θανάτ]ωι. οἱ
μ(ὲν) γ(ὰρ) βάρβαροι θεωρο(ῦν)τ[ες ἐθαύμαζον αὐτοῦ] τὴν   70
ἀνδρείαν. ὁ γ[ο(ῦν)] βασιλ[εὺς   ±10   πυνθ]α-

COLUMN SIX

Heading: Ὑπ[ερβ]άτου φράσεω[ς] κ(ατά)στασις

νόμ(εν)ος ἕτερον ἀλλ᾽ ἢ τοὺς αὐτο(ὺς) λόγο(υς) ἀκούων
ἀγασθεὶς τὴν ἀνδρείαν κ(αὶ) τ(ὴν) βεβαιότητα τῶν
τρόπ(ων), διενοήθη μ(ὲν) αὐτὸν ὅλως ἀφεῖναι νομίζων
[γ]ενόμ(εν)ον αὐτῶι φίλον πάντων ἔσεσθαι χρησι-
μώτατον. ἀντιπ{ε}ιπτόντων δ(ὲ) Βαγώου κ(αὶ)   5
Μέντορος, διὰ τὸ φθονεῖν κ(αὶ) φοβεῖσθαι μὴ πρω-
τεύσηι μᾶλλον ὧδ᾽ αὐτῶν ἀφεθείς, ταύτην μ(ὲν)
πάλι⟨ν⟩ μετεβάλετο τ[ὴ]ν γνώμην, δικάζων δ(ὲ)
τῶν γι⟨γ⟩νομ(έν)ων παρ[᾽ αὐτ]ῶι κακοπαθιῶν ἄμοι-
ρον αὐτὸν ἐποίησε [διὰ τὴν] ἀρετ(ήν). ἡ μ(ὲν) ο(ὖν) τοιαύτη   10
μετριότης ὑπῆ[ρξε παρ]ὰ τῶν ἐχθρῶν παρα-
δοξ[οτά]τ[η κ(αὶ)] π[ολὺ παρὰ τ]ὸν τῶν βαρβάρων
τρό[πον.....] τελ[.....]ν μέλλ[ω]ν· Φιλι-
[±12   ]ον[......]εσάμ(εν)ος ἀλλ[..]
[±12   ]εσκ[.... α]ὐτῶι πρὸ[ς] τοὺ[ς φ]ί-   15
[λους κ(αὶ) τοὺς ἑ]ταίρο(υς) [ἐπισ]τέλλειν ὡς οὐδ[ὲ]ν

tyranny he changed [. . .] a *gentler* rule. For this reason he ruled also
over *all* [the] *neighbouring territory* (60) up to Assos, when [. . .] to the
(above)-mentioned learned men [. . .] the city of (the) Assians. *Of
these he was* most *receptive of* Aristotle (and) [treated] him in a most
friendly way.'

What is more, Kallisthen[es] also has composed an (65) [. . .]
about him (in which) [he says] *especially the following* : 'Not only [was
he] *this sort of man* [when he was outside of] dangers, but also, [when
he found himself] close (to them), he continued to be still the same,
and he afforded (the) *greatest* [proof] of his courage in [death] *itself.*
For, (70) the barbarians [were amazed] *when they saw* his bravery,
while for his part the *King,* (since) *in his enquiries* [. . .]

COLUMN SIX

Heading: (The) figure (is that) of a transposed expression.

he kept hearing [nothing] other than the same accounts/reports,
being full of admiration for his courage and the stability of his
character, was of a mind to let him off entirely, with the thought
that, if he (Hermias) became his (the King's) friend, he would be the
most useful (5) of all men. But when Bagoas and Mentor objected,
out of envy and the fear that, once released, he might become the
foremost (courtier) in their stead, he (i.e. the King) changed his
mind again, but in passing judgement, he absolved him from the
mutilations that were (10) usual at *his* court [because of his] courage.
Now such moderation *was most* unexpected *from* one's enemies and
especially [contrary to] *the way* of the barbarians [. . .] being about
to. [. . .] | [. . .] (15) [. . .] to him to *send a message* to his [friends and
his] companions, (saying) that he had done nothing *unworthy* of philosophy [or] shameful.'

ἀ̣[(νά)ξιο]ν ε̣[ἴ]η φιλοσοφία[ς οὐδ’ ἄ]σχημον δ(ια)πεπρα-
γμ[(έν)]ος." κ(αὶ) ἡ κηδεία δ(ὲ) ἡ πρ[ὸς] τὸν Ἀριστοτέλη

κ[(αὶ)] ὁ γραφεὶς ἐπ’ αὐτῶ[ι Παι]ὰν μαρτυρεῖν αὐ-
τ[ο]ῦ τῆι ἀρετῆι δόξε[ιεν ἄν], κοὐκ ἂν [ἔ]χ[ο]ι φαύ-   20
λως αὐτὸν ἀναγρά[ψαι δι]ὰ τὸ μὴ πολλοῖς
πρὸ χειρὸς (εἶναι), ἔχοντα [ο]ὕ[(τως)]· "⌊Ἀρετ⌋ὰ πολ⌊ύ-
μ⌋οχθε γε-
νει βροτείωι, / θήραμα ⌊κάλλι⌋στον βίωι, / ⌊σ⌋ᾶς π⌊ε⌋-
ρί, πάρθενε, μορφᾶς / κ(αὶ) θα⌊νεῖ⌋ν ζηλωτ⌊ὸ⌋ς ἐν Ἑλλάδι πότμος / κ(αὶ) πόνους τλ⌊ῆ⌋ναι μαλερούς ἀκά-   25
μαντας. / τοῖον ἐπὶ φρέν⌊α⌋ βάλλεις / καρπὸν
ἰσαθάνατον χρυσοῦ τε κρείσσω / κ(αὶ) γονέων
μαλα⌊κ⌋αυγήτοιο θ’ ὕπνου. / σοῦ γ’ ἔνεκεν ⟨καὶ⟩ ὁ δῖος / Ἡ-
ρακ⌊λῆ⌋ς Λήδας τε κ⌊ό⌋ρ⌊οι⌋ / πόλλ’ ἀνέτλασαν ἔρ-
γοις, / ⌊σ⌋αν ἀγρ⌊εύοντε⌋ς δύνα⌊μ⌋ιν, / σοῖς τε πόθοις   30
⌊Ἀ⌋χιλεὺ⌊ς⌋ ⌊Αἴ⌋- / ας τ’ Ἀΐ̈δαο δόμ⌊ο⌋υς ἦλθον· / σᾶς δ’
⌊ἔ⌋νεκε⌊ν⌋ φιλ⌊ίο⌋υ μ⌊ορφᾶς⌋ Ἀταρνέος / ἔντροφος
⌊ἀ⌋λίο⌊υ⌋ χήρωσεν αὐγάς. ⌋ / ⌊το⌋ι⌊γ⌋(ὰρ) ἀοίδιμον ἔργοις /
⌊ἀ⌋θά⌊να⌋τ⌊ό⌋ν τέ μι⌊ν⌋ αὐξήσουσι Μο⌊ῦ⌋σαι, / Μναμοσύ-
⌊ν⌋ας θ⌊ύ⌋γατρες, Δ⌊ι⌋- / ὸς ξενίου σέ⌊β⌋ας αὔξου- / σαι φι-   35
⌊λ⌋ίας τ⌊ε⌋ γέρας β⌊ε⌋βαίου. ⌋" [καὶ μνημεῖον δὲ λέγε]-
[ται] Ἀριστοτέ[λης αὐτῶι ἐν Δελφοῖς ἀνα]-
θ[εῖ]ναι, ὃ δὴ κ[εῖται ±12 καὶ αὐ]-
τ[ὸ]ς ἐγγέγρ[αφε τὸ τοιόνδε]· "⌊Τόνδε ποτ’ οὐχ ὁ⌋-
σίως παραβ⌊ὰ⌋ς μακάρων θέμιν ἁγνήν / ἔ⌊-   40
κτεινεν ⌊Π⌋ε⌊ρ⌋σῶν τοξοφόρων βασιλεύς, / οὐ φα⌊-
νερᾶς ⌊λόγ⌋χη⌊ς⌋ φονίοις ἐν ἀγῶσι κρατήσας⌋, /
ἀλ⌊λ⌋’ ἀνδρ⌊ὸ⌋ς π⌊ί⌋στει χρησάμενος δολίου⌋. [πρὸς ὅν]
φησι Βρ[ύ]ω[ν ἐν τῶι Περὶ Θεοκρίτου ἐπίγραμ]-
μά τι Θεόκριτον [τὸν Χῖον τοιόνδε ἀντιποιῆ]-   45
σαι· "Ἑρμίο⌊υ⌋ εὐ⌊ν⌋ούχου τ⌊ε⌋ κ(αὶ) Ε⌊ὐ⌋βούλου τόδε⌋
δούλου / σῆμα κ⌊ε⌋νὸν⌋ κενόφρων θῆκεν Ἀριστο⌊-
τέλης· / ὃς ⌊γα⌋στρὸς τιμ⌊ῶ⌋ν ἄνομ⌊ον φύσιν εἵλετο ναί⌋-
ειν / ἀντ’ ⌊Ἀ⌋καδημείας βορβ⌊όρου ἐν προχοαῖς⌋."
ἀλλὰ γ(ὰρ) [ἔ]τι διαλλάττουσι κ(αὶ) π[(ερὶ) τ(ὴν) σύλ]ληψιν αὐτοῦ κ(αὶ) τὸν θάνατον· Ἕρμι[ππος] γ(ὰρ) ἐν τῶι Πε-   51
ρὶ Ἀριστοτέλους Β̅ ἐν το[ῖς δεσμο]ῖς φη[σι]ν αὐ-
τὸν τελευτῆσαι. οἱ δ’ ὑπ[ὸ βασιλ]έως βασα-
[νισ]θέντα ἀ(να)σταυρωθῆνα[ι, καθ]άπερ προέκ-
κειται. ο[ἱ δ](ὲ) αὐτὸν ἐσ[±10] μη[δ]ὲν   55

Both his connection by marriage with Aristotle and the [pae]an that was written for him *would* appear to testify (20) to his courage, and *it would not be* insignificant to record it (i.e. the paean) on account of the fact that it is not available to many. It goes *as follows*:

> Virtue, laborious for the mortal race to attain,
> The noblest object of life's hunt;
> For your beautiful form, O virgin,
> To die is a fate sought after in Greece (25)
> And to endure fierce, unwearied labours.
> Such is the fruit, quite divine, that you
> Cast upon the mind, (a fruit) better than gold,
> Than parents, than languid-eyed sleep.
> For your sake the godlike
> Herakles and the sons of Leda
> Endured much (30) in (their) labours,
> As they pursued the prize of your power,
> And out of yearning for you Akhilleus
> And Aias went to the halls of Hades.
> And it was for the sake of your beloved beauty that Atarneus'
> Offspring forsook the rays of the sun.
> Wherefore, the Muses, daughters (35) of Memory,
> Shall exalt his memory in song
> For his accomplishments, and make him immortal,
> As they exalt the majesty of Zeus, god of hospitality,
> And the honour of lasting friendship.

[And] Aristot[le is said] *to have dedicated* [a memorial to him (sc. Hermias) at Delphi], which indeed *is situated* [. . . and] *himself in-scribed* [the following]:

> This man once in (40) unholy transgression of the sacred law of the
>   blessed ones
> Was killed by the king of the Persians who carry the bow,
> Not overcoming him in deadly contest of spear out in the open,
> But employing the trust of a devious man.

Against him (sc. Aristotle) Br[y]o[n in his (book) <u>On Theokritos</u>], says (45) that Theokritos [the Khian] *composed* [the following] *epigram*:

> Of Hermias the eunuch and slave of Euboulos this
> Empty tomb was set up by the empty-headed Aristotle,
> A man, who out of respect for the lawless nature of his stomach,
>   chose to dwell
> At the mouth of 'borboros' instead of the Academy.

(50) And *yet* people *still* disagree about both his *capture* and his death.

[τῶ]ν Φιλίππωι συνεγνωσμ(έν)ων̣ [ὁμ]ολο[γ]ή-
σαντα, καθάπερ ὁ Καλλισθέν[η]ς. ἔτι δ' οἱ
μ(ὲν) ἐν τῆι Αἰολίδι Κατάνηι φα[σὶ]ν αὐτὸν
συλληφθῆναι, οἱ δ' ἑτέρωθι. δόξ[ειε] δ' ἂν ἐν
[..... τὰ] περὶ αὐτὸν διατεθεικ[έν]αι Ἀ-   60
ναξιμένης ἐν τῆι ἕκτηι τ(ῶν) Περὶ Φ[ίλιππ]ον ἱ-
στοριῶν, οὗ τὴν ἐκλογ(ὴν) παρίημι. ο[ὺ γ(ὰρ) ὄφε]λος.

"Ὁ δὴ βάρβαρος, κ(αὶ) κοινὸς κ(αὶ) ἄπασιν ἐχθ̣ρός⌋, κ̣(αὶ) πάντα τὰ τοιαῦτα." ταῦτα ἰδίαι προσιστ[ορεῖ ὡ]ς
παρ' ἔκαστα τῶν Ἀθηναίων τ̣[ὰ τοιάδ]ε [κα]-   65
τὰ τοῦ βαρβάρου λεγόντων. "Ἐγὼ γ̣(ὰρ) ὅτ̣αν τι⌞-

νὰ ἴδω τὸν μ(ὲν) ἐν Σούσοις κ(αὶ) Ἐγβατάνοις ⌞δεδοι⌟κότα
κ(αὶ) κακόνουν (εἶναι) τῆι πόλει φάσκοντα, ὃ̣ς κ(αὶ) πρ̣ότε-
ρον σ(υν)επηνώρθωσε τὰ τ(ῆς) πόλεως πρ̣άγμ̣α̣τα̣ κ(αὶ)
ν(ῦν) ἐπηγγέλλετο, εἰ δ(ὲ) μὴ 'δ(έ)χεσθε ὑμ̣εῖς ἀλλ' ἀ-   70
⌞π̣⌟εψηφίζεσθε οὐ τά γ' ἐκείνου αἴτι̣α, ὑ̣π̣ὲ̣ρ δ(ὲ)
τ̣ο̣ῦ ἐν ταῖς θύραις ἐγγὺς οὕ(τωσ)ὶ ἐν μέσηι⌞ι̣⌟ τῆι Ἑλλά-
⌞δ⌟ι αὐξομ(έν)ου ληιστοῦ τ(ῶν) Ἑλλήν(ων) ἄλλο τι λέγοντα, θαυμάζω, κ(αὶ) δ(έ)δοικα τοῦτον, ὅστις ἂν ἦι ποτε, ἔγωγε,

COLUMN SEVEN

Heading: Τίς ἡ ἐξ ὑπογύ[ου γ]ενηθεῖσα τῶι βασιλεῖ πρὸς Ἀ-
θηναίους [φιλ]ανθρωπί[α]

ἐπειδὴ οὐχ οὗτος Φίλιππον." ὑπερβάτωι τῆι φρά-

σει κέχρηται ἣν καταστατέον οὕ(τως)· ἐγὼ γὰρ ὅ-
ταν τιν' ἴδω τὸν μ(ὲν) ἐν Σούσοις κ(αὶ) ἐν Ἐκβατά-
νοις δ(ε)δοικότα, ὑπὲρ δ(ὲ) τοῦ ἐπὶ ταῖς θύραις ἐγγὺς οὑτωσὶ ἐν μέσηι τῆι Ἑλλάδι αὐξανομ(έν)ου ληι-   5
στοῦ τῶν Ἑλλήν(ων) μηδὲ λέγοντα, θαυμάζω κ(αὶ) δέ-
δοικα τοῦτον, ὅστις ἂν ἦι ποτ', ἔγωγε. φησὶ δ(ὲ) τὸν

βασιλέα κ(αὶ) πρότερον μ(ὲν) ποτ' ἐπανορθῶσαι τὰ
τ(ῆς) πόλεως πράγματα κ(αὶ) νῦν ἐξ ὑπογύο[υ] αὐτὸν
μ(ὲν) φιλοτιμηθῆναι περὶ αὑ[τήν, ἀπ]οψηφίσασθαι   10
δ(ὲ) τὴν πόλιν τὰ διδόμ(εν)α. [τὴν πρ]οτέραν μ(ὲν) ο(ὖν) ἐπα-

For Hermi[ppos] in (book) two of his <u>On Aristotle</u> *says* (that) he died in *imprisonment* . But some (say that), *after he had been tortured by the King*, he was crucified, *just as* was described (55) previously. *Yet others* (say that) [. . .], having confessed to none *of the* plans he had made with Philip, just as Kallisthen[e]s (says). Yet again, some say that he was captured at Katane in Aiolis, others (say that it was) some-where else. But it would seem (60) (that) [the issues] concerning him (sc. Hermias) have been laid out [. . .] by Anaximenes in the sixth (book) of his histories <u>On P[hilip]</u>, the quotation of which I pass by, [for] (it is) *not useful*.

'The barbarian and common enemy of mankind, and all that sort of thing.' He *includes* these examples specifically in his narrative, *alleging that / on the grounds that* (65) the Athenians make *such* state-ments *against* the barbarian on each and every occasion.

'For, as for me, whenever I see someone who is fearful of the man in Sousa and Ekbatana, and who says that he (sc. the man in Sousa) is ill-disposed to the city, even though in the past he helped in put-ting the city's affairs back in order and (70) just recently was making offers—and if you did not accept them, but voted their rejection, it was not his fault—and (when I see this same man) saying something different about the plunderer of the Greeks, who so near at hand, at our doors, in the very centre of Greece has so increased in power, I am amazed and I fear that man, whoever he may be, truly I do,

COLUMN SEVEN

Heading: What was the King's recent act of generosity towards the Athenians?

since he (does not fear) Philip.'

He has employed a transposed way of speaking, which one must construe as follows: For, if I see someone who fears the man in Sousa and in Ekbatana on the one hand, but concerning the plunderer, who is increasing in power at our doors, so near (5) at hand, indeed in the very centre of Greece, is not even saying a word, I am amazed and I fear him, whoever he is, truly I do.

And he says that the King both restored the city's fortunes on some previous occasion and now, recently, he (10) made a display of generosity towards it (sc. the city), but that the city voted to reject what was being offered.

νόρθωσιν ἔ[νι]οί φασιν α[ὐτὸν λ]έγειν τὴν ἐ-
π' Ἀντιαλκ[ίδου τοῦ Λ]άκ[ωνος] καταβᾶσ[α]ν
ε[ἰρήν]ην, οὐ[κ ὀρθῶς ὅσα γο(ῦν)] ἐμοὶ δ[οκεῖ]· ταύτην γ(ὰρ)
οὐ μ[όνον οὐκ ἐδέξαντο] Ἀθ[η]ν[αῖοι], ἀλλὰ κ(αὶ) πᾶν   15
τοὐν[αντίον τὰ διδόμ(εν)]' αὐτοῖς ἀ[πε]ώσαντο, παρ'
[ἣ]ν α[ἰτίαν Φιλό]χορος ἀφη[γεῖ]ται αὐτοῖς ὀνό-
[μ]ασι, πρ[οθ]εὶς ἄρχοντα Φιλο[κλέ]α Ἀναφλύ-
[σ]τιον· "Κ(αὶ) τὴν εἰρήν(ην) τὴν ἐπ' Ἀντ[α]λκίδου κατέ-

π[ε]μψεν ὁ βασιλεύς, ἣν Ἀθηναῖοι ο[ὐκ] ἐδ(έ)ξαντο   20
δ[ι]ότι ἐγέγ[ρ]απτο ἐν αὐτῆι τοὺ[ς τ(ὴν) Ἀσ]ίαν οἰκοῦν-
τ[ας] Ἕλληνας ἐν βασιλέως οἴκ[ωι π]άντας (εἶναι)
[σ]υννενεμημ(έν)ους. ἀλλὰ κ(αὶ) τοὺ[ς πρέσ]βεις το(ὺς)
ἐν Λακεδαίμονι συγχωρήσα[ντας] ἐφυγάδευ-
σαν Καλλιστράτου γράψαντος [οὐ]δ' ὑπομεί-   25
ναντας τὴν κρίσιν, Ἐπικράτην Κ[η]φισιέα, Ἀν-
δοκ[ί]δην Κυδαθηναιέα, Κρατῖνον Σ[φ]ήττιον, Εὐ-
β[ο]υλίδην Ἐλευσίνιον." οὐκοῦν ὅτι μ(ὲν) οὐκ εἰκός (ἐστι)

[τ]ὸν [Δ]ημοσθένη ταύτης αὐτοὺς ὑπομιμνή-
[σκ]ειν τῆς εἰρήν(ης) ἑόραται, ἑ[τ]έρας δ(έ) τινος εὐ-   30
[εργ]εσίας κ(αὶ) [ταχ' ἂν τ(ῆς)] περὶ Κό[νων]α τὸν Τιμοθέ-
[ου, δ(ιὰ) τὸ] τοῦ[τον] τ[αῖς ἐ]κ Φαρ[ναβά]ζου παρασκευ-
[αῖς] χρησάμ(εν)[ο]ν ἐν τ[ῆι π]ερὶ Κν[ί]δον ναυμαχίαι
[Λα]κεδαιμονίους ἀ[νὰ] κράτ[ος νι]κῆσαι. καὶ
[ταῦ]τα π[ιστ]ώσεται Φι[λό]χορος· προθεὶ]ς γ(ὰρ) ἄρχον-   35
[τα Σ]ου[νιάδ]ην Ἀχαρνέ[α ἐν τῆι Ε̄ οὕτως γρ[ά]φε[ι]· "Κ[ο]-
[νων μ(ὲν) ἀπὸ Κύ]πρου μ(ετὰ) π[ολλῶν νεῶν πλεύσας]
[τὸν δ(ὲ) τῆς Φρ]υγίας σα[τράπην Φαρνάβαζον ±7]
[±8]τὸ ναυτ[ικόν   c.18   ]
[....]δου[.] ἔπλευσεν[c.18   ]   40
[.....] Μ̄ τριήρων [c.20   ]
[.....]κόλπου σ[c.21   ]
[......]ων προσήγα[γεν ἐκ τῆς Συ]ρίας[±7]
[...]ας τὴν παραλ[c.19   ]
α[γ]αγὼν δ(ὲ) τὰς ναῦς [τ(ὰς) π(αρὰ) βασι]λέ[ως περὶ Λ]ώρυμ[α]
[τῆς] Χερ[ρο]νήσου κ(αὶ) [ἐν]τε[ῦ]θε[ν ±7] ἐπιπε-   46
σὼ[ν....] τῶι τῶ[ν Λ]ακεδαι[μονίω]ν να[υ]άρχωι
[εἰς] Φύσ[κ]ον κ[(ατ)ενεχθέ]ντι, κ(αὶ) [ναυ]μαχ[ί]ας γεν[ο]-
μ(έν)ης ἐνίκ[ησε κ(αὶ) π]εντήκ[ον]τα τριήρεις [αἱ]-

[By the] *previous* restoration some say *he* means the peace that came down in the time of Antialk[idas, the L]ak[onian], *incorrectly* , [at least as it] *seems* to me. For, (15) not *only* [did] the Ath[e]n[ians not accept] that peace, but entirely *the opposite*, they also rejected [what was being offered] to them, for [the reason which Philo]khoros *recounts* in these very words, after the heading 'the archon (was) Philo[kle]s of Anaphly[s]tos':

'And the King sent down the peace (20) in the time of Ant[a]lkidas, which was *not* accepted by the Athenians, because there had been written in it that the Greeks who were inhabiting [As]ia were all (to be) accounted members in the King's *household*. Furthermore, they banished the *ambassadors*, who gave their consent in Lakedai-mon, (25) on the motion of Kallistratos; and Epikrates of Kephisia, Andokides of Kydathenaion, Kratinos of Sphettos, and Euboulides of Eleusis did *not even* await the judgement/trial.'

Therefore, it has been seen that it is not likely that [D]emosthenes was reminding them of this (30) peace, but of some other bene-faction and [perhaps of the one] involving Ko[non], the [son of] Timothe[os, on account of the fact that] it was by using *the* armaments provided by Phar[naba]zos that *this man overwhelmed* the [La]kedaimonians in *the* naval engagement near Kn[i]dos. (35) Phi[lokhoros] *will confirm these events* as well, for *after the heading* 'the archon (was) [S]ou[niad]es of Akharna[i]', *he writes* [as follows in his fifth book]: 'K[onon . . . from Ky]pros with [. . . Pharnabazos the] *satrap* of [Phr]ygia [. . .] the *fleet* [. . .] (40) [. . .] he sailed [. . .] of 40 ships [. . .] of [the] gulf [. . .] *he brought up/approached* [from Sy]ria [. . .] (45) But/and *after bringing* the ships [provided by] *the King* [near L]orym[a on the] Kher[so]nese and *thence* [. . .] attacking [. . .] the navarch of the [L]akedai[monia]ns, *who had been carried down* [to] Physkos, and, when a *sea battle* took place, *he was victorious* and he *took* (50) fifty triremes *captive* and Peisandros was killed.'

68   TEXT AND TRANSLATION

χμαλώτους ἔ[λα]βε κ(αὶ) Πείσανδρο[ς] ἐτελεύ-   50
τησεν." ἀπὸ δ(ὲ) ταύτης τ(ῆς) ναυμαχίας ὁ Κόνων

κ(αὶ) τὰ [μακρὰ τ]είχη τοῖς Ἀθηναίοι[ς] ἀνέ-
στησεν, ἀκόντων Λακεδαιμονίων, καθάπερ πάλιν ὁ αὐτὸς σ(υγ)γραφεὺς ἱστο[ρ]εῖ· λόγον δ[έ] τινα κ(αὶ) πάνυ πιθανὸν ἔχειν οἶμαι   55
ταύ[τ]ης μνημονεύειν τὸν ῥήτορα τῆς
περ[ὶ] τὴν πόλιν τοῦ βασιλέως φιλοτιμίας.
κ(αὶ) γ(ὰρ) δὴ τὸ φάναι "κ(αὶ) πρότερον συνεπη-
νώρθωσε τὰ τ(ῆς) πόλεως πράγματα" συνω-
δόν πώς (ἐστι) τῶι δοκεῖν τῆι Φαρναβάζου π(αρα)-   60
σκευῆι τὸν Κόνωνα συγχρησάμ(εν)ον Λακε-
δαιμονίους κ(ατα)ναυμαχῆσαι. δύναιτο
δ᾽ ἂν κ(αὶ) ἑτέρας ἀπὸ βασιλέως εἰρήνης, ἣν
ἀσμ(έν)ως προσήκαντο οἱ Ἀθηναῖοι, μνημονεύειν τὰ νῦν ὁ Δημοσθένης, περὶ ἧς πάλιν   65
ὁ Φιλόχορος διείλεκται ὅτι π(αρα)πλήσιον αὐτὴν τῆι τοῦ Λάκωνος Ἀνταλκίδου προσήκαντο, ἀπειρηκότες ταῖς ξενοτροφία[ι]ς
κ(αὶ) ἐκ πάνυ πολλοῦ τοῦ πολέμου τετρυμέ-
νοι, ὅτε κ(αὶ) τὸν τῆς Εἰρήν(ης) βωμὸν ἱδρύ-   70
σαντο. πολλὰς δ᾽ ἂν κ(αὶ) ἄλλας τις ἔχοι παρα[δ]ε[ι]-
κνύναι τοῦ βασιλέως εἰς τὴν πόλιν εὐερ-
γεσίας, [ο]ἷ(ον) τὴν ὑπὸ Καλλίου τοῦ Ἱππον{ε}ί-
κου πρ[υ]τανευθεῖσαν εἰρήνην, κ(αὶ) χρη-
μάτ[ω]ν ἐπιδόσεις ἰδίαι κ(αὶ) κοινῆι τῆι πό-   75

COLUMN EIGHT

Heading: Τίς ἦν χρόνος [ἐ]ν ὧι ταπεινωθέντες P̄
καὶ Λ̄ μ[όν]ον τά[λαν]τα προσόδ[ο]υ ἐλάμβα-
νον.
Περὶ το[ῦ] Ῡ τάλ[α]ντα προσόδ[ο]υ λαμβάνειν
τοὺς [Ἀ]θηναίους.

λει, ὧν τάχ᾽ ἂν αὐτοὺς ὁ Δημοσθένης ὡς ἐν
κεφαλαίωι τὰ νῦν ὑπομιμνήσκοι. κ(αὶ) περὶ
μ(ὲν) τῆ[ς] πρότερον ἐπανορθώσεως τῆι πόλει
πρα[γ]μάτων ἀρκεῖν οἶμαι κ(αὶ) ταῦτα, τὴν

As a result of this sea battle Konon also restored the [Long] Walls for the Athenian[s], *against the will* of the Lakedaimonians, as the same writer records once again. And (55) I think that there is an argument, even (a) very persuasive (argument) that this is the act of generosity of the King towards the city that the orator is mentioning. For, indeed, his saying 'even though in the past he helped in putting the city's affairs back in order' is (60) somewhat in accord with the opinion that Konon defeated the Lakedaimonians at sea by availing himself of Pharnabazos' armament.

But Demosthenes could in this instance be making mention of another peace initiated by the King, one which the Athenians (65) were glad to agree to. Philokhoros has discoursed about this peace also, (saying) that they agreed to it, (though it was) very similar to that of the Lakonian, Antalkidas, because they were exhausted by the cost of maintaining mercenary troops and were worn out from the war (being) very long. (70) At this time, too, they set up the altar of Eirene. One could produce many other examples also of the King's benefaction towards the city, as, for example, the peace that was put to the vote on the motion of Kallias, the son of Hipponikos, and (75) contributions of cash at both the private and public level to the ci-

COLUMN EIGHT

Heading: What was the time when they were reduced (to the point where) they only received 130 talents in revenue?
Concerning the fact that the Athenians received 400 talents in revenue.

ty, of which Demosthenes was perhaps reminding them on this occasion in a summary fashion.

Well, I think that the above is sufficient on the subject of the restoration of the city's affairs in the past, and I must proceed to give

δ' ἐξ [ὑ]πο[γ]ύου, περὶ ἧς φησι, "Κ(αὶ) ν(ῦν) ἐπηγγέλλετο,   5
εἰ δὲ μὴ ἐδ(έ)χεσθε ὑμεῖς ἀλλ' ἀπεψηφίζεσθε,
οὐ τάδ' ἐκείνου αἴτια", ἐξῆς ἀφηγητέον· πρὸ
τοίν(υν) ἐτῶν πέντε τοῦδε, τοῦ Φιλίππου ἐπὶ ἄρχοντος Λυκίσκου Ἀθήναζε περὶ εἰρήνης
πέμψαντος, βασιλέως πρέσβ[ει]ς συμπροσ-   10
ήκαντο οἱ Ἀθηναῖοι, ἀλλὰ ὑπε[ρο]πτικώτε-
ρον ἢ ἐχρῆν διελ[έ]χθησαν αὐτ[οῖ]ς. εἰρηνεύ-
σειν [γ]ὰρ πρὸς α[ὐτὸν ἔφασ]αν, ἐὰν μ[ὴ] ἐπὶ τὰς
Ἑλλην[ίδας] ἴηι [πόλεις. ἀφηγο](ῦν)ται τ[αῦτ]α Ἀνδρο-
τίων, ὃς κ(αὶ) [±10   Ἀνα]ξιμ(έν)εις. ἔ[χο]ι δ' ἂν   15
ἄμεινον [τὰ τοῦ Φι]λοχόρου παραγράψαι.
προθεὶς γ(ὰρ) οὗ[τος ἄ]ρχοντα Λυκίσκ[ον] ὑποτί-
θησιν· "Ἐπὶ τούτου βασιλέως πέμ[ψ]αντος

Ἀθή[να]ζε πρέσβεις κἀξιο(ῦν)τος τὴν [φι]λίαν
[δ(ια)μένει]ν ἑαυτῶι τ(ὴν) πατρώιαν, ἀπε[κρί]νατο   20
[τοῖς π]ρέσβεσιν Ἀθήνησι διαμε[νεῖν] βασι-
λε[ῖ τὴν φιλ]ίαν, ἐὰν μὴ βασιλεὺς ἐπ[ὶ τὰς] Ἑλλη-
νίδ(ας) ἴηι πόλεις." σαφῶς ἐν τούτοις τὰ [μ(ὲν) ἀ]πὸ τοῦ
βασιλέως καταπεμπόμ(εν)α εἰρηναῖα ἦν κ(αὶ) φι-
λάνθρωπα, τὰ δ' ἀπὸ τοῦ δήμου πᾶν τοὐναντί-   25
ον βαρύτερα κ(αὶ) ἀπηνῆ. στοχάσαιτο δ' ἄν τις τ(ὴν)
τοῦ βα[σ]ιλέως πρὸς τὸν Ἀθηναίων δῆμον φι-
λοτιμ[ία]ν γεγονέναι διὰ τὴν κατὰ τοῦ Μα-
[κ]εδό[νο]ς ὑπόν[οι]αν, πρὸς ὃν ἐξοίσειν ἔμελ-
[λε πόλεμο]ν δ(ιὰ) τὸ [πυθέσθ]αι παρ' Ἐ[ρ]μ[ί]ου τοῦ Ἀ-   30
[ταρνέ]ως τὴν [τ]οῦ πρ[ὸς] αὐτὸν [π]ολ[έ]μου π(αρα)-
[σκευήν]. "(Ἔστι) τοίν⌞υ⌟⌞ν⌟ τι πρ⌞ᾶγμ⌟α κ(αὶ) ἄ⌞λ⌟⌞λ⌟ο, ὃ λ⌞υ⌟μαί-

---

ν⌞ε⌟ται τὴν πό⌞λ⌟ιν ὑπὸ βλασφημ⌞ί⌟ας ἀ⌞δ⌟ίκου⌟ κ(αὶ) λό-
⌞γ⌟ων οὐ πρ⌞οσ⌟η⌞κ⌟ό⌞ν⌟των δ(ια)β⌞ε⌟βλημ⌞μ⌟(έν)ον, εἶτα τοῖς
⌞μ⌟ηδὲν τῶν δικαίω⌞ν⌟ ἐν τῆι πο⌞λ⌟ι⌞τ⌟⌞ε⌟ίαι βουλομέ⌞-⌟   35
⌞ν⌟οις ποιεῖν πρόφασι⌞ν⌟ π(αρ)έχε⌞ι⌟· κ(αὶ) ⌞πά⌟ντων, ὅσ' ἐκ⌞-⌟
⌞λ⌟είπει, δέον παρά⌟ του γίγνεσθαι, ἐπὶ τοῦθ'⌟
⌞ε⌟ὑρήσετε τ⌞ὴ⌟ν αἰτ⌞ί⌟αν ἀν⌞α⌟φε⌞ρ⌟ομένην⌟." [.....]
[....τὸ θεωρι]κὸν αἰνίτ[τ]ε[τ]αι τ[±8]
[±10   ]προτερ[.....]χε[±8]   40
[±11   ]μ(εν)ο[.]ν[...]μ(ὲν) γ(ὰρ) [±10   ]
[±9   ]φ[...]πωσο[.]κεδ[.]κι[±9]

an account of the (5) recent instance, about which he (sc. Demosthenes) says: 'and just recently he was making offers, and if you
did not accept them, but voted their rejection, it was not his fault.'
Well now, five years before this, in the archonship of Lykiskos,
when Philip sent (an embassy) to Athens concerning peace, (10) the
Athenians also gave audience to the ambassadors of the King, but
their verbal exchange with them was more arrogant than it should
have been. For *they said* (that) they would live at peace with *him*,
provided he did not attack the Hellen[ic cities]. *These matters are recounted by* (15) Androtion, who also [. . . Ana]ximenes. But it would
be better to add [the words] of [Phi]lokhoros, for, after the heading 'the archon (was) Lykiskos' he goes on: 'In this man's archonship, when the King sent ambassadors to Athe[ns] and was asking
that his ancestral (20) *friendship* continue to exist, reply was made
[to his] ambassadors at Athens that the King *would* continue to
have [their] *friendship*, so long as he not attack [the] Hellenic cities.'
Clearly in these (negotiations) the proposals sent down by the King
were peaceful and (25) generous, while the reaction of the People
(was) quite the reverse, excessively heavy-handed and abrasive.
One could guess (that) the King's munificence towards the Athenian people was generated by his suspicion about the Macedonian,
against whom he was about to initiate (30) [hostilities] as a result
of (his) *learning* from He[r]m[i]as of A[tarne]us about that man's
(i.e. Philip's) *preparations* for hostilities against himself.

'Then there is something else as well, that is being assaulted by
unjust slander and unbecoming language, (and in this way) is harm-
ing the state, (and) furthermore (35) is providing an excuse for those
who are unwilling to perform any of their just obligations under
the constitution. Moreover, you will find that this is the reason put
forward for every failure (to perform) what is required to be done
by anyone.' [. . . the] *theoric fund* is being alluded to cryptically [. . .]
(40). **Too little remains of lines 41 and 42 for translation.**

[.....βλ]ασφημεῖν φησι τοὺ[ς....]ετησ
τι[.....]πο⟨ι⟩οῦντας. "Ἦν ποτ' οὐ π‸άλαι παρ'‸ ὑμῖν

‸ὅ‸τ' οὐ π‸ρ‸ο‸σ‸ή‸ι‸ει τ‸ῆι πόλει τάλαντ‸α ὑπ‸ὲρ ‸τ‸ριά-   45
κοντα κ(αὶ) ἑ‸κ‸ατόν. κ(αὶ) οὐδείς (ἐστι) τῶ‸ν τρ‸ιηραρχεῖν
δυναμ(έν)ων οὐδὲ ‸τῶ‸ν εἰσφέρε‸ι‸ν ὅστις οὐκ ἠ-
ξίου τὰ καθήκ‸ον‸τα ἐφ' ἑαυτὸν ποιεῖν, ὅ-
τι χρήματ' οὐ περιῆν." εἴη ἂν οὗτος ὁ κ(αι)-

ρὸς ἐν ὧι περὶ Αἰγὸς ποταμοὺς ἡττη-   50
θέντες ἐταπεινώθησαν κ(αὶ) εἰς βρα-
χὺ ὁ δῆμος συνεστάλη τῶν ἐξ‸ω‸[τ]ι-
κῶν προ[σό]δων περικοπεισῶν. [σ]α‸-
φὲς δ(ὲ) τοῦτο πο⟨ι⟩ήσει

A space of about ten lines is left uninscribed.

"‸Μ‸ετὰ ταῦτα ἡ τ‸ύ‸χη, καλῶς ποιοῦσα, πολλὰ πε-   55
π‸ο‸ίηκε τὰ κοινά, κ(αὶ) τετρακόσια ἀντὶ τῶν ἑκατὸν ταλάντων προσέρχεται, οὐδενὸς οὐδὲν ζη-
μιουμένου τῶν τὰς οὐσίας ἐχόντων." πε-
[ρὶ] τοῦ τετρακόσια τάλαντα πρόσοδον ἔ-
χειν τοὺς Ἀθηναίο(υς) κατὰ τοὺς Φιλίππου   60
χρόνους κ(αὶ) Θεόπομπος ἐν τῆι ἑβδόμηι
[κ(αὶ) εἰ]κοστῆι τῶν Περὶ Φίλιππον ἐπιμαρτυρεῖ,
[ἐν] οἷς Ἀριστ[ο]φῶν ὁ δημαγωγὸς αὐτῶι πα-
ρ[ά]γεται λέγ[ω]ν ταῦτα· "Ἐνθυμεῖσθε δ' ὡς

COLUMN NINE

Heading: Ὅτι B̄ Ἀρι[σ]τομήδεις, ὁ μ(ὲν) Φεραῖος, ὁ δ' Ἀ-
θηναῖο[ς] ὁ Χαλ[κ]οῦς ἐ(πι)καλούμ(εν)ος.

πάντων ἂν ποιήσαιμ(εν) ἀνανδρότατον εἰ
τὴν ε[ἰ]ρήν[(ην)] δ(ε)ξαίμεθα π(αρα)χωρήσαντες Ἀμφιπό-
λεως, μεγίστην μ(ὲν) πόλιν τῶν Ἑλληνίδ(ων) οἰκο(ῦν)-
τες, πλείστους δ(ὲ) συμμάχο(υς) ἔχοντες, τριακοσί-
ας δὲ τριήρεις κεκτημ(έν)οι κ(αὶ) σχεδὸν τετρα-
κοσί[ω]ν τα[λ]άντων προσόδους λαμβάνοντες,   5
ὧν ὑπαρχόντ(ων) τίς οὐκ ἂν ἡμῖν ἐπιτιμή[σ]ειεν

(43) [. . .] he says (that) slanders are being spoken by/against the men who [. . .] are doing.

'There was a time for us (45) when the income to the state was no more than one hundred and thirty talents; yet there is no one of those capable of undertaking the trierarchy nor of paying the eisphora, who thought it right not to do the duties that concerned him because there was no surplus revenue.'

It could be that this (50) occasion was when they were humbled after the defeat near Aigospotamoi and the people were reduced to short commons, since (their) foreign revenue had been cut off. This will clarify (the point)/he will make this clear. **A space of about ten lines is left uninscribed.** (55) 'Subsequently, when fortune prospered, the public revenue became large and the income was four hundred talents instead of one, without any of the propertied class suffering any loss.' Concerning the fact that the Athenians had revenues of four hundred (60) talents in Philip's time there is also the testimony of Theopompos in the twenty-seventh (book) of his <u>On Philip</u>, where Arist[o]phon, the demagogue, *is introduced* speaking the following (words) to it/him (them?): 'Consider that

COLUMN NINE

Heading: That (there were) two Ari[s]tomedes, the one Pheraian, the other Athenia[n], nicknamed 'the Brazen'.

we would be doing the most cowardly of all things, if, in agreeing to the peace, we should cede Amphipolis, we who inhabit the greatest of the Greek city-states, we who have very many allies, we who (5) possess three hundred triremes and receive revenues of almost four hundred talents. Since these are (our) resources, who would not reproach us, if we should yield anything contrary to justice out of fear for the power of the Macedonians.'

εἰ τ(ὴν) Μακεδόνων δύναμιν φοβηθέν[τ]ες συγ-
χωρήσαιμέν τι παρὰ τὸ δίκ(αι)ον." "Ἀλλὰ ποῦ σ(υν)-

τρίβεται τὸ πρᾶγμα κ(αὶ) ποῦ δυσχεραίνεται; ὅταν τὸ   10
ἀπὸ τῶν κοιν(ῶν) ἔθος ἐπὶ τὰ ἴδια διαβιβάζοντας
ὁρῶσί τινας, κ(αὶ) μέγαν μ(ὲν) ὄντα π(αρ᾽) ὑμῖν εὐθέως
τὸν λέγοντα, ἀθάνατο⌊ν δ᾽⌋ ἕνεκ᾽ ἀσφαλείας, ἑτέραν δ(ὲ) τὴν κρύβδην ψῆ⌊φον τοῦ φα⌋νερῶ⌊ς θ⌋ορύ-
βου. τ⌊α⌋ῦτ᾽ ἀπ⌊ισ⌋τίαν, τα⌊ῦτ᾽ ὀργὴν ἔχ⌋ει." ἄξι[ον] δια-   15
πορήσειν τίνα [ποτὲ οἱ δημαγ]ωγοὶ πρ[άτ]τον-
τές σφισιν μ(ὲν) α[ὐτοῖς ὠφελί]αν κ(ατ)εσκεύαζον ἐκ
τοῦ πλήθους, τ[ὸ δ(ὲ) τῆς] π[ό]λεως συμφέρον ἠφα-
νιζον. κ(αὶ) [(ἔστιν)] ὅσα δ[οκ]εῖν ὃ βούλεται λέγ[ει]ν
τοιοῦτο· [ὅ]σα κοίν᾽, ἅπερ ἦν ὄντως τοῦ [δ]ή-   20
μου, κ[οι]ν[ὰ] ταῦτ᾽ οὐκ ἠξίουν διανέμ[εσθ]αι,
ἀλ[λ᾽ ἐπε]μ[η]χανῶντο κ(αὶ) τῶν οὐ δικ(αί)ω[ν ...]ας
[.]ρ[.... οὐσί]αν δημοσίαν αἰτιώμ(εν)οι [κατ]έ-
χειν τοὺ[ς] ε[ὐ]πόρο(υς) ἢ μὴ δικ(αί)ως τὰ κοιν[ὰ] δι-
οικεῖν ἢ ἄ[λ]λον τινὰ τρόπον ἀδικεῖν, ἐμβα-   25
λόντες δ᾽ ἂν εἰς ἀγῶνας κ(αὶ) γραφὰς δημοσίας
οὓς αὐτοῖς δόξειεν εἰς ἐκκλησίαν κ(αὶ) τὸ δι-
καστήριον ἦγον. ὁ δ(ὲ) δῆμος ἐπὶ ταῖς αἰτίαις
φανερῶς μ(ὲν) [ἐ]θορύβει κ(αὶ) δεινὰ πάσχειν ἐβόα
τ[ο]ὺς εὐπόρ[ο(υς)], κρύφα δ(ὲ) κατεψηφίζετο κ(αὶ)   30
π[ο]λλῶν ἐ[τί]μα χρ[ημάτω]ν. ταῦτα δ(ὲ) ἐγί-
γνε[τ]ο[.....]τ⌊ο[ῖ]s[....]ουμ(έν)οις τὰ [π]ο-
λιτε[ύ]ματα ταῦτα πολλὴ[ν] ἀσφάλει[αν] π(αρ)-
εῖχε [κ(αὶ)] με[γάλ]ας δυναστείας[...]⌊α⌋τα τ(ῶν) π[...]σι
ωνε[±7]υτ[..]η τὸ μέρο[s] οἴεται[...]   35
του[±10 πολι]τεύματο[s ἐ]πανο[ρθω]-
σ[±15]δως εἶχε κατα[.....]
"⌊Καίτοι λοιδορίας⌋ χωρίς, εἴ τις ἔροιτ᾽, ⌊εἰπέ⌋
⌊μοι, τί δὴ γιγνώ⌊σκ⌊ων⌋ ἀκριβῶς, Ἀριστό⌊μηδες⌋,
⌊οὐδεὶς γὰρ τὰ τ⌋οιαῦτα ἀγνοεῖ, τὸν μ(ὲν) ⌊τῶν ἰδι⌋-   40
⌊ωτῶν βίον ἀσφ⌊αλῆ κ(αὶ) ἀ⌋π⌊ρ⌋άγμονα κ(αὶ) ἀκίνδυν⌊ον⌋
⌊ὄντα⌋, τ⌊ὸν δ(ὲ) τῶ⌋ν πολιτευομ(έν)ω⌊ν⌋ ⌊φιλαί⌋-
⌊τιον κ(αὶ) σφ⌊αλ⌊ερόν⌋." δύο Ἀριστομήδ[ε]⌊ι⌋ς (εἰσίν), [ἕ]-
[τερος μ(ὲν)] ὁ Φε[ρ]αῖος ὁ συμπολεμῶν τοῖς [βα]-
σιλ[έ]ω[ς] στρατηγοῖς Φιλίππωι, περ[ὶ οὗ] ἄλ[λοι]   45
τε κ(αὶ) αὐτὸς [ὁ] Φ[ίλ]ιππος ἐν τῆι πρὸ[ς Ἀ]θη[ν]αί-
ους ἐπιστολῆι διείλεκται κ(αὶ) Θεό[πομπος]

'But where (10) does the matter make (them) sore and where does it cause annoyance? Whenever they see certain people carrying over from public affairs the practice (established there) to their private business and (whenever they see) a man of words becoming great in your eyes overnight, (and not just great but) even immortal because of his security, and (whenever they see) your secret ballot differing from the fuss (you make) in public. (15) That creates a lack of trust, that (creates) anger.'

It is right that the question should be raised (about) what [ever] (it was) [the] *demagogues* were doing to provide benefit for themselves at the expense of the populace, yet on the other hand to destroy the city's advantage.

And this is, as far as it appears, the sort of thing he means to say: (20) So much property (as was) public, that which truly belonged to the People, this they did not think fit to divide amongst themselves, but (?) they *made plans against/ devised* [. . .] even of the not-just (undeserving?), accusing the *wealthy* of *retaining* state property or of administering public moneys in an unlawful way (25) or of doing wrong in some other way and, by involving (them) in lawsuits and public prosecutions, they kept bringing before the Assembly or the law courts any person whom they saw fit. And the People, whilst in public they made an outcry at these charges and shouted (that this was) a terrible way to treat (30) the *wealthy*, in secret cast their vote against (them) and fined (them) much *money*. This kept happening [. . .] **Lines 32–7 are too poorly preserved for coherent translation. See commentary for suggested restorations.** (38) 'And yet, invective apart, if someone should ask (you), "Tell me, Aristomedes, why, indeed, when you know precisely, (40) for there is not anyone who is ignorant of such things, (that) the life of the private citizens is secure and uninvolved and free from danger, whilst that of those in politics is contentious and insecure . . .".' There are two Aristomed[e]s, [one], the Phe[r]aian, who fought the war on the side of *the* (45) *King's* generals against Philip. About [this man] *others* have discoursed and in particular Ph[il]ip himself in his letter to (the) [A]the[n]ians and Theo[pompos] in the 48th

ἐν τῆ[ι] Ἦ καὶ Μ̄ τῶν Περὶ Φίλιππον, τῶ[ι]
Ἀλεξάνδρωι δὲ περὶ Κιλικίαν ἀντιτα-
ξάμ(εν)ος σὺν Δαρείωι εἰς Κύπρον διέδρα,　　　　50
καθά φησιν Ἀναξιμ(έν)ης ἐν τῆι Θ̄ τῶν Περὶ Ἀλέξανδρον. ἕτερος δ(ὲ), πρὸς ὃν ν(ῦν) ὁ Δημοσθένης διέξ⟨ε⟩ισιν, Ἀθηναῖος ὁ Χαλκοῦς
λεγόμ(εν)ος, περὶ οὗ ἄλλοι τε κ(αὶ) Δείναρ-
χος ἐν τῆι Δοκίμου Ἀπολογίαι ὑπὲρ τοῦ ἵπ-　　55
που φησὶν οὕ(τως)· "Ἐπεὶ δ' ὑπ' Ἀριστομήδους τοῦ
Χαλκοῦ κ(αὶ) Χαιρεστράτου τοῦ ἑαυτοῦ θείου
προήχθης οὐ δίκ(αι)α ποιῶν ἐγκαλεῖν ἐμοί,
τηνικαῦτα δ(ὲ) κ(αὶ) τῶι μ(ὲν) δίκην ἔρημον ἀπε-
γράψατο κατ' ἐμοῦ ἀποδημοῦντος κ(αὶ) ταῦ-　　60
τ' ἐν Θετταλίαι." κ(αὶ) οἱ κωμικοὶ δ' αὐτοῦ μνη-

μονεύουσι, καθάπερ Φιλήμων μ(ὲν) ἐν Λι-
θ[ο]γλύφωι· "Πρὸς τῶι μυροπωλίωι γὰρ ἀν-
θρώπων τινῶν / ἤκουσα Χαλκοῦν περιπα-
τεῖν κλέπτην τινά· / ἄπειρος ὢν δὲ τοῦ λε-　　65
γομ(έν)ου πράγματο[ς] / Ἀριστομήδην ἠρόμην
παριόνθ' ὁρῶν. / ὁ δ' ἐνήλατ' εὐθύς μοι παρα-
στὰς τῶι σκ[έ]λει / παίει τε λὰξ πύξ, ὥστε μ'
ἐκθανεῖν· ἐπεὶ / μόλις γε φεύγων ἐξέπεσον
ἄλληι λά[θρ]α." Τιμοκλῆς δ' ἐν Ἥρωσιν· "Ἑρ-　　70

μῆς δ' ὁ Μαίας ταῦτα συνδιακονεῖ /

COLUMN TEN

Heading: Χρόνοι κ(αὶ) π[ό]λεις τ[ο]ῦ λόγου.

Ὅτι Ἀναξ[ι]μέν[ο]υς (ἐστὶν) ὁ λόγος.

ἂν ἦι πρόθυμος· κ(ατα)βέβηκεν ἄσμ(εν)ος / χαριζό-
μ(εν)ός γ' Ἀρ[ι]στομήδηι τῶι καλῶ⟨ι⟩, / ἵνα μηκέτ'
αὐτὸν ὁ Σάτυρος κλέπτην λέγηι." κ(αὶ) ἐν'{Ε}Ι-

καρίοις· "Μαρσύαν δ(ὲ) τὸν φ[ί]λαυλον Αὐτο-
κλέα δ(ε)[δ]αρμ(έν)[ο]ν / γυμνὸν ἑστάναι καμ{ε}ί-　　5
νωι προσπεπατταλευμ(έν)ον, / Τηρέα τ' Ἀριστο-

(book) of his <u>Concerning Philip</u>. Furthermore, after campaigning against Alexander throughout Kilikia (50) at Darius' side, he ran away to Kypros, as is told by Anaximenes in the ninth (book) of his <u>On Alexander</u>. And the other one, against whom Demosthenes is expounding on this occasion, (was) an Athenian, nicknamed the Brazen. About this man others (have written) and in particular Deinarkhos (55) in the <u>Defence of Dokimos: Concerning the Horse</u> speaks as follows:

'Since you were induced by Aristomedes the Brazen and Khairestratos, his own uncle, to act unjustly and bring a charge against me. And at that time also for one (of them) he brought a suit (60) against me that he won by default, since I was out of the country and, at that, in Thessaly . . .' The comic playwrights also make mention of him, for example Philemon in <u>Sculptor</u>:

> Beside the perfume-seller's I heard some
> Men (saying) that Brazen, a thief, was on the loose.
> Being quite ignorant of the point of the statement,
> I asked Aristomedes, (whom) I saw passing by.
> And he, forthwith, standing beside me, set upon my leg
> And beats (it) with foot and fist, so I almost fainted dead away.
> When, escaping with real difficulty, I departed (70) secretly by
> Some other way . . .

And Timokles in <u>Heroes</u> (writes):

> Hermes, the son of Maia, aids in conducting these things,

COLUMN TEN

Heading: Circumstances and cities of the speech.
That the speech is (by) Anax[i]men[e]s.

> If he is favourable. He gladly came down as
> A real favour to Ar[i]stomedes the Fair, to prevent Satyros
> Calling him a thief any longer.

Also in <u>Ikarians</u> (he says):

> . . . (that) Autokles (is) 'Marsyas the Flute-lover', when he had his hide tanned
> (And) stood naked, pinned on the furnace,

μήδην.—διὰ τί Τηρέα λέγεις;—/ διότι τηρ[ε]ῖν
δεῖ π(αρ)όντος τοῦδε τὰ σκεύη σφόδρα. / εἰ δ(ὲ) μή,
Πρόκνη γενήσῃ⟨ι⟩, κνώμενος τὸ κρανίον /
ἂν ἀπολέσῃς.—ψυχρόν.—ἀλλὰ πρὸς θεῶν ἐπί[σ]χε-   10
τε / μηδὲ συρίξητε."

[Ī]Ā

"Ὅτι μ(ὲν), ὦ (ἄνδρες) Ἀθ(ηναῖοι), Φίλιπ⌐πος οὐκ ἐποιήσατο
    τ(ὴν) εἰρή⌐ν(ην)⌐
πρὶ⌐ὸ⌐ς ἡμ⌐ᾶς⌐, ἀλλ' ἀνεβάλετο τὸν πόλεμον, π⌐α⌐-
σιν ὑμ⌐ῖν φα⌐ν⌐ε⌐ρὸ⌐ν γέγονεν." οἱ χρόνοι το[ῦ]   15

───────

λόγου σ[α]φεῖς τέλεόν (εἰσιν). τέως μ(ὲν) γ(ὰρ) ἦσαν οἱ [λό]-
γοι τῶι Δημοσθένει ὑπὲρ τοῦ τὸν Φίλιππον
ἐ(πι)βουλεύειν δ(ια)νοεῖσθαι τοῖς Ἕλλησι παρα-
κινο(ῦν)τα τὴν ε[ἰρ]ήν(ην) κ(αὶ) τοὺς ὅρκο(υς) π(αρα)βαίνο[ν]-
τα· νυνὶ δ(ὲ) λαμπρῶς ἤδη συνερρωγότο[σ]   20
τοῦ πολέμου [γε]⟨ν⟩νικώτερόν φησιν [ὁρᾶν]
τί πο[ι]ή[σ]ωσιν αὐτῶι ἄντικρυς ἀπαγγε[ί]-
λαντ[ι] διὰ τῆς [ἐπισ]τολ(ῆς) τὸν π[ρὸς] αὐτ[ο]ὺς πόλεμον. ἐπὶ γο(ῦν) τ[έλ]ει τῆς [ἐ(πι)]στολ[ῆς] φησι· "Πρ[ο]-
υπαρχόν[τ]ων ο(ὖν) ὑμῶν κ(αὶ) διὰ τὴν [ἐμὴ]ν εὐλά-   25
βειαν μᾶλ[λον ἐπ]ικειμ(έν)ων κ(αὶ) διὰ τέλους ὡς
μάλιστα [δύν]ασθ[ε] πρα[γ]ματευομ(έν)ων ὅπω[σ]
[ἔ]λ[οι]τ' [ἂν] ἐμὲ πο[λέμωι τὸ]ν πρότερον ὑ[μᾶς]
[c.18   μ](ετὰ) τοῦ δικ(αί)ου ἀμ[υ]-
[νοῦμαι   ±12   ] ἀντιπ(αρα)ταττόμ(εν)ο[σ]."   30
[±7   ] δ[ὲ τ]ῆς συμβουλ(ῆς) κατὰ τ[άδε]·
"⌐Ὅτι μὲν⌐, ὦ (ἄνδρες) Ἀ⌐θ(ηναῖοι), Φί⌐λιππος οὐκ
        ἐποιήσ⟨ατο⟩ τ(ὴν) εἰρή⌐ν(ην)⌐
⌐πρὸς ἡμᾶς⌐, ἀλλ' ἀ⌐νεβά⌐λετο τὸν πόλε(μον), πᾶσιν ἡ-
⌐μ⌐ῖ⌐ν φα⌐ν⌐ε⌐ρὸν γέγ⌐ονεν⌐. "ἐξήφθη δ' ὁ π[ρὸ]ς
[τὸν] Μ[α]κεδόνα π[ό]λεμος Ἀθηναί(ων) [....]   35
[...τ]ἆλλα μ(ὲν), ὅσα Φίλιππος εἰρήνην [πρ]οσ-
ποιού[μ(εν)ο]ς ἄγειν ἐπλημμέλει, το[ὺς] Ἀ-
θηναίο(υς), μάλιστα δ' ἡ ἐπὶ Βυζά[ν]τι-
ον κ(αὶ) Πέρινθον αὐτοῦ στρατεία. τὰς ⟨δὲ⟩
πόλεις ἐφιλοτιμεῖτο παραστήσασθαι   40
δυοῖν ἕνεκα, τοῦ τε ἀφελέσθαι τὴν σιτο-
πομπίαν τῶν Ἀθηναί(ων) κ(αὶ) ἵνα μὴ πόλεις

And (that) Aristomedes (is) 'Tereus'.—Why do you call (him)
  Tereus?—

Because, when he's around, you've got to be terribly careful of
  your bags.

Otherwise, you'll become Prokne, scratching your head (10),

If you lose (them).—(That's a) frigid (joke).—(I know) but, by the
  Gods, be patient

And do not hiss.

(Speech) 11

'So, men of Athens, that Philip did not make peace with us, but
(just) put off the war, (15) has now become clear to you all.'

The circumstances of the speech are perfectly clear. For hitherto
Demosthenes' speeches were concerned with the fact that Philip
was intending to plot against the Greeks by disturbing the peace
and transgressing the oaths, (20) but now, since the war had obviously already broken out, he says (that) [he sees] what more *noble*
course of action they should take against him, since he has openly
reported in his *letter* his war *against* them. At any rate, at the *end* of his
letter he (i.e. Philip) says:

'Since (it is) you, (25) therefore, (who) are taking the initiative and
are more aggressive as a result of *my* caution, and are all the time to the
best of your *ability* exerting yourselves *to the end that* you [might] *take*
me *by war, your* former [. . .], *with* justice *I* (30) *shall defend myself* [. . .],
marshalling my forces against (you).'

And [. . .] of his counsel (is) as *follows* : 'So, men of Athens, that
Philip did not make peace with us, but (just) put off the war, has
now become clear to you all.' And a match was put to the (35) war
of the Athenians *against* [the] M[a]cedonian [. . .] on the one hand
all the other ways Philip offended the Athenians whilst (he was) pretending to live in peace, and, in particular, his expedition against
Byza[n]tion and Perinthos. These cities (40) he was anxious to bring
back to his side for two reasons: both to deprive the Athenians of
their grain supply and so that they might not have coastal cities
that were providing bases for their fleet and places of refuge for the

ἔχωσιν ἐπιθαλαττίους ναυτικῶι προΰ-
χοντες ὁρμητήρια κ(αὶ) καταφυγὰς τοῦ
πρὸς αὐτὸν πολέμου, ὅτε δὴ κ(αὶ) [τὸ] π(αρα)- 45
νομώτατον ἔργον διεπράξα-
το τὰ ἐφ᾽ Ἱερῶι πλοῖα τῶν ἐμπόρ(ων) κατα-
γαγ[ώ]ν, ὡς μ(ὲν) ὁ Φιλόχορος Ā πρὸς τοῖς δι-
ακ[οσ]ίοις, ὡς δ᾽ ὁ Θεόπομπος R̄Π, ἀφ᾽ ὧν
ἑπτακοσία τάλαντα ἤθροισε. ταῦτα δὴ 50
[...]εσι διαπεπρᾶχθαι ἐπὶ Θεοφράστου
[τ]οῦ μετὰ Νικόμαχον ἄρχοντος, καθά-
[π]ερ ἄ[λ]λοι τε κ(αὶ) Φιλόχορος οὑτωσί φη-
[σιν]· "Κ(αὶ) Χάρης μ(ὲν) ἀπῆ{ι}ρεν εἰς τὸν σύλλο-

γ[ον] τῶν βασιλικ(ῶν) στρατηγῶν καταλι- 55
πὼν ἐφ᾽ Ἱερῶι ναῦς, ὅπως ἂν τὰ πλοῖα τὰ
ἐκ τοῦ Πόντου συναγάγωσι. Φίλιππος
δ᾽ α[ἰ]σθόμ(εν)ος οὐ παρόντα τὸν Χάρητα τὸ μ(ὲν)
[π]ρῶτον ἐπειρᾶ{ι}το πέμψαι τὰς ναῦς τὰ
[π]λοῖα κ(ατα)γαγεῖν· οὐ δυνάμ(εν)ος δ(ὲ) βιάσ- 60
[σ]θαι, στρατ[ι]ώτας διεβίβασεν εἰς τὸ
πέραν ἐ[φ᾽] Ἱερὸν κ(αὶ) τῶν πλοίων ἐκυρί-

COLUMN ELEVEN

Heading: Τί τὸ ὀρρωδεῖν.

—————

Π(ερὶ) Νικαίας.

—————

Π(ερὶ) τοῦ σκορακίζειν κ(αὶ) τῆς Ἐς
κόρακας παροιμίας.

ευσεν. ἦν δ᾽ οὐκ ἐλάττω τὰ πάντα διακοσίων
κ(αὶ) τριάκοντα. κ(αὶ) ἐπικρίνων τὰ πολέμια διέ-
λυε κ(αὶ) τοῖς ξύ[λ]οις ἐχρῆτο πρ[ὸ]ς τὰ μηχανώματα, κ(αὶ) σίτου [κ](αὶ) βυρσῶν κ(αὶ) χρημάτων πολλῶν ἐγκρατὴ[ς] ἐγένετο." Χρόνοι μ(ὲν) δὴ τῆς 5

—————

συμβουλ(ῆς) κ(αὶ) πέρας τῶν Φιλιππικῶν τοῦ-
τ᾽ ἂν εἴη. ὑπ[ο]τοπήσειε δ᾽ ἄν τις οὐκ ἀπὸ
σκοποῦ συμ[π]εφωρῆσθαι τὸ λογίδιον

(45) war against him; and at that time, indeed, he committed [his] greatest transgression by seizing the merchants' ships that were at Hieron. According to Philokhoros (they were) two hundred and thirty (ships), while Theopompos (says they were) one hundred and eighty, and from these (50) he amassed seven hundred talents. (That) these actions were perpetrated *the year before* in the archonship of Theophrastos, the archon after Nikomakhos, as (is reported by) others and, in particular, Philokhoros, who says the following:

'And Khares sailed away to a meeting (55) of the King's generals, leaving behind warships at Hieron for the purpose of gathering together the cargo ships from the Pontos. And Philip, when he perceived that Khares was absent, at first attempted to send his (own) warships to (60) seize the boats, but, being unable to capture (them), transported (his) soldiers over to the other side against Hieron and gained control of the cargo

COLUMN ELEVEN

Heading: What (is the meaning of the word) 'orrodein'?
Concerning Nikaia.
Concerning the (word) 'skorakizein' and the proverbial saying 'to the crows' (es korakas).

boats. Altogether (the vessels) were not less than two hundred and thirty. And, determining (that they were) prizes of war, he broke (them) up and applied the timbers towards his siege weapons. He also gained possession of grain and hides (5) and much money.'

Well now, (these are) the circumstances of his speech of advice and this would be the culmination of the <u>Philippics</u>. One would not be off target to suspect (that) this little speech has been cobbled

ἔκ τινων Δημοσθένους πραγματ⟨ει⟩ῶν ἐ-
πισυντεθέν. κ(αὶ) (εἰσὶν) οἵ φασιν Ἀναξιμ(έν)ους　　　10
(εἶναι) τοῦ Λαμψακηνοῦ τὴν συ[μ]βουλήν, [...]
δ[.] ἐν τῆι ἑβδόμηι τῶ[ν Φιλιππ]ικ(ῶν), ην ὀ-
λίγου δεῖν γρ[ά]μμασιν α[ὐτοῖς ἔ]ντετ[ά]-
χθ[αι]. ἔνιοι δ(ὲ) [..]νομ[..]φο[...]κωτερω[.]
ἡρμήνευσαν, καθά[πε]ρ τὸ ὀρρωδεῖν ἥ-　　　15
κιστα Δημο[σθ]ενικὸν ὂν κ(αὶ) εἴ τινα ἄλ[λ]α
ὅμοια τούτω[ι]. "Ὅτι δ(ὲ) χρὴ μήτε ὀρρωδεῖν

ἡμᾶς τ(ὴν) ἐκείνου ⌞δ⌟ύναμιν μήτε ἀγεννῶς
⌞ἀν⌟τιταχθ⌞ῆ⌟ναι πρὸς αὐτόν." ὀρρωδεῖν δε-
δο[ι]κέν[αι (ἐστίν), ἀπὸ] δ(ὲ) τοῦ συμβεβηκότος　　　20
τοῖς δ(ε)δι[ό]σι [π]εποίηται· τοὔνομα γ(ὰρ) περὶ
τὸν ὄρρον [...] ὡς {ε} ἴδεδροι. Ὅμηρος· "Ἴδιον
ὡς ἐνόησα, δ(ε)δάκρυνται δ(έ) μοι ὄσσε." κ(αὶ) ὁ κω-
μικὸς Ἀριστοφάνης ἐν Βατράχοις ἐπὶ τοῦ
κατεπτηκότ[ο]ς Διονύσου· "Χὠ πρωκτὸς　　　25
ἰδίει πάλαι."—"⌞Ὑ⌟ποπτεύεται δ' ὑπὸ τ(ῶν) Θη-

βαίων Ν⌞ί⌟κ(αι)αν μ(ὲν) [φ]ρούραι κ(ατ)έ[χ]ων, εἰς δ(ὲ)
τὴν Ἀμφικτυο⌞νία⌟ν εἰσδεδυ[κώ]ς." Ν{ε}ίκαι-

α ἐπιθαλ[ά]σσιό[ς (ἐστι)] πόλις Θερμ[ο]πυλῶν
ἀπέχουσα σταδίους Κ̄, περὶ ἧς Τιμοσθέ-　　　30
ν[η]ς ἐν τῶι Περ[ὶ] Λιμ(έν)ων Ē φησὶ [τρό]-
[πον] τοῦτον· "Ἐκ [Θερμοπ]υλῶν δ(ὲ) κομισ[θέν]-
[τι πλο]ῦ[ν] ὡς [στ]αδί[ων Κ̄ (ἐστὶ) π]όλις Ν{ε}ίκαια,
[πεζεύοντι δὲ ὅσον πεν]τήκοντα· ἀπὸ [δὲ]
[ταύτης μάλιστ]α σταδίους Ē ἄκρα　　　35
[κ]ει[ται ψα]μμώδης ἐπὶ σταδίους τέττα-
[ρα]ς [ἔχουσα νηὶ] μακρᾶι ὕφορμον." κ(αὶ) Φιλόχ[ο]-
[ρο]ς δ' [ὅτι Λοκ]ροῖς Φ[ί]λιππος αὐτὴν ἐκέ[λευ]-
[σε] π[αρὰ] Θ[η]βαίων ἀποδοθῆναι διὰ τῆ[ς]
ἔ[κ]της φησι τὸν τρόπον τοῦτον· "Φιλ[ίπ]-　　　40
[που] δ[(ὲ) καταλα]βόντος Ἐλάτειαν κ(αὶ) Κυτίν[ιον]
κ(αὶ) πρέσβ[ει]ς πέμψαντος εἰς Θήβας Θε[ττα]-
λῶν Αἰν̣[ι]άνων Αἰτωλῶν Δολόπων Φθι-
ωτῶν κ(αὶ) ἀξιο(ῦν)τος Νίκαιαν Λοκροῖς
παραδιδόναι παρὰ τὸ δόγμα τὸ τῶν　　　45
Ἀμφικτυόν(ων), ἣν ὑπὸ Φιλίππου φρουρου-

together, a cumulative accretion from some of Demosthenes' treat-
ments (10) of the issues. And there are those who say (that) the speech
of advice belongs to Anaximenes of Lampsakos [. . .] in the seventh
(book) *of his* [Philipp]ika [. . .] has been inserted in almost *the very*
words. And some people have interpreted [. . .](15), for example,
the (word) 'orrodein' as being not at all Demo[sth]enic, and any
other words like it.

'And that it is right for us neither to break out in a cold sweat
(orrodein) at his power nor to oppose him ignobly.' To 'break out in
a cold sweat' (orrodein) (20) is/means to be afraid; it (i.e. the word)
is created as a result of what happens to those who are afraid. For
the word about the bum [. . .], as 'people with sweaty bums.' (To
quote) Homer: 'When I recognized (him), I broke into a sweat, and
my eyes filled with tears.' And the comic playwright Aristophanes
in Frogs, at the expense of (25) the cowering Dionysos, (makes him
say): 'And my arse has been exuding moisture for a long time.'

'And he is suspected by the Thebans for retaining Nikaia with a
garrison and for having wormed his way into the Amphiktyony.'
Nikaia is a coastal city, (30) twenty stades distant from
Therm[o]pylai. And Timosthen[e]s writes about it this way in the
fifth (book) of his On Harbours: 'And, *for a person travelling* [by sea]
from [Thermop]ylai, the city of Nikaia [is situated (at a distance
of) about 20] *stades*, [but for a person on foot it is as much as] *fifty*.
(Separated) from (35) [this by about] 5 stades *lies* a *sandy* promontory, four stades in extent [with] anchorage for a [ship] of war.' And
[the fact that] Ph[i]lip *ordered* it to be given back to (the) Lo[k]rians
by (the) Th[e]bans is stated by Philokh[oro]s (40) in his sixth (book)
as follows: 'After Phil[ip] *had captured* Elateia and Kytin[ion] and
had sent to Thebes *ambassadors* from (the) The[ssa]lians, (the)
Ain[i]anians, (the) Aitolians, (the) Dolopians (and the) Phthiotians,
and was demanding (that they) give Nikaia (45) back to the Lokrians
in contravention of the resolution of the Amphiktyons—(Nikaia

μ(έν)[ην], ὅτ᾽ ἐκεῖνος ἐν Σκύθαις ἦν, ἐκβαλόν-
τες [τ]οὺς φρούρο(υς) αὐτοὶ κ(ατ)εῖχον οἱ Θηβαῖ-
οι, τούτοις μ(ὲν) ἀπεκρίναντο πρεσβείαν
ὑπὲρ ἁπάντων π[ρὸ]ς Φίλιππον διαλεξο-   50
μ(έν)ην ⟨πέμψειν⟩." (εἰσὶν) δ(ὲ) καὶ ἄλλ[αι] Ν{ε}ίκαιαι, περὶ ὧν οὐ-

κ οἶμαι ἀ[να]γκ[αῖον] νῦν λέγειν. "Ἔτι δ(ὲ)

τῶν πολλ(ῶν) ἐὰν ἁμάρτ⌐ηι τις, ζ⌐ημίαν κ(ατὰ) τ(ὴν) ἀ-
ξ⌐ίαν⌐ εἴληφεν. οἱ δ(ὲ) ὅ⌐τ⌐αν μ⌐ά⌐λιστα κατορ-
θ⌐ώ⌐σι, τότε μάλιστα σκορακίζονται   55
κ(αὶ) ⌐πρ⌐οπηλακίζονται." παρὰ τὸ ἐς κόρα-
[κα]ς πεποίηται τοὔνομα, ὅπερ εἰώθα-
[μ(εν) κοινῆι] λέγειν κατὰ τῶν μετὰ βλα-
[σφ]ημ[ί]ας ὁποίποτε ἀπιόντων. μνη-
μονεύει δ᾽ αὐτῆς Ἀριστοφάνης ἐν   60
Ὄρ[ν]ισιν· "Ἐς κόρακας ἐλθεῖν κ(αὶ) π(αρ)εσκευ-
⌐ασμ(έν)⌐ους." θέλει μ(ὲν) γ(ὰρ) λέγειν εἰς τὰ ὄρνεα,
[χα]ριεντίζεται δ(ὲ) εἰς τὴν παροιμίαν,
[ἥ]ν φησιν ὁ Δήμων διαδοθῆναι
ἐνθένδε γράφ(ων) τὸν τρόπον τοῦτον· "Τοὺς   65
Βοιωτούς φασιν ἀναστάτους ὑπὸ Θραι-

COLUMN TWELVE

Heading: *ἰδὲ μὴ νεμομένους
Π(ερὶ) τῶν Φιλίππου τραυμάτων.

κῶν γενομ(έν)ους εἰς τὴν τότε μ(ὲν) Αἰολίδα ν(ῦν) δὲ
Θετταλίαν ὀνομαζομ(έν)ην στρατεύσασθαι,
κ(αὶ) τοὺς τὴν γῆν νεμομένους ἐξελάσαντας   *
τὴν ἐκείνων κατέχειν χώραν. πολεμο(ύν)των
δ(ὲ) πρὸς αὐτοὺς τῶν Αἰολέων κ(αὶ) τοὺ[ς] καρ-   5
πούς το(ὺς) ἐπετείους αἰεὶ φθειρόντων, πέμ-
ψαντες εἰς Δ(ε)λφοὺς ἐπηρώτων πότ⟨ερον⟩ μένω-
σιν ἐπὶ ταύτης ἢ ἑτέραν χώραν ζητῶσι.
τοῦ δ(ὲ) θεοῦ φήσαντος λευκοὺς κόρακας
πρότερον φανεῖσθαι ἢ τοὺς Βοιωτο(ὺς) τῆς   10
γῆς ταύτης ἀποβαλεῖν, θαρρήσαντες ἐ-
πὶ τ[ῶ]ι χρησμῶι τὴν ν[......]ν ἀγορὰν ἐν-

was a place) that the Thebans themselves had taken, after expelling Philip's garrison that was holding it, when he was in Scythia— to these (ambassadors) they (the Thebans) replied (that) an embassy (50) ⟨would be sent⟩ to Philip to negotiate about all issues.'

And there are other Nikaias also, but I do not think it *necessary* to speak about them at this point.

'Furthermore, if one of the rank and file makes a mistake, he receives a punishment that accords with his crime, but, in the case of these men, it is at the moment when they are most successful (55) that they are treated with the most contemptuous (skorakizein) and insulting language.'

The word (i.e. skorakizein) has been created on the basis of the (expression) 'es korakas' ('to the crows'/'to Hell'), which we are accustomed to use [commonly] against those who are being dismissed to some place with a curse.

It is used (60) by Aristophanes in <u>Birds</u>: 'And ready to go to the crows (Hell).'

He means to refer to the birds (i.e. the crows), but the joke relates to the proverb, *which* Demon says arose (65) from the following circumstance, (which) he narrates this way:

'The story goes that, when the Boiotians were displaced

COLUMN TWELVE

Heading: *If not, 'nemomenous' ('inhabiting'/'farming').
        Concerning Philip's injuries.

by the Thracians, they marched into the territory that was then called Aiolis but now is Thessaly and, after driving out those who were inhabiting the land, took possession of these people's country. And (5) the Aiolians kept waging war against them and kept on destroying their annual crop. (So the Boiotians) sent (a delegation) to Delphi to enquire whether they should remain on that land or search for another. And, when the God replied that white crows (10) would be seen before the Boiotians would be ejected from that land, they took heart at his response and eagerly convened the [. . .] assembly, which the Thessalian people even now [. . .]. Well, when

τόνως συνῆγον ἦν κ(αὶ) νῦν [...]ͅγειν τὸ τῶν
Θετταλ(ῶν) ἔθνος. [μ]εθ[υσ]θέντ[ω]ν ο(ὖν) τ(ῶν) νεανί-
σκων τινὲς ἀ̣[να]θηρ[εύ]σαντες κόρακας   15
κ(αὶ) τούτους γυ[ψ]ώσαντες ἀφῆκαν πέτε-
σθαι πρὸς κακίαν μ(ὲν) οὐδ(ε)μίαν, παιγνίας
δ(ὲ) κ(αὶ) γέλωτος τοῦτο πράξαντες. περιπετα-
μέν(ων) δ(ὲ) τ[ὰς πόλε]ις αὐτῶν κ(αὶ) πάντων τὸ γε-
[γ]ονὸς θαυ[μα]ζόντ(ων), κ(αὶ) τῶν μ(ὲν) τετελέσθαι   20
τὸν χρησμὸν φασκόντων, ἐγχωρίωι
δ(ὲ) τινι ἰδιώματι λεγόντων ἄλλο τοιοῦτο   /
γενέσθαι ⟨...⟩ παρὰ τὸν Παγασιτικὸν κόλπον
κατώικησαν, ὅθεν φασὶν ἀπ᾽ ἐκείνου
κληθῆναι τοὺς ἐκεῖ Κόρακας. οἱ δ᾽ Αἰολεῖς   25
τεταρα[γ]μ(έν)οις τ[οῖ]ς Βοιωτοῖς ἐπιπεσόν-
τες ἐκείνους μ(ὲν) ἐξήλασαν, τὴν δ(ὲ) χώραν ἀπέλαβον. τοὺς δ᾽ ἀδικ[ο](ῦν)τάς τι κ(αὶ) φυ-
γῆι ζημι[ο]υμ(έν)ους ἐπὶ πολὺν [χρ(όνον)] εἰς τοὺς
Κόρακας λεγομ(έν)ους ἐκείνους ἀπέστελ-   30
λον, ὅθεν [τοῖ]ς ἀπορ{ε}ιππτουμ(έν)οις τὸ [ἔπο]ς
[τοῦτ᾽] ἐ̣[σ]κορακί[ζει]ν ἔτι κ(αὶ) ν(ῦν) ἐπιφέρ[ε]-
[ται......].”—“⌐Κἀ⌐κεῖ̣νοι μ⌐(ὲν) Ἀθηναίοις φό⌐ρους⌐
⌐ἤνεγκαν, ἡ δ᾽ ἡμ⌐ετέρα πόλις οὐδ(ε)νί ⌐πω τῶν ἁ-⌐
⌐π⌐άν⌐τω⌐ν.” ὅτι Μακεδόνες Ἀθηναίοις φό-   35
ρου[ς ἐτ]έλο(υν) ἐν τῶι Περὶ τοῦ στεφάνου δεδη-
λώκα[μ]ε[ν]. “ἀλλὰ τὸν μ(ὲν) ἐκ Μακεδονία⌐ς⌐

⌐ο⌐ρ⌐μώμ(εν)⌐ο⌐ν οὕ(τως) (εἶναι) φιλ⌐ο⌐κίνδυνον ὥσθ᾽ ὑπὲρ
τ̣οῦ μ⌐εί⌐ζω ποιῆσαι τὴν ἀρχὴν κ(ατα)τετρῶσθαι
πᾶν τ⌐ὸ σῶ⌐μα τοῖς πολεμίοις μαχόμ(εν)ον.” πε-   40
ρὶ ὧν ἔσχε τραυμάτων ὁ Φίλιππ[ος ε]ἴρη-
ται μ(ὲν) ἡμῖν ἐντελῶς· κ(αὶ) νυνὶ δ᾽ εἰς β[ρ]α-
χὺ ὑπομνηστέον. περὶ μ(ὲν) γ(ὰρ) τὴν Μεθώ-
νης πολιορκίαν τὸν δεξιὸν ὀφθαλ-
μ[ὸ]ν ἐξεκόπη τοξεύματι πληγείς, ἔ[ν] ὧι   45
τὰ μηχανώματα κ(αὶ) τὰς χωστρίδας λε-
γομ(έν)ας ἐφεώρα, καθάπερ ἐν τῆι Δ̄ τῶν
περὶ αὐτὸν ἱστοριῶν ἀφηγεῖται Θεόπομπος, οἷς κ(αὶ) Μαρσύας ὁ Μακεδὼν ὁμο-
λογεῖ. ὁ δ(ὲ) Δοῦρις, ἔδει γ(ὰρ) αὐτὸν κ(αὶ) ἐνταῦ-   50
θα τερατ[ε]ύσε[σθαι, Ἀ]στέρα φησὶ (εἶναι) τοὔνομα τοῦ τὸ ἀκ[όντιον καιρίως] ἐπ᾽ αὐτὸν

the young men got drunk, (15) some (of them) caught crows and covered them with white chalk and (then) let them loose to fly.

'They did this with no evil intent, but merely for a joke and a laugh. But, when these flew around the cities and everyone (20) was astounded at what had happened, some were declaring (that) the oracle had been fulfilled and were saying in the local idiom that "something like it" had happened

'⟨. . .⟩ settled beside the gulf of Pagasai, as a result of which, so the story goes, from that time (25) the (people) there got the name "Korakes" (i.e. Crows). And, when the Boiotians were in disarray, the Aiolians fell upon them and drove them out and took back the land. And for a long time (after that) those men who had committed some crime and were under the penalty of exile were (30) sent to the so-called "Korakes". For this reason still today [this] *expression* "eskorakizein" *is applied* to those who are outcasts [. . .].'

'And those men have paid tribute to Athens, but our city alone (has) not yet (paid tribute) (35) to anyone.' That the Macedonians *used to pay tribute* to Athens, we have demonstrated in our (work) <u>On the Crown</u>.

'. . . but that a man who originates from Macedonia is so fond of danger that, to enlarge his domain, he would suffer wounds (40) to all his body in the course of fighting his enemies . . .'

Concerning the wounds that Philip received, we have given a full account, and at this time it must be abbreviated. In connection with the siege of Methone he had his right eye (45) knocked out, when it was struck by an arrow while he was supervising the siege engines and the so-called (tortoise) sheds. This is the way it is recounted by Theopompos in the fourth (book) of his histories about him (i.e.the <u>Philippika</u>), and Marsyas the Macedonian (50) concurs. But Douris (of Samos), for even on this occasion he had to *talk marvels*, says (that) the name of the man who cast the *missile* at him [in this opportune way] was [A]ster (Shooting Star), even though almost *all those who*

ἀφέντος, [τ]ῶν [συνεστρα]τευκότων
αὐτῶι σχε[δ]ὸν [πάν]των τοξεύμα[τ]ι
λεγόντων [a]ὑτὸ[ν] τετρῶσθαι. τὰ μ(ὲν) γ(ὰρ)   55

περὶ τῶν αὐλητ(ῶν) ὁμολογεῖται κ(αὶ) παρὰ
Μαρσύαι, διότι συντελοῦντι μουσικοὺς
ἀγῶνας αὐτῶι μ{ε}ικρὸν ἐπάνω τῆς
συμφορ(ᾶς) κ(ατὰ) δαίμονα συνέβη τὸν Κύ-
κλωπα πάντας αὐλῆσαι, Ἀντιγενείδην   60
μ(ὲν) τὸν Φιλοξένου, Χρυσόγονον δ(ὲ) τὸν
[Στ]ησιχόρου, Τιμόθεον δ(ὲ) τὸν Οἰνιάδου.
τὸν μ(ὲν) ο(ὖν) ὀφθαλμὸν οὕ(τω) φασὶν αὐτὸν ἐκ-
κοπῆναι, τὴν δ(ὲ) κλεῖν τ(ὴν) δ(ε)ξιὰν ἐν Ἰλ-
λυριοῖς λόγχηι τὸν Ἰλλυριὸν Πλευ-   65
ρᾶτον διώκοντα, ὅθ᾽ ἑκατὸν μ(ὲν) καὶ

COLUMN THIRTEEN

Heading: [Ὅ]τι οὐκ (ἔστι) τ(ῶν) Φιλιππικῶν ὁ λό[γος],
Δημοσθένους δ(ὲ) ἄλλως.

π[ε]ντήκοντα τῶν ἑταίρ(ων) τραυματίζον-
τα[ι], τελευτᾶι δ(ὲ) Ἱππόστρατος ὁ Ἀμύντου.
τ[ρ]ίτον τραῦμα λ[α]μβάνει κατὰ τὴν
εἰς Τριβάλλους ἐμβολήν, τὴν σάρι-
σάν τινος τῶν διωκομ(έν)ων εἰς τὸν   5
δ(ε)ξιὸν αὐτοῦ μηρὸν ὡσαμ(έν)ου κ(αὶ) χω-
λώσαντος αὐτόν. δόξειε δ᾽ ἂν περὶ τὰ
τραύματα κ(αὶ) τὰς πληγὰς ἀμείνονι
τύχηι κεχρῆσθαι τοῦ πατρὸς ὁ Ἀλέξαν-
[δ]ρος. δέκα γάρ π[ο]υ λαβὼν καιρίους   10
πληγὰς ἄπηρ[ος διέ]μεινε, Φιλ[ί]ππωι
δ(ὲ) τὸ [ὅλ]ον σῶμα δι[ε]λελώβητο.

ΙΒ

"Πε⸤ρὶ μ(ὲν) τ⸥οῦ π(αρ)όντος ἀργυρίου κ(αὶ) ὧν τ(ὴν) ἐκ-
κλ⸤ησία⸥ν ποιεῖτε, ὦ (ἄνδρες) Ἀθ(ηναῖοι), οὐδ(έ)τερόν μοι δο-   15
κεῖ τῶ⸤ν⸥ χαλεπῶν (εἶναι)." κ(αὶ) τοῦτον ἔνιοι

And some people include this speech amongst the <u>Philippics</u>, not correctly, in my opinion at any rate. For there is not any mention whatsoever of Philip in it, (20) nor, moreover, of (the) Macedonians nor of the cities which he had taken in transgression of the treaty and his oaths—Perinth[os, O]lynthos, (and) Poteidaia—(whilst there is mention), on the other hand, *of the* freedom of (the) Rhodians and of (the) Mytilenians, though the Macedonian was involved in neither case. (25) And, perhaps, [D]emosthenes *composed* this *speech* after the peace with Philip, *at a time when* [things] *were* quiet [for the Ath]e[ni]ans *on the* Macedonian *front*, but affairs in As[ia] *kept them very* (30) busy. At any rate the following (is what) he says about *the situation* at the time: 'For if it was sufficient for you to be inactive and if you were not in the habit of expending extra effort on the condition of Greek affairs, it would be another story. But, as it is, you claim to be leaders and (35) to set limits on others regarding their rights, and yet you neither have equipped ⟨nor are equipping⟩ a force that is keeping watch or will be on guard, but during your gross inactivity and in your absence the popular government at Mytilene has been dissolved, during your gross inactivity (40) the (popular government) at Rhodes (also).'

But one could detect that the date of the speech was the archonship of K[a]llimakhos, the (archon) after Apollodoros. Why, do you suppose? Because he mentions the action taken by the Athenians against the Megarians over the Sacred Orgas. This (45) happened during the archonship of Apollodoros, as is recounted by Philokhoros, writing as follows:

'Because the Athenians had a dispute with the Megarians over the delimitation of the Sacred [O]rgas, they entered (the territory of) Megara *with* (50) Ephialtes, the general for the homeguard, and marked out the limits of the Sacred Orgas. With the Megarians' agreement the men who marked out the boundaries were Lakrateides the Hierophant and Hierok[l]eides the Dadoukhos. And the edge-lands, too, around the Orgas, (55) were consecrated by them,

καθιέρωσαν τοῦ ἱεροῦ χρή{ι}σαντος λῶι- 55
ον κ(αὶ) ἄμεινον ἀν⟨ε⟩ῖσι κ(αὶ) μὴ ἐργαζομ(έν)οισι.
κ[(αὶ)] ἀφώρισαν κύκλωι στήλαις κατὰ [ψ]ήφι-
σμα Φιλοκράτους." τούτων ἑοραμ(έν)ων

ε̣ἴη ἂν μετὰ τόνδε τὸν ἄρχοντα συντε-
ταγμ(έν)ος ὁ λόγος, διακέλευσιν ἔχων τῶν 60
εἰς τοὺς πολέμο(υς), εἴπερ ἄρα ἔσοιτο
π(αρα)σκευάζων. ζητεῖται δ' ἐν τῶι λόγωι

COLUMN FOURTEEN

Heading: Π(ερὶ) τῆς Ὀργάδος.

Διὰ τί τοὺς Μεγαρέας κ(ατα)ρά-
τους ἔφη.

οὐδὲν ὅτι μὴ λόγου τινὸς ἐν τοῖς πρὸ τοῦ
τέτευχεν. ὅμως περὶ τ(ῆς) Ὀργάδος εἰς βρα-

χὺ δηλωτέον. λέγεται τοίνυν ὀργὰς
κοινότερον μ(ὲν) ἅπαν χωρίον δενδρῶδες
οἷ(ον) ἄλσος, πεποιημ(έν)ου τοῦ ὀνόματος πα- 5
ρὰ τὸ ὀργᾶν κ(αὶ) τινα ὁρμὴν εἰς τὸ βλαστά-
νειν ἔχειν. οὐ(τωσ)ὶ γ(ὰρ) ἔλεγον ὀργᾶν τὸ πρὸς ὁτι-
ο(ῦν) ὁρμὴν εἰς ἑτοιμότητα ἔχον, καθάπερ
κἂν τῶι βίωι φαμ(ὲν) ὀργάσαι τὸν πηλὸν ἐ-
πὶ τοῦ π(αρα)σκευάσαι πρὸς τὰς ἀλοιφάς. Σοφο- 10
κλῆς ἐν [Ποιμ]έσιν· "Ἔμισ[γ'], ὅσον δ(ὴ) [π]ηλὸν
ὀργάσαι κ[αλό]ν." κ(αὶ) Αἰσχύ[λ]ος ἐπὶ τῶν πρὸ
τῆς Καδμείας νεκρῶν τ[ῶ]ν πρὸς τὴν
ταφὴν ἑτοίμως ἐχόντων· "Ὤργα τὸ
πρᾶγμα, διεμύδαιν' ἤδη νέκυς." Τὰς 15
δ' ὀργάδας ἄλματά τε κ(αὶ) ἄλση προσηγό-
ρευον ἀπὸ τῆς εἰς τὸ μῆκος ἄλσεως. "Ἔν-
θα Τρώιον ἄλμα κ(αὶ) ἤρια Μυνειτοιο." τοι-
οῦτόν (ἐστι) κ(αὶ) τὸ παρ' Ὁμήρῳ λεγόμ(εν)ον· "[Ὁ δ'] ἀνε-
δραμεν ἔρνεϊ ἶσος." ἐνθένδ(ε) κ(αὶ) ὁ ὄρπηξ πα- 20
ρὰ τὸ ἕρπειν κ(αὶ) αὐτὸς πεποιημ(έν)ος.
περὶ μ(ὲν) ο(ὖν) τῆς κοινότερον λεγομ(έν)ης

after the sanctuary had responded (that) it was more profitable and better (for them), if they left (them) untilled and did not farm (them). And they fenced (it/them) around with stelai according to the decree of Philokrates.'

In view of these facts, it could be (that it was) after this man's archonship (60) (that) the speech was composed, since it contains an exhortation for war preparations, preparing in case there should, in fact, be (a war). And there is found in this speech

COLUMN FOURTEEN

Heading: Concerning the Orgas.
Why did he say 'the Megarians (are) accursed'?

nothing except (what) has received some mention in the (works) before this. Nevertheless, a brief clarification of the Orgas should be given. Well, the term 'Orgas' is used more commonly to denote all wooded spaces, (5) like a grove. The word is formed on the basis of (the verb) 'to get ready to grow'/ 'to ripen' (organ) and of (the concept) of having some impulse towards growth. Thus, people are in the habit of using the word 'organ' with respect to that which is in a state of readiness for an impulse toward anything; as, for example, in everyday life we say (that) we 'soften' (orgazein) the mortar (10) with a view to preparing (it) for application. (For example), Sophokles in [Sheph]erds (writes): 'He was mixing, in the same proportion as (is) *good* for softening mortar.' And Aiskhy[l]os, over the corpses in front of the Kadmeia that were ready for burial, (writes): 'The situation (15) was becoming ripe; the corpse was already putrefying.' And people are in the habit of calling both hallowed places and sacred groves 'orgades' on the basis of the growth in length. 'There (was) the sacred grove of Tros and the tomb of Mounit[os].' Similar is the saying found in Homer: '[And he] (20) shot up like a young plant.' Hence the word 'sapling' has itself also been created on the basis of (the word meaning) 'to begin to move.' Well now, that (is what I have to say) about the more common usage of the word 'orgas.'

ὀργάδος ταῦτα. λέγεται δ(έ) τις ἰδίως
παρὰ Μεγαρεῦσιν Ὀργὰς ὀνομαστι-
κῶς, καθάπερ Ἴδη ἥ τ᾽ ἐν Ἰλί[ω]ι κ(αὶ) τὸ   25
δενδρῶ[δ]ες χωρίον, κ(αὶ) πάλιν Αἰγιαλὸς
ἥ τε ἠιὼν κ(αὶ) ἡ οὕτωσὶ λεγομ(έν)η χώρα
κ(αὶ) ἡ Ἀκτὴ ⟨τῆ⟩ς Ἀττικῆς κ(αὶ) τὸ παραθαλασ-
σίδιον ἅπαν χωρίον, κ(αὶ) Ῥίον τὸ μ(ὲν) Μο-
[λ]ύ[κ]ρειον, τὸ δ(ὲ) κοιν[ό]τερον ἤδη πᾶσα ὄ-   30
ρου[ς] κορυφή, κ(αὶ) ἄλλα τούτ[οι]ς ὅμο[ι]α. κ(αὶ) (ἔστιν) ὁ
λόγος τὰ νῦν τῶι Δη[μ]οσθένε[ι π]ερὶ τῆς
Μεγαρικῆς Ὀργάδ[ος], ἧς κ(αὶ) Καλλίμα-
χός που μνημονεύων φησ[ί]· "Ν{ε}ισαί-
ης ἀγλῖθες ἀπ᾽ Ὀργάδος." διείλεκται δ(ὲ)   35
περὶ ταύτης τ(ῆς) Ὀργάδος κ(αὶ) Ἀνδ[ρ]οτίων
ἐν τῆι Ζ̄ τῶν Ἀτθίδ(ων) γράφ(ων) οὕτως·"Ὡ-
ρίσαντο δ(ὲ) κ(αὶ) Ἀθην[αῖο]ι πρὸς Μεγαρέας
τὴν Ὀργάδα διὰ τ[οῖ]ν θεοῖν ὅπως βού-
λοιντο· συνεχώρησαν γ(ὰρ) οἱ Μεγαρεῖς   40
ὁριστὰς γενέσθαι τὸν ἱεροφάντ(ην)
Λακρατ⟨ε⟩ίδην κ(αὶ) τὸν δαιδοῦχον Ἱερο-
κλείδην. κ(αὶ) ὡς οὗτοι ὥρισαν ἐνέμει-
ναν. κ(αὶ) τὰς ἐσχατίας ὅσαι ἦσαν πρὸς τῆι
Ὀργάδι καθιέρωσαν, διαμαντευσά-   45
μ(εν)οι κ(αὶ) ἀνελόντος τοῦ θεοῦ λῶιον κ(αὶ)
ἄμεινον (εἶναι) μὴ ἐργαζομένοις. κ(αὶ) στήλαις
ὡρ[ί]σθη κύκλωι λιθίναις Φιλοκρά-
τους εἰπόντος."—"Οἷον ἃ πρὸς τοὺς κ(ατα)ρά-

τους ⌞Μ⌟εγαρεῖς ἐψηφίσασθε ἀποτε-   50
μνομ(έν)ους τὴν Ὀργάδα, διεξιέναι, κω-
λύειν, μὴ ἐπιτρέπειν." καταράτους
   εἶπε τοὺς Μεγαρέας παρ᾽ ὅσον δυσ-
   νόως εἶχον αὐτοὶ κ(αὶ) Βοιωτοὶ πρὸς
   Ἀθηναίους, καθάπερ ἐν τῆι Κ̄Σ̄   55
   Θεόπομπος ἀπομαρτυρεῖ, ἐν οἷς
   Φιλοκράτης ὁ δημαγωγὸς αὐτοῖς παράγεται λέγων ταῦτα· "Ἐν-

θυμεῖσθε τοίνυν ὡς οὐδ(ὲ) καιρὸς
οὐθείς (ἐστι) φιλονεικεῖν· οὐδ(ὲ) κα-   60
λῶς ἔχειν τὰ πράγματα τῆς

But, amongst the Megarians (something) is called an Orgas idio-matically as a name, (25) just as Ida (signifies) both the (mountain) in Ili[o]n and 'the wooded place', and, again, Aigialos is both 'the beach' and the place so named, and Akte (denotes part of) Attika and every place along the seashore, and Rhion (signifies) on the one hand (30) Mo[l]y[k]reion, but more commonly now (denotes) every *mountain* peak, and (there are) other (examples) similar to these. And the speech of De[m]osthene[s] (that we are) presently (concerned with) is about the Megarian Orga[s], which even Kallimakhos has mentioned somewhere, (when) he says: 'Cloves of garlic (35) from the Orgas at Nisaia.'

And[r]otion, too, has written about this Orgas in the seventh (book) of the <u>Atthides</u>. He writes as follows: 'But the Athenians, too, marked the boundaries of the Orgas in the direction of the Megarians on account of the Two Goddesses, in whatever way they (40) wanted. For the Megarians agreed (that) the boundary markers had been the Hierophant, Lakrateides, and the Daidoukhos, Hiero-kleides. And they abided by the boundaries as these men had marked (them). And the edge-lands, as many as were beside the (45) Orgas, were consecrated by them, after they had consulted the oracle and after the God had replied (that) it was more profitable and better for them, if they did not cultivate (them). And the bound-ary was marked off in a circle with marble stelai, on the motion of Philokrates.'

'Just like the motions you approved (50) against the accursed Megarians, when they were encroaching on the Orgas, namely to march out (against them), to stop (them), not to allow (it).' He called the Megarians accursed to the extent that they and the Boiotians were ill-disposed towards (55) the Athenians, as Theopompos attests in the 26th (book), where the demagogue Philokrates is introduced speaking the following (words) to them:

'So, consider that there is not even any time (60) for factional rivalry; nor are the city's affairs

COLUMN FIFTEEN

πόλεως, ἀλλὰ πολλοὶ κ(αὶ) μεγάλοι κίνδυ-
νοι περιεσ[τ]ᾶσιν ἡμᾶς. ἐπιστάμ[ε]θα
γ(ὰρ) Βοιωτοὺς κ(αὶ) Μεγαρεῖς δυσμ(εν)ῶς ἡμῖν
διακειμ(έν)ους, Πελοποννησίων δὲ
τοὺς μ(ὲν) Θηβαίοις, τοὺς δ(ὲ) Λακεδαιμο-   5
νίοις τὸν νοῦν προσέχοντας, Χίους
δ(ὲ) κ(αὶ) Ῥοδίους κ(αὶ) τοὺς τούτων συμμά-
χους πρὸς μ(ὲν) τὴν πόλιν ἐχθρῶς
[δι]ακειμένους, Φ[ι]λίππωι δ[ὲ] περὶ φιλίας διαλεγομένους."   10

— ΔΙΔΥΜΟΥ —
ΠΕΡΙ ΔΗΜΟΣΘΕΝΟΥΣ
— ΚΗ —
ΦΙΛΙΠΠΙΚΩΝ Γ

Θ̄   Πολλῶν, ὦ ἄνδ(ρες) Ἀθ(ηναῖοι)
Ῑ   Καὶ σπουδαῖα ν[ο]μίζ(ων)
Ῑ   [Ᾱ] [Ὅ]τ[ι] μ(ὲν) ὦ (ἄνδρες) Ἀθ(ηναῖοι) Φ[ί]λιπ(πος)
ῙΒ̄   Περὶ μὲ[ν τ]οῦ π(αρ)όν(τος)

COLUMN FIFTEEN

in good health, but many great dangers surround us. For, we know (that) the Boiotians and Megarians are ill-disposed to us, and of the Peloponnesians (5) some are obedient to the Thebans, some to the Lakedaimonians, and (that) the Khians and the Rhodians and their allies are on hostile terms with the city and (10) are negotiating friendship (philia) with Ph[i]lip.'

DIDYMOS'
ON DEMOSTHENES
28
OF THE PHILIPPICS 3

9 Although many (speeches), men of Athens . . .
10 And because I *consider* serious . . .
11 *That,* men of Athens, Ph[i]lip . . .
12 Regarding the *revenue at hand* . . .

COMMENTARY

COMMENTARY

[Heading]: As indicated in the Introduction, each column begins with a heading, which states the topic or issue that Didymos is either in process of discussing or will begin discussing at some point in it. Nothing is extant of this heading, which appears to have covered three lines, but something can be inferred about its content. It is clear from line 26 (below) that this has to be the last passage in speech 9 (*Third Philippic*) discussed by Didymos. Precisely which statement attracted Didymos' attention is not so clear, however. The surviving commentary is mainly concerned with Euboia, specifically the Athenian intervention there in 342/1 and 341/0 which led to the removal of the 'tyrants', Philistides of Oreus and Kleitarkhos of Eretria. Whilst their removal from power had manifestly not been effected by the time the speech was delivered (see e.g. Sealey (1993): 261), Euboian affairs are to the forefront from section 57 of the speech onward, and for this reason D-S² (p. 4) identify that section as the point of reference here. They are followed in this by P-S and Gibson (101–2). On the other hand, a few lines below Didymos cites a passage from Demosthenes' *On the Crown* (18.79), that refers to his diplomatic activity in addition to the military intervention in Euboia. A reference to the need for diplomatic initiatives to create a coalition of resistance against Philip can be found at 9.71. More generally, however, the context is about Philip's aggressions and Athens' (Demosthenes') countermoves and suggests that Didymos might have been reacting to nothing more specific than the rhetorical question, 'So, while we are still intact . . . what are we to do?' and Demosthenes' response, 'I shall tell and I shall propose . . .' (9.70). Since 'propose'/'make a proposal' (*grapho*) is the main verb of the passage cited from *On the Crown*, I incline towards this last explanation (cf. Foucart (1909): 54). Osborne (58–9) prefers section 63 or 65, because Eretria and Oreus are mentioned together there. The choice is not helped by the ambiguity of the word *symmakhika*.

tyrant became: The remains of lines 1–5 are exiguous. Line 1 most likely has the word 'tyrant' (though in fact only two letters of that word are visible to all editors), followed by the first three letters of what could be the word 'became'. The genitive of the place name, Eretria, is all that can be discerned in line 3, and 'campaigns' in line 4. These remains are hardly sufficient to provide a solution to the question raised in the previous note, though they are often associated with the reference to Macedonian expeditions to Eretria in 9.57–8.

matters related to alliance: This is the least prejudicial translation of the word *symmakhika*. In different contexts it can mean 'treaty of alliance' (e.g. Thuc. 5.6, in the singular) and 'the allied forces' or 'the allies' (frequently in the singular, but also in the plural in Xen. *Cyr.* 3.3.12). Obviously, it would make an important difference to the identification of Didymos' theme, if we could tell which sense is being used here, but unfortunately we cannot. I am unable to agree with Osborne (62) that the 'logical reference' is to the alliance between Athens and Khalkis mentioned in line 15 (though see now Gibson: 102). It is no more clear to me than to Wankel (1987: 217) how P-S interpret this word in their restoration of the passage (cited below).

of [. . .]phon: This is usually restored (e.g. by D-S² and P-S) as the name [Ktesi]phon. Since the word is in the genitive case and considering the quotation that follows, it is not unreasonable to conclude that this is part of the title of Demosthenes' famous speech *On the Crown* (*Or.* 18), which was normally referred to by the ancient scholars as 'the defence of Ktesiphon' (Dion. Hal., *Demosthenes* 4) or 'the speech on behalf of Ktesiphon' (Dion. Hal., *Demosthenes* 31) or simply 'the on behalf of Ktesiphon' (Harpokration: *passim*). Didymos is not, however, consistent in this, since he gave his own monograph on this speech the title, *On the Crown* (see col. 12.36).

of [Phi]lip: It is fairly certain that the name of Philip of Macedon in the possessive form stood here. On the other hand, it is not at all clear in what context. Between his name and Ktesiphon's can be read the letters OILOG, which suggest the restoration (H)OI LOGOI ('speeches'/'words'). P-S restore the whole passage to read: '[a more precise report] of the *symmakhika* [is given by the speech on behalf of Ktesi]phon [than by these] speeches/words, de[tailing all the actions] of [Phi]lip.' But this restoration is most hypothetical and serious questions have been raised about it by Wankel (1987:

217), not least in regard to the personification of the word LOGOS as subject of the verbs 'report is given' and 'detailing'. More crucially, it is not clear how their restoration relates to the passage from speech 18 that follows, especially since it involves Didymos in the logical inconsistency of saying that the passage from Demosthenes provides details, which he then needs to supplement with information from the historian Philokhoros (cf. Gibson: 102).

And first the embassy: The following passage is from Demosthenes 18.79. I have followed P-S (here and elsewhere) in using half-brackets in the Greek text of quotations from extant authors to enclose letters that are missing, but can be supplied with confidence. The missing letters of the quotation fit neatly into the spaces between the preserved ones. In the papyrus the whole line 'the embassy to the Peloponnese was my proposal, at the time when that man' is lacking. Its absence can be explained by a very simple palaeographical error (haplography), since that line and the one beneath both begin with the same word 'Peloponnese'. It is not possible to tell whether this mistake was made by our copyist or was in his exemplar, but it can be deduced from it that the arrangement of words in the original was the same as in our copy, at least at this point. That suggests that our scribe was copying the format of his original.

I feel that Didymos' inclusion of this passage, in which Demosthenes is boasting of his initiative in responding to each of Philip's moves (cf. Wankel (1976): 449), provides the best clue to the section of the *Third Philippic* he was commenting on (see above under **[Heading]**).

was making his initial attempt: This is surely to be identified with Philip's intervention on behalf of Messene and Argos in 344 and Demosthenes' consequent embassy, all of which is detailed in the *Second Philippic* (6.13 ff.). Cf. Wüst (1938): 54–6; Wankel (1976): 386, 450; Sealey (1993): 170–1. The alternative view of Weil (1883: 458), followed by Mathieu (1947: 50) that the embassy here was 'sans doute' that referred to as 'the embassies of last year' in the *Third Philippic* (9.72) is chronologically impossible, whether speech 9 is dated to the archonship of Sosigenes or Nikomakhos (Osborne: 65–6). The charge that Demosthenes was lying and that 'between 344 and 342 Philip did not intervene in Greece' (Cawkwell (1978): 127; cf. Cawkwell (1963): 200–5) has been refuted by Griffith ((1979): 474–9. Cf. Sealey (1993): 307, n. 30).

the embassy to Euboia: This is probably a reference to the
embassy that Demosthenes says (9.66) was rejected by the Eretrians
in a context related to the rise to power of Kleitarkhos in that city,
even though he does not there claim responsibility for its being dispatched. In that case it should be dated to the year 343/2 (Sealey
(1993): 260, 264). I am inclined to believe that it is identical to the
embassy to Oreus and Eretria that Aiskhines says (3.100) was proposed by Demosthenes, but that is a hotly debated issue. Cf. Cawkwell (1963): 210–13 and (1978): 56–66; Brunt (1969): 255–9; Griffith
(1979): 545–52 and Sealey (1993): 262–4.

when he was laying hold of Euboia: Philip's first intervention in Euboia, the expedition of Hipponikos of 343/2, is mentioned
at 9.57–8 and 19.87 and 204 (see Ryder (2000): 76).

the expedition . . . to Oreus and the one to Eretria: see the
next note.

established tyrants in those cities: Philistides had been
established as tyrant in Oreus in 342 with aid provided by Parmenion
(9.59–62; Athen. 11.508d–e, citing Karystios of Pergamon). Kleitarkhos had risen to power in Eretria sometime after the the expul-
sion of Ploutarkhos (by the Athenians under Phokion) in 348 (9.57–
8), but had benefitted from Hipponikos' expedition.

[. . . in Philo]khoros testifies: The standard restoration of the
missing letters in all editions is 'to which (events) also the (narrative)
in . . .' For the Atthidographer Philokhoros, see the Introduction
(Sources). Didymos always used Philokhoros when he wanted to
establish a date, as did his contemporary Dionysios of Halikarnassos (e.g. *Ad Ammaeum* 1.9, 11).

[that went out]:   The surviving letters are consistent with this
restoration, which was first adopted in D-S² on the suggestion of
Blass and has been accepted since (see P-S and Wankel (1987):
217).

after the heading 'the archon (was) Sos[i]ge[nes]':   The
Atthidographers organized their material, at least for the historical
period, by the magistracies of the Athenian archons (see Harding
(1994): 3). The formula that Didymos uses here is his standard way
of reflecting their introductory phrase, 'in the archonship of x'.
Sosigenes was archon for the year 342/1.

Athenians *made* an alliance with (the) Khalkidians: Phil-okhoros' statement is unequivocal: the Athenians made an alliance with the people of Khalkis some time in 342/1. In fact, he even specifies the month, as we shall see below. But his language does not suggest that this was a renewal or a repeat of a recently made alliance. This presents a difficulty for those who, like Cawk-well ((1963): 210–13; (1978): 56–66) believe that (1) the Athenians were in alliance with Khalkis already in the previous archon year (343/2, when he wants to date the combined diplomatic activity of Demosthenes and Kallias of Khalkis referred to in Aiskh. 3 (*Against Ktesiphon*) 89–105) and that (2) Athens and Khalkis renewed alliance sixteen months later. On the other hand, the counter-view of Brunt (1969: 255–9) and Griffith (1979: 545–52), that the reference here and in Aiskhines are to the same situation, entails equally great, or even greater, difficulties. See the review in Sealey (1993: 262–4). I merely note that it would not be uncharacteristic of a chronicler, as Philokhoros was, to neglect to make an association between the two alliances (if they took place). There is, of course, always the possibility that he did write 'again' (*palin*), but that Didymos did not recognize its significance and left it out. Indeed, that something has been left out, either by Philokhoros or Didymos, is confirmed by the report in Stephanos of Byzantion (*Ethnika* s.v. 'Oreus') that the historian Charax (*FGrHist* 103 F19) stated in his *Chronika* (book 6) that the Megarians also took part in the liberation of Oreus (see Harding (1985): no. 91).

in the month of [Skiropho]rion: That is the last month of the Athenian administrative year, roughly June-July on our calendar. The date is crucial for establishing the chronological relationship between the liberation of Oreus and that of Eretria. The restoration of the name of the month is based upon a scholiast to Aiskh. 3.85, which runs: 'His (sc. Mnesarkhos') sons, Kallias and Taurosthenes, together with Kephisophon, general of the Athenian force, cam-paigned against Oreus (and) killed Philistides, when Sosigenes was archon at Athens, in the month of Skirophorion, in the nineteenth year of Philip's reign.' Cf. Ryder (2000): 78.

Kephisophon was the general: Kephisophon, son of Kephal-ion, of Aphidna (*APF* no. 8410), was an important Athenian official in the 340s. He was elected *strategos* in 345/4, which was probably when he campaigned at Skiathos and was crowned by the Samo-thracians (*IG* ii² 1443. 106ff.; *AO* 324) and honoured with *proxenia* by Thasos and Paros (*IG* XII. v (1) 114; *APF* 292). In 343/2 he was a commissioner of the Theoric Fund (*IG* II² 223c.6). Subsequently, he was elected general twice more, in 342/1 when he commanded this campaign, and in 340/39 when he shared the command of the Athenian forces at Byzantion with Phokion (*IG* II² 1628. 438; 1629. 959; *AO* 332, 338).

Phi[listid]es the tyrant died: That Philistides came to be viewed as a tyrant is quite possible. Tyranny was not an official position, had no defined powers or limits, and could, therefore, become just a matter of perception. He certainly had popular support when he came to power (Dem. 9.59–62). Exactly how he died is not known.

'the archon (was) Nikomakhos':   The year was 341/0.

In *this man's archonship*:   According to Jacoby (*Atthis*: 94 f.; *Text*: 532. Cf. Harding (1994): 3, 163) the chroniclers used this formula to signify the first entry under the heading of a particular archon's name. The practice is intrinsically rational and illustrated in Androtion (*FGrHist* 324 F44) and frequently in Philokhoros, especially when he is cited verbatim by Didymos (*FGrHist* 328 F157 and F160) and Dionysios of Halikarnassos (*Ad Ammaeum* 1.9 = *FGrHist* 328 F49, and 1.11 = *FGrHist* 328 FF54 and 56). The same passages, but especially 1.9 (*FGrHist* 328 FF49–51), support the additional conclusion that other entries under the same archon's name were not introduced by this phrase (*pace* Brunt (1969): 256 and n. 4). Thus, the liberation of Eretria followed almost immediately upon that of Oreus, which took place in the last month of the previous magistracy (see above), and suggests a coordinated plan. This issue is well reviewed by Osborne (76–9).

with Phokion as their general: For Phokion, son of Phokos, see *APF* no. 15076. His deme might be Potamos (Tritle (1981): 118–32, but see *AO* 291). His long career as politician and general (according to Plut. *Phokion* 8.1 he was general forty-five times) was distinguished, but controversial. His reputation for justice was popularized by the Peripatetics, though it originated with Aiskhines (2.184). Despite that, he was put to death in 318 as a traitor to democracy. His life has been the subject of several recent studies. See e.g. Bearzot (1985), Gehrke (1976), and Tritle (1988). In the late 340s his career appears to have intersected with that of Kephisophon. At least, they campaigned together at Byzantion in 340/39, and the close chronology of the two campaigns mentioned here might suggest collaboration between the generals (*APF* 292). On the other hand, there is no strategic reason why the Athenians could not have liberated both Oreus and Eretria in one campaign and it seems to me that the fact that they mounted two separate expeditions so close together requires explanation. The person of Kallias, leader of the Khalkidians, might provide a clue. Philokhoros specifically associates the Khalkidians with the liberation of Oreus and fails to mention them in Phokion's campaign against Eretria. This may not be accidental and the Khalkidians may not have taken part, not only 'for fear of provoking antagonism in a city that was their neighbour' (Sealey (1993): 262), but out of deference to Phokion, who cannot have had fond memories of Kallias and his brother, Taurosthenes, who had betrayed him in 348 (Aiskh. 3.86; cf. Ryder (2000): 56).

besiege Kleitarkhos: Surely on the acropolis (cf. A. Philippson, *RE* 6.1 [1906]: 422–4, s.v. 'Eretria').

was a factional rival of Ploutarkhos: Ploutarkhos had been dominant in Eretrian politics from at least 349. He had influential supporters in Athens, like Meidias (Dem. 21.110, 200; *APF* no. 9719) and the Euboulos group. When his position was challenged by a rival group (schol. Dem. 5.5) led by the political exile Kleitarkhos (schol. Aiskh. 3.86, and for this meaning of *antistasiotes* see Hdt. 4.164 and Xen. *Anab.* 1.1.10), Athens sent out a force to help him under the leadership of Phokion. This force almost met disaster at the battle of Tamynai (Plut. *Phokion* 12–14; Aiskh. 3.85–8). Most responsible for this situation had been Kallias and Taurosthenes of Khalkis (Aiskh. 3.85–7), traitors in Athenian eyes, nationalists to Euboians. After the battle of Tamynai Phokion expelled Ploutarkhos (Plut. *Phokion* 13.4) and, according to Demosthenes (9.57–8), the *demos* was in control at Eretria, until the expedition of Hipponikos helped Kleitarkhos to power in 343/2. What this probably signifies is that in the intervening period Kleitarkhos was merely one of several contenders for supremacy in the state.

became tyrant: Kleitarkhos, like Ploutarkhos, is consistently referred to as a tyrant, by Philokhoros (here), by Demosthenes (9.58) and in the scholion to Aiskh. 3.103 (cf. Schaefer (1885–7): ii. 295). The situation was probably somewhat less precise (Sealey (1993): 260), though the fact that he had outside support from Philip, as Ploutarkhos had had from Athens, was surely what created the perception. See the preceding note and on Philistides (above).

overcoming him by siege: Philokhoros does not say what happened to Kleitarkhos, but the scholion to Aiskh. 3.103 says he was killed by the Athenians. In any case, we hear no more about him.

Note on the text of speech 9

Speech 9 is one of those where there exist major differences between the textual tradition represented by manuscript S (Parisinus Graecus 2934) and that of the other main MSS (FAY). In this case S is usually shorter, lacking several words and even extended passages that are in the other manuscripts. Opinion is divided whether both versions go back to the original publication, or whether one (S) is the original, the other a later, edited version (see, most recently, Sealey (1993): 233–5). Two of the more controversial passages are amongst those canvassed here as possibly the subject of Didymos' attention (9.58 and 9.71). Unfortunately, nothing in his discussion throws any light on this textual problem.

Speech 10

And because I consider: These are, of course, the opening words (for which see Hajdu (2002): 83–4) of the *Fourth Philippic*, quoted here by Didymos not for specific comment themselves, but to introduce his discussion of the speech as a whole. As Gibson (103) astutely observes, there is a certain redundancy in identifying the speech both by number and its opening sentence. His conclusion, that the numeral was put there by the copyist, since 'there is no evidence that Didymus himself ever referred to Demosthenes' speeches by number', is somewhat presumptuous. Someone assigned numbers to the speeches in this papyrus, including in the summary at the end, and the burden of proof rests upon those who believe it was not Didymos.

glimpse **[the]** *circumstances* **of the speech:** The first thing Didymos is concerned to do, when he begins discussion of a new speech, is to establish its date and historical context. This part of his discussion appears to have continued at least to line 3 of col. 2 (cf. Gibson: 103–5) or even to line 23 (see below, p. 116), but probably not as far as line 39, as P-S have suggested. Elsewhere, at this point in his presentation, he will also grapple with issues of authenticity and classification whenever they are relevant, as he does, for example, at the beginning of his treatment of speeches 11 (authenticity) and

13 (classification). His failure to do so here suggests that, like his contemporary Dionysios of Halikarnassos, Didymos accepted the authenticity of the *Fourth Philippic*, as do many modern scholars (see e.g. Körte (1905): 388–410; Daitz (1957): 145–62; Pearson (1976): 155–7; Worthington (1991): 425–8; Sealey (1993): 232; Hajdu (2002): 44–9; *contra* Milns (1987): 287–302; the position of Buckler (1994): 106 is confused. Sharply critical of Didymos on this, as on other issues, is Badian (2000): 10–11). It is also probable that he did not find any prior discussion of the topic.

Line 30: *the archon* **was Nikomakhos:** this is surely the last part of the formula Didymos uses for introducing a citation from the Atthidographer Philokhoros to establish a date. The text should, then, be restored: '[. . . from what Philokhoros (says) after the heading] *the archon* was Nikomakhos.' Since it is invariably Didymos' practice to follow this formula with a quotation from his source, it is likely that a passage from Philokhoros stood in the missing lines that follow. Similarly, we should suspect that another quotation from Philokhoros is missing, when the formula is repeated in line 53. Jacoby, however, strangely treats the whole passage down to line 60 as one fragment (Philokhoros, *FGrHist* 328 F161) and is of the opinion that 'it is not certain whether this is a quotation proper' or simply a summary of relevant material from three archon years (Jacoby, *Text*: 537).

Given the very bad state of preservation of the text, it is difficult to follow much of Didymos' argument, but it does look as though he, like Dionysios of Halikarnassos (*Ad Amm.* 1.10), dated the speech to the archonship of Nikomakhos (341/0) and rejected the views of those who put it either in the following year (Theophrastos' archonship, 340/39) or the preceding (Sosigenes, 342/1). The perceived discrepancy between the date of 341/0 and Demosthenes' reference in 10.9 to Philip's activity in Oreus prior to its liberation, which Didymos above dated to the last month of 342/1, troubled Körte (and others, see Hajdu (2002): 40 n. 199), but was dismissed as 'not adequate to discredit Dionysios' by Cawkwell (1963: 134–6). Dionysios' dates have been defended by Sealey ((1955): 77–120; (1993): 232–3, but see Lewis (1997): 230–51 and Lane Fox (1997): 167–203). It should also be noted that both the amount of space devoted by Didymos to the question and the systematic way the case is presented are signs of original scholarship, not compilation (cf. Foucart (1909): 54–5; Osborne: 91–2).

neither *wishing* nor: This restoration, with the participle in the nominative, masculine singular, is by P-S. It is consistent with what can be seen on the papyrus.

[Philistides the] Oreitan: The restoration of these next two lines down to the punctuation mark is quite hypothetical. Beyond doubt there is a reference to an Oreitan and an Eretrian (both in the genitive). Little else is certain. Even the phrase 'in the time of So[sigenes]' could be quite misleading. Nevertheless, it has often seemed tempting to follow Foucart (1909: 55 n. 1) in restoring Philistides as the Oreitan and Kleitarkhos as the Eretrian (cf. Jacoby, *FGrHist* 328 F161; P-S ad loc.; Hajdu (2002): 40 n. 199). Dispute now centres around the participles that are assumed to belong to each name (genitive absolute), both of which have to be entirely restored. Foucart's original suggestion failed to account for the space after the name Nikomakhos, but the modification proposed by Crönert (1907: 380) and accepted by Jacoby (*FGrHist* 328 F161) is quite impossible, because it requires several more letters than the space available. P-S avoid the difficulties with their restoration: '(since) [Philistides the] Oreitan [died] in the time of So[sigenes], and [Kleitarkh]os the Eretri[an was expelled in the time of Nikom]akho[s].' After all that, it is not clear in what context Didymos introduced these people into his argument, since, as Foucart was quick to notice (1909: 56), Demosthenes nowhere mentions the liberation of Oreus or Eretria in the *Fourth Philippic* and in two places assumes they are still hostile (10.8–9, 68). This is, indeed, an argument for dating the speech to the archonship of Sosigenes (*pace* Cawkwell (1963): 134–6; Sealey (1993): 233; Hajdu (2002): 40–3), though it was probably not the date Didymos was supporting (*pace* P-S: 4). Attempts to explain the text as restored by P-S are offered by Osborne (91) and Gibson (104), but it is wise to remember that the confusion is generated by the restoration of two names that could be quite wrong. So often what appears to be inconsistency on the part of Didymos is created by modern restoration.

these things . . . *speech*:   Restorations of this badly mutilated passage (lines 49–51) are numerous. D-S[1] proposed: '. . . [At any rate Philokh]o[r]os *adds* (these things) *clearly* at the end of Nik[omakhos' magistra]cy.' Jacoby, on the other hand (*FGrHist* 328 F161), following Crönert (1907: 380) reads: '[And] these things *will confirm* [that those things (happened?) much] *before* [the events] at the end of Niko[makhos' magistrac]y, *but* [in particular the] *speech* (i.e. will

confirm this).' That contorted sentence has quite deservedly failed
to find favour. No more likely to do so is the attempt of P-S: 'These
things also [Philokh]oros *will confirm* [as having happened] at the
end of Nik[omakhos' magistrac]y, which things [the] *speech* [is not
yet aware as having taken place].' Not the least objections to this
restoration are the uncharacteristic (for Didymos) personification
of 'speech' (cf. Wankel (1987): 217) and the fact that a mention of
Philokhoros would normally be followed by a quotation (Wankel
(1987): 221). Furthermore, if the restoration of Philistides and Kleitarkhos in the previous sentence is accepted (though see previous
note), it is hard to see the relevance of the reference to the 'end of
Nikomakhos' magistracy,' since Philistides had already died in the
preceding year and Kleitarkhos surely died early in 341/0 (Nikomakhos' archonship). Even Jacoby's suggestion (*Text*: 537) that
Didymos was claiming that all the events mentioned in this section
had happened before that time hardly makes them relevant.

well then . . . seen: At first sight restoration of these lines (51–3)
looks quite practicable. No doubt Didymos was summing up this
part of his argument about the date of the speech. In the space
before 'has been seen' it makes little difference whether we restore
'sufficiently' with P-S, following Foucart and Arnim (cf. Foucart
(1909): 55 n. 1) or 'clearly' with Fuhr (1904: 1130), though the remains favour the former. But the crucial information for clarifying
which date Didymos was advocating is lost and current restorations yield two very different results. Jacoby, adopting Crönert's
text, reads: 'Well, then, that the *speech* has been written [not later
than] the magistracy [of Sosigen]es, [not that (it was written) after]
Niko[makhos], has [now] been seen *sufficiently*.' This text cannot
be correct, since the last letters of the name Sosigenes conflict with
the remains on the papyrus. Recently, however, still in the belief
that Didymos was dating the speech to Sosigenes' year, P-S restore:
'Well, then, that the *speech* has been written [before the afore-
mentioned] magistracy (i.e. before the year of Nikomakhos), [not
that (it was written) after] Nik[omakhos], has [now] been seen *sufficiently*.' But lines 2–3 of column 2 suggest strongly that Didymos
did not follow those who dated the speech to Sosigenes' archonship.
Besides, it makes little sense to say that something happened *before*
the year of Nikomakhos, not *after* it, without refuting the possibility that it happened *at* his time. For that reason, I think Foucart
(1909: 55 and n. 1) was more on the right lines in arguing that

Didymos dated the *Fourth Philippic* to Nikomakhos' year, and this is, indeed, the majority opinion today (cf. Gibson: 104; Hajdu (2002): 40–3). Foucart's restoration runs: 'Well, then, that the *speech* has been written [not later than the afore-mentioned] magistracy (i.e. Nikomakhos'), [but at the time of] Nik[omakhos], has been seen *sufficiently*.' Less satisfactory, but along the same lines, is Osborne's suggestion: 'Therefore, it has been *sufficiently* seen that the *speech* was written [after these events in this] archonship (i.e. Nikomakhos'), [not after] Nik[omakhos].'

Lines 53–7: *under the heading*:   This reading is certain. In association with it we should expect an author's name, surely Philokhoros', or a reference to him in some form (e.g. 'the same man', as in col. 1.19).

Nikoma[khos]:   Considering that the next part of Didymos' discussion is clearly concerned with the archonship of Theophrastos (340/39) and in light of the fact that Didymos appeared to be concluding the preceding part of his argument a few lines above, it is reasonable to look for some formula that will include Theophrastos here. The restoration: '[Theophrastos, the one after] Nikoma[khos . . . .]' is, therefore, very likely. I would even follow D-S[1] in their suggestion that the word 'was archon' should follow the name Nikomakhos (D-S[1] ad loc.; cf col. 1.68 and col. 10.51). At the same time it should be noted that this particular formula cannot have originated with the Atthidographer, for whom it was redundant to state that one archon followed another. The formula must be a feature of Didymos' argument.

***will show*:**   Almost all restorations require a main verb at this point. The remains suggest the verb 'show' in the future tense, and a sentence, 'Philokhoros, under the heading . . . will show . . .', would be quite appropriate. But, the final letter of line 54 is most likely a nu and P-S, following D-S[2], give the infinitive 'to be going to show'. But this would require another finite verb to depend upon, and it is not easy to think of one. I suspect, therefore, that the final nu is the first letter of another word.

***concerning* the [peace] with Philip:**   Lines 55–6 are too corrupt for plausible restoration, but the remains suggest some inferences. In the first place, one would expect this section to contain a direct quotation from Didymos' usual source for dating purposes, namely Philokhoros, but in this case it may be that the quotation is delayed until line 70, since the section that begins at the end of line 67 appears to be resumptive (note the 'now' for the Greek *MEN OYN*) and the archon formula, usual before a quotation, is absent there. Second, since, as pointed out above, Didymos paid special attention to establish the chronological relationship between the two archons, it is not surprising to learn at the end what it was about Theophrastos' archonship that was so important: that it was in his time that the treaty with Philip was broken and war was declared. Echoes of this fact can be found in the remains of lines 55–7 (cf. 56–7, 'and the *stele* regarding the treaty').

So, the logic behind Didymos' argument from col. 1.53 to col. 2.2 appears to be somewhat as follows:

1. Lines 53–60. Reference to Philokhoros will prove that peace was broken and war declared in the archonship of Theophrastos, who followed Nikomakhos; but peace still existed when the *Fourth Philippic* was delivered.

2. Lines 61–6. Demosthenes himself attests to this in 10.17, which is then quoted.

3. Lines 66–7. So, the Athenians were still at peace then.

4. Lines 67–9. Didymos restates his point that war was declared in Theophrastos' archonship, to prove which he gives the citation from Philokhoros (line 69– col. 2.2), which he promised at the beginning of his digression.

I find this interpretation more plausible than the one implied by P-S (p. 4) in their suggested restoration of lines 55–8: '[The Athenians kept] *their* [oaths] regarding the [peace] with Philip and the *stele* regarding the treaty [that concerned the] *peace* [still stood] in the archonship of Theophrastos . . . .' This seems to me to be totally against the flow of Didymos' argument.

***as/that* I . . . :** Whether the first word ([ὡ]ς) is to be translated 'as' or 'that' depends upon the verb (beginning with alpha) that is to be restored in the space after 'I'. P-S, following D-S[1], restore ἀ[ποδείξω], '[shall show]', which requires the translation 'as'. Probably better is the restoration ἀ[ληθεύω], '[speak truth]', adopted in D-S[2] on the suggestion of Blass and supported by Wankel ((1987): 221; cf. (1976): 286–7), who points out that this is a common formula in the orators when introducing witnesses. In that case the translation 'that' is necessary. Anyway, here we have a clear example of Didymos' personal involvement with the argument. Note, however, that this is the only place in the papyrus where Didymos uses a passage from elsewhere in the same speech to elucidate a *lemma*.

'So, because . . . :   The passage is #17 of the *Fourth Philippic*. The restorations are assured.

For he . . . *peace*:   This sentence makes quite clear the logic of Didymos' argument that the *Fourth Philippic* was delivered while Athens was still at peace with Philip and, therefore, before the archonship of Theophrastos.

[that the treaty] *was broken*:   Fuhr's restoration (1904: 1130) is preferable to Wilamowitz's, '[the stelai] *were destroyed*'.

suffice (to quote) Phil[o]khoros: *FGrHist* 328 F55b. Precisely the same passage is cited by Dionysios of Halikarnassos in *Ad Amm.* 1.11 (*FGrHist* 328 F55a), whose text has been used to restore this passage. For the use of similar passages of Philokhoros by both Dionysios and Didymos see the Introduction under Didymos the Scholar.

had heard [the letter]:   A letter from Philip has been preserved as speech 12 in some manuscripts (i.e. F and Y) of the Demosthenic corpus. That this is more or less an authentic work by Philip has been accepted since the studies by Pohlenz (1929: 41–62) and Wüst (1938: 134–6) early in the twentieth century. See the reviews by Hammond (1994: 13–20), who argues for total authenticity, and Griffith (1979: 714–16), who has some reservations. Compare Ellis (1976: 176–80), Osborne (96–7), and Sealey (1993: 239–40). But, as everyone except Cawkwell (1978: 127) recognizes, that letter is not the one referred to here (see now Gibson: 105). The situation at the time of writing of [Dem.] 12 is too early in 340, probably by a couple of months: Philip had escorted his ships through the Khersonese with his army (12.16), but had not yet put Perinthos under siege. The context envisaged here is essentially the one responded to by [Dem.] 11 (*Reply to the Letter of Philip*), by which time the siege of Perinthos had failed and Philip had turned his attention to Byzantion (Dion. Hal. *Ad Amm.* 1.11 = Philokhoros, *FGrHist* 328 F54 and 55a). Reflections of that situation can perhaps be discerned in the exiguous remains of col. 2.2–23, where a reference to 'Sky[th]ians' (line 21) and 'Byz[ant]ion' (23) are most likely. For more on the context and authorship of speech 11 and the circumstances under which war was declared see below on col. 10.34 ff. (pp. 210–12).

Demosthenes had exhorted: This is clear testimony to the fact that Demosthenes did make a speech in response to Philip's final letter. That speech has, however, probably not survived, if the one preserved as speech 11 in the corpus was composed by Anaximenes (see below on col. 11.10 ff., pp. 219–21).

to destroy the stele: The Athenian equivalent of tearing up a document. Compare, for example, *IG* ii² 116 = Harding (1985): no. 59.

COLUMN TWO

Heading: The four lines of the heading do not necessarily raise four independent issues related to four separate passages in the text of Demosthenes. Two can, however, be assigned with some confidence. The first ('Who are the supporters . . .') probably relates to 10.4–5 ('those of that man's persuasion' or 'those who control the government through him'); the last ('That ill-disposed . . .') almost certainly refers to 10.11 ('that Philip is ill-intentioned and inimical to the whole city'). The second ('Concerning the suspicion . . .') could well be an elaboration of the first line. The relevance of the third ('Thebans *alliance/allies* . . .') is not clear. At any rate, we can be sure that the last *lemma* that was dealt with in column 2 was from 10.11. Thus, I find the speculations of P-S in their apparatus criticus (pp. 6–8), that line 9 began a discussion of 10.29 and lines 28–30 of 10.33, unpersuasive (cf. Gibson: 105).

In contrast to the opinion expressed above about the issues raised in the heading is the suggestion of Milns (1994: 87 n. 35) that the first two entries should be restored as 'What (were) the [circumstances that] en[compassed the *demos*]' and 'Concerning the suspicion [that the speech was not Demosthenes']'. This would allow Didymos to have considered the question of the authenticity of the oration. This idea is not uninteresting, but it comes up against the obstacle that Didymos had begun discussing the date of the speech already by line 29 of the previous column and there is no other instance where the heading refers back to a discussion in progress.

[to man] a fleet: Philokhoros used the technical term. There is no reason to believe that he cited the number of ships, though the *psephisma* probably did. Neither the number of ships sent by Athens nor the total marshalled for the defence of Byzantion against Philip is stated by any of our main sources. Only Hesykhios (*FGrHist* 390 F 1.28) gives a figure of forty triremes for Khares' original squadron. This figure is quite consistent with other naval forces sent out by Athens at this time (Hammond (1994): 16). Later, Phokion and Kephisophon were dispatched with an unspecified number of additional triremes (Plut. *Phokion* 14.3–4). These were joined by ships from Khios, Rhodes, and Kos (Diod. 16.77.2). A document, preserved in Demosthenes 18.90, claims that the total of ships (*ploia*) reached 120. The document is a forgery (Wankel (1976): 497–8), but some find the figure credible (e.g. Jacoby, *Text*: 331; Osborne: 98).

***But* some . . . [Sos]ig[e]nes:**   This very plausible restoration was suggested by Wilamowitz (app. crit. ad loc. in D-S²) and is still accepted by P-S and others (e.g. Milns (1987): 287 n. 4; Gibson: 84). If correct, it shows that Didymos continued his discussion of the date of the *Fourth Philippic* on to column 2, perhaps as far as line 23, where there is a reference to Byzantion, followed by an introductory formula ('And concerning . . .'). Sosigenes was archon in 342/1, before Nikomakhos. The formula used here ('some say . . .') is regularly employed by Didymos to advert to opinions that he disagrees with or to arguments that are different from his own (see Introduction). In this case he was surely disagreeing with the date. He was probably correct in doing so (see above on col. 1.30 and 51–3). It would be interesting to know what arguments were put forward by these unnamed predecessors, but at least this oblique reference to them shows that controversy existed on this point.

Col. 2.3 to the end of column 3 are too poorly preserved for intelligible translation and, consequently, for commentary. Attempts to reconstruct the argument (e.g. Foucart (1909): 56–7) or identify *lemmata* (as in P-S, pp. 6–10) are unconvincing. As already mentioned, the best that can be said is that Didymos probably continued his argument on the date to 2.23; that it is unlikely that any passage beyond 10.11 was discussed in column 2 (the quotation of 10.17 was not a *lemma*); that the *lemma* Didymos was treating at the end of column 3 preceded 10.32 and may well have been from 10.31 (see the discussion immediately below).

COLUMN FOUR

Heading: The four-line heading is poorly preserved, but the reference to Atarneus, combined with the subsequent narrative (lines 48 ff.), is sufficient to prove that the topic is Hermias of Atarneus and the context is 10.32 ('Next, the man who is the agent and confidant of all Philip's preparations against the King has been dragged up-country to the King . . .'). On this basis speculative restorations for the heading have been advanced, the boldest of which is in P-S: 'Who was the man dragged up-country to the King and the one who revealed Philip's preparations against him? Concerning Hermias of Atarneus what do those who have written about him say?' Whilst quibbles can legitimately be raised against some of the readings (see Wankel (1987): 220), this restoration must be essentially on the right lines.

But, before it gets to Hermias, the narrative of column 4 picks up some way through a discussion that began in the previous column. Given the poor state of the papyrus at this point, it is not possible to establish conclusively what passage Didymos was commenting on, though the choice must be a passage that lies somewhere between 10.11 (the last verifiable *lemma*) and 10.32. The choice is not helped by the surviving commentary, which is largely concerned with a decree of the Delphic Amphiktyony, responding to a request from the Messenians and Megalopolitans to be admitted into the Amphiktyony and registered as 'benefactors' *(euergetai)*, and probably continues on to include a quotation from Aristotle's *Nomima* (see below and cf. Osborne: 106 and Gibson (2001): 45–7). Unfortunately, there is no reference to Delphi, Messene, or Megalopolis in the relevant part of speech 10. In fact, the closest Demosthenes comes to Delphi at any point in this speech is an oblique reference to the Pylaia in 10.67. This led Diels (D-S[1] p. 14) to the view that Didymos' point here was to note that *King Philip of Macedon* was declared a 'benefactor' of the Amphiktyony. This suggestion, of course, completely fails to explain the presence of the decree quoted and the absence of any mention of Philip in it, except on the unlikely hypothesis that the part of the decree that related to Philip had not been preserved. In this desperate view Diels was followed by von Pomtow, who edited this inscription for the third edition of Dittenberger's *Sylloge Inscriptionum Graecarum* (298–9). On this interpretation we would have to agree with Diels that the decree was 'inapposite' and that its presence created 'new obscurity'.

Paradoxically, there is a speech of Demosthenes, whose subject matter might appear to provide a quite apposite context for the decree. That is speech 5 (*On the Peace*), where the danger that 'people who call themselves Amphiktyones' might be 'given an excuse (*prophasis*) for making a common war on Athens' (5.14) and the fear that various states, like Messene and Megalopolis, might combine against Athens out of hostility to Sparta (5.17) led Demosthenes to conclude with a memorable reference to 'the shadow at Delphi' (5.25). The apparent relevance of this speech has led P-S to suggest that Didymos was, in fact, commenting upon it in an excursus (pp. xiii–xiv). But this theory is no less desperate than Diels', especially since the only support they can adduce for their idea of an excursus to a different speech is the presence of the word *prophasis* in line 43 of column 3. The recent revival of this idea to include the possibility that Didymos' aim was to 'clarify the view that the Megalopolitans and Messenians were somehow considered benefactors of the Persian king' (Gibson (2001): 55–6) lacks credibility on historical grounds (see below). To be sure, Didymos did comment on the expression 'the shadow at Delphi' (Harpokration, s.v. *ΠΕΡΙ ΤΗΣ ΕΝ ΔΕΛΦΟΙΣ ΣΚΙΑΣ*; cf. Schmidt (1854): 311; Maehler (1992): 625–33), but there is no reason to believe that he did not do so in the appropriate place, namely, as part of his commentary on Dem. 5.25.

Much more positive and far more in keeping with Didymos' practice is the suggestion of Osborne (104–5) and its subsequent elaboration by Gibson (2001: 43–56) that the connection lies in the title 'benefactors' (*euergetai*) that is requested from the Amphiktyons, since it also appears in a unique usage in 10.31. There, Demosthenes states that 'the people, whom the King (i.e. of Persia) trusts and has accepted as his "benefactors", these hate Philip and are at war with him.' In fact, A. B. Bosworth has suggested *per litt.* that the Persian title for benefactors—*ὀροσάγγαι*, mentioned in Herodotos (8.85)—might be identified at the beginning of column 3, line 41 [*ὀροσ*]*άγγ*[*αι*]; cf. Hajdu (2002): 260.

Exactly whom Demosthenes might have been alluding to is in dispute. For a review of the suggested candidates see Gibson (2001: 51), who adds the Megalopolitans and Messenians to the list, as noted above. See also Sealey (1993: 184) for the view that Demosthenes is referring to Mentor and Memnon of Rhodes, and their brother-in-law, Artabazos. Hajdu (2002: 258–60) restricts the reference to Mentor alone. But it is surely the euphemistic use of the word 'bene-factor' for 'supporter' or 'agent' that is just the sort of thing to have caught the eye of a lexicographically inclined scholar like Didymos. Furthermore, if the historical context that most plausibly explains their request is correct (see below), the Messenians and Megalo-politans are using the word in a similarly euphemistic way, since they were hardly *euergetai* in the accepted sense, but were looking to curry favour with the champion of Apollo (Philip of Macedon) in their struggles with Sparta. Finally, this interpretation provides a context for the quotation from Aristotle, either because Didymos proceeded to compare Greek usage with that of other nationalities (Osborne: 105), or for the more narrowly historical reason that the subject of Aristotle's reference was known as a 'benefactor' of the Great King (Gibson (2001): 49–56).

The general context of the Amphiktyonic decree is hardly in doubt, though the precise date is not agreed upon. In fact, it *is* the situation described in Demosthenes 5 (*On the Peace*). The Peace of Philokrates that ended the Third Sacred War in midsummer 346 had repercussions on the whole international scene in Greece. This was not least the case in the Peloponnese, where Sparta, which had been restricted in power by the Thebans and circumscribed by Epameinondas' two creations (Messene and Megalopolis) and was now even more outcast as a result of having supported Phokis, was still trying to regain control of the Peloponnese. With the decline of Theban power, Philip was the man for former Theban dependen-cies, like Messene and Megalopolis, to look to for help. Whether they did so right away in the autumn of 346 (Foucart (1909): 117; Ellis (1976): 134) or some time in 345/4 (von Pomtow, *SIG*³ no. 224, p. 298) or in the autumn of 345 (Wüst (1938): 25, n. 3) or, even later, in 344 (Griffith (1979): 481) cannot be determined with certainty. What is generally agreed, however (*pace* Ellis (1976): 134), is that the Amphiktyons did not admit them (Griffith (1978): 481; Londey (1990): 252; Rhodes with Lewis (1997): 133; Lefèvre (1998): 96) and that may explain why they joined the Athenian alliance of 343/2 (schol. Aiskh. 3.83; *IG* II² 225 = Harding (1985): no. 89).

Before passing on to specific points in the text, it is important for our estimation of Didymos' scholarship to ask where he found this document. Only Foucart makes a reference to this, when he com-ments that Didymos' text of the decree was not a direct copy from the stone, because he spelled Amphikt*y*ony with an upsilon, not an

iota, as he maintains was always the case in coins and inscriptions
of the fourth century (Foucart (1909): 113 n. 2). But this point is not
crucial. In the first place, it is incredible to imagine that Didymos
went to Delphi to look at inscriptions. He certainly consulted a collection, the author of which may well have changed the spelling
of the word to conform with the standard literary form, which has
upsilon. Or, Didymos himself may have altered the format to accord
with his own usage, much as Thucydides could do, when quoting
documents, especially if he was quoting from memory. But, more
importantly, Foucart's statement is incorrect. Whilst the spelling
with iota was usual in the fourth century, the practice was inconsistent even then and became increasingly so in subsequent centuries.
See, for example, the Amphiktyonic Law of 380 BC (Rougement
(1977): no. 10, p. 90), where the two different spellings are extant
only four lines apart.

Regardless, the most likely answer to the question posed above
must be that Didymos found this inscription himself in some collection of Delphic or Amphiktyonic decrees. The alternative, that
he found it already cited in an earlier commentary on this passage
or in some other unrelated work, is not credible and has not, to
my knowledge, been advanced even by those who believe he was a
'mere compiler'. In fact, especially if we accept that Didymos was
commenting on the word *euergetai*, the citation is so apposite and
the point so idiosyncratic as to make it almost certain that this is
Didymos' own work. In that case, one can only be most impressed
by the huge extent of his reading.

[of the A]mphiktyons: This sentence holds the key to the context of the inscription that follows. Unfortunately, it is too poorly
preserved to be helpful and, in one way, has been responsible for
much of the confusion surrounding this part of the text. Halfway
along the line is a word that all editors have read as $META\Sigma X\Omega N$,
the masculine nominative singular aorist participle of the word
'share', 'have a share in'. This reading would require a masculine
singular subject for the sentence and has led to the view that it was
Philip of Macedon. On that assumption D-S restored the preceding words as '[benefactor of the god and of the A]mphiktyons and
having a share in the [Amphik]tyo[n]y [according to] the following
decree'. In order to explain why Philip should be the subject of this
sentence, but not mentioned in the following decree, they devised
the ingenious theory (discussed above) that the part of the decree

concerning Philip had fallen out. Similarly, P-S even more creative-
ly restore: '[The Megalopolitans and the Messenians did not get
what they wanted, but Philip increased in power, being flattered
by the A]mphiktyons and having a share in the [Amphik]tyo[n]y.
[And the] decree (is) as follows.' This is marginally better, in as much
as they do not have to believe in a disappearing document, but still
makes for a rather awkward introduction to a decree that makes
no mention of Philip. Furthermore, their explanation of Didymos'
thinking (or lack of it) here (discussed above) is based upon a purely
fictitious connection (Wankel (1987): 220).

Of course, what is needed at this point in the text is not a reference to Philip of Macedon but to the subject matter of the decree,
i.e. to the request of the Megalopolitans and Messenians, and, in
fact, that is not hard to find. Close scrutiny of the last, only partially
preserved, letter(s) of the word 'share' shows that it ends not in a
nu but in a sigma iota. Thus, it becomes $ΜΕΤΑΣΧΩΣΙ$, the third
person plural aorist subjunctive and translates, '. . . they may have
a share in the [Amphik]tyo[n]y'.

[. . .] following decree: We do not have enough of the previous sentence to be able to choose between '[in accordance with the]
following decree' (D-S) and '[And the] decree (is) as follows' (P-S).

Resolved by the Amphikty[o]ns: This is a recognized enact-
ment formula found in Amphiktyonic inscriptions (see Rhodes with
Lewis (1997): 132–40; Lefèvre (1998): 183–91). The absence of reference to the Pylaia or the *hieromnemones* is not without parallel, if this
was a meeting of the *ekklesia* (for which see Aiskh. 3.124) and not of
the *synhedrion*. Alternatively, if, as seems likely, it was passed at a
meeting of the *synhedrion* (Lefèvre (1998): 167, 190), we can explain
the absence of the dating formula and the list of participants as
editing on Didymos' part, since they are quite irrelevant to his
purpose.

since: D-S restored '[and] *since*', in order to justify their supposition that an earlier part of the decree dealing with Philip of Macedon
had fallen out. This is quite unnecessary, as we have seen.

benefactors **of the god:** The title of benefactor (*euergetes*) was a
standard honorific title bestowed by Greek states from the fourth
century onward upon individuals and states that had performed
them distinguished service (Henry (1983)). The only service
the states involved here can have performed for Delphi was the

contribution of funds for the rebuilding of the temple (von Pomtow, *SIG*³ no. 224, p. 299). But there is little doubt that there was an ulterior motive to their request and that they were really hoping to gain the support of Delphi (and its champion, Philip) against Sparta (Griffith (1979): 481).

[…] Amphiktyons: If this line began beneath the one above, as is usually but not always the case, there is space for a word of eight (or possibly nine) letters before 'Amphiktyons'. D-S read *NAI* as the last three letters and restore the infinitive *ΚΛΗΘΗΝΑΙ* ('to be called/named'). Von Pomtow (*SIG*³ no. 224, p. 299) rightly points out that the formula for becoming a member of the Amphiktyony simply uses the verb 'to be' (*EINAI*) and cites in support Demosthenes 19.111 and 327. Of the same opinion is Lefèvre (1998: 166–7). Whilst this is surely the case, that word (*EINAI*) is too short for the space (cf. Wankel (1987): 220). In fact, to my eye the remains of the letter before *AI* are not consistent with *N*. Indeed, P-S claim to see quite different letters in these last three spaces, namely *EIN* (all dotted) and they may be correct (Wankel (1987): 220). On this basis they restore [*EINAI ΔOK*]*EIN* ('to be decreed/held to be'). This is probably the best suggestion so far. At any rate, all are agreed that the request was to become members of the Amphiktyony, though it is not clear whether this meant that each city wanted a vote or just to be attached to the Peloponnesian group (cf. Lefèvre (1998): 167 n. 63).

***refer* the matter … to the cities:**   This was obviously too serious an issue for the *hieromnemones* to decide for themselves. For a good discussion of the process involved see Londey (1990: 251–4). Cf. Lefèvre (1998): 183–91.

reply … Pylaia: The Pylaia was normally held twice a year in spring and autumn (Lefèvre (1998): 197–204). For the location (Thermopylai and/or Delphi) see Lefèvre (1998): 193–6). Since the year of this decree cannot be determined with certainty, it is not possible to tell which was the occasion of the request and which the reply. Griffith (1979: 481) sees in this reply 'temporising and diplomatic language' (cf. von Pomtow, who calls it a 'mitior recusatio'), but Londey (1990: 252–3 and n. 67) argues that it was normal procedure. As noted above, there is common agreement that the request for membership was rejected, even though the honorific title 'benefactor' was granted.

answer shall be made [. . .]:   It is generally agreed amongst editors that the name of some other party should be restored here, to whom the title 'benefactor' was also granted. Foucart (1909: 114 n. 2) accepted Arnim's suggestion 'to the Argives', though reluctantly, because it involved too many letters for the space, while Crönert (1907: 381) proposed 'to the Eleans' (cf. von Pomtow, *SIG*³ no. 224). Neither the Argives nor the Eleans are known to have made donations to the *Naopoioi*, but the Eleans had performed the service of destroying the remains of Phalaikos' mercenaries (Diod. 16.63). The most recent view is that it is not possible to identify the party concerned (Lefèvre (1998): 167 n. 63).

And . . . Aristo[tle]:   It is important to decide whether this mention of Aristotle indicates that Didymos is starting a new topic or not. P-S, following Crönert (1907: 381), see a punctuation point before Aristo[tle] and restore: 'And [of the things concerning these matters so much]'. This would suggest a change of subject. But the formula is not quite right and it would be very strange to introduce a new topic with a quotation from Aristotle, but no reference to a passage in Demosthenes. The evidence is in favour of those who believe that Didymos is continuing his discussion of 10.31, which probably began at the very beginning of column 3. See Osborne (104–5) and Gibson (2001: 48–56).

[in] *the* third (book):   All editors identify the work cited as Aristotle's *NOMIMA BARBARIKA* (a treatise in four books, presumably on the institutions and customs of non-Greek peoples). For the few fragments see Gigon (1987: 559–61, 750–4), though he makes no reference to this passage. Nothing of the title is extant and there is only space to restore the first part (*NOMIMA*). Nevertheless there is considerable agreement that the passage should be restored to read '. . . Aristo[tle in] *the* third (book) [of the *Nomima*, which is about the customs] of the Scythians, says . . .', with the slight exception that Gibson would replace 'customs' by 'tribes'. This is part of his explication of the whole passage as a reference to the story in Diodoros (17.81.1–2; cf. Curtius 7.3.1–3, Arrian 3.27.4–5) of the way the Arimaspians (or Ariaspians), a Scythian tribe according to Stephanos of Byzantion (s.v. Εὐεργέτης), came to be called 'benefactors' by the Persians, in the time of Cyrus the Great (Gibson (2001): 43–56). In fact, he may be right in detecting the name '*the* Ari[maspians]' at the end of line 18 and '*the* be[nefactors . . . Arim]aspians . . .' in lines 19–20.

Hermias, ruler of Atarneus and Assos in northern Asia Minor

This individual is the subject of a major excursus by Didymos, beginning at least at col. 4.59 and probably several lines earlier (see below) and extending to column 6.62. He is an intriguing figure. Educated at Plato's Academy (though not by Plato), he took over control (*c.*355 BC) of the territory around the gulf of Adrammytion, formerly controlled by a Euboulos (about whom we know nothing reliable), and expanded his little kingdom to the point where he dominated most of northern Asia Minor, maintaining his independence from the Great King. He established a sort of school for philosophers at Assos, first (supposedly on the advice of Plato's *Sixth Letter*) for the Platonists Koriskos and Erastos, then in 348/7 for Aristotle, Kallisthenes and others, after they left Athens. Aristotle was particularly close to Hermias, since he married his niece and adopted daughter, Pythias. His reign was eventually ended by Mentor of Rhodes, who captured Atarneus and took Hermias as a prisoner to the King (Diod. 16.52.5–7; cf. Strabo 13.1.57 C610, who mistakenly names his captor Memnon, Mentor's brother). He was probably tortured and put to death, likely in 341 BC (Diod. gives the date as 349/8, but is certainly wrong).

Column 4, lines 20–58:   Though nothing intelligible remains of the next part of the papyrus up to and including line 58, the few letters that can be discerned in lines 47–9 could yield the words 'captured' (47), 'deceived' (48), 'of Rhodes and to the king' (49). P-S, following a suggestion originally put forward by Crönert (1907: 382), take this as part of a narrative of the deception and capture of Hermias of Atarneus by Mentor of Rhodes and his dispatch up-country to the King (cf. Diod. 16.52.5–7; Strabo 13.1.57 C610). Given the allusion in the Heading and the material in the following columns, this suggestion is surely correct and is universally accepted. It is likely that Didymos discussed this individual in his commentary on Demosthenes 10.32 (the *lemma* for which must consequently have been introduced before line 47) and that he identified Hermias as the man there referred to as the 'agent and confidant of all Philip's plots against the king'. This identification can also be found independently in the scholia to this passage (see Dilts (1983): 152). It has spawned some extravagant modern theories about close political intrigue between Philip II of Macedon and Hermias, and Aristotle's role as matchmaker (e.g. Jaeger (1948):

119–21; Chroust (1972): 170–1; Ellis (1976): 97–8, 172–3; Cawkwell (1978): 53–5; Griffith (1979): 487, 518–21; Hammond (1994): 130). The only real disagreement amongst these scholars is whether the initiative came from Philip, because he wanted to use Hermias' territory as a bridgehead, or from Hermias, because he needed support against the reviving powers of the Persian Empire. On that point, the latter view (most strongly expressed by Cawkwell and Griffith) is more convincing. More recently, however, the very idea of any liaison between Philip and Hermias has been challenged in a provocative article by R. D. Milns (1987: 287–302, esp. p. 301), aimed at proving that the *Fourth Philippic* was not an authentic Demosthenic speech (on that question see now Hajdu (2002): 44–9). But, though Milns makes some good points, his arguments fail to convince. The likelihood that there was some contact between the two rulers (with or without Aristotle's involvement) is intrinsically too strong to be ignored (but see contra, Briant (2002): 688–90, 1005–6), and is surely confirmed by the view attributed to Kallisthenes, who knew him well, in col. 6.55–7 (see note ad loc.), despite the scepticism of Bosworth (1980: 18 n. 44 and reiterated forcefully *per litt.*). Whilst there may be no reason to talk of bridgeheads (Buckler (1994): 107) or even to assume that Philip was already planning his invasion of the Persian Empire (Errington (1981): 76–83), Philip certainly could not have overlooked the strategic usefulness of having an ally in Asia. Hermias, on the other hand, like the Attalids who later ruled in the same area, would always need outside help against a strong or resurgent Persia. I find the alternative, that there was no 'relationship', they were just 'good friends' (most clearly enunciated by Errington (1981): 76–83), naive.

Second, there is a potential point of contact between the two, that is not often brought into this discussion, in the institution of the 'companions' (*hetairoi*). This well-known part of the Macedonian court can also be found in Hermias' administration. At least, that is the natural conclusion to be drawn from an inscription (*SIG*³ 229, Tod 165, Harding (1985): no. 79, Stauber (1996): ii. 53–6; Rhodes and Osborne (2003): no. 68), preserving part of a treaty between Hermias and Erythrai, in which he is always named together with his 'companions' (e.g. lines 12–13: 'The oath shall be sworn by the Ery[thraian]s to Hermias and his companions'). They appear to share in his government (Tod 189; Rhodes and Osborne (2003): 345) and may be the rulers of the dependent *poleis* (Stauber (1996): ii. 55), that are referred to by Diodoros (16.52.6–7). If so, this could be an indication that Hermias modelled his court on Philip's (that Philip was the imitator is obviated by the chronology. For the history of the *hetairoi* in Macedon see Kienast (1973): 273–81 and Griffith (1979): 395–414). But, this evidence is often not interpreted in this way. The alternate view is that the *hetairoi* of the inscription are the group of philosophers who gathered around Hermias at Atarneus and Assos (cf. Wormell (1935): 59–61; Ellis (1976): 97–8; Cawkwell (1978): 54–5, who even sees the influence of Athenian intellectuals on both Philip and Hermias as a sign that they were 'thoroughly Greek', and Milns (1994): 73–4, who actually restores the word *hetairoi* in the text at col. 5.53). For the evidence that *hetairos* was a term used amongst Platonists see Brunt (1993: 284 n. 7), but there is nothing to suggest that the relationship went beyond the philosophical or that it involved sharing in administrative and political functions. On Hermias' 'companions' see below on col. 6.16 (p. 152).

Lines 59–60: [a very great] *difference of opinion***:** After what was probably a brief narrative of the capture and death of Hermias, Didymos here passes on to a discussion of his character, about which he found disagreement. He explores this controversy with several extensive quotations about Hermias (both for him and against), taken from the accounts of contemporaries. These quotations form one of the most valuable parts of his commentary. Controversy exists over the question where Didymos found them. Many believe he found them collected in the works of a predecessor, the Hellenistic biographer Hermippos. But, this view has been challenged recently and, in my opinion, those who believe he was himself responsible for these quotations are surely correct. See Osborne (22–30), Yunis (1997: 1052), Bollansée (2001: 97–8, with reservations), Gibson (107), and, in general, the Introduction under Didymos the Scholar.

the fondness for listening to/of . . . : This very literal translation purposely reveals the ambiguity of the Greek, which could mean either 'since I (i.e. Didymos himself) enjoy listening to those who . . .' (so, Yunis (1997): 1050) or 'to gratify the receptive ears of those who . . .' (Gibson: 85). Context favours the latter. For a similar usage in Polybios see e.g. 7.7.8; 9.1.4.

[those who even now] busy themselves: The restoration is convenient and is as old as the first edition, but it is just a restoration. It is dangerous to make assertions on the strength of it, such as that of Düring (1957: 275) that this could not have been written by Didymos, because 'it is not likely that the Hermias episode was much discussed in Didymus' time', and that, consequently, it must have been written by his source, who he believed was Hermippos. Even if the restoration is correct and even though Hermias had clearly been of interest to Didymos' predecessors, there is clear evidence that he remained a 'hot topic' in Didymos' time. After all, besides Didymos himself, his close contemporaries Diodoros (16.52.5–7), Dionysios of Halikarnassos (*Ad Amm.* 1.5), Demetrios of Magnesia (in Diogenes Laertios, *Life of Aristotle* 5.3) and even Ovid (*Ibis* 319–20) wrote about Hermias.

I think . . . [more extensively] on these topics: Once again, the restoration fits the space and has been accepted since the first edition. If it is correct, it might indicate that Didymos was dissatisfied with the work of his predecessors. Even if it is not correct, the use of the first person indicates Didymos' independence of his sources in authoring this digression.

Theopompos: For this famous fourth-century historian from Khios see the Introduction under Sources. It is triply appropriate that he should be cited on the negative side. First, he was habitually critical of the people he wrote about. Second, as a Khian, he may well have had particular reason to dislike Hermias for his interference in Khian affairs (see further on this below, pp. 130–3). Third, he was hostile to the members of the Academy, especially Plato and Aristotle, with whom Hermias had close relations. See Wormell (1935): 67–71 and Flower (1994): 87–8.

[. . .]-sixth (book) of his Concerning [Phili]p: The *Affairs concerning Philip* is Didymos' variant for the more usual *Philippika*. He uses it again at col. 8.62 in a totally different context. This is further evidence that he is not deriving this whole section from one source, like Hermippos, but that the citations are his own. The book number has always been restored as '[forty]-sixth' since the first edition. It also suits what can be inferred about the arrangement of the *Philippika*, since the other fragments of book 46 are datable to 341, the year of Hermias' death, which is the most likely context for Theopompos to have written about him (see Shrimpton (1991): 63; *pace* Jacoby, *FGrHist* 2b, comm. p. 393).

he *writes* [as follows]:   The quotation is fragment 291 in Jacoby, *FGrHist* 2b, pp. 598–9, though the text given there needs to be corrected.

though he was **a eunuch [and B]ithy[n]ian:**   Enough of the word 'Bithynian' can be read to put this restoration beyond doubt. Crönert's suggestion (1907: 382), '*mutilated* in [appearance through the process of cauteriza]tion', adopted by Jacoby in *FGrHist*, is impossible. The accuracy of this information is another question. It was suspected already by Wormell (1935: 73), on the grounds that Hermias was surely Greek, because of the evidence of Aristotle's poem (see below) and because the Eleians proclaimed the Olympic truce for him (below, col. 5.29–30). Furthermore, about the only information we are provided about Euboulos (the *Souda*, s.v. Euboulos) is suspiciously similar: i.e. that he was a banker and a Bithynian. Besides that, most of the charges Theopompos levels against Hermias are the stock-in-trade of rhetorical invective, the influence of which on Theopompos is strong. They originated in the comic theatre, where they often lacked any factual basis; similarly, in the orators such invective can be shown to be false. See Owen (1983: 16); Flower (1994: 206–8); Harding (1987: 25–39) and (1994b: 196–202). But, the charge that he was a slave and a eunuch was repeated by (or originated with?) Theokritos of Khios (below) and became canonical (cf. Strabo 13.1.57 C610). See Mulvany (1926: 155) for the suggestion that those charges were based upon Herodotos' account of Hermotimos of Pedasa (Hdt. 8.104–6), discussed below at col. 5.23. In that context it should be noted that to brand a man as a eunuch was an effective way of denigrating him in the eyes of a Greek audience, even though it cannot have been an unusual experience for Greeks under Persian rule to suffer castration (cf. Strabo 13.4.1 C623 on the fate of Philetairos of Pergamon and see Bosworth (1997): 297–313). For a recent discussion of eunuchs in the Persian court and Greek attitudes to them see Briant (2002): 268–77.

And/but third . . . :   The last lines of this column are corrupt, but the remains are consistent with the expectation that Theopompos continued his review of Hermias' career with an account of his rise to power. The most extensive restoration is by Crönert and adopted by Jacoby: 'and third, *after he had associated* for *unjust purposes* [with his master], *when he was sick*, he took [As]sos [as (his) heir].' But this is too far-fetched. Not much safer is P-S's speculation that the letters *ΔΕ* after 'third' are the beginning of the word *ΔΕΣΠΟΤΗΝ* (master), presuming that the reference to a 'third master' (sc. for Hermias) reflects the tradition that appears later in Harpokration (s.v. Hermias) that Hermias was 'thrice-bought'.

In the last line between 'seized' and 'Assos' P-S restore '*with* Eub[oulos]', in the space where Crönert had '[as (his) heir]'. I cannot see any of the letters P-S see in this space. The papyrus at this point is in tatters. Nevertheless, some reference to Euboulos here may be appropriate, since he is referred to as Hermias' predecessor and master (see below on the epigram of Theokritos). The demonstrative in line 1 of col. 5 needs a referant.

As]sos: A strongly fortified hill on the coast of the Troad opposite Lesbos. It is the modern Turkish village of Behram. A settlement here has been traced back to the early Bronze Age and has been identified with Homeric Pedasos (but see Cook (1973): 245–6). It has also been linked to the Hittite Assuwa. It was colonized by Greeks from Methymna (Strabo 13.1.58 C610), probably around 600, if the remains of the temple on the acropolis have been correctly dated to the sixth century. It was a tribute-paying member of the Athenian empire. The temple was restored in the first half of the fourth century, about the same time as the extensive fortifications were built. Both are likely the work of Euboulos and Hermias, who probably made Assos the base of their power (that Assos was Euboulos' base is assumed by Griffith (1979): 518; Trampedach (1994): 68), until Hermias turned it into a school for expatriate Platonic philosophers in the 340s. Subsequently, it was the birthplace of the Stoic philosopher, Kleanthes. The town was considerably enlarged in the Hellenistic period, when an agora with stoas and several civic buildings was developed on the terraced slope between the acropolis and the harbour. The steepness of this slope may have suggested the pun on the name of the place and the word 'nearer' (both *asson*), attributed to the Athenian citharist, Stratonikos, 'Come to Assos/ nearer so that you may more quickly reach the fulfilment of death' (cf. Homer, *Iliad* 6.143; Strabo 13.1.57 C610). The town continued to be inhabited into the late-Roman (there was a statue of Constantius II in the agora) and Byzantine periods. In the nineteenth century it attracted a great deal of attention from travellers and archaeologists. It was the first site excavated by the Archaeological Institute of America between 1881 and 1883. Their publication of the site is still fundamental (see the reports in Clarke (1882), (1898), and, for the plans of the site, (1902–21)). More recent accounts can be found in Leaf (1923: 289–300), Cook (1973: 240–50) and by U. Serdaroglu and others in *Asia Minor Studien* (vol. 2 (1990); vol. 10 (1993); vol. 21 (1996)).

P-S speculate that the scribe missed a line at the end of this column, that recounted the death of Euboulos. They suggest 'and after the death of Euboulos, he succeeded to the estate of that man'. But that leaves the problem of what to read in the space after 'of that man'/'that man's' (see below).

COLUMN FIVE

There is no Heading. This indicates that the discussion continues from the previous column and, also, carries on to the next.

that *man's*:   The possessive is virtually certain, and probably in the singular. Crönert's suggestion of 'fort and' in the following space fits the gap and the sense. P-S make no restoration here, for the reason given above.

Atarneus: The other place associated with this little kingdom in our sources. It had been under Khian control since the time of Cyrus the Great (Hdt. 1.160.4) and once again after the Peloponnesian War (Xen. *Hell.* 3. 2. 11). It probably passed into the hands of the Great King as a result of the King's Peace of 387/6 (see Hornblower, *CAH* ² vi. 94). Some time before the mid-fourth century it was taken over by Euboulos, probably during the course of (or as a result of) the satraps' revolt of 366–360 BC (Arist. *Pol.* 2. 1267a; Weiskopf (1989): 41, 95). Wormell (1935: 68) considers this the reason for the hostility of Theopompos and Theokritos toward Hermias, since both of them were from Khios (cf. Flower (1994): 87–8). The place, once a centre of power, became uninhabited and Pausanias could not identify any visible remains when he visited it (7.2.11). Consequently, it has not been easy for modern scholars to agree upon its location. For a review of the suggestions and the evidence see Lambrianides et al. (1996: 190–4). He concludes that it is to be identified with the fortifications on the hill at Kale Agili, 4 km north-east of modern Dikili, located on the opposite side of the bay of Edremit (Adramyttion) from Assos and well to the south, on a line between Mytilene and Pergamon, roughly where it is located on the Barrington Atlas (p. 56 D3). Possession of Assos and Atarneus would have given Hermias control of about 150 km of coastline along the bay of Adramyttion and the states situated there. Diodoros claims Hermias was 'in control of many strongholds and cities' (16.52.5). See further Stauber (1996: i. 263–9).

nearby territory. [For of] *all men*: I follow P-S here. The punctuation point after 'territory' is clearly visible and renders all restorations that treat the following words as part of the preceding sentence invalid, e.g. Crönert's '. . . nearby territory all (of it), [ruling] *most unjustly* and basely' (1907: 382) and Grenfell-Hunt's 'nearby territory, [having done] *everything most unjustly* and basely' (P-S, app. crit. ad loc.).

always *behaved* **most [cruel]ly . . .** : This charge is, of course, part of the standard depiction of a tyrant. It is completely contrary to the characterization presented below by Aristotle and Kallisthenes. It is not easy to judge between them without any other descriptions. Philosophers were more favourably inclined towards autocrats and could be no less tendentious in their presentation than historians (even one as malign as Theopompos). In this case they had particular reason to distort the facts, given their close association with Hermias (Trampedach (1994): 67–70).

[citizens]: P-S, following Macher (1914: 8). This is probably a more likely restoration than D-S's 'friends'.

[all of them]: This is the suggestion of P-S in place of the more popular 'harshly' (Wendland in P-S, app. crit. ad loc.) or 'most cruelly' (Crönert (1907): 382). It, at least, has the advantage that it is consistent with the altered punctuation.

[by the noose he did away with]: This is the restoration proposed by Crönert and accepted by both Jacoby and P-S; the latter see more of the word 'noose' than I can.

[And of the] territory . . . : This is an important passage for an understanding of Theopompos' point, but once again some crucial words are missing and interpretation is difficult. The two most extensive attempts at restoration are by Crönert (1907: 382), who is followed by Jacoby (*FGrHist* 115 F291) and Wormell (1935: 70), and by P-S. Unfortunately, as so often, Crönert's restoration is over-enthusiastic and, in several places, does not conform to the preserved lettering (for a rendering see Harding (1985): 114), whilst P-S, on the other hand, produce a text that is more consistent with what can be read, but rather contorted Greek. Their version goes as follows: '[And of the] territory, which the Khians and the Mytilen[ians were disputing], *after* they established him [ruler/protector, many times together with] his unpaid soldiery, he [treated with drunken abuse] and insulted very many of the Ionia[ns].' For a more elegant translation of this restoration, that attempts to iron out the wrinkles, see Shrimpton (1991: 126).

[. . .] to be of the unpaid soldiery/campaigns: Not the least of the difficulties with the restoration discussed above is the text and meaning of this phrase. First, I have to agree with D-S that the abbreviation for the word immediately preceding 'of the unpaid soldiery/campaigns', that P-S interpret as the word *meta* ('together with'), looks more like the sign for the verb 'to be' , which is how I have translated it. That being the case the text might have read: '*after* they established him **to be** [chief and leader (*ΠΡΟΣΤΑΤΗΝ K' ΗΓΕΜΟΝΑ*)] of unpaid soldiery/campaigns.' Next, what does this mean? Certainly, the more natural translation of the word *strateumata* is 'campaigns', but it does not fit well with 'together with'. It is more at home with 'to be'. And, what is the significance of either soldiery or campaigns being 'unpaid'? It would help answer this question, if we could decide whom Theopompos was blaming for failure to pay. P-S seem to think Hermias was being accused (see also Osborne: 113), while Wormell (1935: 71) attributes the failure to pay to the Khians. Perhaps, the key to this lies in the word that P-S restore as 'he treated with drunken abuse'.

[. . .]:   P-S restore in this space, [he treated with drunken abuse]. It is safe to say that there is absolutely no palaeographic justifica-tion for this restoration, since only the first letter, dotted at that, is preserved. Nor does it make good sense. Better is the suggestion of Rusten (1987: 265), 'he acted unlawfully' (cf. Gibson: 85), but even that seems to me to be off-track. More likely is a word that can gov-ern the first word of the sentence that is in the genitive, a word like *para-* (*or kata-*)*lambano* ('seize', 'take hold of'). Then the passage might read: '[And the] territory, which the Khians and Mytilen[ians were disputing, *after* they established him to be [chief and leader] of cam-paigns that they failed to pay for, he seized (*ΠΑΡΕΛΑΒΕ*); and he treated very many of the Ionia[ns] with abuse.'

After all that, the historical situation is hardly less difficult to de-duce. The territory concerned is not likely to have been on the islands of Khios and Lesbos themselves, as some (e.g. Wormell (1935): 70) have thought, but must surely have been on the mainland, opposite Khios and Lesbos, their *peraia*. It could have been on the tip of the Erythraian peninsula and had something to do with the decline of the Hekatomnid dynasty to the south and Hermias' expansion into the area. Inscriptions from Erythrai might provide some support for this view. During the heyday of Mausolos of Halikarnassos (377–353 BC) Erythrai acknowledged his authority (*SIG*³ 168; Tod 155; Rhodes and Osborne (2003): no. 56). This submission extended to his successor, Idrieus, who ruled until 344. He was honoured by Erythrai, maybe early in his reign (Varinluoglu (1981): 45–7; Harding (1985): no. 28; Rhodes and Osborne (2003): no. 56). Some time thereafter, however, Erythrai found it expedient to make an agreement with Hermias (*SIG*³ 229; Tod 165; Harding (1985): no. 79; Rhodes and Osborne (2003): no. 68), which might indicate that he now controlled the whole area south from Assos to Erythrai. But recently Hornblower has doubted that the inscriptional evidence will bear this conclusion (*CAH*² vi. 94). He suggests, instead, that the area in contention might have been Atarneus itself, since it had once belonged to Khios (Hdt. 1.160.4; Xen. *Hell.* 3.2.11). This suggestion is not very plausible. In the first place, there is no evidence that Mytilene had any claim on Atarneus and, second, we would have to believe that Hermias was deviously campaigning against a town of which he was the master!

For, being a *bought slave* ... money changers' *table*:   The punctuation is secure, thanks to the presence of the particle (ΓΑΡ—'for'), which follows the first word of a clause that usually explains the preceding sentence—in this case probably the statement that he 'treated very many of the Ionians with abuse'. The tradition that Hermias began his career as a slave and employee of the banker, Euboulos, is strong. The representation is consistent with what we know of the banking business in the Greek world of this time (Bogaert (1968): 242); the most obvious analogy is with Pasion (*APF* no. 11672), himself originally a slave, and Phormion, the slave who succeeded him in his business at Athens. On the other hand, the arguments in favour of Hermias' being a Greek are cogent and militate against the tradition (Wormell (1935): 73). The money changers' tables were a regular feature of any agora (see e.g. Harding (1985): no. 45.5). It is, in fact, not unlikely that money changing was the basis of the banker's business (Millett (1991): 216–17).

composed ... **of misfortunes /** *beset* **by calamities:**   This is another place where radically different restorations have been put forward. All are agreed that we are still dealing with circumstantial clauses that provide the background to the action (found in the main clause 'he did not rest') that Theopompos considered abusive to the Ionians. One approach is to assume that the subject is still Hermias and restore something like 'and [entirely] *the product* (*composed*) of misfortune' (Wendland ap. D-S²). Another changes the subject to 'disasters' (genitive absolute) and restores, 'when disasters *were contrived* (*composed*) [for the Khians]' (P-S, followed by Gibson (85), who translates without reservation, 'when disasters befell [*sic*] the Chians').

Lines 11–16: he did not rest: This restoration is hardly questionable, but little more than that about these lines is certain. There is a reference to 'propriety' or 'decency.' P-S print this word in the dative case and it looks as though they would take it with 'at the same time/together with' that immediately precedes. This has the support of grammar, but little else. Their reading cannot be confirmed by my own examination of the papyrus; in fact, what I see is consistent with the original reading of D-S, namely the nominative, or more likely accusative, singular (*ΤΟ ΠΡΕΠΟΝ*). Furthermore, 'together with propriety' appears to be quite out of keeping with the tone of Theopompos' description of Hermias. 'Contrary to (*ΠΑΡΑ*) propriety/decency' would be more in line and suits the accusative, but is not supported by the remains of the letters that precede 'propriety'. Crönert's suggestion (1907: 382), 'simultaneously defaming decency', may not be totally off the mark.

A new sentence probably begins at 'And of many' (because of the particle *de*), and maybe another (or at least a new clause) with 'but amongst (?) some . . .' (for the same reason). It is not impossible that Macher (1914: 8) was on the right lines in inferring that Theopompos was contrasting Hermias' treatment of two separate groups, the former of which might have suffered the loss of their property, while the latter experienced the dissolution (if the last word is correctly restored) of their existing constitutions. The far more ambitious restoration by Crönert, adopted by Jacoby in his text of this passage (*FGrHist* 115 F291), is unfortunately too imaginative.

And yet he did not escape scot-free . . . : At this point the text becomes more readable and the restoration put forward by Diels and Schubart has been standard, except for the substitution of '[did it go totally] *unnoticed*' by P-S for their '*maintain* [his office]'. The narrative of Hermias' capture is in Diodoros and Strabo and, of course, alluded to in Demosthenes 10.32 (see above on col. 4.20–58, p. 124). While Demosthenes emphasizes a connection between Hermias and Philip of Macedon as Artaxerxes' motivation for arresting him, Diodoros, though quite wrong about the date, more plausibly attributes it to Hermias' defection from Persian control and treats it as part of Artaxerxes' aggressive reassertion of Persian dominance in Asia Minor (see Sealey (1993): 183; Briant (2002): 688–9). But Philip is not totally absent from Diodoros' narrative. Mentor, Hermias' captor, had managed to win the favour of the Great King by his campaigning in Phoenicia and Egypt and was now able to negotiate the return of his brother, Memnon, and his brother-in-law, Artabazos (former satrap of Phrygia), from the court of Philip of Macedon, where they had been in exile (Diod. 16.52.3–4). Furthermore, one can suspect there was no little family interest for Mentor in eliminating Hermias' dominance of the important Gulf of Adramyttion, which had sometimes been a part of the Phrygian satrapy.

after he had been dragged up-country to the King: Osborne (115) follows Düring (1957: 275) in drawing attention to the 'remarkable coincidence of language' between Theopompos' account (*ΑΝΑΣΠΑΣΤΟΣ ΓΕΝΟΜΕΝΟΣ*) and Dem. 10.32 (*ΑΝΑΣΠΑΣΤΟΣ ΓΕΓΟΝΕ*). Though the vocabulary is not un-common and technically correct, and the coincidence hardly, therefore, 'remarkable', given Theopompos' familiarity with Demosthenes' opinions (Shrimpton (1991): 157–80), it remains possible that Theopompos was, at least, aware of Demosthenes' wording (cf. Hajdu (2002) ad loc.). If so, it suggests that a person as contemporary as Theopompos recognized Hermias as the person alluded to by Demosthenes.

after he had endured . . . *crucifixion*: There was no agreement on the manner of Hermias' death in antiquity, as can be seen from Didymos' summation at col. 6.50–9. See the discussion there pp. 160–2).

And the *same* (author, i.e. Theopompos) **. . . *letter to* Phi[lip]:** This is the only fragment we have from this letter; indeed, it is the only reference to its existence, unless the name 'Philip' is to be restored after 'Letter to [. . .]' in the list of Theopompos' works in the Rhodian Booklist (*FGrHist* 115 T48). Since the *Philippika* was probably not finished much before 323 BC (Shrimpton (1991): 7; Flower (1994): 32), the excursus on Hermias was written long after his death, rather like an obituary. The *Letter to Philip*, on the other hand, was surely written before Hermias' death, as is shown by the use of the

present tense for the verbs (Wormell (1935): 66; Flower (1994): 39).
And the context is not difficult to arrive at. It was no doubt Theopompos' contribution to the intense competition amongst the intel-
lectual elite in the 340s for the favour of Philip, on which see Markle
(1976: 80–99) and, in general, Owen (1983: 1–25). Whether he sent
his letter to Philip before Aristotle was chosen to be Alexander's
tutor (343/2) in order to advance his own candidacy by calumni-
ating his rival (Shrimpton (1991): 6), or after Aristotle's selection
to counter the growing influence of the Academy at Philip's court
(Flower (1994): 88–9) is impossible to judge, but it is unlikely that he
was playing the role of a Macedonian secret agent (Wormell (1935):
71), or even posing as one (Shrimpton (1991): 5).

the reputation . . . *amongst* [the] Hellenes: Since it is unlikely that Hermias was known to very many Greeks (Milns (1994):
81), the 'reputation' that Theopompos is concerned to refute must
be amongst those very philosophers who had resided with him and
whose opinion Didymos cites in his favour, especially Aristotle and
Kallisthenes. These were, of course, the very people Theopompos
aimed to discredit in the eyes of Philip, by means of this attack upon
Hermias.

**Lines 23–30: [. . .], yet [. . .] being refined . . . truce [for
him]:**   After 'refined' D-S restore 'fond of culture' (*philomousos*),
while P-S suggest 'fond of honour' (*philokalos*). Foucart is alone in
his feeling that Theopompos is giving a different, more moderate judgement of Hermias in this passage (1909: 127, 129). Others
follow Wormell in recognizing its strongly antithetical style, whereby Theopompos 'introduces into each favourable statement a
contrasting and damaging qualification' (1935: 71). In fact, we
can surely be confident that he created the negative comments in
response to the positive propaganda put out by Hermias' friends. It
is possible, as Mulvany suggested (1926: 155) that he and his fellow
Khian, Theokritos, based their hostile characterization of Hermias
upon the story of Hermotimos of Pedasa, who was castrated and
sold into slavery in Persia by a Khian, named Panionios, but later
took an awful revenge upon him (Hdt. 8.104–6), but more likely, in
my opinion, that they were just employing standard rhetorical techniques of *diabole* (Owen (1983): 10 ff.). For example, the antithesis,
'though he is not of Greek origin, he studies in the company of the
Platonists', is really designed to communicate the idea: Platonists
consort with barbarians. Any attempt to restore the beginning of this

passage must proceed on this basis and lead us to expect a negative statement to balance 'refined and *fond of honour / culture*'. Furthermore, the lost clause should contain a finite verb, since the positive view is contained in a subordinate relative clause. Thus, Theopompos would have created a chiastic arrangement between his two opening antitheses, having a negative main clause balanced by a positive subordinate clause, then reversing the relationship with a negative subordinate clause ('though he is not of Greek origin') balanced by a positive main clause ('he studies in the company of Platonists'). That assumption seems to exclude Foucart's suggestion, '[(being) savage by nature], yet [feignedly] being refined . . .' (1909: 128), because there is no main verb in the restored clause (Crönert (1907): 383). Furthermore, 'feignedly' destroys the antithesis. On the other hand, the restoration of P-S, '[For he was a eunuch], yet [in like manner] being refined . . .', that has gained acceptance (see e.g. Gibson: 85; contra Osborne: 117), may not be right either. It needs to be demonstrated that being a eunuch is a suitable antithesis for 'being refined and fond of honour/culture', but more importantly the past tense 'was' that this restoration requires is out of keeping with the tenses of the remaining verbs and the word translated as 'in like manner' is unsatisfactory both grammatically (a comparison usually requires similar clauses) and logically ('in like manner' to what?). [Professor Bosworth has suggested to me that, if *philokalos* is the correct reading, it may be a 'sarcastic echo' of Perikles' usage in the Funeral Oration (*Epitaphios*) at Thuc. 2.40, with the connotation that the barbarian Hermias is aping the ways of the ideal Athenian.]

not *of Greek origin*: This is, of course, another version of the charge that he was Bithynian, discussed above, and manifestly untrue (see also below under **truce**). But it may be worth noting the possibility that Hermias might have been born in Bithynia, though of Greek parents (or at least a Greek father). The case of Demosthenes himself would be an analogy (cf. Mulvany (1926): 155; Osborne: 118).

studies **in the company of the P[lato]nists:** But not, it seems, of Plato himself (*pace* Strabo 13.1.57 C610). The *Sixth Letter* attributed to Plato (accepted by Jaeger (1948): 111; Guthrie (1975): 400–1; rejected by Trampedach (1994): 70–2) was addressed to Hermias (amongst others), but in it Plato claims never to have met him (*Ep.* 6.323a).

with expensive (racing) teams: The *Sixth Letter* (322d) confirms that Hermias was wealthy, and sufficiently so to indulge in the very expensive business of entering teams of horses in the four-horse chariot competitions at the international festivals. The author (Plato?), however, advises Hermias that trusty friends with clean characters would stand him in greater stead than all the horses, military alliances, or money in the world.

possessing (only) rocky crags *and little* [lands]:   This is another charge that comes into conflict with the evidence. Diodoros, probably basing his account upon Theopompos' contemporary Ephoros, says that Hermias was 'in control of many strongholds and cities' (Diod. 16.52.5). Foucart was surely right to see that Theopompos' purpose was to 'diminish the importance of (Hermias') principality' (1909: 129).

he got the [. . .]:   No satisfactory restoration for the missing word has been suggested. It has to be something that would contrast with possession of rocky crags. Blass's proposal of 'title of benefactor' (*EYEPΓETHΣ*) is the most appealing, but would be three letters short of the left-hand margin.

***persuaded* [the] city . . . (Olympic) truce [for him]:**   Elis was in charge of the games at Olympia throughout most of the Classical period, though it had briefly lost control between 365 and 360. The proclamation of the sacred truce (*EKEXEIPIA*) was a prelude to the celebration of all the international festivals of Greece. The process involved the sending out of *spondophoroi* to proclaim the truce in each participating city or region. Only after they had visited did the truce take effect. This was a Greek practice and the truce was extended exclusively to Greeks to enable them to attend the Greek international festivals and contests (Golden (1998): 16–17). Thus, the natural inference to be drawn from this statement, which even Theopompos does not deny, is that Hermias was considered a Greek by the administrators of the Olympian games; and, for this and other reasons, he is universally so considered by scholars today (see e.g. Foucart (1909): 131; Mulvany (1926): 155; Wormell (1935): 73; Owen (1983): 16; Flower (1994): 86, 206–8).

when that man was *celebrating the festival*:   I do not see as many letters of 'was celebrating the festival' as P-S claim to do, but I do see enough to support that reading. This invalidates previous restorations. The context is, however, unfortunately unclear.

Lines 53–63: Nothing useful can be read between lines 31 and 53, though this did not prevent the ever creative Crönert (1907: 383) from proposing for lines 32–3: '[. . . when Plat]o [sent out some students, he held] *discussions* [especially about . . .]'. When the papyrus becomes readable again at the beginning of line 53, it is clear that the quotation from Theopompos has finished and that we are now dealing with a different source, more favourable to Hermias (*pace* Gibson: 108–9, who considers that lines 53–63 are a continuation of the previous quotation). Most editors from D-S to P-S have suspected that the Hellenistic biographer Hermippos was the author of this passage and they have been followed by the commentators, though there has been some disagreement about which work of his was involved (whether it was his *On Aristotle* or a work entitled *On those who converted from philosophy to tyranny and the exercise of power*). For a thorough roll-call of those who hold the view that the author was Hermippos and the different works of his they advocate see Bollansée (2001: 92 n. 89).

But this view has little to be said for it and has been soundly disposed of by Milns (1994: 78–81). His suggestion that the author may have been Theophrastos is felicitous and has met with some approval (e.g. Bollansée (2001): 95). Indeed, in its favour is a revealing observation made by Wormell (1935: 80), especially because he believed the author was Hermippos. He remarks: 'The passage is the most moderate in tone of all the evidence preserved by Didymus, and the detailed knowledge of its author, together with his scientific manner, justifies us in using it as a chief source in reconstructing the history of Hermias.' Furthermore, it has been suggested (Owen (1983): 7; Gaiser (1985): 12, 21; Trampedach (1994): 73) that Theophrastos' name should be read in line 54, as one of those who were invited to Assos (see below ad loc.).

It should be noted, however, that this is no longer the only reliable source for Hermias and the sojourn of the Platonists at Assos. Another account can be extracted from the fragments of a section of Philodemos' *Syntaxis Philosophorum* that has been recovered in two papyri from Herculaneum, no. 1021, col. v, lines 1–22 and no. 164, fr. 5. For a text see Gaiser (1985): 13, or better (1988): 161–2. If he is correct in his surmise ((1985): 16; (1988): 380–6) that Philodemos' source at this point was the Atthidographer Philokhoros, we would have a trustworthy account that has the additional advantage of being independent of the partisan literature that Didymos cites.

For the sake of reference I offer here a translation of the text of this passage, as restored by Gaiser (1988: 161–2):

[And] *'stars'* amongst philosophers [came] to Herm[i]as, (like) planets. And Her[mi]as, who had sent for them *in a most friendly manner* on a previous occasion, at that time urged (them to come) *all the more* on account of the *death* of Plato (i.e. 347 BC). After they had arrived, *he shared* all his property with them, and in particular [gave] (them) *a city*, As(s)[o]s, to inhabit. And they *spent their time* there in philosophical pursuits, associating in one *covered walkway* (peripatos), and Hermias, *of course*, provided for *all their needs*. *They considered that* [cities that were ruled by despots] *had changed* under the influence of philosophy to rule by the individual *most worthy of esteem*. *By proposing to hold a contest for politicians* [concerning] *'the best'*, *they confirmed* Pla[to's] saying, where (he said that) one land [would show] them [through] *eternity* (as) *very* [useful politicians].

Lines 52–63: Many attempts have been made to restore the text of these lines. Amongst the most influential are those by D-S, Jaeger (1948: 114 n. 2); Düring (1957: 273); P-S; Rusten (1987: 267) and Milns (1994: 72–8). See also Gaiser ((1985): 12; (1988): 380). These will be referred to by name only in the commentary that follows, wherever pertinent.

the *of* Plat[o] . . . : Milns makes the boldest attempt to restore this line. He puts a punctuation point after Plato and continues: '[At that time, then, Herm]ias was commander of the people round about.' In this he is followed by Gibson (85), although he translates 'was commander of' as 'ruled'. Unfortunately, although they may seem logical, Milns's readings of -*IAΣ* (the end of Hermias' name) in place of the *EIΣ* seen by both D-S and P-S and of the abbreviation for the plural genitive of the definite article (*T'*) in front of 'round about' instead of that for the accusative feminine singular (*T`*) are clearly not based on personal examination of the papyrus. My own examination supports the reading printed in P-S and I have translated accordingly. More consistent with the remains, but less logical (and grammatically questionable) is Gaiser's suggestion: *'Having abandoned* Plat[o's school/way of life], he generalled the (country) roundabout.'

[. . .] and Erastos and Aristot[le . . .]: All editors agree in placing the name of Koriskos (of Skepsis) before that of Erastos. Not only is he usually named in the same breath as his fellow philosopher from Skepsis (e.g. by Plato (?), who pairs them consistently in his *Sixth Letter)*, but the second *K* of his name can clearly be read in the antepenultimate position. These two students of Plato had returned from Athens to Skepsis, a small city in the Troad about thirty miles north-east of Assos (as the crow flies), shortly before Plato wrote to them (the precise date is hard to arrive at; it was obviously before Plato's death in 347, but not by much, perhaps, since he admits to being old in the letter, 322d). They are depicted in the letter as naive young graduates, full of the Theory of Ideas, but lacking in worldly experience, who would benefit from association with the pragmatic and powerful Hermias, as he conversely would be improved by their company. They are often looked upon as indicative of the practical side of the educational purpose of the Academy (see e.g. Guthrie (1975): 23). Koriskos, of course, was father of Neleus of Skepsis, the man to whom Theophrastos bequeathed his library, which contained the major writings of Aristotle (see Strabo 13.1.54 C608; Guthrie (1981): 59–65).

But there is less agreement about what should precede. Since it has to be entirely restored, it is not altogether easy to decide between 'he invited from Athens . . .' (P-S; Rusten), 'he made into his friends . . .' (Jaeger, Düring; cf. Wormell (1935): 80) or 'he invited as (his) companions' (*hetairoi*, Milns, followed by Gibson), though Milns is probably right in rejecting the first, on grounds that Erastos and Koriskos were already in the Troad. On the other hand, I find it difficult to support Milns's argument for the reading '*hetairoi*' that they are 'epigraphically attested in a treaty between Erythrae and Hermias' (for reasons given above, see **Column 4, lines 20–58**, p. 124).

Aristot[le]:   Aristotle went to Asia Minor after the death of Plato in 347 and stayed there until 345/4, when he moved across the water to Mytilene, probably in the company of Theophrastos. His connection with Hermias is well attested, not least by the material contained in this papyrus, and has been the subject of many studies, most of which have been referred to already. See further below.

In the space following Aristotle's name most editors (including, most recently, Milns (1994: 73) and Gibson (85) restore the name of Xenokrates of Khalkedon, student of Plato and Head of the Academy from 339 to 314 (on whom see Diogenes Laertius 4.6–15), but as noted above, serious reservations have been raised about the possibility that Xenokrates ever went to Asia Minor with Aristotle (Owen (1983): 6–10) and the name of Theophrastos of Eresos, pupil of Aristotle and his successor in 323 (on whom see Diogenes

Laertius 5.36–57) is becoming an increasingly popular restoration for this space (Owen (1983): 7; Gaiser (1988): 12.21; Trampedach (1994): 73). P-S, by contrast, do not restore a name at this point, but propose 'to live with (him)', and they are followed by Rusten.

for which reason, indeed, *all these men* **[. . .]:** There is common agreement on the sense of the words that should follow 'men', even though the precise wording differs. 'Spent time with him/ Hermias', originally suggested by Foucart (1909: 157), is favoured by Jaeger, Düring, and Rusten. 'Came to Hermias' (Milns, Gibson) or 'came to Assos' (P-S, Gaiser) are also options.

[and] later, [when others] *had come*: This is the text proposed by P-S and accepted by most recent scholars (e.g. Rusten, Gaiser, Milns, Gibson). Also possible is: 'And later, when more had come by invitation' (Düring, Wormell).

he gave *them* **[some territory]** *as a gift*: This restoration, proposed by P-S, fits the legible remains and is currently accepted (see Rusten, Milns, Gibson). If it is correct, the place they were given (presumably to live and study in) must have been just a plot of land and was surely not the town of Assos (*pace* Gaiser, who restores after 'had come' '[And he writes that] he gave *them* [the city] *as a gift*.'), since that was almost certainly assigned to them later.

Lines 57–9: [. . .], and [. . .]: Clearly visible on the papyrus are *paragraphoi* between lines 56 and 57 and again between lines 57 and 58; also line 57 is indented. As Rusten (1987: 267) has pointed out, these are indications that one quotation ended and another began in line 57. Previous attempts to restore these lines have ignored this evidence and treated the quotation as continuous (e.g. by P-S, who restore 'when Euboulos had died' after 'gift'). They are invalidated for this reason. At the same time the tone of the narrative before and after this break is similar and there is not enough space to introduce the author and title of a new source. Rusten's conclusion, that it is necessary to assume a 'two-part quotation from the same author', is therefore inescapable and he has been followed by Gaiser ((1985): 12; (1988): 380), Milns (1994: 73), and Gibson (86). The first part of the quotation is usually assumed to end at 'gift' (probably correctly, *pace* Gaiser, who restores '[the city]' after 'gift') and the next part must begin near the end of line 57 with 'And' (in the translation, but with the word that precedes it in Greek, because the particle in Greek that translates as 'and' always follows the first word in its clause). This leaves eighteen or nineteen spaces for the transitional clause and the first word of the next part of the quotation. Two letters of that word are preserved (-$E\Sigma$). These are taken by P-S (followed by Rusten and Gaiser) as the preposition 'into' ($E\Sigma/EI\Sigma$), but by Milns and Gibson (following D-S) as the last two letters of the adverb 'on purpose' ($E\Pi IT H\Delta E\Sigma$). Against the former, Milns's argument that the non-Attic form of the preposition ($E\Sigma$) is inconsistent with the Attic form ($EI\Sigma$) that P-S restore two lines above, though not definitive, is not to be dismissed lightly. Furthermore, the restoration proposed by P-S (and adopted by both Rusten and Gaiser) for the rest of this clause, 'having changed into the tyranny, [he exercised] a *gentler* rule', is unnatural Greek (Milns (1994): 76–7; Bollansée (2001): 92–3 n. 89). Far better Greek, that is also more consistent with what we are told about Hermias, is the original proposal of D-S (adopted by Düring, Milns, and Gibson): 'And *on purpose* he changed the tyranny [into] a *gentler* rule.' The reading 'on purpose' leaves only thirteen letters for the presumed resumptive statement in line 57, for which either '[And he says this too]' (Milns (1994): 73) or '[And he further recounts]' (Gaiser (1985): 12) would be acceptable.

For this reason . . . Assos: This is the text adopted by all editors and commentators. For the territory controlled by Hermias see the notes above on Assos and Atarneus.

when . . . Assians: There are two gaps in the text of this sentence. The first, of about thirteen letters, is clearly, on the basis of its ending, a nominative participle, surely modifying Hermias. It has been variously restored as '[having handed over everything] to the (above)-mentioned learned men' (P-S); '[having put everything at the disposal of] the (above)-mentioned learned men' (Gaiser); '[being very pleased] with the (above)-mentioned learned men' (D-S, Düring, Rusten); '[having completed his education], to the (above)-mentioned learned men . . .' (Milns, followed by Gibson). The choice is, to some extent, affected by the restoration of the space in the following line. This must contain a main verb. Only two suggestions have been put forward: '[he went away to] the city of the Assians' (P-S); '[he assigned] the city of the Assians (to them)' (D-S, Düring, Rusten, Gaiser) or 'to the (above)-mentioned learned men [he assigned] the city of the Assians' (Milns, Gibson). Of these, P-S's 'he went away' is untenable, if for no other reason than that Hermias continued to rule from Atarneus, where he was eventually captured by Mentor. The reading 'assigned' is probably correct. If so, it makes 'having handed over everything', or the like, rather redundant. Consequently, one of the other suggestions for the first space is to be preferred. Along with Gibson, I incline towards Milns's explication of this whole section of the papyrus from lines 55 to 62 (Milns (1994): 74–8).

***Of these* . . . most friendly way':** The closeness of the relationship between Aristotle and Hermias is nowhere better attested than in Aristotle's own words that are cited later on in the papyrus. As is well known, there was also a marriage that bound them, that is of Aristotle to Pythias, who was variously reported in antiquity to be Hermias' niece and adopted daughter, his real daughter or granddaughter, or his mistress (on the tradition see Wormell (1935): 87–9). For good general accounts of Aristotle's stay in Assos see Jaeger (1948: 105–23); Guthrie (1981: 26–36); Gaiser (1985: 21–4).

What is more Kallisthen[es]: A *paragraphos* after line 63 indicates the end of the preceding quotation, and another at line 66 marks the beginning of the next. Between the two *paragraphoi* are three indented lines, in which Didymos introduces, as is his practice, the author and the work he will cite next, in this case Kallisthenes of Olynthos, nephew of Aristotle. For this historian (*FGrHist* 124) see the Introduction under Sources. That he was amongst the group of intellectuals at Assos is assumed by all commentators (e.g. Wormell (1935): 75; Jaeger (1948): 115) and is intrinsically plausible, given his relationship to Aristotle and the detailed knowledge of Hermias revealed by this passage. Jacoby prints this as fr. 2 in his collection of Kallisthenes' fragments and assigns it the otherwise unattested title of *Hermias* or *Hermias or On Arete* (based on the title of Theophrastos' later eulogy of Kallisthenes himself, which was entitled *Kallisthenes or On Sorrow*. See Diogenes Laertius, 5. 44).

composed an [. . . . .] about him: Missing, unfortunately, is the word that would indicate what sort of work he wrote. Neither D-S nor P-S were able to see any letters in this space and both suggest the neutral *ΣΥΝΓΡΑΜΜΑ* = written work/book. This fits the space, but to say that Kallisthenes 'composed a book' would represent a departure from Didymos' usual practice, which is either to give a specific title for a work (e.g. 'Anaximenes in the sixth [sc. book] of his histories *On Philip*' in col. 6.61–2) or to name a genre (e.g. Aristotle's poem is called a paean in col. 6.19 and Theokritos 'composed an epigram' in col. 6.45) or to use a specialized report-ing verb (e.g. Philokhoros 'testifies' in col. 1.13). For that reason, I am inclined to sympathize with those (e.g. Jacoby in *FGrHist* 124 F2; Wormell (1935): 75; Düring (1957): 274) who adopt Crönert's sugges-tion (1907: 383) of 'enkomion', although I cannot confirm the final *N* of that word that he claims to see, and for the sake of accuracy it should be noted that Blass was the first to propose this restoration (1906: 290).

A further consideration leads in the same direction, that is the question 'when' and 'why' Kallisthenes composed this work. Jacoby (in his commentary on *FGrHist* 124 F2) is, of course, correct in point-ing out that this favourable account of Hermias' last days cannot have been designed to refute the negative depiction presented by Theopompos in his *Philippika* (*FGrHist* 115 F291), because it was surely written soon after Hermias' death and, therefore, before the *Philippika*. But that does not exclude the possibility that Kallisthenes was reacting to the characterization of Hermias in Theopompos' earlier *Letter to Philip*, discussed above (pp. 135–6). Jacoby's own suggestion, that Kallisthenes wrote the work in Philip's interest to counteract political viewpoints, like that of Demosthenes (10.32), gives that veiled reference a significance it hardly deserves. More attractive than these political interpretations is Wormell's develop-ment of an idea originally thrown out by Wilamowitz (1893: ii. 405 and n. 3), that Kallisthenes wrote this eulogy to accompany Aristotle's paean as part of the memorial ceremony in honour of Hermias (Wormell (1935): 76–7).

Lines 66–71: The gist of these lines is quite clear and agreed upon; only minor disagreements exist in the actual wording of the texts proposed by a number of scholars. The text that I have offered (and translated) is a compromise between the suggestions of D-S and P-S. I agree with P-S in seeing the kappa of $KATA\Sigma TA\Sigma$ (trans. 'when he found himself') in line 67 and the gamma of $MEΓI\Sigma THN$ ('greatest') in line 68. On the other hand, I find the restorations of D-S in lines 66 ('outside of') and 69 ('in death itself') to be either more acceptable Greek or more logical (or both). Both editors follow the suggestions of Usener and Buecheler in restoring lines 70 and 71.

'Not only [was he] *this sort of man* . . . : This is a clear indi-cation that the section that Didymos has excerpted was preceded by a favourable characterization of Hermias' life, most probably developing his key virtue—*arete*, which appears in line 69 (translated as 'courage') in the face of death. By emphasizing this particularly Greek quality, Kallisthenes may be tacitly responding to those who, like Theopompos, charged Hermias with barbarian birth. More importantly, he was certainly aligning himself with (and probably preparing the way for) Aristotle's hymn or paean to Arete (discussed below). This common theme unites the passages that Didymos has chosen to excerpt from Kallisthenes and Aristotle in such a way as to support the idea that they were united in purpose (Wormell (1935): 76–7).

For, the barbarians [were amazed]:   All editors restore some word signifying amazement or stupefaction in the missing space (though Crönert's more fulsome wording, accepted uncritically by Wormell and Jacoby, is too long for the space). It is a nice rhetorical antithesis to have barbarians stand in awe of Hermias for his demonstration of quintessential Greekness.

while for his part the king: Discernible to my eyes is the delta of the particle $ΔE$ ('on the other hand', 'for his part'), which produces a more acceptable response to the particles (MEN $ΓAP$) with 'barbarians' than the 'at any rate' suggested by D-S[2] and P-S (cf. Blass (1906): 290; Crönert (1907): 383; Wankel (1987): 219). The last half of the line is badly mutilated, though 'in his enquiries' ([$ΠΥΝΘ$]A-$NOMENOΣ$) is quite certain. The alpha at the end of the line is clear and renders Crönert's restoration, which I find opaque in any case, untenable. Less certain is what to restore between 'king' and 'in his enquiries'. The word 'nothing' is required by 'other than the same words/reports'. In the remaining six letter spaces both D-S and P-S restore 'about him', yielding a translation: '(since) *in his enquiries* [about him] he kept hearing [nothing] other than the same reports . . .'. Alternatively, we might read 'from him', as Körte suggested (1905: 394), which would produce the following meaning: '(since) *in his enquiries* he kept hearing [nothing from him] other than the same words' (i.e. he stuck to his story). As Körte points out, this would be consistent with the view, attributed to Kallisthenes in col. 6.55–7, that Hermias did not confess to the plans he had made with Philip, even under torture.

The King, of course, was Artaxerxes III (Ochus), who came to the throne in 359/8, after the death of his father, the long-reigning Artaxerxes II. Ochus ruled until 338. See Briant (2002): 612–90, especially 680–90.

COLUMN SIX

Heading: The heading signposts a new topic that will be addressed in this column, beginning at line 66 and continuing on to col. 7.7. Strangely, Didymos fails to indicate in this heading another *lemma* (from Dem. 10.33) that he discusses, albeit very briefly (col. 6. 63–6), between the end of this long excursus on Hermias and the beginning of the one mentioned here.

being full of admiration ... of all men: The text is not in question. The assertion is, of course, tendentious, since it was not possible for Kallisthenes to know what the Great King's thoughts or intentions were.

Bagoas and Mentor: The name Bagoas is misspelled, having a lambda in place of the gamma.

In Kallisthenes' dramatized account of the death of Hermias these two are cast in the role of villain. By all accounts they were well suited for the part. Bagoas was probably of Egyptian origin. In our sources he is depicted as the archetypical evil eunuch (Briant (2002): 269–70). It is useful to follow Theophrastos in naming him 'the former Bagoas' (*HP* 2.6.7) to distinguish him from a younger Bagoas, gift of Nabarzanes, who became a favourite of Alexander the Great. Most of our information about the 'former' Bagoas comes from Diodoros (probably following Ephoros). According to his account Bagoas was a man of great influence in the court of Artaxerxes III, eventually rising to the position of vizier (denoted in Greek by the title *khiliarch*: see Diod. 17.5.3). Diodoros attributes this to his close relationship with the Greek, Mentor of Rhodes, with whom he is often associated (as here), but that relationship was surely more beneficial to the latter. Bagoas was the one whom Artaxerxes trusted most (Diod. 16.47.4), so that in the latter days of his reign he would do nothing without consulting Bagoas, who was the real master of the kingdom (Diod. 16.50.8). But Bagoas was also a man distinguished by his daring and lawlessness (Diod. 16.47.4), 'a eunuch in outward appearance, but base and warlike by nature' (17.5.3). In 338 he poisoned Artaxerxes III, whose youngest son, Arses, he placed on the throne in his stead (in the process eliminating Arses' brothers). When Arses proved less tractable than Bagoas had hoped, he poisoned him also, and engineered in 336 the accession of Dareios III (Codoman), the later opponent of

Alexander (cf. Briant (2003): 99–100, 199–200). But Dareios turned
the tables and brought an end to Bagoas' life of crime by poisoning
him (Diod. 17.5.3–5). Whilst Diodoros' account may be naive and
Bagoas might have been more an abetter than an instigator (see
Briant (2002): 769–76), it does show the generally negative view that
Greeks had of this individual. Of course, it is true that Bagoas' more
nefarious activities were performed after the death of Hermias, but
the Greeks had already witnessed his perfidy during the course of
Artaxerxes' reconquest of Egypt in 343–342, during which time
he entered into a close relationship with Mentor of Rhodes (Diod.
16.47–50), to whom I now turn.

We know nothing of Mentor's origin or parentage, except that
he came from Rhodes. This is not surprising in this turbulent time,
when great opportunities awaited the ambitious. And ambition was
not a quality lacking in this family. He had a brother, Memnon,
who was later to coordinate the campaign against Alexander in the
Aegean until his unfortunate death on Lesbos in 333. He also had
at least one sister. Like so many women in ancient history she is
nameless, but significant. Sometime in the 360s, when her brothers
first appear in the record (Dem. 23.154–7), they are already referred
to as relatives-in-law and supporters of Artabazos (son of Pharnabazos and the Achaemenid princess Apame). They had achieved
this distinction as a result of their sister's marriage to him (probably in 363, when he came out to replace Ariobarzanes as satrap
of Phrygia). She bore him eleven sons and ten daughters, some of
whom lived for a while at the court of Philip of Macedon, when
Artabazos was in exile there (Diod. 16.52.3–4) from the late 350s
to 343 (Sealey (1993): 183–4; Briant (2003): 406–7). One of these
was assuredly a daughter, named Barsine, whose life was tossed
upon the waves of this stormy period. She suffered the fate of being
married to both her uncles, first to Mentor, then, when he died
(the date is unknown, but was perhaps not long after the Hermias-
affair), to Memnon. After Memnon's death in 333, she turned up
amongst those captured at Damascus following the battle of Issos,
and became the mistress of Alexander (Plut. *Alex.* 21.7–10), whom
she had probably known as a child in Pella, and the mother of his
first child, Herakles (romanticized by Lane Fox (1973): 50, 176–7).
She was killed together with Herakles by Polyperkhon in 309, both
victims of the struggle for Alexander's empire.

Mentor's own career was hardly less chequered. When Artabazos fell out of favour with Artaxerxes and fled with his family,

and Memnon, to the court of Philip at Pella (*c.*353), we do not know if Mentor went with them, since the next we hear of him he is commander of 4,000 mercenaries, sent by Nektanebo from Egypt to help Tennes of Sidon in his revolt from Artaxerxes (Diod. 16.42.2). There, he distinguished himself by aiding and abetting in the betrayal and utter destruction of the city (Diod. 16.45; cf. 16.47.4, where he is called 'the man who betrayed Sidon'), as a result of which he was able to change sides and join the Persian army that was preparing to invade Egypt. This is where he first met Bagoas, since they were put in joint command of the third contingent (Diod. 16.47.4). In the invasion he trapped Bagoas in a life-threatening situation, which he had engineered but from which he proceeded to rescue him, on condition that they work together for mutual advancement for the future (Diod. 16.50). As a result of this collaboration, says Diodoros, they both attained the greatest influence at Artaxerxes' court. Mentor, for his part, arranged for the reconciliation of Artabazos and Memnon with Artaxerxes, so that they returned from Macedon, and had himself appointed chief commander of the Asia Minor coast. It was in this capacity that he campaigned against Hermias, who was his guest-friend, and captured him by a trick (Diod. 16.52.5–6). For the prosopography see Hofstetter, nos. 63 (Barsine), 215 (Memnon), and 220 (Mentor). For interpretation and context see Parke (1933: 165–9); Ellis (1976: 172–3); Griffith (1979: 518–22); Bosworth (1980: 112–13); Weiskopf (1989: 45–64, 94–9); Sealey (1993: 183–5); Briant (2002: 656–75, 681–90).

objected: In writing this word the scribe made his second careless mistake in three words, unless the errors were already embedded in his exemplar. In addition to misspelling the name Bagoas (mentioned above) he here inserted a gratuitous epsilon, writing -*ΠΕΙΠ*- instead of -*ΠΙΠ*. On this error (iotacism) see Introduction (under The Papyrus).

out of envy ... in their stead: Once again Kallisthenes is tendentiously attributing to Bagoas and Mentor thoughts that he could not have known, but which suit his purpose, by emphasizing that Hermias' virtue was so great that it became the object of envy even from evil men (cf. Wormell (1935): 76–8). More realistically, we can see that both Mentor and Artaxerxes had pragmatic reason for eliminating Hermias; the king, because he wanted to regain control of territory that had long been troublesome and had been lost to him since the time of Orontes (Weiskopf (1989): 69–99), Mentor, because he had family interests in the region, since the time of his sister's marriage to Artabazos (Dem. 23.154–7).

in passing judgement . . . courage: For the first word all editors read the future participle ($\Delta IKA\Sigma\Omega N$), which would yield a translation 'about to call to trial' (*vel sim.*). P-S object (p. xi) that this is more a Latin use of the future participle than Greek. In addition they find the whole situation illogical, especially the idea that a person who has been tortured (which they, as I, assume that Kallisthenes implied, though he nowhere explicitly says so) can be said to be excused from mutilation, as the next part of the sentence seems to say. For these reasons they despair of making sense of this passage and obelize it. But their difficulty with the logic of the sentence is exaggerated. Torture to extract information was practised by the Greeks, but some truly exquisite forms of mutilation as punishment were peculiar to the Persians (e.g. Hdt. 7.39; 9.112). The distinction is real. There remains the problem of the future participle. Attempts have been made to solve that by eliminating it. Wilamowitz is accredited with the emendation $A\Pi A\Sigma\Omega N$ (= 'of all'), making it into a genitive plural adjective modifying 'mutilations' (cf. Bodin, ap. Foucart (1909): 216). More recently, Rusten has suggested that $\Delta IKA\Sigma\Omega N$ is a corruption for $AIKI\Sigma M\Omega N$, which is the technical term for mutilation. With the addition of an 'and' in the next line he produces a translation that runs: 'he exempted him from the maltreatment and suffering that are customary at the king's hands' (1987: 268). Both these emendations make sense (cf. Gibson: 110), but to my eye are unnecessary. I see quite distinctly the bottom part of a zeta in the antepenultimate letter space of the word $\Delta IKAZ\Omega$, which produces the present participle ($\Delta IKAZ\Omega N$ = 'in passing judgement') that Blass wished he could read (1906: 290). Finally, the fact that it was Hermias' courage (*arete*) and steadfastness that earned him this reward, despite the envy and fear of his enemies, demonstrates once again the tendentious purpose of the narrative (i.e. his virtues would have saved his life, if the villains had not intervened, but at least it won him this saving grace), and renders questions of logical consistency and detail of fact somewhat irrelevant.

such moderation . . . enemies: The account goes on in the same vein, i.e. his courage now makes barbarians behave in unexpected ways. Together with P-S, I read the dotted tau that confirms Blass's suggestion (1906: 290) of the superlative 'most unexpected.'

Instead of 'from' one's enemies, Rusten (1987: 268) has argued for 'toward'. His suggestion fits the space and is reasonable, but not necessarily any better than the restoration 'from' that has been favoured by previous editors.

and *especially* . . . barbarians: This restoration, suggested by Blass (1906: 290) and adopted by P-S, fits the extant remains best. Moderation was, of course, a Greek value, praised since the time of Solon. It was also essentially Aristotelian (e.g. *EN* 2.1104a11–27, 1106a26–1109b26).

Lines 13–15:   These lines are in a bad state and there are consequently many problems with the text. The change in gender of the participle [. . .]*ΕΣΑΜΕΝΟΣ* (and surely also *ΜΕΛΛ*[.]*Ν*) indicates that the subject has changed from 'moderation' to 'Hermias'. This requires some sort of punctuation after 'barbarians' (either a comma or a period) and the restoration of some phrase for 'but he' in the next space. The remains of the word before *ΜΕΛΛ*[.]*Ν* ('being about to') strongly suggest a form of the word *ΤΕΛΕΥΤΑΩ* ('die') in the infinitive (an infinitive is in any case required by the grammar; 'of the Greeks' proposed by D-S makes no sense). There are not enough spaces for the future infinitive favoured by Blass (1906: 290); Crönert (1907: 383); Wormell (1935: 76), and Jacoby (*FGrHist* 124 F2), so the present infinitive of P-S (following Fuhr) is to be preferred. This would yield reasonable sense as, 'But he, being about to die, . . .'. Unfortunately, the scribe has complicated the issue by putting a colon after the word *ΜΕΛΛ*[.]*Ν*. This has to be assumed to be another mistake on his part, though in the English punctuation a comma at this point would be quite appropriate. The last four letters of line 13, that belong to the beginning of the first word of the next clause, are *ΦΙΛΙ*. These have occasioned the most speculation. They should belong with the second subordinate participle that ends in -*ΕΣΑΜΕΝΟΣ*, which is restored by all commentators as a compound of *ΚΑΛΕΣΑΜΕΝΟΣ*, 'called', compounded either with *ΕΙΣ*- 'had called in' (Blass (1906): 290; Crönert (1907): 383; Wormell (1935): 76; Jacoby, *FGrHist* 124 F2), *ΜΕΤΑ*- 'summoned' (Rusten (1987): 268–9) or *ΕΠΙ*- 'invoked' (P-S). P-S were unable to see anything at the beginning of the next line (14) and as a result were not willing to speculate how the word continued. My own examination of the papyrus supports their caution. D-S, on the other hand, claimed to see indications of either a pi (D-S[1]), on the basis of which they suggested that Philip of Macedon was being referred to, or a sigma (D-S²) and both these sightings have been exploited by the bolder commentators. Some have restored another name for the person Hermias supposedly called in, e.g. 'Philis[tides his companion]' by Bodin (ap. Foucart (1909): 216), 'Phili[stos to himself]' by Crönert (1907: 383), followed by Wormell (1935: 76) and Jacoby (*FGrHist* 124 F2), or 'Phili[nos to himself]' by Blass (1906: 290), but none justify their choice or explain what this person was doing at the court of Artaxerxes, where these events were presumably taking place (cf. Strabo 13.1.57 C610). More recently Rusten has revived the reading Philip (in the genitive), followed by the word 'messenger' and advocated 'summoned a messenger of Philip' (1987: 268–9). All these attempts fail the test of historical plausibility, as is pointed out by P-S (p. xii), Wankel (1987: 219), and Gibson (110). Despite that, P-S's own attempt ('invoking') only raises new problems (Wankel (1987): 219) and something along the lines suggested has to be assumed by the restoration of lines 15–18 (beginning), which D-S² advocated (based as they acknowledge upon suggestions by Blass; cf. Blass (1906): 290), a restoration that is accepted by all subsequent editors, including P-S. In sum, someone has to be supplied to whom (under some conditions) Hermias '[said nothing] *else*, [but enjoined upon] him to *send a message* to his [friends and his] companions, (saying) that he had done nothing *unworthy* of philosophy [or] shameful.' The suggestion that that person was Artaxerxes himself (Jaeger (1948): 117) has something to be said for it. But, in the final analysis it is more likely that we are in the realm of rhetorical fantasy, where the famous last words of dying men need not conform to any rules of historical reason.

companions: I see no reason to believe that this word is being used as a technical term here, nor do I think it can be used to support the idea that the 'companions' (*ETAIPOI*) of the inscriptions (see above under **Column 4, lines 20–58**, p. 124) were the same as Hermias' philosopher-friends. There is no evidence or suggestion in our sources either that Hermias gave up governing for the life of the philosopher, not that Aristotle and company became involved in the political administration of his little kingdom.

connection by marriage with Aristotle: That is, his marriage to Pythias. See above on col. 5.63 (*Of these . . .* **friendly way**', p. 144). For the ancient sources see Diogenes Laertius, *Aristotle* 5.2.3–4 and Strabo 13.1.57 C610. The assertion that Aristotle's marriage to a woman related (however distantly) to Hermias attests to Hermias' virtue (courage) is elliptical, to say the least. Unless Didymos was writing very loosely, he must be thinking that Aristotle would only have married into a virtuous family!

[pae]an: Didymos reveals no doubt about calling the poem that follows a 'paean ' (a choral song, often associated with Apollo; for the genre see the Introduction to Rutherford (2001)), but others in antiquity were not so sure and modern scholars have debated the issue hotly. The dispute arose in antiquity in the context of the trial of Aristotle at Athens for impiety in 323, following the death of Alexander, when Athens was in open conflict with Macedon. Though the trial was clearly motivated by the political situation (Aristotle was identified as pro-Macedonian), Demophilos, the accuser, used as his pretext the charge of impiety, on the grounds that Aristotle had composed a 'paean' to a mortal, Hermias, and instituted a daily singing of it in the commons at the Lykeion (the charge may have been based partly upon the similarities between Aristotle's poem and that of Ariphron (see below), which would have the effect of suggesting that Hermias was on a par with *Hygieia*, a personified deity). The tale is told in Athenaios' *Deipnosophistai* (15. 696a–697b), where Demokritos of Nikomedia, one of the deipnosophists, dismisses the idea that the poem was a paean and considers, instead, that it was a kind of *skolion* (drinking song). Similar details are reported in Diogenes Laertius 5.3–9. Modern views range even more widely, from paean to *skolion*, *threnos* (lament for the dead) to dithyramb, or often, more casually, hymn or ode. The reality is that these genre designations in antiquity were imprecise and a definitive choice may not be possible. This may especially be the case if, as some think (e.g. Bowra and Renehan below), Aristotle has broken new ground by blending genres. On the other hand, it has been well demonstrated that he was inspired by and modelled his poem upon the 'paean' to *Hygieia* (Health) of Ariphron of Sikyon (Athenaios 15.702a–b). See the discussions in Wilamowitz (1893: ii. 404–12); Wormell (1935: 62–5); Bowra (1938: 182–9); Jaeger (1948: 118–19); Guthrie (1981: 32–4); Renehan (1982: 251–74).

***it would not be* insignificant to record it:** As elsewhere, the use of the potential optative here indicates that this is Didymos' own opinion. See Osborne: 32–3, 129; Gibson: 30–2.

not available to many: though this poem has been handed

down to us in its complete form by two other authors, Athenaios (15. 696a–697b) and Diogenes Laertius (5.7–8), both of whom are later than Didymos, I think we have to take Didymos' word that the text was not readily available at his time. I would find it obtuse to suggest that Didymos took over this statement about the work's unavailability (along with the text of the poem itself) from a hypothetical source, like Hermippos. Indeed, since that Hellenistic biographer is thought to be the source for Athenaios' text (Bowra (1938): 182), the difference between it and Didymos' (for which see the apparatus criticus in Page (1962): 444, no. 842) constitutes a further argument against the idea that Hermippos was Didymos' source for his whole entry on Hermias. The same argument holds true in reverse, of course: Didymos could not have been the source for the discussion in either of the later authors.

The paean (?) to *Arete* (Virtue):   Many modern texts of this poem are available in print, e.g. Wilamowitz (1893): ii.406–7; Macher (1914): 21; Wormell (1935): 62–3 (with translation); Jaeger (1948): 118 (translation only); Page (1962): 444–5, no. 842; Page (1968): 230–1, no. 432; Guthrie (1981): 32–3 (translation only); Renehan (1982): 252–3. It is even included in the *Oxford Book of Greek Verse* (no. 459). Page (1962: 444–5, no. 842) provides the most detailed apparatus criticus.

   Text: the papyrus agrees in substance with the other versions in Athenaios and Diogenes Laertius (both of which disagree in details), but contains some errors and one important improvement: in line 23 $BPOTEI\Omega I$ ('mortal') lacks the first iota; line 25 $\Pi OTMO\Sigma$ ('fate') was originally written $\Pi OTMON$, but corrected; line 26 has $AKAMANTO\Sigma$ incorrectly for $AKAMANTA\Sigma$ of Diogenes Laertius; in line 27 $I\Sigma ATHANATON$ ('quite divine/immortal') confirms Wilamowitz's emendation and improves on the readings in the other texts; in line 28 the papyrus reads the less poetic genitive $-OY$ for the coined word $MA\Lambda AKAYTETOIO$ ('languid-eyed') and at the end of that line (where the text is in any case questionable) the papyrus has gibberish; in line 29 it has $KOPOI$ for $KOYPOI$ and has corrupted $\Pi O\Lambda\Lambda'$ $ANET\Lambda A\Sigma AN$ ('endured much') into an incomprehensible $\Pi O\Lambda\Lambda ENE\Pi\Lambda A\Sigma AN$; in the first half of line 30 the letters that can be read after the first gap ($E\Pi ONTE$) are not consistent with the preferred reading of the other versions ($AFPEYONTE\Sigma$ = 'pursuing the prize' in Athenaios); in line 32 the name $ATAPNEO\Sigma$ is clearly misspelled $ATEPNEO\Sigma$ and in line 33 the scribe has transposed the second and fourth letters of *XHPΩ* to *XΩPH*. These are the most notable distinctions. They are sufficient to show: (1) that Didymos was following a different textual tradition from that (or those) used by our other sources; (2) that errors had been introduced (probably by someone who had no sensitivity to metre) into Didymos' text in the course of transmission, such that (3) our scribe could not understand what was written and probably made further errors in transcription as a result. I have printed (and translated) a corrected text.

Critical commentary is provided by Wilamowitz (404–12), Macher (16–21), Wormell (62–5), Jaeger (118–19), Guthrie (32–4), Renehan (251–74) and, in addition, by Bowra (1938: 182–9). The metre has been analysed by Macher (17–18), Bowra (184), and Renehan (258) as basically dactylo-epitritic with the exception of the opening, which may be aeolic or anapaestic. It is virtually identical to the metre employed by Ariphron in his paean to *Hygieia* (Health), quoted in Athenaios 15.702a–b. This is one of the arguments used to support the view that Aristotle modelled his poem on Ariphron's; the others are verbal, grammatical, and thematic (see Renehan: 258–64). But, as Renehan has shown, Aristotle went beyond mere imitation to create new and significant meaning. Where Ariphron was celebrating a personified abstraction, whose benefactions were physical and felt during life, Aristotle was invoking a principle, whose rewards were spiritual and to be enjoyed after death. But, though *Arete* is the main topic of the poem, the immediate purpose was surely to celebrate Hermias (referred to obliquely as 'Atarneus' offspring'), by likening him to Herakles, Akhilleus, Aias, and Kastor and Polydeukes, great Greek heroes, who preferred to die nobly in the laborious pursuit of *Arete,* rather than to live ignobly. [Professor Bosworth makes the interesting point that most of these heroes, especially Herakles, the Dioskouroi, and Akhilleus, had associations with *apotheosis* and were used in the Alexander historians as precedents for Alexander's own divinity; this connection may not have escaped the Athenians at the time of Aristotle's trial in 323, when they were fighting the Lamian War against Macedonian domination.]

Time and place: the most likely occasion, in my opinion, for Aristotle to have composed this poem is at the time of Hermias' death in 341, when he and Kallisthenes (at least) held a religious celebration for Hermias, for which Kallisthenes provided the encomium (discussed above) and Aristotle the hymn (that the poem was designed to be sung by a choir has been accepted since it was first suggested by Wilamowitz (1893): ii. 405). The first performance could have taken place in Macedon (where both Aristotle and Kallisthenes were at that time), but I think it not unlikely that it happened at Delphi, where a tomb to Hermias was dedicated, on which was inscribed the epigram (also written by Aristotle) that Didymos cites below. The celebration later became an annual ritual at the Lykeion (Athenaios 15.696a), but this is hardly likely to have been the occasion of the first performance, since there is no reason to believe that Kallisthenes went to Athens with Aristotle, when he returned and established his school in 335 (cf. Diogenes Laertius 5.4–5), and, of course, Kallisthenes left for Asia with Alexander in the spring of 334, never to return.

sought after in Greece: This reference, combined with the association of Hermias with Greek national heroes, like Herakles, supports the view that Hermias was a Greek.

the sons of Leda: Kastor and Polydeukes, the Dioskouroi.

forsook the rays of the sun: A strong image. The verb actually means 'make a widow of'. Aristotle nicely reverses the traditional metaphor and depicts the sun as the bereaved party.

Zeus, god of hospitality: This is a reference to the Greek code of *xenia*, the relationship beween guest and host (on which see Herman (1987)), which was overseen by Zeus, king of the gods. Mentor had transgressed this code, when he lured Hermias, with whom he had a guest-host relationship, into a trap and so disgraced 'the honour of lasting friendship'.

[And] Aristot[le is said] *to have dedicated* **[a memorial to him at Delphi]:** This restoration is securely based upon the testimony of Diogenes Laertius 5.6 and the epigram of Theokritos below. The only point of contention concerns the word 'memorial', since Diogenes claims that the epigram was inscribed upon a statue at Delphi. On that basis Foucart (1909: 132) suggested that $A\Gamma A\Lambda MA$ ('statue') should be restored in place of the $MNHMEION$ ('memorial'), that had been proposed by D-S. But his arguments against the obvious implication of Theokritos' epigram are unconvincing and I keep the reading that has been adopted by all other editors. On the other hand, that a statue was erected as part of the dedication is not at all unlikely. The memorial has not survived.

***is situated* [. . .]:** Foucart suggested tentatively 'beside the altar' for the space. His suggestion has not been followed, probably because it adds an unlikely cultic connotation to the dedication.

The epigram to Hermias: The text has been restored on the basis of Diogenes Laertius. For a modern edition see Page (1975): 622–6. Wormell finds the tone 'one of unalleviated bitterness' and the lines 'somewhat uninspiring' by comparison with the paean (1935: 61). It certainly has a different focus, concentrating on the unholiness and perfidy of Hermias' captors, rather than celebrating his triumphant virtue.

Persians who carry the bow: A standard indication of non-Greekness. Since the time of the so-called hoplite revolution Greek males had been taught to fight with the spear (and sword); those who fought with the bow and arrow were considered less than manly. The distinction can be seen clearly as early as Homer's *Iliad*, in his treatment of the half-brothers Aias and Teukros (8.266–72). Of course, this is a good example of the inconsistency that changing historical circumstance can generate in societal attitudes, since the weapon of choice for Greece's greatest hero, Herakles, was the bow and skill in its use had undoubtedly been valued earlier in Greek tradition, as the story of Odysseus shows.

in deadly contest of spear out in the open: The papyrus' reading has the adjective ('out in the open') agreeing with the noun ('spear'), while Diogenes has: 'in deadly contest openly by means of the spear'.

the trust of a devious man: A blatant oxymoron. Mentor of Rhodes is the person referred to.

Br[y]o[n in his (book) <u>On Theokritos</u>]: Nothing is known about the author of this work and even his name has been questioned, since Diogenes Laertius (5.11) calls him Ambryon. On this point Didymos is more likely to be correct. The name Ambryon is unknown outside of Thebes, while a Bryon is attested amongst the ambassadors of Khios, who negotiated a treaty with Athens in 384/3 (*IG* II² 34.42; Tod no. 118; Harding (1985): no. 31). Foucart (1909: 151) perceptively pointed out that a grandson of this man would have been a contemporary and fellow-countryman of Theokritos of Khios, the author of the epigram. (The name Bryon also appears in a inscription from Iasos, *SIG*³ 169.24, and there are two men of that name in fourth-century Athens, listed in *LGPN*. The variant, Bryson, proposed independently by Blass (1906: 291) and Crönert (1907: 384) is not required by the space, as they thought.)

Foucart may also be correct in his surmise that Bryon's book, *On Theokritos*, was mainly a collection of witty (and scurrilous) maxims (*Khreiai*), such as Theokritos was reputed to have written (cf. the *Souda*, s.v. Theokritos; Wormell (1935): 74). In fact, as Laqueur has suggested, Bryon may have been responsible for preserving Theokritos' work for posterity (*RE* 5A:2, s.v. Theokritos aus Chios), by making this collection. In this context it is important to note that both Didymos and Diogenes Laertius cite Theokritos' epigram indirectly (i.e. from Bryon's book) and, furthermore, that this is the only place in the papyrus where Didymos quotes an author at second hand (Foucart (1909): 150; Osborne: 132). This may support the idea that Bryon's was the only collection extant. (Other citations of the epigram in Eusebios and Plutarch, whilst they attribute the epigram to Theokritos, do not indicate a source and, consequently, neither support nor refute this suggestion.) Alternatively, since Diogenes did not consult Bryon's work at first hand (as his misspelling of the name reveals) but took the reference from another source, the similarity in the two citations may indicate dependence upon a common source and raise the spectre of Hermippos. A possible resolution of this issue would be available, if only Diogenes had quoted the whole epigram. Strangely, since his purpose was to demonstrate how Theokritos ridiculed Aristotle, he gives only the first two lines; the last two are added by editors from the text given in Eusebios, even though it disagrees quite substantially in line 3 from the text that must be read in the papyrus (see below). If we could be confident that Diogenes really did have the same text as Eusebios, we could be absolutely certain that his source was different from Didymos'. Unfortunately, as things stand, the question must remain open.

Theokritos [the Khian]:   See the Introduction under Sources. His hostility to the Platonic school (and, by extension, Aristotle), has now been given a historical background by Dusanic (1999: 6–7), who argues for an association between Theokritos' ancestors and Isokrates.

epigram: This pair of couplets is extant in one other complete text (Eusebios, *Praeparatio Evangelica* 15.2.12), which agrees in most respects with the version of the papyrus, except that it reads 'memorial' at the beginning of line 2 instead of Didymos' 'tomb', and disagrees on the wording of the first half of line 3 (see below). The first two lines are also quoted by Diogenes Laertius (as cited above), who supports the papyrus text in reading 'tomb' in line 2, but disagrees with Eusebios in line 1, notably by having 'at the same time' where he reads 'this'. Eusebios is surely to be preferred in that case (Macher (1914): 22–3) and the papyrus is restored on that basis. Finally, Plutarch (*Mor.* 603c) cites the final line and a half. Modern texts can be found in Page (1975: 627–30) and Lloyd-Jones and Parsons (1983: no. 738, which has the fullest apparatus criticus).

Commentators ancient and modern recognize that the epigram was directed at Aristotle rather than Hermias, who was only the immediate cause for the abuse. We are surely right to envisage it as a reaction to Aristotle's own dedicatory epigram on the memorial to Hermias at Delphi (Macher (1914): 22–3; Düring (1957): 277; Runia (1986): 532). [There is also, as Professor Bowsorth has pointed out to me, some play on philosphical terminology in the juxtaposition of *nomos* and *physis* (cf. *anomon physin* in line 3) and the implication that Aristotle is guilty of *akrasia* ('lack of self-control'), a fault Aristotle himself criticizes in *EN* 1145a16.] Interpretation of these lines has been obfuscated by Plutarch, who, in an attempt to explain the word 'borboros', created a river where none existed, and directed the reference to Macedon, when it must be to Asia Minor (perhaps the alluvial plain of the Caicus River, as suggested by Bosworth (2002): 352 n. 16), if the Hermias context has any point (cf. Runia (1986): 533–4).

Of Hermias the eunuch and slave of Euboulos: Theokritos, though not on good terms with Theopompos politically or personally, repeated the same stock charges against Hermias; they are no better founded for that. See above, col. 4.69: ***though he was a eunuch [and B]ithy[n]ian*** (p. 128).' Theokritos does, however, have the distinction of being the earliest extant source to provide the name of Hermias' predecessor, Euboulos.

Empty tomb . . . empty-headed: A rather uninspired pun.

who out of respect for the lawless nature of his stomach: This restoration, originally proposed by D-S, is adopted by P-S and is hardly to be doubted. It disagrees verbally, though not in sense, with the text found in Eusebios ('on account of the uncontrolled nature of the stomach') and usually supplied in Diogenes (though see

Düring (1957): 275). The grammar and metre, though different, are
acceptable. There is, consequently, no easy way of deciding which
was the original text, unless Runia (1986: 532–4) is correct in finding
allusions to Platonic thought (in this case 'control' of appetite) in the
last two lines. Nevertheless, the fact that Didymos has preserved an
alternative text for this line demonstrates that he was following a
distinct textual tradition and goes some way to support the otherwise reasonable conclusion that he was doing original research.

**to dwell | At the mouth of 'borboros' instead of the
Academy:**   This is clearly an allusion to Aristotle's departure
from Athens in 347, when he went to stay with Hermias. It is in
that context that its meaning must be explicated. Plutarch's idea
(*Mor.* 603c) that Theokritos was ridiculing Aristotle, because he
enjoyed his stay in Macedonia with Philip and Alexander (which
led Wormell (1935: 74) to suggest that the epigram was really aimed
at Alexander), is wide of the mark and leads to his imaginative
suggestion that Borboros was the name of a river near Pella. The
translation 'at the mouth/outpourings of filth' (borboros) is far
more vigorous and in keeping with the tone of the poem. Several
commentators (e.g. Wormell (1935): 75, n. 34; Runia (1986): 532–3;
contra Düring (1957): 277) see an obscene reference and the implication of unseemly homosexual activity between Hermias and Aristotle is not unlikely, given the genre (see now Bosworth (2002: 352
n. 16). Runia adds another dimension to the epigram by discover-
ing a further Platonic allusion here to the 'filth' (barbarian, at that)
in which the unphilosophical soul lies (*Phd.* 69c5; *Rep.* 533c7–d2)
and suggests that the point was that Aristotle, by moving 'from the
serenity of the Academy to the filth of Asia Minor', was turning his
back on Platonic principles (cf. Gibson: 111). But that may be giving
Theokritos credit for more learning than he deserves. He might,
after all, have been thinking no further than Aristophanes, *Frogs* 145.

And *yet* people . . . his death: Didymos concludes this long
excursus on Hermias of Atarneus by canvassing some remaining
views on the place and manner of his death. Osborne (133) draws
attention to the summarizing function of this kind of resumé in
ancient scholarship (cf. Gibson: 112).

For Hermi[ppos] in (book) two of his <u>On Aristotle</u>:   For
the Hellenistic biographer, Hermippos, see the Introduction under
Sources. Didymos' specific reference to author, book, and title is in

keeping with his practice elsewhere, when he is introducing a new source. It is quite obtuse to extrapolate from this the notion that Hermippos was Didymos' source for the whole Hermias episode, as was done by Wormell (1935: 82) and others, like Düring (1957: 275), who have followed him. In fact, the specific nature of the citation suggests precisely the opposite conclusion. Other sources ('But some . . . yet others . . .') are alluded to below without being named, because they support views that have already been attributed to Theopompos and Kallisthenes (with specific references), but Hermippos is cited for a new position, not previously attested, namely that Hermias 'died in *imprisonment*'. For that reason he needed to be properly credited in a manner that puts him on a par with other major sources. See the Introduction under Didymos the Scholar. But see Bollansée (2001): 83–9.

after he had been tortured by the King, he was crucified: The view of Theopompos (*FGrHist* 115 F291), cited above.

Yet others (say that) [. . .]: Various restorations have been suggested for the eleven-letter space, all along essentially the same lines, i.e. that he died. P-S claim to see enough letters to restore, 'he experienced extreme suffering', but I am unable to confirm their sightings (see also Wankel (1987): 221).

having confessed . . . as Kallisthen[e]s (says): In the extant portion of the passage from Kallisthenes (discussed above) there is no mention of Philip or plans. Nevertheless, it is reasonable to credit Didymos with knowing what Kallisthenes said on the subject. This testimony is very important to the resolution of the question whether there had been any negotiations between Hermias and Philip (see above, though it is often overlooked by those who believe there were none). Kallisthenes was well placed to know what relationship existed between the two kings.

some say he was captured at Katane in Aiolis: Both Diodoros (16.52.6) and Strabo (13.1.57 C610) narrate that Mentor lured (invited) Hermias to a meeting, at which he arrested him. Where that meeting took place they do not say, but it is quite probable that it was not too far from Atarneus, Hermias' base. This reference in Didymos (unfortunately from an author or authors unnamed) is the only extant attempt to name that place, though Didymos claims he knew of others. Sadly it is unhelpful, since no place of that name has been located on the map of Aiolis, though Stephanos of Byzantion (s.v. Katane) mentions a Katanai (in the plural) 'opposite Lesbos'. Macher (1914: 23), in desperation, suggests that both Didymos and Stephanos are wrong and that the place they meant was Kanai, which is a few miles down the coast from Atarneus, under the mountain of the same name. See on this Rigsby (1998: 137–8), who argues in support of Didymos' reference.

Lines 60–2: have been laid out [. . .] by Anaximenes . . . *not useful*:   For Anaximenes see the Introduction under Sources. The key to understanding this passage lies in the six- or seven-letter word (the first two letters of which are *EN*) that follows 'laid out'. Setting aside P-S's unique suggestion (*ENTYΠΩΣ*), because its usage is unattested and its meaning in this context unclear (Wankel (1987): 221), we are left with two clear alternatives: *ENTEΛΩΣ* ('completely') by D-S and *ENΔEΩΣ* ('deficiently') by Foucart (1909: 134). As Gibson (112–13) has well argued, only the latter (or a word of similar meaning) suits the context. Didymos is saying that it would not be useful to quote the relevant passage of Anaximenes' work, because 'it would seem' (i.e. in Didymos' opinion) that he had laid out the issues in a deficient manner. That makes sense, while the alternative ('Anaximenes has laid out the issues completely, so it will not be useful to quote him') is illogical (*pace* Macher (1914): 23 n. 4). No doubt Didymos can be unintelligent at times, but it is not fair to foist unintelligibility upon him through restoration.

'The barbarian and common enemy of mankind . . .':   This new *lemma* is from Dem. 10.33. Textually it exemplifies perfectly the relationship of the papyrus to the manuscript tradition of Demosthenes (see Introduction under Didymos and the Text of Demosthenes). In the opening words (*O ΔH*) it agrees with the best manuscripts (SAFY), whilst further along the same line it misses out the *O* (in S) before *KOINOΣ* and adds a gratuitous *KAI* ('and') after it.

   Didymos has correctly appreciated Demosthenes' point, which is in fact so obvious that it hardly needed explication. Athenian orators, Demosthenes maintained (correctly), were in the habit of maligning the King of Persia ('the barbarian') with stock phrases, two specific examples of which he cites, at every opportunity they got. Indeed, it has long been recognized as one of the themes of Athenian national propaganda, associated with the so-called Panhellenic movement, that Greeks should unite under Athenian leadership (though later other leaders were canvassed) in a war against their great enemy, the Persians. The most notorious exponent of this view is thought to have been Isokrates (see e.g. Bringmann (1965): 19–27). Demosthenes was advising his fellow-citizens to moderate their language and their policy toward the King, out of his belief that Philip of Macedon was the greater danger and that the King could be a useful ally.

As noted above (under **Heading**) this *lemma* is exceptional in not being signposted by a heading at the top of the column. It is hard to tell what that might signify, but I find it hard to believe that it supports Gibson's suggestion that the commentary, as we have it, is a series of excerpts from Didymos' original, made by a researcher with a special interest in history, who was himself responsible for the headings (Gibson: 51–69). I find it less likely that such a person would forget to make this reference to his own excerpt than that an original heading had fallen out in the course of transmission. On the other hand, Osborne's observation that this note surely originated with Didymos (i.e. it was not borrowed from some source), because Didymos did not refer to any 'author, controversy or earlier scholar' (135–6) is well taken. In fact, if we use Didymos' topics as an indication of the interests of prior scholarship, as I think we can, then this was not one of them.

'For, as for me, whenever . . . truly I do . . .': This long *lemma*, which continues to the first line of the next column, is from Dem. 10.34 (see Hajdu (2002): 276–8). It was announced by the heading at the top of the column ('The figure [is that] of a transposed expression'). The commentary on that topic begins at the top of the next column and extends to line 7, though, in reality, the commentary on the whole *lemma* continues all the way to col. 8.32. On the way, however, Didymos changes the topic to the one announced at the top of column 7, namely 'What was the King's recent act of generosity towards the Athenians?' Thus, here, Didymos provides two headings for two separate topics of discussion that arise from the same passage from Demosthenes.

The missing parts of the passage are restored on the basis of the text of Demosthenes. Nevertheless, in the mainly extant portions of the quotation it is possible to detect a similar pattern in the relationship of the papyrus-text to our manuscripts of Demosthenes as was noted above. The papyrus sometimes agrees with one reading, sometimes with another. Usually, however, it has the preferred text. Only in two places does it have a totally original reading (*EN* for *ΕΠΙ ΤΑΙΣ ΘΥΡΑΙΣ*, 'within' instead of 'at our doors', and the aorist participle, 'has increased', for the present participle, 'is increasing', of the manuscripts). Even then, strangely, when he later paraphrases the passage, Didymos gives the reading of the manuscripts in both cases, and, even more strangely, sides with the worse manuscripts in spelling Ekbatana with a kappa instead of the gamma he used previously (but see Hajdu (2002): 277, who prefers the reading with kappa) and introducing the preposition 'in' before it. This can only show that the readings in the *lemma* were those of the text he had before him, since, if it had provided the readings he clearly wanted (as indicated by his paraphrase), he would not have altered them.

I shall discuss this passage in the context of Didymos' commentary, which begins at the top of column 7.

COLUMN SEVEN

Heading: The issue raised by the heading to the previous column has only just begun with the quotation of the *lemma,* and the commentary on it follows in the first seven lines of column 7. Only after that does Didymos address the topic of this heading, the identification of a recent benefaction of the King of Persia to Athens, alluded to in 'just recently was making offers' (col. 6.70). Even then he gets side-tracked on an explication of the phrase 'in the past he helped in putting the city's affairs back in order' (6.69) and only gets to his proclaimed topic in column 8 (lines 5–32).

He has employed a transposed way of speaking: Use of the periphrasis 'transposed way of speaking' / 'transposed expression' is rare and otherwise late (see Gibson: 114, who calls it 'peculiar'). But hyperbaton itself was a well-known figure of speech in antiquity, especially amongst verse writers. In its simplest form it involved the insertion of one or more words between two that logically and grammatically belonged together (thus they were transposed). The result was that emphasis was thrown upon one of the two separated words. Some prose authors, like Thucydides, however, took this to extremes and inserted whole clauses between related parts of a sentence to heighten the listener's (or reader's) suspense. The danger was, of course, that excessive suspense could produce frustration. This is the fault that two of the major ancient critics of literary style found with Demosthenes' use of the figure (see Dion. Hal., *Demosthenes* 9; Longinus, *On the Sublime* 22). This sentence is a good example of their criticism. In his paraphrase, designed to demonstrate the figure, Didymos is able to cut out the whole central digression from 'and who says that . . .' to 'it was not his fault' without losing the sense. Of course, students of Demosthenes will lament the consequent loss of effect and the complex interweaving of ideas that is one of the characteristics of the great orator's periodic style (see, for example, Harding (1994*b*): 217–18), but it is not Didymos' purpose to praise or blame, merely to elucidate the workings of the figure, which he does not even attempt to define. And, that this was Didymos' own comment (not one he took from a predecessor) has been well shown by Osborne (138). Cf. Gibson (113–14).

Finally, it should be noted (with Gibson: 113) that this is the only entry in the commentary that could be viewed as rhetorical in emphasis (or grammatical, cf. D-S[1], p. xv), as distinct from philological or historical. This is not surprising, since, as Gibson has well demonstrated (22–3), 'it is unlikely that Didymos ever wrote extensive rhetorical commentaries on Demosthenes'. I cannot help but feel that this observation, well-founded as it is, undermines his theory that the historical bias of the majority of the entries in the papyrus suggests the work of an excerptor with an interest in history, as he himself concedes (69, n. 60).

Column 7, line 7 to column 8, line 32: The previous . . . benefaction: No part of the papyrus has provided more ammunition for those who view Didymos as a careless and incompetent scholar than this section, where he tries to explain the two references in Demosthenes 10.34, one to some previous occasion when the King restored Athenian affairs, the other to a recent benefaction (both topics are introduced in col. 7.7–11). I begin with 'the previous restoration' (col. 7.11–30).

some say *he* means the peace . . . Antialk[idas, the L]ak[onian]: Didymos begins his analysis by treating the suggestion of some, or maybe just one (the plural can be generalizing), of his predecessors that the reference is to a peace that is identified by the name of Antalkidas (for the spelling see below), the Spartan. It is important to note right away that, whichever of the two possible candidates for this peace is the correct one, neither can seriously be considered a benefaction to Athens and that consequently Didymos is justified in rejecting this argument.

There are two candidates for this peace, both of which are referred to by Xenophon. The first was an abortive negotiation that took place at Sardis, in 392/1, as a result of an initiative of Antalkidas to Tiribazos, the satrap of Ionia (Xen. *Hell.* 4.8.12–15); the second was the infamous Great King's Peace of 387/6 (often referred to as the Peace of Antalkidas, or 'the *Koine Eirene* of Antalkidas' in Diod. 15.5.1, and see Stylianou (1998): ad loc.), the terms of which were handed down by Tiribazos (on behalf of the King) at Sardis also, and were probably quite similar to those put forward by Antalkidas in 393/2, since he and the Spartans were the Greeks who benefitted most from it (Xen. *Hell.* 5.1.30–6; Diod. 14.110.3–4). There is, however, another peace negotiation known from this period, that involved different participants and took place at a different venue, Sparta, though probably in 392/1, about the time of the first, abortive, meeting at Sardis. It is the subject of a speech by the Athenian orator-politician (*rhetor*) Andokides, his third extant speech, *On the Peace*. It was also a failure. The relationship of this negotiation to the one at Sardis of the same year was in dispute even before the discovery of the papyrus and, unfortunately, Didymos' contribution (or at least the interpretations of it) has not helped matters. In fact, one recent scholar has expressed the opinion that 'things were reduced to chaos by the publication' of the Didymos papyrus (Badian (1991): 27). Others (especially Osborne: 141–8; Keen (1995): 1–10; (1998): 375–8; and Pownall (1995): 140–9) have taken a more positive position and acquitted Didymos of the worst of crimes. As will become apparent in the subsequent notes, I find that this latter approach is attractive and more upon the right lines.

Antialk[idas, the L]ak[onian]:   The spelling of the name here (with an iota) is aberrant and must be an error of the copyist. It is in opposition to the spelling in all our extant sources and even contradicted later in the papyrus (col. 7.67). Nevertheless, on its basis both D-S and P-S restore the iota in the spelling of the name in the passage from Philokhoros below (col. 7.19). But the space there is 1.5 mm less than it is here and, therefore, the restoration of the iota is unjustified. Unfortunately, this mistaken spelling was adopted with enthusiasm by Jacoby as the way Philokhoros actually spelled the name and he used it throughout his discussion of this fragment (*FGrHist* 328 F 149; *Text*: 515–21; *Notes*: 413–19). His view has been countered by Whitehead (1979: 191–3).

Antalkidas (Poralla no. 97) was an elite Spartiate, probably close-

ly related to King Agesilaos II (Cartledge (1987): 145–6), who played
an important role in Spartan affairs as ephor, ambassador, and navarch. He is most famous for his negotiations with the Persians in
393/2 and 388/7–387/6, the latter of which led to the Great King's
Peace and the conclusion of the Corinthian War. Much has been
made by modern scholars of Plutarch's statement (*Ages.* 23.3–4) that
Antalkidas was the personal enemy of Agesilaos, the king. This has
formed the basis for many recent interpretations of Spartan politics and foreign policy, according to which they were influenced
by factional strife between Agesilaos, who was in favour of war
with Persia for the liberation of the Greek cities in Asia Minor, and
Antalkidas, who was prepared to surrender those cities in order to
win Persian support for the war in Greece (see Cawkwell (1976):
68–9; DeVoto (1986): 191–202; Hamilton (1991): 111 f.). This view
has been criticized, correctly in my opinion, by Cartledge (1987:
195), who believes that there was no disagreement between the
two and that Spartan policy was, instead, responding to changed
circumstances. The issue is thoroughly reviewed in Urban (1991:
59–78). Most recently the idea of personal conflict between the two
has been dubbed a 'Hellenistic invention' by Keen (1995: 7 n. 42).

incorrectly, [at least as it] *seems* to me: That the phraseo-
logy indicates quite clearly that this is Didymos' own opinion is
maintained by Osborne (140), surely correctly.

not *only* **[did] the Ath[e]n[ians not accept] that peace:**
This restoration was proposed by D-S and is accepted by P-S
without question. It suits both the space and the context and is
certainly right. It shows, beyond doubt, that Didymos took his
predecessors' theory to relate to the failed negotiations of 392/1
and, consequently, that he thought the quotation from Philokhoros
did also. Whether he was right or not is another question, but one
that we cannot answer, although it is not infrequent to find him
accused of 'misunderstanding' their meaning (e.g. by West (1970)
295; Hajdu (2002): 279).

they also rejected . . . Philo]khoros recounts: The text here
is corrupt and a variety of restorations have been put forward for
the two gaps in it. For the first gap the suggestion of P-S, '[what
was being offered]', is more attractive than others, both because it
provides a direct object for the verb 'rejected' and because it picks
up the vocabulary of line 11. This is not the case, however, with their

restoration for the second space, 'in [the way which]'. As has been remarked (Wankel (1987): 221), it is hard to see what this means. D-S's suggestion, 'for [what reason]', still makes more sense and has not been invalidated by re-examination of the papyrus (cf. Wankel, ibid.). A quite different approach to this sentence is taken by Crönert (1907: 388), who is followed (as usual) by Jacoby (*FGrHist* 328 F149a): 'they rejected (it) [as an impious] *transgression* against themselves, [as Philo]khoros *recounts* . . .'. This is, however, no more credible than the majority of Crönert's imaginative restorations (cf. West (1970): 288 n. 3). R. Bauman's uncritical acceptance of Crönert's text has led him seriously off-track in his discussion of the charge that was used against the ambassadors (1990: 88–9) and shows the danger of ignoring the square brackets around a restoration.

in these very words: Osborne's understanding of this expression (i.e that it 'shows that what Did. found in Philochoros was very similar or even identical' to the view of the people he was criticizing) is wrong in sense and grammar, as Gibson has noted (115). The word *ONOMA* fundamentally means 'name' (so Gibson, who translates 'naming names'), though it is frequently used in the sense of 'word,' as for example by Didymos at col. 11.14. I find the latter more natural (cf. Bruce (2001): 57), since I cannot see what point Didymos would be making by asserting that the quotation from Philokhoros contained names, but Gibson's suggestion might find some support if it is the dative of accompaniment with *ΑΥΤΟΣ* (Smyth §1525, 'names and all') that Didymos intended here.

after the heading: see above (p. 104) under **after the heading 'the archon (was) Sos[i]ge[nes]'.**

'the archon (was) Philo[kle]s of Anaphly[s]tos': The year was 392/1 (*AO* 212). We know little else about this man and he does not merit an entry in *APF*. The name is very common in Athenian prosopography, as can be seen from the long entry in the *LGPN* (ii. 454–5). We cannot even tell if he was in any way related to the Philokles who was elected general after Arginousai (Xen. *Hell.* 1.7.1) and was captured and killed at Aigospotamoi (Xen. *Hell.* 2.1.30–2), because Xenophon does not give that man's demotic.

And the king sent down the peace: As mentioned above (p. 166), there are two peace negotiations reported for the year 392/1, one at Sardis, the other in Sparta, the relationship of which to each other is very controversial, since neither refers to the other (the otherwise detailed discussion of this issue in Urban (1991): 59–78 unfortunately does not devote much attention to this passage). The meeting at Sardis was arranged between Antalkidas and Tiribazos. It was gatecrashed by other Greek states, not least Athens, whose ambassadors were Konon, Hermogenes, Dion, Kallisthenes, and Kallimedon (Xen. *Hell.* 4.8.13. Cf. *AO* 211–12, who places it under the archon year 393/2, wrongly in my opinion; see Strauss (1986): 147 n. 62; Urban (1991): 60; Pownall (1995): 140 n. 2). This negotiation came to nothing, because the terms (on which see the next note) were unacceptable, especially to the Athenians, and even the Great King found something about them not to his liking (maybe just that they were unsuccessful), since he replaced his agent (Tiribazos) with a man (Strouthas), who followed a different policy.

A second, most likely later (despite the doubts of Badian (1991): 32; see Ryder (1965): 32, 165–9; Strauss (1986): 147 n. 62; Urban (1991): 60; Pownall (1995): 143 n. 15), negotiation took place at Sparta. We know of this primarily from Andokides' speech 3 (*On the Peace*), though the hypothesis to that speech and the quotation from Philokhoros cited here provide additional detail. Xenophon does not mention this meeting, but neither does Andokides refer to the negotiations at Sardis. We do not know what part, if any, Antalkidas played in these later negotiations, nor if the King of Persia's interests were represented. Indications are that they were not, however, and that this was largely a Greek affair, although the status of the Greek cities in Asia was part of the discussion. If this fragment from Philokhoros has been correctly cited by Didymos, we know the names of the Athenian ambassadors, and they were different from those at Sardis. These negotiations also were abortive.

Strictly speaking, neither of these negotiations can be called a 'peace that the King sent down', since those at Sardis were carried on by Tiribazos and rejected or abandoned by the King with his replacement of Tiribazos by Strouthas, and those at Sparta appear to have been mainly a Greek initiative (Ryder (1965): 31–3). For this reason some (e.g. Bruce (1966): 272–81 and (2001): 57–62; Hamilton (1979): 237–9; Badian (1991): 29 f.) have taken the view that Didymos was describing the Great King's Peace of 387/6 and had somehow looked up the wrong archon's name in Philokhoros. But, though it is not impossible that the scholar(s) Didymos was criticizing did believe that Demosthenes was referring to the Great King's Peace, the idea that, in attempting to refute that theory, he looked up the archon for a different year, is implausible (see Cawkwell (1976): 276 n. 25; *pace* Badian (1991): 33 n. 18, whose attempt to explain Didymos' 'confusion' by the unfounded suggestion that Philokhoros might have written up the account of the peace negotiations from 392/1 to 387/6 in one connected narrative involves a radical revision of the present understanding of the annalistic format of the *Atthis*, for which see Harding (1994): 6–8). And, of course, the major obstacle to this theory is the hard fact that the Athenians did not reject the peace of 387/6. There is really no way to elude this difficulty, not even the creative suggestion of Badian (1991: 32) that the Athenians first rejected, then accepted, the peace terms in 387/6, an idea which he extracts from two most unreliable sources (Plato, *Menexenos* 245d and Aelius Aristeides, *Panath.* 293). It is obtuse to argue that Didymos would base his whole analysis upon a temporary rejection that was soon reversed—if, that is, it happened at all.

Anyway, as Keen ((1995): 3; (1998): 376) has well pointed out, from the Greeks' point of view Tiribazos would be seen as the agent of the King, so the terms he proposed could easily be seen as 'sent down by the King', despite the fact that the King later appeared to repudiate them (see also Strauss (1986): 137). The same cannot, however, be said of the negotiations at Sparta, at which we have no evidence for Persian involvement physically. That fact and the presence of different ambassadors leads to the conclusion that the two negotiations were separate initiatives (Ryder (1965): 27–33), only connected, if at all, by the possibility that the meeting at Sparta was the result of the reaction of the Greek states to the failure of the negotiations in Asia (this does not, of course, exclude the possibility that some of the same terms and issues were on the table, cf. Strauss (1986): 137–9). [Professor Bosworth has suggested that the meeting at Sparta might be a continuation of the first and that Xenophon (or, at least, his text) has run the two together. He finds support for this in a textually difficult (and possibly corrupt) place in Xenophon's narrative (at *Hell.* 4.8.15), where the sentence 'in the view of the other side these were mere words' is 'patent nonsense' and based upon a reading in Stephanos that is in opposition to that in all the manuscripts. He suspects a substantial lacuna in Xenophon's account at this point, large enough to include a move to Sparta to enable the Greeks to debate the terms announced at Sardis. The continuation of Xenophon's narrative, beginning with the Athenian reaction, would then, in his view, have taken place at Sparta.]

because there had been written ... in the King's *household*: i.e. one of the terms debated at Sparta was that the Greek cities in Asia Minor be surrendered to Persian control. The expression 'members in the King's household' is alien to Greek diplomatic vocabulary (Lewis (1977): 146 n. 68), but its meaning is clear, since it is surely a euphemism for the Persian Empire (Cawkwell (1981): 72 n. 10). The use of that term does, however, show that some part of one of these negotiations originated on the Persian side, i.e. was 'sent down by the King'. This is in favour of the interpretation given just above that 'some of the same terms and issues were on the table'. It might also provide support for Bosworth's suggestion.

This reason for the Athenians' rejection of the peace terms is different from that given by Xenophon (*Hell.* 4.8.15), where it is fear of losing Lemnos, Imbros, and Skyros that is cited. But this problem may be more apparent than real. There is no doubt from Xenophon's account that the freedom of the Greeks in Asia was a major issue, as indeed it had to be, since regaining control of the Asia Minor seaboard was a fundamental demand of Persian policy. Antalkidas, like Lysander and other Spartan negotiators before him, was prepared to grant Persia's demand (*Hell.* 4.8.14), whenever it was expedient, in return for funding and support. By contrast, Athenian policy from at least the time of the foundation of the Delian League, but almost certainly earlier under Peisistratos (and maybe Solon), had been to champion the independence of those states, by claiming to be their metropolis. There is no sign that Athens was willing to cede this stance at this time, as she had to in 387/6. I see no reason to believe that this was a pose on Athens' part (*pace* Pownall (1995): 143 and n. 14). Before the signing of the Great King's Peace many Athenians (not least Thrasyboulos) clearly hoped for a revival of Athens' imperial past (Cawkwell (1976): 270–7).

But Antalkidas very cleverly threw out another principle (*Hell.* 4.8.14), to resolve the war in Greece (the Corinthian War) in Sparta's interests, namely that the mainland (that must be the meaning of 'other') cities and the islands (i.e. of the Aegean) should be independent. This disconcerted several members of the anti-Spartan coalition, especially Thebes (sensing this was aimed at her control of the Boiotian League), Argos (because of Corinth), and Athens. The Athenians feared the loss of the islands mentioned above, which were crucial to their access to the Hellespont and beyond. As a result the Athenian ambassadors probably protested against both clauses at Sardis. Xenophon chose to emphasize one objection,

Philokhoros chose the other (that is, if we have his full account; see below). Alternatively, since obviously we have only a very abbreviated account of the negotiations and the procedures, the Athenians may have said one thing for public consumption at Sardis, another at home in Athens, as Keen suggests (1995: 5–6).

Provocatively, Andokides in his speech regarding the negotiations at Sparta makes no mention of this issue. Maybe he decided the issue was too unpopular to touch upon. If not, it is rather difficult to see how he could avoid doing so, unless the freedom of the Greeks in Asia was not raised at that conference (but see Pownall (1995): 142). This would conform to the possibility, mentioned above, that the two negotiations were quite separate (*pace* Jacoby, *Text*: 515 f., who is followed by Lewis (1977): 146 n. 68), but it does conflict with the next sentence in the text, as it stands (see below).

On the history of the slogan 'the freedom of the Greeks in Asia' and arguments to suggest that it became regularly exploited for political purposes in the period 400–386 see Seager and Tuplin (1980: 141–54).

Furthermore . . . in Lakedaimon: As the text stands, the clear implication is that the negotiations in Sparta were a continuation of those in Sardis, or that only the negotiations in Sparta were being narrated. The word 'furthermore' ('but also') seems to suggest some connection between rejection of the terms and the exile of the ambassadors for giving their 'consent'. In that case, some such supplement as 'to the terms' is required after 'gave their consent' and is frequently supplied (see e.g. Harding (1985): no. 23). But an alternative solution, proposed allusively by Jacoby (*Text*: 518), has now found favour (Keen (1995): 8–9; Pownall (1995): 142–3), that is that there is something missing between 'household' and 'furthermore'. This something may well be another fragment from Philokhoros (numbered by Jacoby F149b) that is cited in the hypothesis to Andokides, *On the Peace*. After referring to the conference at Sparta, the author of the hypothesis reports that the Spartans sent ambassadors to Athens, where the *demos* was to have forty days to decide. Then he goes on: 'Philokhoros says that the ambassadors both came from Lakedaimon and returned without accomplishing anything, since Andokides did not succeed in persuading (i.e. the Athenians).' If this fragment belongs before the sentence beginning with 'furthermore', it would change the reference from 'consenting' to 'persuading' and put a different interpretation on the passage: i.e.

'Andokides did not succeed in persuading. Furthermore they banished the ambassadors . . .' (Keen (1995): 9). On this view, Didymos was excerpting parts of Philokhoros' account for the archonship of Philokles of the reaction in Athens to the peace terms proposed by Antalkidas and Tiribazos at Sardis and combining it with his account of their reaction to the negotiations at Sparta, but leaving out a substantial amount of intervening material (Keen (1995): 8–9; Pownall (1995): 142–3). Admittedly, this would be a departure from his practice elsewhere in the papyrus (but see below under '[S]ou[niad]es of Akharna[i]'), where he regularly marks a break in a quotation by a *paragraphos* and the indentation of a resumptive phrase (such as 'and later the same author says:'). A similar practice is employed by Dionysios of Halikarnassos in excerpting three passages from Philokhoros' account of the Olynthian War (Dion. Hal. *Ad Amm.* 1. 9; Harding (1994): 6–8). We would have to assume that on this occasion, had Didymos been a modern scholar, he might have used dots between his excerpts, but since he did not, he has created confusion for us and a reputation for confusion for himself (a universal charge: see West (1970): 295; Harris (1989): 37; Keen (1995): 9, who are all too quick to conclude that Didymos did not understand what his predecessor(s) meant, without any evidence to support their assumption). He, however, knew what he was doing: producing evidence to disprove the obviously misguided suggestion of one of his predecessors that the reference in Demosthenes to a previous benefaction of the Great King to Athens involved these peace negotiations of 392/1, by showing how negatively the Athenians reacted to them both. This interpretation of the passage may be the most economical explanation of the problems that have been seen in it (*pace* Badian (1991): 31).

on the motion of Kallistratos: This Kallistratos is usually identified with Kallistratos of Aphidna (*APF* no. 8157). Identification of individuals by name alone, without patronymic and/or demotic, is not as safe as is often assumed (see Thompson (1974): 144–9), especially when the name is as common as this (there are three and a half columns in *LGPN* 252–3), but if this is the correct identification in this case, then this politically motivated trial is the first known act in the long and illustrious career of Kallistratos of Aphidna. On his career see Sealey (1956: 178–203) and for the politics behind the trial see Strauss (1986: 140 f.). Exactly what procedure Kallistratos followed is unclear. The word used in the Greek

is the standard vocabulary for a proposal before the Assembly, not
for an indictment (see below, p. 175).

Epikrates of Kephisia: (*APF* no. 4859). The same caution
applies here as above (only in reverse), since this name also was
very popular in Athens (there are three columns in *LGPN* 148–9).
Despite this, this man is usually identified with the Epikrates mentioned (without demotic) by Demosthenes (19.277) as a *demotikos*,
who helped restore the democracy in 403, and in the *Hellenika Oxyrhynchia* as the leader of the popular faction before the Corinthian
War together with Kephalos (see *Hell. Oxy.* 6.2; cf. Bruce (1967):
56; Strauss (1986): 140; Sealey (1956): 185, who claims 'there is
no reason to question the identification'). About the same time a
man of the same name, but nicknamed *beard-bearer* (σακεσφόρος),
was prosecuted for some sort of financial misdemeanour (Lysias
27.3) and was generally accused of taking bribes (Lysias 27.3; Plato
Comicus fr. 119; schol. to Aristophanes, *Ekkles.* 71; cf. Florian (1908):
10–11). All are treated, perhaps rightly, as the same powerful politician (*rhetor kai demagogos*). It is no obstacle to this identification that
in 397 he was in favour of war with Sparta (*Hell. Oxy.* 6.2) and in 392
went on an embassy to negotiate peace, since political factions in
Athens were not defined by policy so much as by personality (Sealey
(1967): *passim*; Strauss (1986): 11–41). His personal allegiance may
have been to Konon, son of Timotheos (Strauss (1986): 134).

The statement made here that Epikrates of Kephisia was exiled
at this time (and possibly condemned to death, if we believe Demosthenes 19.277) has been questioned by Bruce ((1966): 272–81 and
(2001): 57–62) and Badian (1991: 29) on the basis of a passage in
Aelius Aristeides (*Panath.* 293, with scholion), where it is stated that
the Athenians were the last to accept the Great King's Peace and
even condemned those who persuaded them (one of whom is identified as Epikrates by the scholiast). This evidence forms a basic part
of Bruce's attempt to show that the peace referred to in this passage
of Didymos was the peace of 387/6. But, quite apart from the other
reasons for rejecting that idea (mentioned above, pp. 169–70), we
would have to conclude that Andokides and the others named here
also took part in negotiating the King's Peace and were exiled in
386 not 392 (cf. Badian (1991): 29 f.). This is very hard to accept (see
below) and runs into the obstacle that Kallias, son of Hipponikos,
was quite probably one of the ambassadors who negotiated the
King's Peace and is not mentioned here (see below at col. 7.73). In

a situation where we have a disagreement between a respected historian, like Philokhoros, and a scholiast to a late orator, like Aelius Aristeides, preference should be given to the historian (Cawkwell (1976): 276 n. 25). There may, however, be no disagreement if Epikrates of Kephisia was allowed to return from exile sometime between 392 and 387, as might be indicated by an early fourth-century tombstone for a man of the same name and demotic (*IG* II² 6444; *APF* no. 4859).

Andokides of Kydathenaion: The son of Leogoras (*APF* no. 828) surely needs no introduction. Member of one of the leading aristocratic families in Athens, he was forced to leave Athens, as a consequence of his involvement with the mutilators of the Hermai, by the decree of Isotimides. After an unsuccessful attempt to return in 411/10 , for which he delivered the speech *On the Return*, he finally came back to Athens in the general amnesty after the Peloponnesian War. He survived prosecution by, amongst others, Kallias, son of Hipponikos, and Agyrrhios of Kollytos, uncle of Kallistratos of Aphidna (*On the Mysteries*). Politically, his one main initiative, and his last, was to go on this peace embassy to Sparta in 392, for which he wrote his speech *On the Peace* (on Andokides' place in Athenian politics see Strauss (1986): 99–103, 138–143; on this speech see Missiou-Ladi (1992): 55–86, 168–82). That he was again exiled on this occasion is confirmed by Plut. *Mor.* 835a. The suggestion of Badian (1991: 29 f.) that Andokides was not exiled at this time, but remained active in Athenian politics and took part in the negotiations for the Great King's Peace, at which time—along with Epikrates and the others mentioned here—he was exiled, is quite unsupported by the evidence. See the resumé of Andokides' career in MacDowell (1962: 1–6).

Kratinos of Sphettos: The scribe misspelled the demotic, writing a sigma in place of the first tau. This man is otherwise unknown (see *LGPN* 272).

Euboulides of Eleusis: This man is usually, perhaps over-confidently (e.g. Sealey (1956): 185), identified with the Euboulides (without demotic) known from several sources as the archon of 394/3 (*IG* II² 16 fr. A, *IG* II² 18; *AO* 208).

did *not even* await the judgement/trial: As mentioned above (see **on the motion of Kallistratos**), it is hard to know exactly what procedure was followed, or what action was brought against the ambassadors. They had probably not agreed to anything (Bruce (1966): 274; Keen (1995): 10; contra, Pownall (1995): 147–9), even though they were designated 'autokratores' in the hypothesis (for the significance of that designation, 'plenipotentiary', in general see Mosley (1973): 30–8, and for this specific case see Pownall (1995): 144–7), otherwise the debate in Athens was irrelevant. In fact, we are told explicitly that they, together with a delegation from Sparta, brought the terms to Athens (Philokhoros, F149b) and that the *demos* was allowed forty days to deliberate. Yet somehow they had departed from the instructions they had been given (*On the Peace* 35) and it has recently been suggested that their transgression was to give provisional agreement to Sparta's terms under pressure from a change in the balance of power after the Spartan capture of Lechaion (Pownall (1995): 147–9). This is, of course, pure speculation.

In the end, as we know, the people were persuaded to reject the terms. Thus, the situation was not similar to that which followed the Peace of Philokrates (346/5), when the political trials resulted from the disillusionment of the *demos* with the terms that it had accepted on the advice of the ambassadors. If there is any parallel between the two procedures, it would seem to be with the earlier stage in the negotiations of 346/5, when the ambassadors returned from Macedon with Philip's representatives to present the options to the people. It is more likely that Andokides and his colleagues simply lost the debate over the Spartan proposal to their opponents in the Assembly, amongst whom was Kallistratos, who at some point took advantage of the people's decision against the terms to propose some action against the ambassadors, who promptly fled into self-imposed exile (see Strauss (1986): 138–43, 150–1).

As for the charge(s) that were brought against the envoys, they could range over the whole gamut of stock accusations against ambassadors for *parapresbeia*, some idea of which can be gleaned from Demosthenes (19.277): i.e. disobeying instructions, making untruthful reports to the *boule*, sending untruthful dispatches, bearing false witness against allies, or taking bribes. Specificity is not possible, though I find unlikely the recent suggestion (Bauman (1990): 88–9) that the charge was impiety (*asebeia*), for the reason already stated above (under **they also rejected [what was being offered] to them**, pp. 167–8).

But Philokhoros' vocabulary strongly suggests that Kallistratos moved a motion in the Assembly and Bauman (1990: 88) may be correct in interpreting this as a possible reference to the stock charge of 'unconstitutional proposal' (*graphe paranomon*). Finally, we cannot even be sure that a trial took place, since the ambassadors fled into exile before it could happen.

Lines 28–62:   Didymos concludes his refutation of his predecessor(s)' theory with an argument from likelihood and moves on to present his own idea of what Demosthenes was referring to. That what follows was his own idea is clear from his summation in lines 55–62 (see Osborne: 151–2; Gibson: 115). Just as his judgement was surely correct in rejecting the preceding view, so one has to admit that his own suggestion qualifies as the best candidate for Demosthenes' reference (even acknowledged by Harris (1989): 37; cf. Hajdu (2002): 278–9). That being said, once again it is the details that have been thought to present problems. In essence, the issue may be a variant of that raised in the last discussion, since Didymos begins his presentation of the process that led to the naval victory of Pharnabazos and Konon at Knidos over the Spartans in 394/3 (the archonship of Euboulides) with a citation from Philokhoros from the year 397/6 (the archonship of Souniades). This has led to the view that either he or Philokhoros (see e.g. Foucart (1909): 161; Badian (1991): 33 n. 18; Gibson: 115–16) has compressed the details of four years into one entry under the year 397/6. On this, I shall make two preliminary points: (1) It is important to be sensitive to Didymos' argument, which is that it was the King's *support* that was the benefaction that led to the restoration that followed the victory at Knidos. He precisely, and valuably (Jacoby, *Text*, 513), dates this, by citing Philokhoros' entry under Souniades. (2) The belief that this is all one entry is questionable. The left-hand margin of the papyrus from line 28 to line 45 is missing and as a result we cannot tell where one quotation stops and another begins, since we lack the *paragraphoi*. It is not impossible, as we shall see, that Didymos ended one citation from Philokhoros and began another at some point in this passage, with a transitional phrase such as the one that has been restored in column 5.57 on the basis of the extant *paragraphoi*.

Ko[non], the [son of] Timothe[os]:   For the career of this famous Athenian see Barbieri (1955: *passim*); Davies (*APF* no. 13700); Harding (1985: no. 12); Strauss (1986: *passim*); Seager (*CAH*[2] vi. 97–109). First mentioned as commander of Naupaktos in 414 (Thuc. 7.31), he had some considerable involvement in the last phase of the Peloponnesian War, restoring morale in the fleet in 407 after

Notion (Xen. *Hell.* 1.5.20), blockaded by Kallikratidas at Mytilene in 406 and thereby missing the battle of Arginousai (Xen. *Hell.* 1.6.38) and distinguishing himself at Aigospotamoi by being the only commander alert enough to escape the disaster (Xen. *Hell.* 2.1.28–9). He fled to Kypros, where he took refuge with King Evagoras of Salamis, by whom through the agency of Ktesias he was introduced to the Persian high command (Diod. 14.39.1; Photius, *Bibl.* 44b20–38). From 397 to 394 he collaborated with Pharnabazos in training a Greco-Persian fleet that eventually defeated the Spartans (under Peisander) in a naval engagement off Knidos in 394. Following that, in 393 he returned to Athens and helped in restoring the fortifications (cf. Harding (1985): no. 17) and fortunes of the city. For a short time he was the most influential man in Athens (Strauss (1986): 127–8). But in 392 he was a member of the Athenian embassy to Tiribazos, by whom he was imprisoned. He escaped to Kypros, but died there soon after (probably 389). He was admired by the rhetorician, Isokrates (4.142, 5.62–4, 9.52–7), who claimed his son, Timotheos, as his most famous student. By contrast he was not on good terms with Thrasyboulos, whose position as the restorer of democracy was eclipsed by Konon's great military achievements and financial contributions (Strauss (1986): 108). Konon bequeathed to his son a considerable fortune (Lysias 19.39–41; *APF* 508–9).

the armaments provided by Phar[naba]zos: Didymos appropriately (cf. Osborne: 149) notes that it was the provision of financial and military support that constituted the King's benefaction. Diodorus (14.39) provides the detail that Pharnabazos brought 500 talents of silver and ordered the kings of Kypros to prepare one hundred triremes. Konon did not, however, wait for these to be ready, but began his campaign by sailing off to Kaunos with forty ships.

Pharnabazos, son of Pharnaces, was the satrap of Hellespontine Phrygia, based upon Daskyleion (on which see Briant (2002): 697–700). He was closely related to the royal household, since his earliest known ancestor was Arsames, brother of Hystaspes, who was father to Darius the Great. Pharnabazos' grandfather, Artabazos, had been put in charge of the Hellespontine region by Xerxes in 479 and the family had governed it since then. Pharnabazos himself was in control of the region from 412 (at least) to 387/6, when he was summoned to court to marry Apame, daughter of Artaxerxes II (Briant (2002): 339). During the last years of the fifth century and the first years of the fourth he was in frequent competition with his colleague Tissaphernes, satrap of Ionia, over the leadership of the Persian involvement in Greek affairs (cf. Thuc. 8.6.1, 8.8.1, 8.99, 8.109; Briant (2002): 592–6). He is usually named as the man who encompassed the assassination of Alkibiades (Diod. 14.11.1; Plut. *Alk.* 39.1–9; Nepos, *Alc.* 10.2–6).

in *the* naval engagement near Kn[i]dos: Other accounts of this battle are offered by Diodoros (14.79–85) and, with considerably less detail, Xenophon (4.3.10–13).

***after the heading*:** See above (p. 104) under **after the heading 'the archon (was) Sos[i]ge[nes]'**.

[S]ou[niad]es of Akharna[i]: The demotic renders the restoration of the name of the archon beyond question (cf. Jacoby, *Text*: 513–14). Other evidence confirms the spelling of his name (see *AO* 205), despite Diodoros' aberrant Lysiades (14.47.1). There are only six Athenians on record with this name and this is by far the earliest (*LGPN* 402). The year was 397/6. Diodoros dates the beginning of Konon's activities to 399/8, in the archonship of Aristokrates (14.38.1). Presuming that this is what Philokhoros is recording, his date is to be preferred. It is consistent with the information provided by the *Hellenika Oxyrhynchia* (6.1; cf. Bruce (1967): 50–1; Harding (1985): no. 11A).

***he writes* [as follows in his fifth book]:** This restoration is confirmed by Jacoby's analysis of the contents of book five of Philokhoros' *Atthis*, i.e. from 403 down to 360/59 or 357/6 (Jacoby, *Text*: 252). The following narrative is listed by Jacoby as *FGrHist* 328 F144–5.

K[onon . . . the *fleet*: It is tantalizing to have this important fragment concerning the movements of Konon in such a corrupt condition. There have been numerous attempts at restoration, but they are all quite hypothetical. Sufficient survives, however, to enable us to establish that Philokhoros is probably starting his narrative at the point covered by Diodoros 14.39, in which Konon sailed with forty ships from Kypros to Kaunos in Karia. Given the context, Konon must be assumed to be the subject and enough of 'from Kypros' can be read to suggest that a word like 'set out' or 'sailed' is needed. After 'with' all editors supply 'ships' coupled with some modifier. Based upon the account in Diodoros, Foucart (1909: 164) wanted to read 'forty', but the only preserved letter of the word (the first—a pi) precludes this. D-S read 'many' (*ΠΟΛΛΩΝ*), and P-S follow them, but this seems to me unsuitable. Simply put, Konon did not have 'many' ships. Better is Lenchantin's 'all (*ΠΑΣΩΝ*) his ships' (1921: 23–7). In the next line the last letters of 'Phrygia' and the first two letters of 'satrap' show that Pharnabazos was, as one would have suspected in any case, also mentioned, but it is not clear in what context or even in which grammatical case (D-S and P-S both put him in the accusative, as do most others; only Lenchantin prefers the dative). I think it quite unlikely, however, that Philokhoros is here referring to the incident reported by Diodoros at 14.81.4–5 (*pace* Gibson: 116). In line 39, 'the fleet' (Fuhr (1904): 1130) is surely to be preferred to the rather opaque suggestion of D-S², but whether we are to supply 'the royal' after it (Foucart (1909): 164) or end the sentence there with P-S, is unclear. If all this is correct, some mention of Kaunos is to be expected.

Lines 39–44: he sailed . . . [from Sy]ria: Four or five letters in from the left margin (presuming it started in the offset position) of line 40, D-S read the letters *Δ*(?)*OY*, which they took to be the last letters of the name Euboulides, the archon for 394/3, in the genitive case. They saw in this the formula 'in the time/year/archonship of Euboulides' and assumed that a new part of Philokhoros' narrative was being excerpted. Jacoby (*Text*: 513), who also believed that more than one citation from Philokhoros was involved, was reluctantly led to reject this reading, by accepting (as always) the assertion of Crönert (1907: 384–5) that the first letter was not a delta but a xi. Crönert's confidence was, however, misplaced; P-S think the choice between the two is uncertain and my own autopsy finds xi less likely than delta (clearly visible is a horizontal line at the bottom of the letter space, consistent with delta). Despite that, I do not think that this is the appropriate place for a new entry and I think P-S are probably correct in seeing instead a reference in lines 40–2(?) to the incident at Kaunos, reported by Diodoros (14.79.4–5) under the year 396 (but likely still in 397, see Bruce (1967): 73–5), when Konon, still with only forty ships (Crönert's certain reading in line 41), was blockaded by Pharax, the Spartan navarch for 398/7, who operated out of Rhodes. This would have the great advantage of preserving the temporal unity of this citation from Philokhoros, all of which could have been included under the one archonship. The following lines could then contain a reference to the aid that was brought to

Konon at Kaunos by Pharnabazos and Artaphernes, which forced Pharax to retire to Rhodes, though this may have been in summary form, as P-S suspect, rather than a verbatim quotation.

Lines 45–51: But/and *after* . . . was killed': It is quite clear that Didymos has at this point moved on to Philokhoros' narrative of the battle of Knidos, which took place in August of 394/3, if the ancient synchronization with the battle of Koroneia is correct (cf. Xen. *Hell.* 4.3.10; Plut. *Ages.* 17). I follow P-S in the view that a new citation begins at this point and have no difficulty with the idea that some such typically Didymean introductory expression as 'the same author says' or 'later he says' preceded in the missing last two-thirds of line 44 (see above under **Lines 28–62**, p. 177). There is no reason to believe that Philokhoros recounted the battle under the year 397/6 (*pace* Badian (1991): 33 n. 18; Gibson: 115).

The text of this section is restored by P-S (largely following Crönert (1907): 385). Ultimately, it is based upon the account in Diodoros (14.83.4–7), to which it shows considerable similarity. Both accounts agree on the name of the Spartan navarch (Peisander, brother-in-law of Agesilaos, the king; see Cartledge (1987): 146), the number of Spartan ships captured and the topographical points— Loryma and Physkos. The only real difficulty in reconstructing the movements of the two fleets involves the reference to Physkos. There was a well-known town of this name in the region. It was situated almost midway between Kaunos and Loryma, at the southern end of the main road northwards to Ephesos (Strabo 14.2.4 C652; 14.2. 29 C663; Barrington Atlas, map 65). Unfortunately, accepting this location could, depending on the translation of the verb, create the tactical unlikelihood that Peisander sailed right past Konon's position at Loryma (and back again almost to Knidos), without either commander seeing the other. The verb concerned ($KATA\Phi EP\Omega$) is used by both Diodoros and (probably) Philokhoros. In the passive (as here) its basic meaning should be 'carried down', though it is translated as widely as 'moved' (Gibson: 89) and 'put in' (Oldfather in the Loeb Diodoros, vol. vi, p. 241), which is its usual meaning in a naval context in Diodoros (cf. 13.3.3; 20.96.2; 27.12.1). With either of the former the sense could simply be directional, i.e. 'was carried down/moved in the direction of Physkos' (adopting the restoration of $\Pi PO\Sigma$ at the beginning of line 48, in agreement with Diodoros 14.83.5), without any implication that he reached the place. He was on his way, when he was attacked by Konon's fleet from

Loryma. This is the solution proposed by Foucart (1909: 165–6). Unfortunately, Diodoros clearly understood his source to mean that Peisander actually reached Physkos, because he begins the next sentence with 'From there he sailed out . . .' (hence Oldfather's translation, but see Foucart for the suggestion that 'from there' refers back to Knidos). This has led others (e.g. Judeich (1892): 75, followed by Barbieri (1955): 145–7) to suggest that there must have been some other, otherwise unrecorded, Physkos, situated on the Khersonese, somewhere between Knidos and Loryma. In support of this—at first sight incredible—solution, they point to the existence of yet another Physkos, also unknown, referred to by Strabo as near Mylasa (Strabo 14.2.23 C659).

This convenient hypothesis would make the tactical manoeuvres easier to reconstruct, but, given the state of the papyrus and Diodoros' failure to explain Peisander's movement to Physkos, other possibilities exist. For example (as Professor Bosworth has pointed out), it is not impossible that there was some pressing reason for Peisander to sail to the known Physkos and that he took a chance on Konon's fleet being unprepared for action at short notice.

For an analysis of this battle, still fundamental is Barbieri (1955: 144–60). For reactions to the victory in the Greek world (especially in Athens) see Seager (1967: 95–115) and Strauss (1986: 121–49).

Konon also restored the [Long] Walls: See Jacoby, *FGrHist* 328 F146. The traditional view, found in most literary sources, was that Konon had been solely responsible for providing the manpower and money for rebuilding the fortifications of Peiraieus and the Long Walls, after he returned to Athens in 393 (cf. Diod. 14.85.1–3; Dem. 20.68–9 and Xen. *Hell.* 4.8.10, though he, at least, recognized that some of the work was done by the Athenians with Boiotian help). In fact, the documentary evidence shows that the Athenians had begun work on the walls before the victory of Knidos (see Jacoby, *FGrHist* 328 F40 and F146; *Text*: 325, 514; Harding (1985): no. 17).

the same writer records once again: The *paragraphos* in the margin below line 51 shows that the verbatim quotation from Philokhoros ended at 'was killed' and that what follows is only a paraphrase of his account on the building of the walls.

Lines 55–62: I think there is an argument . . . :   As was pointed out above (p. 177), the tentative and personal way in which this summation is expressed is a sure sign that the identification of Demosthenes' reference with the help given to Konon is Didymos' own idea. His nervousness in advancing it is confirmed by the number of alternative possibilities he throws out in the next few lines. This nervousness is all the more surprising, since, as even his strongest critics admit (e.g. Harris (1989): 37), his identification is clearly the right one. Also noteworthy, however, is what this says about Hellenistic scholarship on Demosthenes before Didymos. The clear implication is that none of his predecessors had had the wit to recognize this obvious identification. This should give those pause who see Didymos as representing the nadir of Greek scholarship, and make them think twice before assuming that it is Didymos who has misinterpreted his predecessors (on the assumption that they could not have thought of anything so wrong).

The word he uses for 'in accord with' (lines 59–60) is rather poetical and could be seen as one indication that Didymos had some literary ambitions, as D-S¹ claimed (pp. xxviii–xxix). On the significance of 'generosity' (*ΦΙΛΟΤΙΜΙΑ*) in Greek political culture, but here applied to the Great King's actions, see Whitehead (1983: 55–74).

But Demosthenes could ... peace initiated by the King: Nothing better reveals Didymos' nervousness and insecurity in his own interpretation and his deference to his predecessor's mistaken identification of the King's benefaction with a peace treaty than his addition here of two other peace treaties that were associated with the King (*pace* Foucart (1909): 71, who believes that Didymos was simply making a display of his erudition).

Lines 63–71: the Athenians were glad to agree to: Whilst the Athenians took an ambivalent attitude (at best) toward the Great King's Peace, they were very pleased with the peace of 375/4 (see Jehne (1994): 63–4).

Philokhoros has discoursed about this peace also: Once again Didymos resorts to his regular authority for Athenian affairs, Philokhoros (*FGrHist* 328 F151), though on this occasion he does not cite him verbatim, nor under an archon date. The treaty referred to here can be identified with certainty as the Common Peace (*Koine Eirene*) of 375/4 (Diod. 15.38; Xen. *Hell.* 6.2.1; Isok. 15.109; Nepos, *Timotheus* 2; cf. Jacoby, *Text*: 522–3; Ryder (1965): 58, 124–6; Harding (1985): no. 44; Sealey (1993): 63; Seager, *CAH*² vi. 175–6; Jehne

(1994): 57–64). It was initiated by the King (Diod. 15.38.1), accepted
eagerly by the Athenians, because their finances and manpower
were exhausted (Xen. *Hell.* 6.2.1; cf. Wilson (1970): 302–26), and is
generally agreed to be similar in terms to the Great King's Peace of
387/6 (see, for example, Jehne (1994): 57–64).

from the war (being) very long: I have translated the text as
it stands, with the word 'war' in the genitive. Wankel (1987: 221)
follows Wilamowitz in declaring that the case must be emended to
the dative, giving the sense 'exhausted by the war for a long time'
(Gibson: 89 n. 18).

they set up the altar of Eirene: Despite this clear statement,
there are still those who would argue for the peace of 371, or even
that of 362, as the inspiration for the establishment of the cult of
Eirene and the commissioning of the famous cult statue of Eirene
(Peace) holding the baby Ploutos (Wealth) by the sculptor Kephiso-
dotos (*APF* no. 8334; Ridgway (1997): 258–60), which was set up
in the agora (Pausanias, 1.8.2, 9.16.2). To be sure, the earliest depiction of the statue group (on Panathenaic vases) dates to 360/59
(Eschbach (1986): 58–70; Ridgway (1997): 280 n. 62), and there is,
admittedly, no definitive reason for dating the cult and the statue at
the same time, but the historical situation of 375/4 is, in my opinion,
clearly best suited to the context of both. For a review of the ancient
evidence see Jacoby, *Text* (523–6) and for modern discussions see
Jehne (1994): 63 n. 94; Knell (2000): 73–80. For a representation of
the statue and a detail of a relevant Panathenaic vase see Boardman
(1995): Pl. 24; Knell (2000): 74–5, 77.

the peace that was put to the vote . . . Hipponikos: It is not
clear what Didymos is referring to here. Most recent discussions
(e.g. Osborne: 157–8; Gibson: 118) assume without question that he
has in mind the notorious Peace of Kallias that was believed to belong some time in the mid-fifth century. But there is no way this was
(or could have been) ever considered a 'benefaction' of the King's,
since the tradition was that it was forced upon him by Kimon's
victories. I think it far more likely, given that all other examples
are drawn from the fourth century, that Didymos is here referring
to the Peace of 371/0, for which Kallias, son of Hipponikos and
grandson of the fifth-century Kallias (Kallias III in *APF* no. 7826),
was an Athenian negotiator at the meeting in Sparta (see Xen.
Hell. 4.3.2–20; Diod. 15.50.4; Ryder (1965): 127–30; Jehne (1994):

65–74), or maybe even the Peace negotiation held at Athens in the same year but following the Spartan defeat at Leuktra (Xen. *Hell.* 6.5.1; Ryder (1965): 131–3; Jehne (1994): 74–9), though Kallias is not mentioned in this context.

On a textual point, note that the scribe has added an intrusive epsilon before the iota of -*nikos*, as he did in line 70 (above) at the beginning of the word 'set up'.

contributions of cash at both the private and public level: There is no reason to believe that Didymos had any specific instances in mind (as e.g. the money that Timokrates the Rhodian brought to Greece before the Corinthian War: see *Hell. Oxy.* 7.2). This is just a final, rather desperate, attempt to cover all bases, as a summation to this very lengthy explanation of Demosthenes' reference.

COLUMN EIGHT

Heading: The two topics identified in the heading to column 8 refer respectively to the *lemma* from Dem. 10.37, which begins at line 44, and the *lemma* from 10.38, which begins at line 55. The heading does not make mention of the *lemma* from Dem. 10.35, which is found at line 32.

I think that the above is sufficient: Most people would agree with this observation.

the restoration of the city's affairs in the past: Though the Greek here is not as precise as we might like and editors have suggested inserting the genitive plural definite article either before 'the city' or after it, it hardly deserves to be dubbed 'unverständlich', as it is by Wankel (1987: 221).

I must proceed to give an account of the recent instance: Didymos finally gets down to the topic he announced in the heading to the previous column. Maybe it would have been better for him if he had not, since the answer he comes up with to the recent instance of the King's generosity to Athens has led him into deep trouble with modern scholars (e.g. Harris (1989): 36–44; (1995): 108–9; Badian (1991): 30 n. 14, 33 n. 18) and some glaring inconsistency with his own arguments.

five years before this, in the archonship of Lykiskos:
Lykiskos was archon for the Attic year 344/3 (see *AO* 326). Didymos' problems begin right away. He has established his preferred date for the *Fourth Philippic* as 341/0 (see cols. 1 and 2) and there is no system of reckoning that can find five years between 344/3 and 341/0 (cf. Gibson: 118). Osborne's attempt (160 and n. 39) to excuse the error, by suggesting that one of Didymos' sources (maybe Anaximenes) narrated part of these events under the previous year (345/4), is quite unconvincing. Canfora (1968: 17–19) also lays the blame on Didymos' source, but his solution would involve lowering the date of Hermias' arrest to 340, which is unacceptably late (Hajdu (2002): 281).

Philip sent (an embassy) to Athens concerning peace:
There are several references to Macedonian embassies to Athens in this year: (1) The *hypothesis* to Dem. 6 (*Second Philippic*) states that the speech was delivered (autumn 344 is the accepted date) in response to some ambassadors and that, while the speech does not reveal where these ambassadors had come from, certain *Histories of Philip* make it clear that they had come from Philip, the Messenians, and the Argives. (2) The embassy at which Python of Byzantion was spokesman for Philip and presented his offer for revision (*epanorthosis*) of the Peace of Philokrates ([Dem.] 7.18–26, [Dem.] 12.18, Dem. 18.136). (3) The embassy concerning peace mentioned here.

It is possible that all three references are to the same occasion, in which case they would belong to the setting of the *Second Philippic*, where Demosthenes alone responded to Python as he claimed in 18.136 (Cawkwell (1963) 123–7; (1978): 123–6). Conversely, it has also been argued that (1) and (2) are different, in particular that Python's embassy was distinct and later; furthermore, that (1) might not have been from Philip at all, and that (3) could relate to either or neither of the others (the permutations are numerous: see e.g. Wüst (1938): 64–7; Jacoby, *Text*: 531–3; Wankel (1976): 739–41; Sealey (1978): 300–10; (1993): 170–4; Griffith (1979): 489–95; Buckler (1994): 104–5; Harris (1995): 108–9).

the Athenians also gave audience to the ambassadors of the King: An embassy from Artaxerxes (Ochus) to the major states of Greece, including Sparta and Athens, as a prelude to his invasion of Egypt is recorded by Diodoros (16.44). His date (351/0) is certainly incorrect and the circumstances fit this context well, as is now universally accepted (see e.g. Wüst (1938): 64; Cawkwell (1963):

121–3; Griffith (1979): 484; Sealey (1993): 172; Hajdu (2002): 279–80). The synchronism, however, between the arrival in Athens of that embassy and one from Philip, implied by Didymos, is no longer accepted as readily as it once was (e.g. by Wüst (1938): 64–77; defended by Cawkwell (1963): 121–7; cf. Griffith (1979): 484; Harding (1994): 178; Buckler (1994): 104–5). Jacoby's point (*Text*: 532) that the citation from Philokhoros (below) must be the first entry for the archon year (i.e. right after midsummer 344), because it begins with the formula 'in this man's archonship', has been well taken and has persuaded most scholars that Wüst's chronology (which put the Persian embassy together with Python's in February 343) will not work and that the synchronism must be rejected (see e.g. Wankel (1976): 740–1; Sealey (1978): 300–10; (1993): 172 and n. 32; Harris (1995): 108–9), despite Cawkwell's valiant effort to save it (1963: 121–7).

NB: the word translated as 'also gave audience to' appears only here in the whole corpus of Greek literature. It is not possible to tell whether it originated with Didymos or his source (Jacoby, *Notes*: 428). Wendland's emendation to 'did not give audience to' makes no sense (Jacoby, *Notes*: 427).

more arrogant than it should have been: This judgement is usually attributed to Didymos (e.g. Wüst (1938): 65; Cawkwell (1963): 121; Osborne: 166–9; Harris (1989): 42 n. 22; (1995): 108; Hajdu (2002): 280) or his source, Anaximenes (Jacoby, *Text*: 532; *Notes*: 427, who asserts that Didymos did not make 'historical or political judgments'. Cf. Sealey (1993): 172, n. 33). The idea that it could have been derived from Philokhoros is rejected out of hand by Jacoby (*Text*: 532) and his opinion has not been questioned. It follows that it did not originate with Androtion either, since he was no doubt Philokhoros' source for this incident (Harding (1994): 32–3; *pace* Moscati Castelnuovo (1980): 274). I suspect it was Didymos' own (see below under **heavy-handed and abrasive**, p. 191). There is less unanimity, however, regarding the value of the judgement (see below).

they would live at peace . . . the Hellen[ic cities]: This report of the Athenian response to the King's ambassadors looks like a paraphrase of the citation from Philokhoros, given below, and it would be easy to follow Jacoby (*Text*, 531) in the view that Didymos did not consult Androtion's *Atthis* at all, but got a reference to his involvement from Anaximenes. But, given what we know about Philokhoros' dependence upon Androtion for fourth-century affairs, there is no reason to think that Didymos did not find the same sort of entry in Androtion as he later cites from Philokhoros (see Harding (1994): 178). For the significance of this response in the context of the judgement mentioned above see the note on the passage from Philokhoros (below at lines 19–23).

These matters . . . Ana]ximenes: These lines are badly preserved. The restoration adopted by D-S (with input from Wilamowitz) and followed by P-S is quite speculative and has been criticized by both Cawkwell (1963: 131 n. 1) and Harding (1976: 197–8). Cf. Osborne (162–3), Harris (1989: 38 n. 7) and Gibson (90 n. 19). It is probably safe to assume that Didymos was saying that both Androtion (*FGrHist* 324 F53) and Anaximenes (*FGrHist* 72 F28) narrated this incident, but the words following Androtion in both D-S and P-S (i.e 'who at that time proposed the motion') admit of too many alternative supplements (e.g. 'who at that time was present' or 'who at that time was in exile'; Cawkwell (1963): 131 n. 1) to form the basis for any such theory, about Androtion's involvement and subsequent exile, as that put forward by Jacoby (*Text*: 90). See Harding (1994: 13–25, 178–80). For both authors see the Introduction under Sources.

it would be better: Another potential optative, indicating a tentative preference by Didymos himself. Given a choice, Didymos will, sensibly, always prefer to cite Philokhoros in full. The text printed by P-S, following D-S, is not possible. For the correct reading see Harding (1976: 198). Cf. Osborne (164).

Lines 19–23: Philokhoros, *FGrHist* 328 F157:   The discussion of this fragment of Philokhoros' *Atthis* by Jacoby (*Text*: 531–3; *Notes*: 426–30) is fundamental. He makes several crucial points: (1) The entry must be at the very beginning of the archon year, i.e. soon after midsummer 344. This observation has changed the discussion of the chronology, as noted above. (2) The citation from Philokhoros mentions only the embassy from Artaxerxes and says nothing of a simultaneous delegation from Macedon (or anywhere else). It is a justifiable inference that Philokhoros was not, therefore, responsible for the synchronism, because Didymos would surely have quoted him, if he were (*pace* Cawkwell (1963): 124). (3) The idea of the synchronism is either to be attributed to Didymos himself or to one of his other sources, Androtion or Anaximenes. Of these possibilities, the latter is clearly preferable, and of Androtion and Anaximenes, the one with the motive, opportunity and inclination to create such a dramatic encounter was Anaximenes (cf. Sealey (1993): 172 n. 33).

asking that his ancestral *friendship* continue to exist: Friendship (*philia*), proposed by Crönert (1907: 385, who saw part of the lambda, as do I) is surely the correct reading (over [As]ian, D-S). It and the designation 'friend' (*philos*) were important tools in the administrative technique of the Persian hierarchy both in domestic and foreign relations (see in general Briant (2002): 302–54). As with many other aristocratic elites (not least the Greek, cf. Herman (1987): *passim*) the system involved gift-giving (benefactions) and reciprocal obligations. On this basis, the Great King could lay claim to 'friendship' with Athens since at least the time of Konon, if not back in the 390s, when his financial support helped fuel the Corinthian War. It is an interesting, but unanswerable, question whether the request here implied an offer of some sort (e.g. subsidies in return for military assistance against Egypt). If it did, Didymos may not be quite as guilty of illogicality, in treating a Persian 'request' as though it were a 'benefaction', as Harris suggests (1989: 39–41). This Persian practice is also not irrelevant to an evaluation of the King's attitude to the Athenian reply. What exactly was the King asking for? Philokhoros only says that he requested assurance of *philia*, but the context for his diplomacy that is described by Diodoros (16.44) was to secure military support for his invasion of Egypt. He was successful in acquiring an offer of troops from Thebes and Argos, but the Spartans and Athenians only committed themselves to neutrality, at best, and, in the Athenian case, conditional neutrality. Some modern scholars consider that neutrality was what Artaxerxes had in mind when he asked for *philia*, and that, consequently, he got what he wanted (e.g. Harris (1989): 41; Sealey (1993): 172; Buckler (1994): 104; Hajdu (2002): 281). In that case, it was the attached condition that Didymos considered 'arrogant'. Others scholars are more sensitive to the underlying implication of the request for *philia* and consider that the Athenians were being asked for their active support (e.g. Griffith (1979): 488; Osborne: 164–6). In that case, their whole response was a definite rebuff to the King.

Alternatively, the possibility should not be entirely excluded that Artaxerxes' intentions were quite different and that he was thinking

ahead to eliminating renegade principalities in Asia Minor, like
Hermias', many of whose subject cities were Greek. In that case,
the Athenian response would have sounded like a warning, which
he was entitled to take as an insult.

reply was made [to his] ambassadors at Athens: Though
the verb 'reply' is not in the passive, I have translated this way to get
around a textual problem, namely that the papyrus has the third
person singular here, i.e. 'he/it replied'. P-S assume, on no apparent basis, that the understood subject is Androtion. Osborne thinks
that 'the People' (*O ΔHMOΣ*) would be a more natural subject
to understand (166). D-S, more reasonably assuming scribal error,
suggested the verb be emended to the plural (i.e. 'they replied') by
the simple insertion of a nu before the final tau omicron. Unnecessary is Foucart's further attempt to create a subject for the verb by
emending 'at Athens' to 'Athenians'.

so long as he did not attack [the] Hellenic cities':   There
can be no doubt about the wording of the Athenian reply, since it
comes with the authority of Philokhoros. It raises important questions about Athenian policy at this time. They cannot seriously
have contemplated contesting the King's control of the Greek cities
in Asia Minor (which must be meant here); that had been conceded
in the Great King's Peace of 387/6 and not questioned thereafter
(Harding (1994): 179; *pace* Ellis (1976): 147). Yet, given the obvious
importance that the King attached to his possession of those cities,
it is difficult to see this as other than a rather provocative clause
that deserved Didymos' censure (*pace* Harris (1989): 41). No doubt
there existed at Athens a certain anti-Persian sentiment, reflected
not least in the allusions in Dem. 10.33 (cited above at col. 6.63–6).
It is usually identified with the Panhellenic movement, of which
Isokrates is often considered a proponent, that supposedly wanted
to see Greece united, maybe even under Philip, in a national cru-
sade against Persia (Bringmann (1965): 19–27; Markle (1976): 80–
99; Hornblower (1982): 217). Later, in his letter of 340, Philip would
interpret what happened at this meeting as an invitation to himself
to lead the Greeks against the King ([Dem.] 12.6). But, as elsewhere,
he is probably arrogating too much to himself (see Cawkwell (1963):
127–31) and the Panhellenic lobby may not have been as strong as
some assume. The fact is the Athenians were walking a fine line,
hoping to get Philip to revise the Peace of Philokrates into a common peace (that the idea of *epanorthosis* was originally an Athenian

initiative is maintained by Sealey (1993): 171–2). They obviously decided that it was worth risking some offence to the Great King at this time, especially since they could be sure he would be tied up in Egypt for quite a while. It was a calculated risk, but typical of the situation Athens found herself in for most of the century (Harding (1995): 105–25). In the case of Persia, it paid off; negotiations with Philip, on the other hand, failed, largely because of the machinations of Demosthenes and Hegesippos. For various views on the issues involved see the discussions in Cawkwell (1963): 127–31; Sealey (1978): 300–10; Griffith (1979): 484–95; Osborne, 166–9; Harding (1994): 178–80; Buckler (1994): 104–5; Harris (1995): 108–14.

the proposals sent down by the King were peaceful and generous: As it has been presented, the King's embassy can hardly be classified as an 'offer' (as is required by the reference in Demosthenes), let alone a generous one. Either Didymos is guilty of poor reporting or he has chosen to identify the wrong situation. This latter is argued by Harris (1989: 36–44) and is probably one of the strongest points in his vigorous attack upon Didymos' negligence (but see above under **asking that his ancestral** *friendship* . . ., p. 189). His case is somewhat undermined, however, by his inability to find any other occasion, closer to the time of the *Fourth Philippic*, when the King made any kind of overture to the Athenians.

reaction of the demos . . . heavy-handed and abrasive: That these are Didymos' own words is clear. Since they confirm and justify the controversial judgement, given above, they could be taken to substantiate the opinion that the judgement was his (cf. Osborne: 169–70). It is, however, also possible that he found the judgement in Anaximenes (as Jacoby surmised) and himself concluded that the evidence he had put forward confirmed it.

One could guess . . . :   As we have seen, this is Didymos' formula for tentatively advancing a theory of his own (cf. Osborne: 170). Unfortunately for his reputation, this particular theory finds him guilty of self-contradiction and inconsistency. The passage from the *Fourth Philippic* (10.34), which called forth the long discursus on Hermias of Atarneus (col. 4.59–6.62), makes it quite clear that Hermias had only been arrested by the time of that speech (341/0); his death either had not happened or was not known in Athens. This is the chronology that Didymos has chosen to follow. It is, then, totally inconsistent for him here to claim that Hermias had been arrested by or during the archonship of Lykiskos in 344/3 (see Harris (1989): 38).

against whom he was about to initiate [hostilities]: If we read the singular form of the verb (with both D-S and P-S, following Arnim), the subject has to be Artaxerxes. This leads Didymos into another implausibility, since in 344/3 Artaxerxes was planning his invasion of Egypt, not Macedon. The situation is hardly better if we read the plural and take the Athenians as the subject (as suggested by P-S in the apparatus to this line), since there is no hint that the Athenians were planning to make war on Philip in 344/3. Furthermore, to suggest here that the King was 'about to initiate [hostilities]' against Philip, as a result of what he had learned from Hermias, would contradict the testimony of Kallisthenes, quoted and not disputed by Didymos in col. 5.66–6.18, that Hermias revealed nothing before he died. If the text has been correctly restored, Didymos certainly seems to have nodded (Harris (1989): 38; Gibson: 119). For an attempt to defend him see Osborne (170–3).

Lines 32–8: The *lemma* is from Dem. 10.35. The text is restored on the basis of the manuscript tradition. Only two textual points are worthy of note: in line 35 the papyrus agrees with the word order exhibited by the majority of manuscripts against the order in S; in line 37 the papyrus has the totally original reading [*ΠΑΡ'*] *ΑΥΤΟΥ* in place of the *ΠΑΡΑ ΤΟΥ* of the best manuscripts (SAO) and the confused offerings of the others.

Lines 38–44: Too little remains of Didymos' note on this *lemma* to allow for meaningful comment, except to note that he correctly identified the *theorikon* (Theoric Fund) as the subject of Demosthenes' allusion. This, however, involved no feat of perspicacity on his part, since Demosthenes names that fund as his topic in the very next section of his speech (10.36), which strangely Didymos chose not to quote (cf. Gibson: 119). The short space he devoted to this passage, only six lines, hardly admits the possibility that Didymos addressed two issues that have bothered modern scholars, namely the unusual (*pace* Harris (1996): 57–76) attitude Demosthenes displays here toward the Theoric Fund and the relevance of that to the question of the authenticity of the *Fourth Philippic*. (In fact, neither of these issues seems to have attracted the attention of Alexandrian scholars, to judge from the similar silence of Dionysios of Halikarnassos, and discussion of them in antiquity only appears in the third and fourth

centuries after Christ: see Schaefer (1885–7): iii. 2.100–1. Cf. schol.
at Demosthenes 10.35. in Dilts (1983): 144.)

In the history of scholarship on fourth-century Athens the Theoric
Fund (on which see in general Buchanan (1962); cf. Harding (1985):
no. 75; to the bibliography there add Hansen (1976): 235–46; Rhodes
(1981): 514–16; Sealey (1993): 256–8; Harris (1996): 57–76; Hajdu
(2002): 292–7) has long been seen as an enervating force that contributed to Athens' defeat at Khaironeia. Not the least responsible for
this reputation is Demosthenes, who elsewhere (e.g. *First Olynthiac*
19–20; *Third Olynthiac* 10–11) treats it as an obstacle that prevented
the Athenians from mounting an adequate resistance to Philip by
funding their military (*stratiotika*). The opinion expressed here has,
consequently, caused some interesting reactions, from malicious
glee on the part of Demosthenes' critics (e.g. Mitford (1838): vii.
68, who attributes the 'change in sentiments' to 'the price of his
revived favour with the many') to embarrassment and surprise from
his admirers (e.g. Leland (1806): i. 222; Grote (1862): viii. 102, who
suggests that Demosthenes was trying to 'mediate' between the rich
and the poor). It has also been used by some as an argument against
the authenticity of the speech (not least by Schaefer (1885–7): iii.
2.100). That argument has been well reviewed by Hajdu (2002:
284–6). Others have either completely ignored it (e.g. Sealey (1993):
232–5 in his defence of authenticity, and 256–8 in his appendix on
the Theoric Fund) or deemed it quite consistent with Demosthenes'
earlier statements (Harris (1996): 57–76, who, however, overempha-
sizes the danger of social revolution in Athens; cf. Harding (1974):
282–9). In line with current opinion, we can accept that Demosthenes, like any politician, could trim his sails to suit circumstance
(cf. Harding (1987): 25–39), in this case the need to promote con-
cord (ὁμόνοια) within the state (cf. Hajdu (2002): 284–5), and, surely,
the unusualness of the opinion is the strongest argument against
forgery. But we do not have to think, like Ulpian (Dilts (1983):
153), that Demosthenes had only criticized the Theoric Fund out of
personal enmity toward Euboulos and was now free to express this
different opinion because Euboulos was dead.

**he says (that) slanders are being spoken by/against the men
. . . :** For the remainder of the sentence D-S² suggest 'the men
who are making *some innovation virtuously*'. P-S more cautiously make
no attempt at restoration. Grammatically, the noun clause could be
either the subject or the object of 'slanders are being spoken'.

Lines 44–49: The *lemma* is from Dem. 10.37. Textually it is worth noting that in several places in this passage the papyrus agrees with the reading in S (and sometimes also F) against the other manuscripts: *YMIN* in line 44 (*pace* D-S); *OYΔEIΣ* (*EΣTI*) in line 46; *EΦ' EAYTON* in line 48.

It could be that this occasion: Another tentative attempt by Didymos to identify a reference. Once again, I think we have to assume that he had no prior treatment to follow (cf. West (1970): 294). Unfortunately, once again, his identification, though not unintelligent, has not met with modern approval. West (1970: 294) is particularly harsh, when she condemns Didymos for his 'lack of historical perspective'. It is all too easy to forget that even 'modern' scholars can make errors, as she herself does on p. 289 (line 4) of her article, by writing 'Book 18' instead of 'Book 28'.

when they were humbled . . . Aigospotamoi: Even though the Peloponnesian War cost Athens dearly (see Strauss (1986): 42–69), the idea that Demosthenes' reference here was to the period after the end of the Peloponnesian War cannot be right (see especially Cawkwell (1963*b*): 61 n. 85; Hajdu (2002): 301). Osborne (175–6) is one of the few to believe that Didymos' identification is correct, though even he finds problems with it. More reasonable is the idea that Demosthenes is referring to the desperate financial situation of Athens after the Social War (358/7–355/4), on which see Schaefer ((1885–7): i. 179 ff.; (1858): iii. 2.102); Sealey (1955*b*: 74–81); Cawkwell (1963*b*: 61–5); Burke (1985: 258–9); Harding (1995: 110–13). Cf. Hajdu (2002: 301).

This will clarify (the point)/ he will make this clear: Undoubtedly, this is one form of the formula that Didymos uses to introduce a quotation from a source to confirm a theory. Either translation is possible, but the second is preferable (cf. Gibson: 91), inasmuch as it is not Didymos' usual practice to cite a passage without naming the author. In this case, two related questions arise: (1) which author did he have in mind and (2) why is the quotation left out and a space of ten lines left uninscribed?

Regarding the first question, two hypotheses are advanced. The first (P-S, following D-S²) places a punctuation point after 'clear' (cf. Gibson: 91) and assumes that Demosthenes is the subject, though without offering any suggestion for a relevant passage from his works. The other, observing that there is no punctuation point in the papyrus, prefers the suggestion that Didymos intended to name some other authority (maybe even Philokhoros), but could not find the reference he needed (Foucart (1909): 73; West (1970): 293–4). Either is possible, though the absence of the punctuation is a point in favour of the second hypothesis, in my opinion.

More interesting is the second question. Here, the issue is whether the lacuna originated with Didymos or the scribe of the papyrus. One theory (mentioned above), that is predicated upon Didymos' presumed speed of production, combined with comparable information about scholarly publication in antiquity, holds that he failed to find the quotation he wanted, and either delegated a student to find it or himself intended to return to the topic, when the errant passage came to mind. A space was left for the expected quotation, but the work was published before it was found (Foucart (1909): 37, 73; West (1970): 293–4; see also Introduction under The Scribe and his Work). The supporters of this theory argue that the papyrus is a precise copy of the original and ask us to believe that the scribe of the papyrus reproduced his original so faithfully that he included the lacuna (cf. Gibson: 120). Another theory, put forward by D-S[1] (p. xvii) and followed by Gibson (120), argues that the passage became damaged in the course of transmission and that the scribe left it out, because he could not read it, but left the space in the hope of finding another copy to take it from. This theory is essential to the argument of those who believe that the commentary, as we have it, is only an excerpt from the original, because it would not make sense for an excerptor to excerpt a lacuna (Gibson: 120), but it requires our accepting that the exemplar was damaged only at this point and in a manner that is hard to explain (cf. West (1970): 293). Neither theory is free from difficulty, but on the whole I incline toward the first (see Introduction under The Scribe and his Work).

Lines 55–8: The *lemma* is from Demosthenes 10.38. There are no significant textual issues, except that the papyrus does not elide the final alpha on *TAYTA* and *TETPAKOΣIA*, as the manuscripts do.

Concerning the fact that the Athenians . . . : No one questions that Didymos has correctly identified the fact that by the time of the Peace of Philokrates (346/5), at least, the finances of the Athenian state had improved considerably (thus confirming the hypothesis of Schaefer (1858): iii. 2.103; see now the discussion in Hajdu (2002): 304–5) and his identification has become a fundamental element in modern theories about the economic plan implemented by Euboulos after the end of the Social War in 355/4 (on which, see especially Cawkwell (1963*b*): 53–65. Cf. Burke (1984): 111–20, though his emphasis on the importance of metics to the Athenian economy rather overlooks the part played by the Athenian investor, on which see Thompson (1978): 403–23, and prominent politicians like Agyrrhios, on whom see the salutary remark of Stroud (1998): 25). It is all too easy for modern scholars to belittle their Hellenistic counterparts, especially when they make mistaken identifications, but they are not so quick to praise. In this instance, given the resources Didymos had to work with (basically, the primary texts of the ancient authors) and the conditions under which he worked (dictating his ideas and citing his sources largely from memory: cf. Introduction), it is quite amazing that he was able to pick out this obscure reference to four hundred talents in a work that would hardly be anyone's first choice for information about Athenian finances.

Theopompos in the twenty-seventh (book) of his On Philip: The fragment is no. 166 in Jacoby's *FGrHist*. It is associated with another quotation from the twenty-sixth book (*FGrHist* 115 F164), cited by Didymos in col. 14.55–15.10. Both are considered to belong to the same context, namely the debate in the Athenian Assembly about the terms of the Peace of Philokrates, that took place on the 18th and 19th of Elaphebolion 346 (see Shrimpton (1991): 84–5; Sealey (1993): 147).

Arist[o]phon, the demagogue: Aristophon, son of Aristophanes, of Azenia (*APF* no. 2108) was truly one of the grand old men of Athenian fourth-century politics. He was born *c*.430, lived for ninety-nine years and four months (schol. to Aiskh. 1.64), and died somewhere between 340/39 (*IG* II² 1533.11) and 330 (Dem. 18.162; Aiskh. 3.139). He is represented as boasting that he had survived prosecution for unconstitutional proposals (*graphe paranomon*) seventy-five times (Aiskh. 3.194). He may have been the only Athenian politician still alive in 346/5 who could claim to have participated in the restoration of the democracy in 404/3 (Dem. 20.148). Though we hear little or nothing of him for the next forty years, this does not mean that he was in retirement (see Whitehead (1986): 313–19). He was most active politically from the late 360s to *c*.350 (Plut. *Mor.* 844d), during which time he appeared to be close to Khares and, in the latter years, opposed to Euboulos. Ideologically, he is hard to characterize, but he certainly was the leader of a faction (see Sealey (1955): 74–81; Harding (1976): 193–4). Apart from this citation by Didymos we would have had no reason to guess that he participated in this debate over the Peace of Philokrates, where he is the only named politician known to have spoken in opposition (Sealey (1993): 147). This is another reminder of the inadequate state of our evidence (cf. Stroud (1998): 16–25, for the recent discovery of an inscription that shows that Agyrrhios, a politician whose career had been thought to terminate in the early 380s, was still active in 374/3).

is introduced **speaking the following (words) to it/him (them?):** The text here is restored, based largely upon column 14.57–8, where it looks as though the same introductory formula is used. The only obstacle arises with the word 'to it/him', which lacks a reference. The later passage has the plural 'to them' (i.e. the Athenians), which makes good sense. I suspect scribal error and that the plural is the correct reading here, too.

Column 8 line 64 to column 9 line 9: 'Consider that . . . Macedonians: It is hardly likely that Theopompos was able, or would even have bothered, to access the original text of this speech, or that of Philokrates, that he included in his twenty-sixth book (see col. 14.55–15.10). The style of the two speeches is similar enough and the arguments so contrary (Philokrates arguing in accord with the present realities of the situation, Aristophon invoking Amphipolis, the pipe-dream of Athens' past) that the conclusion must be that Theopompos created them himself as an antilogy (cf. Shrimpton (1991): 84–5).

COLUMN NINE

Heading: The heading looks ahead to the *lemma* from Dem. 10.70, which begins at line 38.

Lines 9–15: 'But where does the matter make (them) sore . . . : The *lemma* is from Dem. 10.44. It is not indicated by a heading, though it could be considered to be a continuation of the previous discussion, since it provides the reason for the discontent of the rich to balance the concerns of the poor that Demosthenes has described in 10.38–42.

Textually, in line 11 the papyrus has the same form of the verb 'carrying over' ($\Delta IABIBAZONTA\Sigma$) as manuscript S against that found in the other manuscripts. In this case Didymos and S are probably in error (see Hajdu (2002): 324).

Lines 15–31: Didymos here attempts to explicate Demosthenes' contorted logic. He recasts the argument in his own words, much as he did in his note on 'hyperbatic phrasing'. He shows, at least, that he understood the thrust of what Demosthenes was saying (so, also, with reservation, Hajdu (2002): 322–3).

The text I have adopted is, for the most part, that of P-S. Besides minor points (like $TOIOYTO$ for $TOIOYTON$ in line 20), it disagrees in only one major respect with that proposed by D-S. In line 20 for 'so much property (as was) public, that which truly belonged to the people . . . .' D-S² suggest 'so much public property ⟨as was surplus⟩, that which truly belonged to the people'. The supplement is not justified and was not in their earlier text (D-S¹), which has the same as in P-S.

The situation is different in the case of lines 22–3. There are so many difficulties there that no proposed restoration makes sense. As a result I have chosen to leave the key spaces blank. D-S¹ originally tried 'but they devised some lawsuits against (reading $KATA$ for KAI) the not-just, accusing . . .' but changed their minds in D-S² and offered 'but they (the demagogues) devised some tricky schemes against the (allegedly) "unjust" charging . . .' (trans. Gibson: 91, who adopts this restoration). The latter seems to me most implausible, but the alternative suggestion by P-S ('but they made plans against the private resources even of the "unjust"') has rightly been dubbed 'unverständlich' by Wankel (1987: 221). I have a certain fondness for the original proposal of D-S ('devised some lawsuits'), but the reading 'and' (KAI) instead of 'against' ($KATA$) is clear and would have to be emended. The real problem is the meaning and the reference of the expression 'the not-just'. See the discussion in Gibson (121).

Lines 31 (end)–37: Didymos clearly continues on the same topic (*pace* D-S² who think he might now be commenting on 10.45), since the next *lemma* begins at line 38, but the text is so mutilated that his point cannot be recovered. It does, however, appear that he is treating the 'speaker' ($\lambda\acute{\epsilon}\gamma\omega\nu$) of Demosthenes, which is clearly referring to the 'politician' (*rhetor*) in the Assembly, as though it meant the prosecutor of the property of the wealthy in court (see Hajdu (2002):

324–6). The most ambitious attempt at restoration is by D-S[1] (following Wilamowitz), who propose 'These things (this) kept happening *to such an extent* [that] it provided great security [and] *great* powers *to those who were proposing* these policies . . . .' for lines 31–4, but even they gave up after that. Subsequently, in D-S[2], they withdrew '*to such an extent* [that]', on the basis of letters that they thought they saw, but which are apparent to neither P-S nor myself. In lines 36–7 Arnim (in the Supplement to D-S[2]) is reported to have proposed '[to be necessary] *for a revision* of the *policy* [concerning the theorika]', but this is wishful thinking.

'And yet, invective apart, if someone . . . insecure . . ."': The *lemma* is from 10.70. Didymos does not finish the sentence, which continues '. . . full of lawsuits and troubles day by day, (why) do you choose the life embroiled in danger, rather than the life of ease?' The invective (*loidoria*), for such it is, continues through to section 74. It is well discussed by Hajdu (2002: 426–42). This is the last passage from the *Fourth Philippic* that Didymos selects for comment. The name of the person under attack has been restored here from the manuscript text, but is fully confirmed by the later references to it in the papyrus. Clearly Didymos' text read the correct name, Aristomedes, in agreement with manuscripts S and A (*pace* Gibson: 121) against the obvious, but pervasive, corruption, Aristodemos (see the similar confusion of the names in Buckler (1994): 108), that is preserved in all other manuscripts and was the standard reading in texts published before Bekker's Oxford edition of 1823. On the morphology of the name see Hajdu (2002: 429). On the other hand, the disposition of words at the beginning of the quotation differs from that in S, which is preferred by most modern editors (see Hajdu (2002): 427–8).

There are two Aristomed[e]s: Didymos' concern is to identify the person named; he is not interested in the relevance of this passage to the question of the authenticity of the *Fourth Philippic*. This is obviously because its authenticity was not an issue for him. Modern scholars, however, have objected to this passage, since it indulges in personal abuse of a named individual, a practice which can be found throughout Demosthenes' speeches for the law courts (cf. Harding (1994*b*): 196–221), but which was said to be absent from his *Philippics* (Plut. *Mor.* 810c–d) and even against the law (Aiskh. 1.35). The first objection is dismissed by Sealey (1993: 233), though his argumentation may appear rather inconclusive to some (e.g. Gibson: 121). A better treatment of the whole issue is offered by Hajdu (2002: 426–7), who also refutes the objection.

[one], the Phe[r]aian, who fought ... against Philip: Aristomedes of Pherai (Berve (1925–6): no. 128) is best known from his activities in opposition to Philip's son, Alexander (see below), but the testimony Didymos invokes here provides the evidence for the inference that he had joined the Persian forces by, at least, 340 (cf. Parke (1933): 199; Griffith (1979): 524 n. 6, 525; Bosworth (1980): 222) and was probably one of those mercenaries who responded to the Great King's call and went to the defence of Perinthos (Diod. 16.75.1–2; cf. Foucart (1909): 127).

***others* have discoursed and in particular:**   This well-known formula is a rather suggestive indication that Didymos only found the two references that follow.

Ph[il]ip himself in his letter to (the) [A]the[n]ians: There is no reference to an Aristomedes in the extant *Letter to the Athenians*, speech 12 in our corpus. But, then, Didymos does not offer any commentary on that letter. In fact, he ignores it altogether and passes from speech 11 (by our numbering) to our speech 13. This might suggest that speech 12, which is only carried by half (F and Y) of the main manuscripts (S and A do not have it), might be a forgery. The present position of modern scholars, however, holds that it might well be an authentic document from Philip, though not the one referred to here, i.e. he knew of a different letter (see Wüst (1938): 133–6; Griffith (1979): 714–16; Sealey (1993): 239–40; Gibson: 121–2, 131–2; cf. the note on col. 1 at **had heard [the letter]**, p. 114). Whatever is the case, once again we find that Didymos' text agrees with the tradition represented by S (and A).

Theo[pompos] in the forty-eighth (book) of his <u>Concerning Philip</u>:   *FGrHist* 115 F222. We do not know whether Theopompos called his work on Philip *The Philippika* or *The Philippic Histories* at the outset (for this dispute see Jacoby, *FGrHist* 2b Commentary, p. 358; Flower (1994): 29 n. 18), or whether these just became standard ways of referring to this work later in the lexicographic and encyclopaedic tradition (e.g. in authors like Harpokration, Photios, or Stephanos of Byzantion). In any case, earlier authors like Polybios and Diodoros felt at liberty to use different titles. Similarly, Didymos has his own preferred way of referring to that work, namely that used above. His consistent and often idiosyncratic way of referencing his sources is a clear sign to me that he is responsible for his own citations and is not taking them from some earlier compilation.

As Foucart (1909: 127) noted, the only other fragment that is specifically cited from this book (*FGrHist* 115 F221) is a reference to a tribe in Thrace. This may substantiate the supposition (probable in any case) that book forty-eight continued the account of Philip's campaign against Perinthos and Byzantion in 340/39, that began in book forty-seven (*FGrHist* 115 F217; cf. Shrimpton (1991): 63).

after campaigning against Alexander . . . Darius' side: This is a reference to the manoeuvring that led to the battle of Issos (late in 333), at which we can be sure Aristomedes was present in command of 20,000 infantry on the Persian left wing (Curtius 3.9.3). Arrian (*Anab.* 2.13.2–3) mentions him amongst those mercenaries (the others were Amyntas, Thymondas, and Bianor) who fled with Darius to Thapsakos after the defeat (cf. Bosworth (1980): 222–3). Darius is, of course, the third, not the second, as he is incorrectly referred to in Gibson (121).

he ran away to Kypros: Arrian reports that 8,000 troops escaped with Darius (not 4,000 as incorrectly in Gibson: 122), but only 4,000 are recorded in our other sources (Diod. 17.48.2 and Curt. 4.1.27) as going on to Kypros (and thence to Egypt) under the leadership of Amyntas. The citation from Anaximenes here makes it certain that Aristomedes, at least, accompanied Amyntas to Kypros. This has led most modern commentators to conclude that all 8,000 mercenaries went to Kypros, but that the force split up there, some (4,000) going with Amyntas to Egypt, the others going independently to Crete (cf. Parke (1933): 199; Badian (1961): 25; Bosworth (1980): 223; contra, Heckel (1984): 272 n. 58). At any rate, we hear nothing more of Aristomedes.

Anaximenes in the ninth (book) of his On Alexander: *FGrHist* 72 F17. For this author see the Introduction under Sources. It is unlikely that the book number is correct. The two other fragments we have from this work are from books one and two; the latter belongs in 335/4. Jacoby prefers to emend the book number to five (*FGrHist* 2c p. 109). Didymos turns to Anaximenes for this detail because, of course, Theopompos, his preferred source for Philip, did not cover the career of Alexander (cf. Milns (1994): 85).

And the other one . . . an Athenian, nicknamed the Brazen: After gratuitously showing off his knowledge about Aristomedes of Pherai, Didymos turns to the identification of the real object of Demosthenes' attack. He was helped in this by Demosthenes himself, who in 10.73 elaborates on the character of the individual and calls him a 'thief'. But it is Didymos who makes the connection between this person and the character referred to as 'the Brazen', for his thievery, in a speech by Deinarkhos and in two comedies. In so doing, he provides us with several new fragments of known works and one new title. The connection is confirmed by Plutarch in his *Life of Demosthenes* 11.6, where we find both ideas combined. This does not mean, of course, that the person was a thief by trade, as Gibson seems to conclude (122), since he was clearly a politician; such charges were common in Athenian political rhetoric, often without basis, especially when they are introduced by a feigned denial of *loidoria*, as here (cf. Harding (1994*b*): 196–221). Two further questions arise: What is the point of the nickname 'Brazen' and who was this person?

The word 'brazen' (ΧΑΛΚΟΥΣ) signified to a Greek either 'cheap', 'low-class', 'base' (as in the famous analogy of coins to citizens/politicians in Aristophanes, *Frogs* 718–37), or 'hard', 'tough' (as in Didymos' own nickname, Khalkenteros, 'Brazen-guts'). Either or both of these connotations can be intended in this case. As indicated above, the usual approach has been to consider that the epithet belonged to a thief (e.g. Osborne: 182; Gibson: 122, who writes of a 'well-known thief who is nicknamed "Brazen"'). This can lead to an interpretation as unlikely as that proposed by Page (1941: 238–9), who suggested that the nickname meant 'Farthing' (a reference, rapidly becoming equally obscure, to the smallest denomination of English coinage that has long been out of circulation) and carried the connotation that Aristomedes was a thief, who would steal even the smallest coin from his victims. But, if we start, as I believe we must, because of the corroboration from Plutarch, with the assumption that Didymos has made the correct connection, then Aristomedes was first and foremost a politician (as is recognized by Davies, *APF* no. 2108) and, while politicians can be (and frequently are) called thieves, thieves only become politicians in the comic theatre (like the sausage-seller in Aristophanes' *Knights*). So, Aristomedes acquired his nickname in his political career (reflecting, perhaps, the standard charge that he was of noncitizen origin) and this, combined with the equally standard charge that he was dipping into the public purse, was exaggerated by the comic playwrights into his role as a professional thief.

The more important question concerns the identity of this individual. Given that we know the names of more Athenian politicians, major and minor, from the fourth century than from any other period of Greek history, and given that Aristomedes, though not unfamiliar, is not the most popular of Athenian names (there are fifteen listed in *LGPN* 59, only five of whom were active in the fourth century) and given, finally, that this person cannot have been totally insignificant to have received such a personal assault from Demosthenes, it would be surprising if we could not identify him. But such seems to be the case.

The one obvious candidate is Aristomedes, son of Aristophon of Azenia (see above under **Arist[o]phon, the demagogue**, p. 196). Given Aristophon's birthdate of *c*.430, all his three sons could have been born by 400 and become politically active by *c*.370, and one, Damostratos, was (he was an Athenian ambassador already in 371, Xen. *Hell.* 6.3.2). But they could also have been born later. Aristomedes himself is first attested as owing poles (*kontous*) from his service as syntrierarch (with Timotheos, son of Konon) on the trireme *Eunoia*, in a naval record from 356 (*IG* II² 1612.289). He also served on the *boule*, as the representative of his tribe, Hippothontis, some time before 350 (*IG* II² 2377.14). The remaining evidence for his political activity would be that collected here, which is not precisely datable, that is, if he is the same person. The strongest arguments for this identification are his name (but without demotic and patronymic that is a dangerous criterion, see Thompson (1974): 144–9), his age (Demosthenes treats his victim as a rather inexperienced neophyte), and his background (he comes from a family with a reputation that is of at least two generations' standing). The arguments against are considered even stronger by Davies (*APF* no. 2108). They are that in Dem. 10.73 his father is treated as dead (in 341/40 Aristophon was surely still alive) and spoken about as though he had no independent reputation in public life (Aristophon's career was distinguished and, incidentally, elsewhere respected by Demosthenes, cf. 18.70, 162, 219; 19.291, 297; 20.146, 148; 24.11).

On the other hand, Körte's suggestion (1905: 400), cited without disagreement by Davies (*APF* no. 2108), that the person referred to could be an unknown Aristomedes from Kollytos, whose only recorded activity was to be an arbitrator (*diaitetes*) in 330/29 (*IG* II² 1924.9), hardly a sign of political ambition or activity (see Arist. *Ath. Pol.* 53.4), is desperate and does not in any way suit the context (*pace* Hajdu (2002): 438, who points out that there is a Khairestratos from

Kollytos, mentioned in *IG* II² 1541.3, who could be the uncle in the passage from Deinarkhos). More interesting is Aristomedes, son of Meton, of Leukonoion, recently revealed as a *bouleutes* in 371 (*SEG* 28, 148.29; *AO* 250). If his father was the great astronomer, as seems likely, then he had the distinguished background, was dead, and was memorably depicted as a charlatan by Aristophanes in *Birds* (992–1020). Not to be overlooked, however, is Hajdu's suggestion that Demosthenes' account of Aristomedes' ancestry has a hypothetical appearance and that it may have been created as an ironic backdrop to Aristomedes' own career (2002: 436–9).

Deinarkhos in the <u>Defence of Dokimos: Concerning the Horse:</u> This speech is otherwise unrecorded, although there are two references to a speech by Deinarkhos, *Concerning the Horse* (Dion. Hal. *Din.* 12) and one to a speech *Against Antiphanes: Concerning the Horse* (Harpokration, s.v. *OXEION*), which are probably to the same speech (cf. Dover (1968): 17; Worthington (1992): 81). This passage is now listed as frs. LXXI–LXXII no.4 in the Teubner text, ed. Conomis. The speech might belong in the 340s or 330s (Worthington (1992): 81), if Dokimos of Erkhia (*APF* no. 4532) is the defendant, for whom Deinarkhos wrote (Worthington (1992): 81). The names Antiphanes and Khairestratos are both too common to make identification possible (see *LGPN* 38–9 for Antiphanes and 470 for Khairestratos), though see the suggestion about Khairestratos mentioned in the note above.

Since you were induced: Gibson (92) follows Wankel (1987: 221) in changing the verb from the second person to the third ('he was induced'), as was originally suggested by the first editors (D-S¹). This certainly reads better and may be right, but, given the habit of ancient orators to apostrophize their opponents in the second person and given that we are totally ignorant of the context of this passage, P-S may be correct to preserve and defend the reading of the papyrus, which is, after all, the *lectio difficilior*.

And at that time also for one (of them) he brought a suit . . . : Gibson (123) takes the reference of 'one (of them)' to be Khairestratos, following Wankel (1987: 221), who is in turn following D-S² (supplementum, p. 55). Once again, this may be correct, but lacking the context, it is not possible to be confident. I see no need to delete the *KAI* ('also') as Blass suggested.

Philemon in <u>Sculptor:</u> For Philemon see the Introduction under Sources. In the spelling of his name the scribe missed out the iota between phi and lambda. His play the *Sculptor* is otherwise unknown. This is the only fragment. It can be found in Page (1941: 238–9, with translation), in Edmonds (vol. iiiA (1961) no. 40A, 21–3, with translation), in Austin (1973: F206) and in Kassel-Austin (*PCG* vol. vii F41). The plot can hardly be guessed at. A date of 341 has been suggested (Wagner (1905): 27); 326 has also been proposed (Edmonds, vol. iiiA (1961): 23). The humour in this passage is self-evident. Gibson (123) draws a comparison with the story of the man who, not knowing to whom he was speaking, asked Aristeides to write his own name on an ostrakon (Plut. *Arist.* 7.5–6). The text of line 66 has an intrusive theta between 'I asked' and 'Aristomedes.'

Timokles in Heroes: For the author see the Introduction under Sources. This fragment is no. 222a in Austin (1973: 217–18). We have two other fragments of this play, both from Athenaios (6.224a–b and 10.455f). All three can be found together in Edmonds (vol. ii (1959): 610–12), Kassel-Austin (*PCG* vol. vii, Timokles, FF12–14, of which this is the last). Fragment 12 is addressed to a person, who has been the object of Demosthenes' anger. Demosthenes, himself, is depicted as Briareus, the hundred-handed monster; he consumes catapults and spearheads and is looking for a fight. This is typical of Timokles' humour. Athenaios (6.233d) cites the passage, along with a number of others, in the context of Aiskhines' attack (3.83) on Demosthenes for always finding fault with everything Philip did, not least when he offered to *give* Halonnesos to Athens and Demosthenes objected that he should be *giving it back* (see Wankel (1976): 410). This suggests a date for the play between 343 and 341. The reference to Aristomedes in our passage (F14) fits well into that context, since the only mention we have of his participation in the major political issues of the period is this reference to him in the *Fourth Philippic* of 341/0. But, whilst the topical reference to contemporary politics may be reasonably inferred, the overall theme of the play is unknown, though Edmonds sets this scene in the Underworld and makes Charon the speaker (vol. ii (1959): 612).

Hermes, the son of Maia . . . : D-S¹ originally put in their apparatus Wilamowitz's suggestion *Δ[P]OMAIΩΣ* ('on the run') for 'the son of Maia', but later (D-S²) adopted Buecheler's reading of *Δ[E]OMAIAΣ*, which P-S and all others print as *Δ' O MAIAΣ*. Nothing is legible in the space where the unnecessary [*E*] is imagined, and I do not think there is a need to read a letter there.

More felicitous is Wilamowitz's proposal ('aids in conducting') to emend the last word of the line, where the papyrus reading is unattested and incomprehensible, and it (or the alternate form with similar meaning suggested by Körte (1905): 411) is accepted by all editors. Hermes is, of course, most appropriate here, because he was the god of thieves, being himself the archetypal thief, as he is depicted in the fourth *Homeric Hymn*.

COLUMN TEN

Heading: The heading looks ahead to line 13 of column 10, where Didymos begins his discussion of the date and authenticity of speech 11.

If he is favourable: The reading of the papyrus at this point (*ANTIΠ[P]OΘYMΩΣ*) strains credulity in sense and transgresses the normal conventions of comic verse that does not lengthen a short vowel before the letters πρ (see P-S, p. x). Only Page (1941: 240–1) has retained it and translates 'an eager enemy'. All others follow Wilamowitz's emendation (adopted here), which must mean 'if he is favourable' (*pace* Gibson: 92, who translates 'however he wishes').

as | A real favour to Ar[i]stomedes: After the verb meaning 'as a favour' the papyrus has the particle *ΓAP* ('for'), which is unacceptable for several reasons: meaning, word order, and metre. The correction to *ΓE* (which I take to be intensive and translate as 'real', although it is possible, I suppose, that it is restrictive and means 'at least') was made by Blass (1906: 291).

the Fair: This epithet for Aristomedes might suggest that he is an object of desire and, therefore, still young.

prevent Satyros | Calling him a thief: It is usual to identify Satyros with the famous comic actor (on whom see Dem. 19.192; Aiskh. 2.156; MacDowell (2000): 286). It would be very appropriate, should that be correct, since Demosthenes obviously was close to Satyros (cf. Dem. 19.192; Plut. *Dem.* 7). That being the case, it is not stretching things too far to imagine that at some point Satyros was cast in the role of Demosthenes (or some character representing him, like Briareus) on the stage (maybe even in this play) and was assigned this attack on Aristomedes, right out of the orator's mouth, so to speak.

Also in <u>Ikarians</u> (he says): Timokles' play the *Ikarians* or the *Ikarian Satyrs* was already known from four other fragments; this fragment adds a fifth (see Edmonds, vol. ii (1959): 612–19; *PCG* vii. 766–9, Timokles FF15–18. Cf. Page (1941): 240–3; Austin (1973): 218 F222b). All five fragments are replete with topical abuse of contemporary persons, not least Hypereides, the orator (see Whitehead (2000): 11), who was put to death in 322; Pythionike, the famous courtesan and mistress of Harpalos, who died in 326; and Thoudippos, the oligarch eliminated by Phokion in 318. These references suggest a date for the play before 326 (see Edmonds, vol. ii (1959): 613 n. f and 615 n. d; Whitehead (2000): 11 n. 42). The frequency of abuse supports the conclusion of Constantinides (1969: 49–61, whose article is still fundamental for this play and Timokles, in general), that the *Ikarians* or *Ikarian Satyrs* is a comedy, not a satyr play. Constantinides subscribes to the view that the play took its name from the Attic deme Ikaria. She does not, however, venture any suggestions about its plot or theme.

Autokles: Edmonds (vol. ii (1959): 615 n. c) suggests that this might be Autokles, son of Strombikhides, of Euonymon (*APF* no. 4386), who was ambassador to Sparta in 371 (Xen. *Hell.* 6.3.2, 7), was general in 368/7 (Diod. 15.71.3) and again in Thrace in 362/1 (Dem. 23.104), whence he was recalled and prosecuted for *prodosia* (Trevett (1992): 131–3) in a trial, for which one of the speeches was probably composed by Hypereides (Whitehead (2000): 10 n. 38). This identification would add some spice to the implication here that he was flayed and 'pinned to the wall', but at the presumed date of this play that incident would have been old news and the son of Strombikhides would have been over seventy years old. The name is not uncommon (see *LGPN* 80) and identification without patronymic and demotic is not safe. Constantinides (1969: 59–60) equates him with Autokleides, a homosexual character in another play by Timokles, the *Orestautokleides*, and suspects a crude joke.

'Marsyas, the flute-lover' . . . furnace: The mythical satyr, Marsyas, who challenged Apollo to a competition in music, lost, and was flayed alive for his audacity, should need no introduction, but the story can be found in Ovid, *Met.* 6.382–400 and Apollodoros, *Bibl.* 1.4.2. Herodotos (7.26) says that his flayed hide was hung in the market place in Kelainai in Phrygia. This is the backdrop to the joke 'pinned to the furnace', which is at the same time an allusion to the practice of blacksmiths of pinning a doll or dummy on their furnaces to ward off bad luck (Pollux 7.108; cf. Page (1941): 241). 'Flayed' may also have a crude meaning (see Page (1941): 240), suggesting that he was 'circumcised' or 'erect' (not 'bald' as in Gibson: 123; for the meaning of $\Psi\Omega\Lambda O\Sigma$ see Dunbar (1995): 347). This possibility would fit well with the view of Constantinides that Autokles/Autokleides was a notorious homosexual.

Aristomedes (is) Tereus ... scratching your head: The story of Tereus and his wife Prokne, their son Itys, and Prokne's sister Philomela was the subject of a (lost) tragedy, *Tereus*, by Sophokles and, since the three adults were turned into birds, provided material for Aristophanes in his play *Birds*, where Tereus has become the respectable Hoopoe (see Dunbar (1995): 139–42 for full details). It is also recounted by Ovid, *Met.* 6.424–674. Its themes of rape, mutilation and child cannibalism hardly seem suited to a character, Aristomedes, whose only crime is theft, but it is introduced largely to support two puns. Tereus' name suggest the Greek word $TEPEIN$ ('to keep watch', here 'to be terribly careful') and Prokne's can, at a stretch, be translated as 'she scratches at the front', setting up a pun with the word $KN\Omega MENO\Sigma$ ('scratching your head') in the next clause.

If you lose (them): This is the reading of D-S. P-S suggest an indefinite relative clause here, 'whatever she loses', but this is rejected by Wankel as 'an incomprehensible alteration' (1987: 221; cf. Gibson: 93, though his translation 'would' for AN and the subjunctive is wide of the mark).

The conclusion of this discussion is marked by a *paragraphos*, topped by a *coronis* and adorned with flourishes. There follows a space of a few lines.

Line 12: (Speech) 11: Didymos has completed his observations on the *Fourth Philippic* and now turns his attention to the eleventh speech (in his collection, I believe (*pace* Gibson: 103), and also in ours), the *Reply to the Letter of Philip*.

'So, men of Athens, that Philip ...': The *lemma* is Dem. 11.1. Didymos begins his discussion of this speech by quoting the opening lines, even though he will not be commenting directly on them right away. This is similar to his introduction of speech 10 (*Fourth*

Philippic) in col. 1.27. Further down (line 32), when he turns to this passage for specific comment, he quotes it again.

Textual note: in two places in line 14 Didymos' text differs from the vulgate reading and sides with manuscript S: 'peace with us', instead of 'you' and 'put off' (aorist) instead of 'kept putting off' (imperfect).

Lines 15–24: The circumstances of the speech . . . war *against* **them:** As with speech 10, so now, Didymos' first concern is to date the speech. This engages him until col. 11.7, after which he moves on to the question of authenticity (for the possibility that he did this also for speech 10 see Milns (1994): 87 n. 35). He employs his usual method (and, no doubt, that of any predecessors he might have had) of deducing observations of his own from the text and supplementing those with citations from his wide reading knowledge in primary sources, with occasional reference to issues raised in secondary literature (i.e. 'some say . . .'). In this case, his initial observation is unexceptionable, namely that the tone of the speech shows that war has already broken out between Philip and Athens. He then sets out to substantiate that observation, by quoting a passage from Philip's letter to the Athenians, to which this speech was a reply.

at the *end* **of his** *letter***:** The passage that follows can be found in essence at [Dem.] 12.23. The sense is virtually identical as are some key items of vocabulary, but there are differences (the tone is more forceful in Didymos' text) that are often considered significant (see above on col. 1. **had heard [the letter]**, p. 114). The differences, in themselves, are not in my mind sufficient to prove the contention that Didymos had a copy of a different letter, but that view is substantiated by other points of disagreement, noted elsewhere (see above and at col. 9.46–7 **Ph[il]ip himself in his letter . . .**, p. 200. The similarities are more troublesome, since they involve accepting that Philip (if both letters were, as is argued, by Philip) ended two letters with a concluding paragraph that contained almost identical points and much similar vocabulary.

Lines 27–30: exerting yourselves . . . former [. . .]: Unfortunately, at the point where it appears that the text departs most extensively from that in [Dem.] 12.23 (which only has 'since you are doing me as much harm as you can'), the papyrus is most corrupt. Some suggested restorations are: 'exerting yourselves *to the end* *that* you [might] *take* me *by war*, (me) *your* former [benefactor]' (P-S, following Crönert (1907*b*): 268); 'exerting yourselves *to do* me [. . .] *harm*, me *your* former [benefactor]' (Blass ap. P-S, supplementum); 'exerting yourselves . . . and the *others who are making war on* me, *your* former [allies]' (Foucart (1909): 93).

shall defend myself [. . .]:   In the space P-S follow D-S in reading 'by every means'.

Lines 30–4:   Textual note: the scribe hit a bad spot here, three times needing to insert (or have inserted by someone else) above the line letters that he had missed: an abbreviated syllable in the middle of 'marshalling my forces against' (30), a letter in the middle of 'make' peace (32), and the final syllable of 'put off' (33).

And [. . .] of his counsel: P-S follow D-S here (surely correctly) in restoring 'he makes a beginning' in the seven-letter space. Gibson (93) translates 'counsel' (*symboule*) as 'deliberative speech' and treats it as a technical term (124). I think this is unnecessary. Demosthenes took on the role of counsellor (*symboulos*) as his political *persona* (Harding (1987): 36) and, therefore, it is very appropriate for Didymos to use *symboule* to denote the content rather than the technical classification of this speech. Of course, speeches 1–16 in the corpus are *symbouleutic* (addresses to the *demos* on issues of policy), but the important point is that the *Philippics* are treated as a subset within that classification. In this context, whilst modern scholars reserve the designation *Philippic* for only four speeches, ancient scholars, like Didymos, cast their net wider, including speeches 1–11, at least, under that term. Some of Didymos' predecessors even considered Dem. 13 (*On Organization*) as a *Philippic* (see col. 13.16–18. Cf. Dover (1968): 7). Didymos' repetition of the introductory lines of the speech is not redundant, but is called for because he will now comment on the specific reference to 'war'.

a match was put to the war: The tense is aorist, not perfect as in Gibson (93). The verb, which means to 'set on fire', is a not unexpected metaphor for starting a war and is used elsewhere (most famously by Aristophanes at *Peace* 609–10. Cf. Strabo 9.3.8 C420), but any metaphorical language may support D-S's view that Didymos had literary pretensions. In col. 1.66–2.2 (see note there, pp. 113–15) Didymos has already established the date when war was declared (in the archonship of Theophrastos, 340/39), so he now focuses his attention on the immediate cause, which he believes was the seizure of the Athenian grain ships. In this he was surely guided by his further reading in Demosthenes, who, though he did not make that claim in this speech, later stated memorably to Aiskhines in *On the Crown* (18.72), 'And, in truth, it was *he* who broke the peace by seizing the ships, not the city, Aiskhines' (cf. 18.139). Unfortunately, Diodoros, who was surely using the fourth-century historian Ephoros, does not even mention the seizure of the ships and made the siege of Byzantion the occasion for Athens' declaration of war (Diod. 16.77.2; cf. Griffith (1979): 577 n. 1). As is to be expected, modern scholars are similarly divided on the issue; some follow Didymos (e.g. Ellis (1976): 179–80; Wankel (1976): 439–43; Griffith (1979): 574–8; Sealey (1993): 187–90; Hammond (1994): 132; Ryder (2000): 79), others Diodoros/Ephoros (e.g. Jacoby, *Text*: 537–9; Cawkwell (1978): 136–8), while Buckler (1996: 87–9) argues unconvincingly, without even referring to this passage, that Philip had declared war before he wrote his letter.

M[a]cedonian [. . .] on the one hand . . . : There is little doubt about the essential meaning here, but the specific restoration of the six to seven missing letters is not agreed upon. Two suggestions have been made. D-S do not punctuate and propose '[both through], on the one hand, all the other ways Philip committed offences ⟨regarding⟩ the Athenians, whilst (he was) pretending to live in peace, and, in particular, his expedition against Byza[n]tion and Perinthos.' The problem with this is that the nominative 'his expedition' has no verb, unless we accept D-S's assumption that there was a lacuna following, in which some such words as 'stirred them up' should be supplied, as Blass suggested (D-S² p. 24). P-S avoid this problem by punctuating after 'M[a]cedonian' and begin a new sentence with 'stirred up': '[For], on the one hand, both all the other offences Philip had committed, whilst (he was) pretending to live in peace, [stirred up] the Athenians and, in particular, his expedition against Byza[n]tion and Perinthos' (i.e. stirred them up).

all the others ways Philip offended the Athenians: The list of Athenian grievances against Philip for his actions against their interests after the Peace of Philokrates (346/5) was long and included his taking of Halonnesos, his meddling in Euboia and, in particular in this context, his expansion into Thrace and the Khersonese. The best account of all these events is in Griffith (1979: 489–584). See also Sealey (1993: 170–93).

expedition against Byza[n]tion and Perinthos: For Philip's siege of Perinthos, thwarted by the stubborn resistance of the Perinthians with assistance from Byzantion and the local satraps of the Persian Empire, and the subsequent siege of Byzantion, broken eventually by the arrival of an Athenian fleet under the command of Phokion and Kephisophon (on whom see notes on col. 1.17, 20), the main ancient narrative is in Diod. 16.74.2–77.3, who was surely following Ephoros up to 16.76.4. See also Dem. 18.87–94; Plut. *Phokion* 14. Cf. Harding (1985): no. 95, to which add Sealey (1993): 187–90 and Hammond (1994): 131–4.

These cities he was anxious to bring back to his side: Byzantion (Dem. 9.34; 18.87) and probably Perinthos (schol. Aiskh. 2.81) had formal treaties of alliance with Philip, but both had been driven to reconsider them as a result of the consequences of Philip's successful last push to eliminate Kersebleptes and other minor Thracian kings in 342–340 (cf. Diod. 16.71.1–2), possibly because he was getting too close (cf. Griffith (1979): 563–4). For a different view, more sympathetic to Philip, see Cawkwell (1978: 117–18).

deprive the Athenians of their grain supply: The importance of Black Sea grain to Athens' ability to maintain an independent foreign policy was still considerable in the fourth century (see Harding (1988): 67–8; (1995): 108; *pace* Cawkwell (1978): 138).

not have coastal cities that were providing bases for their fleet: This is a strange comment, if the implication is that Perinthos and Byzantion were providing bases for the Athenians, since neither of them had been cooperating with Athens or its fleet since the time of the Social War (cf. Cargill (1981): 180). It was Philip's attack upon them that forced Byzantion, certainly (cf. Dem. 18.302), and Perinthos, probably, back into alliance with Athens, not the other way round.

It would be an obtuse reading of the Greek to take the subject of this second reason as the Byzantians and the Perinthians, even though this would produce a more cogent argument, since one of Philip's complaints in his letter to the Athenians ([12].2) implied that the Byzantians were acting in collaboration with (and probably as) pirates against him (cf. Griffith (1979): 563).

committed [his] greatest transgression by seizing the merchants' ships: See above under **a match was put to the war** (p. 210). The view that this was Philip's 'greatest transgression' is either Didymos' own contribution or came from Theopompos. It does not suit Philokhoros' more restrained narrative (cf. Jacoby, *Text*: 537).

that were at Hieron: Hieron was obviously a key link in the transportation of grain from the Crimea to Greece (Dem. 35.10; 50.17). It was situated on the Asiatic side of the Bosporos (cf. Polybios, 4.50.2), north of Khalkedon, about seven miles from the entrance to the Black Sea (cf. Griffith (1979): 576 n. 1). It can be found at E2 on map 52 in the Barrington Atlas. It was an eminently sensible place for Khares to choose for assembling the grain convoy, given the presence of Philip's forces on the European side of the Bosporos (Griffith (1979): 575). It is not to be confused with the mountain called Hieron (Sacred), which lies west of Perinthos on the European side of the Propontis at A3 on the same map. That had been captured by Philip in 346 (cf. Aiskh. 2.90; Dem. 19.156; MacDowell (2000): 268).

According to Philokhoros . . . seven hundred talents: The most acceptable resolution of the discrepancy between the figures provided by Philokhoros (*FGrHist* 328 F162) and Theopompos (*FGrHist* 115 F292) is that Philokhoros gave the total for the whole convoy (see col.11.1), whilst Theopompos' figure represents the number of merchantmen actually retained and plundered by Philip. The remaining fifty ships were possibly non-Athenian and for that reason released (first suggested by D-S¹ p. 50; cf. Ellis (1976): 179 and n. 101; Griffith (1979): 576; Sealey (1993): 188; Osborne: 191; Hammond (1994): 132). Justin's figure (9.1.6) of 170 is usually emended to be the same as Theopompos'. For the sum of seven hundred talents see below at col. 11.2–5, though it is worth stating here that the large figure is credible and makes incomprehensible Cawkwell's assessment that 'the incident was not of great importance' (1978: 138).

(That) these actions were perpetrated *the year before* in the archonship of Theophrastos: For the sake of discussion I have printed and translated the text of P-S, since it is the one largely accepted and debated, but there are serious problems with it. To begin with the easier part: the verb 'were perpetrated' is unquestionably in the infinitive (*ΔΙΑΠΕΠΡΑΧΘΑΙ*), as in P-S. The claim by D-S¹ (p. 48) that the end of the word in the papyrus was -*ΕΑΙ* (instead of *ΘΑΙ*) and had been altered to *ΕΝ* is simply unfounded, even though it might be thought to yield a more acceptable translation ('he has perpetrated these actions'). Accepting the infinitive, however, involves assuming either that Didymos began to write proleptically in reported speech and forgot before he got to the end of the sentence, when he changed the syntax to a comparative clause, or that a verb of reporting has to be understood or restored at the beginning of the sentence.

The more difficult and more controversial part of the text is the word translated as '*the year before*' ([ΠΕΡ]ΥΣΙ). If this restoration is correct, it has serious implications for Didymos' reputation, because he is made to contradict himself, by implying that the speech was delivered the year after the seizure of the ships, in 339/8, not in 340/39, the date he established elsewhere for the outbreak of war (cf. West (1970): 292; Gibson: 124). Key to this restoration is the upsilon that is reported as the third letter from the end. This was first read tentatively by D-S[1] and has subsequently been accepted as certain. My own examination of the papyrus fails to support such confidence. The left upright of the upsilon is completely lacking, though the papyrus is preserved in that area. There is, however, damage at the centre of the letter, making it possible that either the middle bar of an epsilon or the backward loop of an alpha (the most erratically written letter in the papyrus) is missing (but not omega, as Osborne: 191 n. 46 proposed). If the latter is the case, it is possible that the missing verb of reporting, e.g. ΦΑΣΙ ('they say'), stood in this space. Admittedly that would require the scribe to have written a rather sloppy and oversized phi at the beginning, but this is not as implausible as it sounds. Phi elsewhere sometimes takes up two letter spaces, which may be all there are here, judging by the certain restoration in the same space in the line above. What is to be concluded, at any rate, from this discussion is that the current restoration is a poor basis upon which to build theories of 'Chalcenteric negligence'.

Khares: Khares, son of Theokhares, of Angele (*c*.400–*c*.325/4; cf. *LGPN* 473, Khares no. 17) was one of the five best-known Athenian generals of the fourth century, the others being Khabrias, Timotheos, Iphikrates, and Phokion. His reputation did not fare well in the tradition of our sources (see e.g. Diod. 15.95.3), probably because he was of undistinguished birth (cf. Davies, *APF* no. 15292) and no doubt also because he crossed swords with Timotheos, son of Konon, and thereby incurred the hostility of Isokrates, whose speech *On the Peace* was believed to have been directed against him for his mistreatment of Athens' allies (cf. Cargill (1981): 171–6). He was a soldiers' general, who usually was put in command of professional soldiers rather than citizen militia. Despite the negative tradition he served Athens loyally, was elected general seventeen times between 367 and 338 (*AO* ad locc.), won some important campaigns, fought at Khaironeia and was still actively in command of a company at Tainaron in 325/4 (Plut. *Mor.* 848e). A positive evaluation of his career can be found in Parker (1986). On this occasion he was in charge of a squadron of forty triremes (Hammond (1993): 16) in the Hellespont, where he had been since early in the spring of 340, when he was ordered to take care of the people of Elaious in the seventh prytany of the archonship of Nikomakhos (*IG* II^2 228; Harding (1985): no. 94).

sailed away to a meeting of the King's generals: No other source reports this detail, but it is intrinsically plausible and sensible for Khares to be coordinating the campaign with the Persians, who had been involved against Philip since his attack upon Perinthos in midsummer 340 (cf. Diod. 16.75.1–2), even though his absence was unfortunate in its timing (cf. Griffith (1979): 575).

And Philip . . . cargo ships: The best attempt to analyse Philip's strategy and understand how he pulled off this coup against superior forces is by Griffith (1979: 576 n. 1). In lines 59–60 I have retained the text of the papyrus with two infinitives after 'attempted' (so D-S). P-S emend the first infinitive 'to send' into a participle 'having sent', which is syntactically less harsh and is approved by Wankel (1987: 219) and Gibson (94 n. 24), though neither follow P-S in their further, strange suggestion that there was a lacuna between 'having sent' and 'the ships'.

COLUMN ELEVEN

Heading: The heading raises three topics, the first of which will be introduced at line 14, leading to a *lemma* from Dem. 11.2 at line 17, the second at line 26, with a *lemma* from 11.4, and the third at line 52 with a *lemma* from 11.11.

Altogether...two hundred and thirty: The word 'altogether' supports the view that Philokhoros was giving the overall total of the whole convoy.

prizes of war: Technically, this could be taken to mean that Philip and Athens were already at war, but that seems unlikely (cf. Wankel (1976): 439–43; Griffith (1979): 577–8; Sealey (1993): 188; Hammond (1994): 132; *pace* Cawkwell (1978): 138; Buckler (1996): 77–97). In Jacoby's words, Philip 'was not a man to be held back by the thin thread of a formality' (*Text*: 539). In fact, it was following this action that most scholars believe Philip sent to Athens the letter (his 'ultimatum', Wankel (1976): 442) that Didymos considered Demosthenes 11 was replying to, after which war was declared and the *stele* bearing the Peace of Philokrates was broken (see above at col. 1.67–2.2).

timbers towards his siege weapons: In the fourth century two autocrats, Dionysios of Syracuse and Philip of Macedon, were pioneers in the development and use of siege weapons, especially the torsion catapult. For the kind of artillery Philip used and their construction see Diod. 16.74.4. Cf. Marsden (1969): esp. 58–60, 100–4. For the view that Philip's skill at siegecraft was one of the reasons why 'the end of Greek liberty was inevitable' see Cawkwell (1996: 98–121); for an alternate view see Harding (1995: 125).

grains and hides and much money':   On the nature and value of this booty see Griffith (1979: 576 n. 3) and on booty in general see Pritchett (1971: 53–100).

(these are) the circumstances of his speech: Having finished his discussion of the date, Didymos passes on to the question of the authenticity of speech 11.

culmination of the __Philippics__: As Dover has observed (1968: 7), by Didymos' time some scholars considered that the term *Philippics* embraced speeches 1 to 13 (minus 12, *Letter of Philip*, of course) in our corpus, but Didymos clearly rejected that view. For him the *Philippics* ended with this speech (as they did for Dionysios of Halikarnassos, *Ad Amm.* 1.10). For the kind of criteria he applied to define a *Philippic* see col. 13.18–25.

One would not be . . . And there are those who . . . :   As before, the use of the potential optative in a self-effacing impersonal construction shows that Didymos is cautiously advancing his own position (cf. Osborne: 193; Gibson: 125; contra Lossau (1964): 93). In this case, it has to be inferred that others have come to the same conclusion, but they go even further and consider the speech to be a forgery by Anaximenes. The formula used to introduce that contention is Didymos' regular way of referring to an idea that he rejects, and shows that he is not prepared to endorse their position. At least, that is how I read these two sentences, which I feel have to be taken closely together, if we are to decipher Didymos' opinion (cf. Milns (1994): 87).

this little speech has been cobbled together, a cumulative accretion . . . : This assertion is easily substantiated, especially by comparing 11.8–17 with 2.14–23 (cf. Sealey (1993): 239) and 11.21–2 with 2.23–4. But it is an observation that one could make about many of Demosthenes' themes, namely that they were frequently reused and developed over time. One example must suffice. In the *Second Olynthiac* (2.15) Demosthenes brings up the idea of Philip's ambition for *doxa* (fame) and his willingness to suffer anything, even bodily harm, for it. Later in the same speech (23–4) he develops separately the contrast between Philip's activity and the inactivity of the Athenians, which is itself contrasted with the energy and sacrifice of their ancestors (*progonoi*). These two themes are worked together in a more elaborate development in speech 11 (21–2), where Philip's willingness to suffer bodily harm in the pursuit of greater power has become more specifically a willingness to 'be wounded in all parts of his body' (22). But the most sophisticated version of this theme can be found in *On the Crown* (18.66–9), where Philip is reduced to comic bathos in one of the most justly celebrated passages of the speech (cf. Harding (1994*b*): 217–18). It is more reasonable to see in this development the process whereby Demosthenes himself fine-tuned and perfected this particular theme (and therefore an indication that he was the person who 'cobbled together' speech 11) than to believe that Anaximenes, who wrote his *Philippika* no earlier than 330 and probably later, would forge the less sophisticated version in 11 after the passage in *On the Crown* had appeared (cf. Jacoby, *FGrHist* 72 F11, where the whole of speech 11 becomes a fragment of Anaximenes), or vice versa that Demosthenes would copy a conjunction of his own ideas that had been made by someone else. Consequently, I feel that Didymos' caution is justified, if indeed 'he does not openly express an opinion as to whether the compiler was Demosthenes himself or somebody else' (Milns (1994): 87; cf. Foucart (1909): 85–6; Osborne: 194).

But, if this is his stance, it raises the question of the extent of his engagement with the issue of authenticity. It has been observed that 11 is the only speech whose authenticity Didymos queried in the extant papyrus (Gibson: 125) and also noted with interest (Milns (1994): 87) that he could perceive the derivative character of this speech (though without citing any specific passages, cf. Gibson: 125), but fail to notice the more and obviously closer parallels between speeches 10 and 8 (10.11–27 and 8.38–51; 10.55–70 and 8.52–67) in his discussion of the *Fourth Philippic*. Of course, it is always possible that he did deal with the question of the authenticity of 10 in the missing parts of columns 2 and 3 (as Milns himself suggested (1994): 87 n. 35), but not likely, and certainly there is no indication that he considered that speech 'derivative' or 'composite'. A reasonable inference to draw from this evidence may be that, while Didymos can ask original questions on subjects that interest him (especially historical), the scope of his enquiry into such matters as authenticity was limited by the activity of his predecessors (i.e. he discussed that question in the case of speech 11, because serious and important issues had been raised, but did not in the case of speech 10, because no one before him had expressed any doubts). Moreover, it appears that wherever previous discussion existed, he limited himself to indicating his preference or fine-tuning arguments within the limits set by the existing debate. In this way the papyrus may give us a window on the work and interests of Hellenistic scholarship prior to the late first century BC and makes it possible for us to draw some conclusions about Didymos' own contribution.

cobbled together: It would be irresponsible not to point out that all the above speculation is based upon an emendation that makes a substantial difference to Didymos' meaning (*pace* Milns (1994): 86 n. 34). The word translated as 'cobbled together' ($\Sigma YM[\Pi]E\Phi OPH\Sigma\Theta AI$) is an emendation, first proposed by D-S and adopted by all subsequent editors (including myself). It is a sensible change from an unattested and incorrect verb form ($\Sigma YM[\Pi]E\Phi\Omega PH\Sigma\Theta AI$) to a known one, by the simple substitution of an omicron for an omega. If, however, the form of the verb in the papyrus could be defended, it would have to carry the meaning that the passages were 'detected in theft' (not 'filched' as in Milns (1994): 86 n. 34). To my mind this would exclude the possibility (assumed above) that Didymos thought that Demosthenes could have been the author of 11, since I do not think he would have accused Demosthenes of 'pirating' his own words.

And there are those . . . in almost *the very* words: Quite apart from the question what Didymos said or thought on this issue, the fact that some earlier scholar(s) attributed speech 11 to Anaximenes has convinced most modern scholars to do likewise (see e.g. Jacoby, *FGrHist* 72 F11 with commentary. Cf. West (1970): 295; Sealey (1993): 239, who states categorically 'It follows that speech 11 was composed by Anaximenes . . .'). I have indicated my reservation about the logic of that deduction above (under **this little speech . . .**, p. 217). It is simply incorrect to state that 'If the speech was given practically *verbatim* in Anaximenes' work, then it clearly was not by Demosthenes . . .' (West (1970): 295). Since the probable date for the publication of the *Philippika* was 330 or after, there is no reason why Anaximenes could not have had access to a copy of the original speech by Demosthenes. But fundamental to any discussion of that matter and, indeed, for an understanding of the argument here, is a resolution of the textual problems. There are two points where the text is in dispute, one at the end of line 11 and beginning of line 12, the other at the end of line 12.

In the last three spaces of line 11, though both D-S and P-S claim to discern some letters (albeit different ones), I am unable to see any identifiable letters and a similar experience is reported by Wankel (1987: 221–2) and Milns (1994: 86 n. 33). At the beginning of line 12 the delta is clear, followed by an upright, which could be an iota or the left side of an eta. Next to it, at the top of the space, there also appears to be part of a curved letter (an omicron?), but this could just be damage. Possible in this space, then, are either delta eta or delta iota omicron, but not delta epsilon. In the second disputed passage at the end of line 12 the reading is clear: there is an eta and a nu ($\eta\nu$) before the omicron that begins the next word ($O\Lambda I\Gamma O Y$). The question is what to make of these letters. By themselves they could be a relative pronoun (so P-S). Alternatively, they could be part of a word, whose first letters have dropped out (e.g. ὅλην, 'whole/in its entirety' D-S, following Usener, or αὐτήν, 'it' Milns). A final, desperate, solution is to delete them (Wilamowitz in D-S[1]). Both disputed points are usually taken together in attempts to restore the passage.

Essentially there are two approaches to the issues. One treats the words from the end of line 11 through the beginning of 14 as an extension of the statement that 'some attribute the work to Anaximenes' and takes the infinitive 'has been inserted' as part of the indirect speech. Examples include D-S, who read 'And there are those who say (that) the speech of advice belongs to Anaximenes of Lampsakos, [and now] has been inserted in the seventh (book) *of his* [Philipp]ika [whole/in its entirety] in almost *the very words.*' Crönert's text (adopted by Jacoby in *FGrHist* 72 F11) is similar, except that he has '[and, certainly]' in place of D-S's rather bland '[and now]'. Along the same lines, but more problematic grammatically, is the suggestion of P-S (based upon their observation of dotted tau, eta, nu at the end of line 11) that the feminine accusative singular of the definite article ($\tau\dot{\eta}\nu$) should be read there and the feminine accusative singular of the relative pronoun ($\ddot{\eta}\nu$) at the end of line 12. This produces a translation somewhat as follows: 'And there are those who say (that) the speech of advice belongs to Anaximenes of Lampsakos, [the very (speech)] (that is) in the seventh (book) *of his* [Philipp]ika, which (they say) has been inserted in almost *the very words.*' This has rightly been criticized by Wankel (1987: 222) as awkward.

More importantly, as has been observed (Milns (1994): 83–8; Gibson: 126), this approach to the text, that treats it as an assertion made by those who deny authenticity, has exposed Didymos to the charge that he failed to check his reference, because had he done so, he would have resolved the question of authenticity (e.g. West (1970): 295, 'Why did not Didymos himself consult Anaximenes' work?'). Thus he is made guilty of negligence.

A second, more positive, approach to understanding this passage is to take the words from the end of line 11 onward as an explanation or justification of the attribution to Anaximenes. This can be seen in the proposal of Blass (favoured by Wankel (1987): 221–2) to read the demonstrative 'that' (modifying 'speech of advice') at the end of line 11 and begin a new sentence in the next line with the word *ΔIO* ('wherefore'). Recently, a variant of this, proposed by Milns (1994: 86–7) has won approval (e.g. from Gibson: 94 n. 25, 125–6). Milns restores the dative of the definite article at the end of line 11 and takes it with the infinitive 'has been inserted'. Also, he supplements the eta nu in line 12 with the letters $\langle AYT \rangle$, thereby making the word 'it'. His text translates as: 'And there are those who say (that) the speech of advice belongs to Anaximenes of Lampsakos, [because of the fact that] $\langle$it$\rangle$ has been inserted in the seventh (book) *of his* [Philipp]ika in almost *the very words.*' If this restoration is on the right lines, the articular infinitive ('because of the fact that it has been inserted') becomes Didymos' explanation of the reason why 'some' attribute the speech to Anaximenes and absolves him from the charge of not bothering to check his reference. Whether he had seen the speech in Anaximenes or not (and he probably had, as Milns (1994): 84–6 and Gibson: 126, rightly claim) is irrelevant to what he was saying.

And some people have interpreted [. . .]: A third argument, at least in the traditional view, that other (or the same) scholars (Osborne: 195; Gibson: 126) had advanced against authenticity, was stylistic: some of the vocabulary is not Demosthenic. The word 'orrodein' is cited as an example. Once again Didymos introduces the objection obliquely, without specifically stating his agreement or disagreement. He takes the argument as an opportunity to expatiate on the etymology of the word, which is one of his interests (see Introduction). This and similar excursuses on 'skorakizein' and the 'Orgas' are serious obstacles to Gibson's theory that the papyrus text represents only excerpts from Didymos' commentary, selected by someone with an interest in history (see Introduction under Commentary or Monograph?).

Regardless of the quality of Didymos' speculation, which is more difficult to discern as a result of the state of the text, it might be that he was attempting to demonstrate the classical antecedents of the word. This makes it possible that the tacit subtext of his argument may be that the word is 'respectable' and, therefore, not a reason for denying authenticity. It is also possible, however, that he is just showing off (see below), by discussing a word that he had worked up elsewhere (see Schmidt (1854): 77, 249) in his *Lexis Komike*, as Lossau suggests in his detailed analysis of Didymos' central place in the history of ancient theorizing on the etymology of the word 'orrodein' (Lossau (1964): 99–106, esp. 100–1).

The preserved text of line 14 is usually considered unsound (West (1970): 295 and n. 5). Some improvement has been made over D-S's incomprehensible reading at the middle of the line by P-S's recognition (which I confrim) that some part of the word *ONOMA* ('word') must be intended there. Unfortunately, the adverb 'in a vulgar way' modifying the verb 'have interpreted' is almost certain and it has proved hard for most to believe that Didymos said that 'some people have interpreted [these words] in a vulgar way' (cf. West (1970): 295–6 n. 5; Gibson: 126). P-S's own suggestion that 'some people' should be emended to the neuter 'some [of the words]' does not address that issue and is anyway unnecessary. A recent proposal by Gibson (94 n. 26, 126) holds more promise. Even though it too requires an emendation, in this case it is of the offending word 'in a vulgar way'. He suggests changing the ending to alpha and making it into a neuter adjective agreeing with $T(A)$ $[O]NOM[AT(A)]$. He would translate as 'Some people have interpreted his words (as being) rather vulgar.' This is the best amongst the traditional solutions to date and certainly comes closest to saying what the sense seems to require (but see below under 'to break out in a cold sweat'). The only objection I have is to the possessive 'his'. It is not likely that the critics of authenticity would be criticizing Demosthenes' vocabulary as 'rather vulgar'. The point surely must be that some of *the vocabulary* in 11 is 'rather vulgar' and, therefore, not Demosthenic.

On the significance of the term 'vulgar' in ancient stylistic criticism and the possibility that it was used specifically against Demosthenes as a result of an accusation by Aiskhines (cf. Dionysios of Halikarnassos, *On Demosthenes* 57) see Lossau (1964): 9–21, 78–9 and Gibson: 126–7.

'And that it is right . . .':   The *lemma* is from 11.2. Once again the papyrus agrees with S in reading 'us' rather than 'you'.

To 'break out in a cold sweat' (orrodein) is/means to be afraid: I have translated 'orrodein' in this way in order to highlight Didymos' original, but probably erroneous, etymology (cf. Boisacq (1938): 82–3 s.v. arrodeo; Chantraine (1968–80): iii. 827; Frisk (1955–72): ii. 1.427–8). The verb is, in fact, a perfectly respectable one, denoting 'fear' or 'shrinking back', that was used by many major authors (e.g. Herodotos, Plato, Euripides, and Aristophanes). Thucydides even puts it into the mouth of the conservative Nikias (6.9.2). So, it can hardly be considered 'vulgar' and one has to wonder why (or even 'if') the critics of authenticity did so. To be sure, this is the only place in the extant works of Demosthenes where he can be found using this word (it can be found in some manuscripts at 9.65, but the consensus of opinion is that it was interpolated there, and Harpokration, s.v. ORRODEIN, claims to have seen the noun *orrodia* in Demosthenes' *Prooimia*, but it is not in our texts). So, it is not unreasonable that it attracted comment of some sort. But, if Lossau is correct in his analysis (1964: 99–106), the etymology Didymos presents was his own original theory that he had developed already in his *lexikon* of comic vocabulary and imported here. It differed fundamentally from that put forward by his predecessors. In other words, Didymos was the person responsible for the 'crude' interpretation of 'orrodein', that he is attributing to 'some'.

Has he forgotten his own theory? That line of thought would please the advocates of 'negligence' (e.g. West (1970) and Harris (1989)). Or is it just possible that he is being coy here, saying, as he dictated to his students, 'Some (wink, wink, you know who) interpret words in a rather crude manner, (interpreting), for example, "orrodein" as being . . .'? One hesitates to entertain such an idea, especially since it requires 'some' (*enioi*) to have a reference totally contrary to its use in other places (col. 2.2, 7.12, 13.16), in all of which it refers to views of other scholars which Didymos definitely rejects. But it does enable us to keep the papyrus text and it does have its own perverse logic!

what happens to those who are afraid: Didymos explains the etymology of 'orrodein' as being from *orros* ('rear', 'rump', 'arse', 'bum') and *idio* ('sweat'). His presentation can be seen more clearly in the scholion to Aristophanes, *Frogs* 223. As Gibson well points out (127), neither of the passages cited (from Homer, *Odyssey* 20.204 and Aristophanes, *Frogs* 237) makes clear how the word was formed from these two elements.

In line 22 there is a three-letter space after the word 'rump' and an incomprehensible word *EIΔEΔPOI*. Because the scribe is prone to write epsilon iota (*EI*) in place of iota, for example in the spelling of 'exuding moisture' in line 26 and of 'Nikaia' in lines 28 and 33 (this phenomenon is symptomatic of iotacism), *EIΔEΔPOI* is usually changed into the equally unknown, but etymologically more acceptable *IΔEΔPOI* ('bumsweaters'). (I cannot understand why P-S claim this alteration as their own, since the word appears this way in LSJ). This suggests strongly that the word *idiein* ('to sweat') appeared somewhere beforehand. D-S inserted that verb before 'about the rump', because they thought they read *AEI* ('always') in the space. On this basis they suggested the following: 'The word is created as a result of what happems to those who are afraid. For ⟨they sweat⟩ around the rump *always*, like people with sweaty bums.' P-S, by contrast, do not claim to see any letters in that space, but supply the word for sweating (in the infinitive, understanding 'is', I suppose) in the space. Their text translates: 'For the word (is/means) ⟨to sweat⟩ about the bum, like people with sweaty bums.'

Finally, if Lossau (1964: 100–1) is correct in his opinion (based upon the curtailed explication of the etymology as well as the misspelling of *idedroi*) that the scribe was in doubt about what he was writing down, while we can sympathize with his difficulty, his lack of comprehension would constitute another argument against Gibson's theory that the scribe was excerpting only sections of Didymos' commentary that interested him. He can hardly have been interested in what he did not understand.

'And he is suspected . . .':   The *lemma* is from 11.4.

Nikaia: The scribe has misspelled the name here, *NEIKAIA*, as he does also at lines 33 and 51. Nikaia was a small fortified town in eastern Lokris, situated in the long corridor that constituted the ancient pass of Thermopylai. It can be found in the Barrington Atlas on Map 55 at coordinates D3, where it is located about 30 km east (and slightly north) of Thermopylai itself.

Nikaia probably came under Theban control in the 360s, when Thebes was expanding its influence into Thessaly under Pelopidas. It fell into the hands of the Phokians sometime during the Sacred War (356–346) and was under the control of Phalaikos in the last phase of that war. It became a bone of contention between Philip and the Thebans from 346, when he took it from the Phokians and gave it to the Thessalians (Aiskh. 2.132–3, 3.140; Dem. 6.22) down to 339, when the Thebans recaptured it, as part of the manoeuvring that preceded the battle of Khaironeia (cf. Trevett (1999): 196). Didymos elucidates this *lemma* with two apposite quotations, one (for the location) from the Rhodian geographer Timosthenes, the other (for the history) from Philokhoros.

twenty stades distant from Therm[o]pylai: The figure twenty is clear and on its basis the same figure is restored in the quotation at line 33 (D-S, following Wilamowitz; P-S). This may be correct and, if so, Timosthenes disagreed with the scholiast to Aiskh. 2.132, who has the distance as forty stades. But it is noteworthy that that scholion is almost word for word the same as Didymos' summary except for the numeral and the possibility cannot be excluded that the scholion is ultimately derived from his text. In that case, we would have to assume that an error in transcription of the numeral had occured at some point, either in line 30 (maybe by the scribe) and that Timosthenes gave the figure forty (*M*), or in the scholion. The actual distance is somewhat over thirty stades.

Timosthen[e]s . . . On Harbours: For this Rhodian geographer and his work see the Introduction under Sources.

for a person travelling: P-S, following D-S.

[by sea]:   P-S, following Crönert (1907: 386). D-S have 'by ship'.

lies: Both P-S and I support the restoration first proposed by Crönert (1907: 386).

[but for a person on foot it is as much as]:   P-S, following D-S. Crönert (1907: 386) has 'for those on foot about . . .'.

a *sandy* promontory . . . [with] anchorage for a [ship] of war.':   The supplements to the text here are agreed upon by all editors. This is, of course, the sort of observation one would expect of a naval commander. Unfortunately, given the lack of direction and the fact that today's coastline in this area extends considerably further into the channel than it did in antiquity, it is not possible to identify this topographical point.

Phil[ip] *ordered* it to be given back to (the) Lo[k]rians: That Philip ordered the Thebans to surrender Nikaia to the people of Epiknemidian Lokris, in whose territory it was situated, was unknown before the discovery of this papyrus. Griffith (1979: 590) is probably correct in suggesting that this order was given in 339, after Philip had rendered the position ineffective by bypassing it. That he chose not to demand it back for himself, nor for the Thessalians, but for the innocuous Lokrians may indicate, as Griffith suggests (cf. Ellis (1976): 191), that even at that late hour Philip was trying to give the Thebans a way to back down without loss of face.

Philokh[oro]s in his sixth (book):   *FGrHist* 328 F56b. Philokhoros' sixth book covered the years from 360 or 357 to 322/1 or 318/17. A version (*FGrHist* 328 F56a) of this entry was already known from Dionysios of Halikarnassos (*Ad Amm.* 1.11), though it contains some additional material (including the archon's name) and some significant omissions. Jacoby (*Text*: 332) calls Dionysios' version 'drastically abridged' and considers Didymos' more accurate (cf. Osborne: 199–200). Both can be found at Harding (1985): no. 96.

Phil[ip] *had captured* Elateia and Kytin[ion]:   Didymos does not provide the archon name at the beginning of this quotation from the Atthidographer, as he usually does. Both Osborne (199) and Gibson (128) offer the reasonable explanation that his concern was with the place, not the date. Dionysios preserves the opening of the citation that contains the date, which was 339/8 in the archonship of Lysimakhides.

Modern scholars are more precise, favouring the late autumn (November), following the autumn Pylaia in October, as the time for Philip's capture of Kytinion and Elateia (e.g. Wüst (1938): 153–5; Ellis (1976): 190; Cawkwell (1978): 142; Griffith (1979): 585; Sealey (1993): 192). They are less in agreement about the chronology of the events that led up to his intervention, disagreeing in particular over the occasion of Aiskhines' famous speech against the Amphissans (Aiskh. 3.116–24; Dem. 18.149–51), some placing it at the autumn Pylaia of 340 (e.g. Griffith (1979): 585–8, 717–9), most arguing for the spring Pylaia of 339 (e.g. Wüst (1938): 153–5; Ellis (1976): 187; Sealey (1993): 190).

Kytinion, in Doris, was on the road south and west toward Delphi and Amphissa. Its capture, only recorded by Philokhoros, was therefore not a cause for surprise or alarm. The situation was quite different with Elateia, which lay on the more easterly route (used also by Xerxes in 480, Hdt. 8. 33) toward Boiotia and Athens. Its capture caused a panic in Athens (Ryder (2000): 81) and elicited from Demosthenes a memorable description (18.169–73), which was plagiarized by Diodoros (16.84.2), though under the wrong year (338/7). Cf. Plut. *Dem.* 18.1.

had sent to Thebes *ambassadors* from . . . Phthiotians: With the exception of the Aitolians the delegations mentioned here were all representatives of member-states in the Amphiktyony. The presence of that body at these negotiations was quite appropriate, since ostensibly it was a religious issue (the Amphissan affair) that Philip had come to resolve as *hegemon* in a Sacred War. Most historians (e.g. Ellis (1976): 191; Griffith (1979): 590; Sealey (1993): 196; Hammond (1994): 145) treat this embassy as the one referred to by Demosthenes (18.211) and Plutarch (*Dem.* 18.2, quoting Marsyas the Macedonian, *FGrHist* 135/6 F20), at which Philip's ambassadors— Amyntas, Kleandros, and Kasandros from Macedon and Daokhos and Thrasydaios from Thessaly (but not Python of Byzantion as Diodoros, who is hopelessly confused, has it at 16.85.4)—were already present when Demosthenes arrived. It is noteworthy, however, that Philokhoros does not mention any ambassadors from Philip in this passage, and this has led some (e.g. Jacoby, *Text*: 332; *Notes*: 238; Wankel (1976): 975; (1987): 222) to believe that the embassy described here was an independent venture on the part of the Amphiktyonic states that preceded, if only slightly, the arrival of Philip's delegation at Thebes. This would mean that the request that Thebes hand over Nikaia to the Epiknemidian Lokrians was issued by them, not Philip. But this interesting hypothesis requires that the verbs ('sent' and 'demanding') be changed into the plural (as proposed by Keil, ap. *FGrHist* 328 F56a–b), which is contradicted by the text not only of Didymos, but also of Dionysios.

and was demanding . . . : From this point to the end of the quotation is missing from Dionysios, who continues 'and when the Athenians at the same time sent as ambassadors the delegation led by Demosthenes, they voted to make alliance with them.' There is little doubt that he has left out something, the part quoted by Didymos at the very least.

in contravention of the resolution of the Amphiktyons: This phrase has caused considerable difficulty, because many have found it hard to conceive of a *dogma* of the Amphiktyons that forbade giving Nikaia to the Lokrians. One way to resolve the problem has been to emend 'in contravention of' (*ΠΑΡΑ*) to 'in accordance with' (*ΚΑΤΑ*), as Jacoby does at *FGrHist* 328 F56b (following Blass). The error in transcription could easily have resulted from duplication of the *ΠΑΡΑ* in the compound verb *ΠΑΡΑΔΙΔΟΝΑΙ* that immediately precedes. By contrast, P-S, followed by Gibson (95), adopt the more radical approach of transposing the relative pronoun in line 46 to a position in front of 'in contravention of', thus producing a reading (in Gibson's version): '. . . that they hand over Nicaea—which, contrary to the order of the Amphictyons, had been garrisoned by Philip—to the Locrians; but when he was among the Scythians, the Thebans themselves, kicking out the garrisons, took control . . .'. This makes good sense, but the translation tries to conceal the horrendous syntax and the palaeographically unjustifiable transposition is probably not necessary. The papyrus reading is defended by Foucart (1909: 207–8), as a reference to a decree of the Amphiktyons in 346 at the end of the Sacred War, disposing of the former possessions of the Phokians. This is not inconceivable. Wüst (1938: 160 n. 2), on the other hand, sees the phrase as a reflection of a hostile tradition against Philip, and his explanation is considered adequate by Wankel (1987: 222), despite its scornful rejection by Jacoby (*Notes*: 238). The issue remains open. I have translated the text as it stands.

that the Thebans themselves had taken, after expelling Philip's garrison: Neither the fact that Philip had replaced the

Thessalian garrison in Nikaia with his own, nor that the Thebans had captured it from him, was known before the discovery of the papyrus (cf. Sealey (1993): 190).

⟨**would be sent**⟩: Suggested by Foucart (1909: 204). Some such supplement is needed.

about all issues': I hardly see how the Thebans could claim to negotiate 'on everyone's behalf', as Gibson (95) translates.

there are other Nikaias also, but . . . *necessary* to speak about them at this point: Like any scholar, ancient or modern, Didymos is eager to show that he has more information up his sleeve, but is showing good critical judgement by deeming it irrelevant.

'Furthermore, if . . .': The *lemma* is from Dem. 11.11. Textual note: the papyrus leaves out the particle *MEN* that is in all manuscripts, with 'rank and file', but agrees with SA in reading 'if' in line 53 and 'most' in line 55. However, it sides with AF against S in having the singular 'punishment' in line 53.

The word (i.e. skorakizein) has been created . . . : Once again, it is an unusual word (not found elsewhere in Demosthenes, though used by other late authors) that calls forth an essay into etymology from Didymos, who is not interested in anything else in the passage. The etymology he sets forth will be found in LSJ.

It is used by Aristophanes in <u>Birds</u>: At line 28 Euelpides puns on the well-known curse *ΕΣ ΚΟΡΑΚΑΣ*), in explaining to the audience the predicament in which he and Peisetairos find themselves (see Dunbar (1995) ad loc. pp. 145–6). This quotation serves to establish the usage of the expression, which the long narrative from Demon will illustrate.

Demon: On Demon (*FGrHist* 327) see the Introduction (under Sources). He wrote an *Atthis* with a strong emphasis upon the mythical period, and a work *On Sacrifice*, but his most influential work was his *On Proverbs*, from which sixteen fragments are preserved. This quotation is assigned to that work as fr. 7. The absence of a title or a specific book reference suggests that, while Demon was the ultimate source of this narrative, Didymos himself, who composed a major collection of *paroimia*, was the intermediary. This suggestion finds some confirmation in the facts that this narrative reappears in a virtually identical form in the collection of Zenobios (3.87), for whom Didymos' *Paroimia* was an acknowledged source (see Leutsch and Schneidewin (1839–51): i. 78–9). Furthermore, it looks to me very likely that the summary sentence of the excerpt is by Didymos himself, since it is so suited to his purpose here.

when the Boiotians were displaced by the Thracians: As Jacoby (*Text*: 210) astutely observes, this allusion shows that Demon's fanciful narrative has a historical element that is basically in line with the tradition of Boiotian migration, that begins (for us) with Thucydides (1.12.3) and continues with Ephoros (*FGrHist* 70 F119 = Strabo, 9.2.2–5 C400–3) and Diodoros (19.53.7–8, probably from Hieronymos of Kardia). That tradition places the original home of the future Boiotians near Arne in Thessaly and has them driven from there by the Thessalians into their final home. The only difference here is that Demon appears to trace the Boiotians back to Thrace, from where he has them driven into Thessaly. There were alternative traditions about Boiotian origins. One, on the Spartoi, can be found in Androtion (*FGrHist* 324 F60), on which see Harding (1994: 186–8). Others are reviewed by Buck (1979: 76–84). More speculative explorations can be found in Schachter (1985: 143–53) and Bakhuizen (1989: 65–72).

Demon's imaginative narrative, which continues to col. 12.33, does not merit detailed commentary. It is a good example of the dangers of interdisciplinarity. The study of *paroimia*, in their true sense of pithy *sententiae* containing popular reflections of practical wisdom, began with Aristotle and his school and, in this case, we know his explanation of the term *ΕΣ ΚΟΡΑΚΑΣ* (as it is reported at second hand, from Pausanias Atticista, by Eustathius at *Odyssey* N 408, p. 1746, 62). His account is in terms of religious ritual: 'When a plague was in the land and many crows came, men caught the crows and purified them with incantations, then let them go alive, saying to the plague "Go to the crows." ' By contrast (*pace* Jacoby, *Text*: 210), Demon has combined the antiquarian's interest in local tradition with the onomast's fondness for explaining place names (Korakai), thrown in a theme from foundation oracles (e.g. Pausanias Atticista, cited above, explains that an oracle told the Boiotians to settle wherever they saw 'white crows') and woven it all into an elaborate aetiological *mythos*. It is an unfortunate reflection upon Didymos that he obviously approved of Demon's version.

COLUMN TWELVE

Heading: The Heading refers to the topic of Philip's injuries, which is taken up at line 37 with a *lemma* from Dem. 11.22. It fails to make reference to another topic that is discussed (albeit very briefly) in lines 33–7, with a *lemma* from Dem.11.16. Above the Heading is a backward sigma (*antisigma*, indicated in the text by an asterisk) followed by a comment that draws attention to a word in line 3 by means of a corresponding sign in the margin. This word has been written one way (*NEOMENOΥΣ*) and corrected above the line (*NAIΩMENOΥΣ*). The comment at the top of the column appears to offer a third possibility (*NEMOMENOΥΣ*). Until recently the comment was taken to say something like, 'See (*IΔE*), (if the word is) not *NEMOMENOΥΣ*', but Gibson has challenged that interpretation and advanced an attractive alternative that is more sound in grammar (cf. Mayser (1906–70): i. i, 60–5; Gignac (1976): i. 189–90) and sense (the present reading does not construe). His view, which is accepted here, is that the comment has suffered from iotacism and should begin with *EI ΔE*: 'But if (it is) not (*NEOMENOΥΣ/ NAIΩMENOΥΣ*, then it is) *NEMOMENOΥΣ*' (Gibson: 129; cf. Gibson (2000): 148). The meaning is, however, not radically altered and the advice is followed by all editors, who agree in reading *NEMOMENOΥΣ* in line 3.

would be ejected: This is clearly the sense, as can be seen from Zenobios' *EKΠEΣEIΣΘAI*, but the grammar here (the active verb with the genitive) is strange. D-S suggest that 'that land' might once have been in the accusative.

convened the [. . .] assembly: Clearly the context calls for some sort of public gathering (*ΠANEΓΥΡIΣ*), at which it would be expected for young men to overindulge. Since the first letter of the word preceding 'assembly' is undoubtedly *N*, I suggest restoring 'of young men' (*N[EANIΣKΩ]N*). The space taken by this word in lines 14/15 would fit into the gap precisely. Both Blass (1906: 292) and Crönert (1907: 386) want to read a form of the participle 'existing' 'taking place' in the space before 'assembly'.

even now [. . .]:   Some verb replicating 'convened' (above) is required and D-S's suggestion of the Ionic form of 'gather' (*AΓINEIN*) would suit the need and the extant remains. The infinitive would require the assumption that Demon was understanding a reporting verb, like 'they say'.

I find the approach put forward in the last two notes more satisfactory than D-S's alternative suggestion that two words are missing, one in line 12, the other in line 13, which leads them to the following text: 'taking heart at his response ⟨they sowed⟩ the [land] and eagerly convened the assembly, which ⟨they say⟩ the Thessalian people even now *celebrate*.'

that 'something like it' had happened: This translation (cf. Gibson: 96) makes good sense (i.e. the chalk-whitened crows were very close to fulfilling the prophecy) and renders emendation of the existing text unnecessary. Some (e.g. D-S) have been led into the belief that emendation was called for by the scribe, who put a slash (/) in the margin beside line 22. However, this sign is more appropriately interpreted to indicate a lacuna after 'had happened' (line 23), as P-S observe (cf. Gibson: 96 n. 28; McNamee (1992): 17–18). To fill this lacuna P-S (followed by Gibson) propose, e.g.: '⟨while others were making a fuss, shouting that something terrible had happened, the young men fled in fear and⟩ settled . . .'. Jacoby (*FGrHist* 327 F7), more economically and closer to the text of Zenobios, supplies: '⟨the young men, having fled the fuss in fear⟩ settled . . .'.

still today . . . outcasts [. . .]: The word 'outcasts' has *EI* in place of *I* in the third syllable. In other places the text is not well preserved. P-S tentatively propose the restoration '[this] *expression*'. I follow them in this, as does Gibson (96). I do not, however, understand why they would propose 'at Athens' for the six-letter space at the end of the sentence. Jacoby (*FGrHist* 327 F7), on the other hand, adopts Crönert's suggestion: ' "Skorakizein" *is applied* [mockingly] to outcasts still today [in ordinary language].' Regardless of which restoration one prefers, it is hardly in doubt that this summary sentence refers back to the original point of Didymos' excursus, namely the meaning of the word 'skorakizein'. In this way it is so apposite to his enquiry as to suggest that he was the author.

'And those men have paid tribute . . .': The *lemma* is from Dem. 11.16. It was not listed in the Heading. Textual note: In two places, 'alone' and 'not yet', the papyrus supports the reading of manuscript S against the common tradition, 'alone of mankind' and 'never'.

That the Macedonians . . . On the Crown: This little comment contributes to the discussion of a couple of issues and raises a new one. First, it shows beyond a doubt that Didymos wrote more than one monograph on Demosthenes and that our papyrus is not his only contribution. Second, it makes even more unlikely the excerption theory, recently revived by Gibson. No excerptor in his right mind would excerpt what is in essence just a reference to another work. Third, it raises the spectre of negligence once again, since it has been argued (Bliquez (1972): 356–7) that Didymos must be wrong in his reference and is, consequently, guilty as charged (e.g. by Quintilian 1.8.20 and Athenaios 4.139c) of forgetting what he had written and where. It is true, as Bliquez points out, that it is hard to find a place in the speech *On the Crown* (unless we adopt West's desperate suggestion (1970: 290) that Didymos had a different text from ours) that might have prompted a discussion of Macedonian tribute to Athens (*pace* Osborne: 202, who suggests 18.152). On the other hand, Demosthenes does make an assertion about Macedonian kings being subject to Athens in the *Third Olynthiac* (3.24), and an even more explicit reference to Macedonia paying tribute (*phoros*) to Athens can be found in the *On Halonnesos* (7.12), though that was composed by Hegesippos, not Demosthenes. So, Didymos might have written on the subject in his commentary at either of these two points (Bliquez (1972): 357). Alternatively, he might not, but instead have discussed the issue tangentially to some other comment he was making in his commentary on *On the Crown*, as he says (cf. Osborne: 202; Gibson: 130).

Given our ignorance, it seems unwise to convict Didymos of negligence *ex silentio*.

But what of his statement that the Macedonians did actually pay tribute to Athens? Is there any truth to that? Arrian thought so (*Anab.* 7.9.4). And, the Tribute Lists confirm, at least, that a number of communities within the Thrakian panel, which were on territory nominally belonging to Macedon, paid tribute to Athens in the fifth century, like Berge in Bisaltia and Haison in Pieria and, of course, Methone (cf. *ATL* iii. 217–23; *GHI* no. 65; Bliquez (1972): 356; contra, Gomme in *HCT* i. 214–15, 238 n. 3). Furthermore, it remains a good possibility that Amyntas, the father of Philip, did join the Second Athenian Confederacy (see Cargill (1981): 85–7), in which case he would presumably have contributed *syntaxis*. So, Didymos was probably correct, and there is really no reason to claim that he 'knew the charge that "kings" paid tribute was an exaggeration' (Bliquez (1972): 356) and intentionally changed the 'reference to "Macedonian kings" to the more vague "Macedonians"' (Gibson: 130).

but that a man: The *lemma* is from Dem. 11.22.

Concerning the wounds . . . abbreviated: This is surely another reference to Didymos' own (note the first person) commentary on *On the Crown*, in section 67 of which is found the most celebrated description of Philip's willingness to sacrifice all for his honour and glory, including specific details on his injuries ('his eye knocked out, his collarbone broken, his hand and leg maimed'; cf. Wankel (1976): 397–9). That this was the most likely place for Didymos to have expatiated on Philip's wounds is the common consensus (see e.g. Osborne: 203; Gibson: 130; cf. note above on **this little speech . . .**, p. 217). In fact, Riginos (1994: 103–19) demonstrates that that passage in Demosthenes was the basis of all subsequent elaborations. To judge from the useful (and otherwise unpreserved) information that Didymos provides in this abbreviated version of his earlier study, his fuller version would have been invaluable.

D-S suspect a lacuna between 'account' and 'and'. They suggest supplying 'elsewhere' and are followed in this by Gibson (97 n. 29), but there is no indication of a gap in the text and the sense is perfectly logical and grammatical as it stands. Therefore, I follow the reading in P-S (cf. Osborne: 203 n. 50).

In connection . . . so-called (tortoise) sheds: The first and most celebrated of Philip's wounds was the loss of an eye. That it took place at the siege of Methone is recorded in several other places (e.g. Diodoros 16.34.5; Justin 7.6.14; Harpokration s.v. Methone; schol. 124 to Dem. 18.67. For a full list see Riginos (1994): 106). Only one variant tradition erroneously associates the event with Olynthos (Lucian, *Hist. conscr.* 38; see Riginos (1994): 112–13). Other details are less frequently forthcoming: for example, that it was his right eye (specified here and in Justin); that the weapon was an arrow (surely correct, cf. Griffith (1979): 257 n. 2, but alternatives include the spear, which will be discussed below, and even a bolt from a catapult in Strabo 7. F22) and that the injury took place when he was supervising equipment, not in battle. This information was not provided by Demosthenes and left scope for elaboration. For attempts to use this detail to identify the skull found in Royal Tomb II at Vergina as that of Philip of Macedon and the equally vocal objections see Riginos (1994: 104 n. 3) and Hammond (1994: 179–82, 221–2 nn. 9–24).

The term used for siege engines is the generic *MHXANH*, which can stand for a wide range of offensive devices (Marsden (1969): 50).

The tortoise sheds (*ΧΕΛΩΝΑΙ ΧΩΣΤΡΙΔΕΣ*) were designed to protect the ram and the men who were attacking the walls. According to Ephoros (at Diodoros 12.28.3 and Plut. *Perik.* 27.3–4) the tortoise sheds were first employed by Perikles at the siege of Samos, but this is open to question (Gomme, *HCT* i. 354–5; Marsden (1969): 50 n. 7). No doubt, however, they formed part of Philip's siege technique.

Theopompos in the fourth (book) of his histories about him: *FGrHist* 115 F52. Theopompos needs no introduction. He was one of the authors whom Didymos knew well and whom he quoted on fourth-century affairs (unlike his contemporary, Ephoros), especially when they concerned Philip. The reference is certainly to the *Philippika*, the fourth book of which covered the years 356/5–354/3 (*FGrHist* 115 FF 49–52). Within those years fell the siege of Methone, winter 355–summer 354 (Buckler (1989): 176–86, especially 185). On this occasion, Theopompos is cast in the unaccustomed role of reliable reporter (cf. Riginos (1994): 106–7) in comparison to Douris of Samos.

Marsyas the Macedonian concurs: Didymos corroborates the testimony of Theopompos with this reference to a Marsyas of Macedon. There are two historians known to us in this way (one from Pella, the other from Philippi), whose fragments Jacoby lists together as *FGrHist* 135/6. This is fragment 16. Heckel takes Didymos' imprecise reference to 'the Macedonian' to indicate that he only knew of one historian called Marsyas. This individual is almost certainly Marsyas of Pella (cf. Heckel (1980): 444–62), on whom see the Introduction under Sources. If this is the correct identification, he was well placed to know intimate details about Philip's wounds.

Douris (of Samos):   *FGrHist* 76. This is surely from his *Makedonika*, though no title is specified by Didymos. It is listed as fragment 36. For this author and his reputation for dramatic or 'tragic' history see the Introduction under Sources.

even on this occasion he had to *talk marvels*:   See Kebric (1977: 13) for the observation that this is the first known occasion that an ancient complained about Douris' tendency toward sensationalism. If this is Didymos' original thought, he deserves credit for the insight. On the other hand, as Kebric rightly notes, a virtual contemporary of Didymos, Cicero, considered Douris a man *in* *historia diligens* (Cic. *ad Att.* 6.1.18; *FGrHist* 76 T6, F73). But, then, Cicero was not always right (cf. Plut. *Perik.* 28.2). Riginos (1994: 114 n. 49) suggests that the implication here is that Douris is talking of 'portents', which is consistent with the fateful name he gives to the weapon-thrower.

Osborne (206) asks the reasonable question why Didymos would cite Douris at all, if he did not believe what he said. To his answer, that he was in the habit of recording differing views on controversial issues (cf. the account of Hermias), one could add that he had the instinctive scholar's delight in criticizing his predecessors. It is also possible, as Riginos suggests (1994: 111) that he found the story 'amusing'.

the man who cast . . . [A]ster: 'In this opportune way', the suggestion of Wilamowitz, is accepted by both D-S and P-S. So, too, is the restoration 'missile' (*AKONTION*). This word indicates a hand-thrown weapon, like a javelin or spear. That Douris was attributing the wound to a weapon other than an arrow is implicit in the criticism that follows. By its use Douris introduces a different weapon into the story, which he supplements by adding the supposed name of the thrower. These new elements lent themselves to considerable elaboration, as Riginos has shown under 'Variant 1' to the eye-wounding story (1994: 107–9).

almost *all those who were on the campaign* . . . by an arrow: The restoration is accepted by all editors. Assuming it is correct, Didymos' most likely source for this sort of inside information is Marsyas. An arrow is the only really plausible weapon; a spear or a catapult in the eye would have been fatal (cf. Griffith (1979): 257 n. 2), whilst an arrow wound in that organ can be survived (though not by King Harold at the battle of Hastings in 1066).

as for the story concerning the flute players . . . Marsyas: Intriguingly Marsyas (*FGrHist* 135/6 F17), the man at court, agrees with Douris on this second variant (Riginos (1994): 109–11) to the anecdotes about this injury, though we cannot say whether he just corroborated the basic account, or its interpretation. Presumably, this story circulated in high places. As narrated by Douris, it has an undeniably marvellous touch to it, and is explicitly fateful. Theopompos, however, is not mentioned, so presumably he did not include this story in his history. D-S suggests (p. xxxv n. 1) that Didymos' conjunction of the name of the historian Marsyas with a story about flute players led Ptolemy Khennos (as reported in Photios' *Bibliotheka* 190 p. 149a1) to follow his own narrative of Philip's eye wound with the story of the mythical Marsyas and his competition with Apollo. This is an interesting speculation, for which now see Cameron (2004: 146–7), but, if correct, tells us more about the vagaries of Ptolemy's mind than about Didymos (*pace* Cameron (2004): 147.

as he was celebrating . . . played the *Kyklops*:   Polyphemos, the one-eyed, man-eating monster of book nine of Homer's *Odyssey*, became a model for a buffoon for Euripides (in his satyr play, *Kyklops*) and was subsequently cast in the role of love-lost, bucolic swain, wracked by passion (usually unrequited) for a nymph named Galateia. The story took shape in the dithyrambs of the poets mentioned here, was inherited by the bucolic poets, especially Theokritos (see *Idylls* 6 and 11), and finally passed on to the western tradition by Ovid (*Met.* 13.738 ff.). The theme was clearly very popular in the fourth century and there is nothing implausible or necessarily coincidental about all three flautists choosing to play different versions of the same dithyramb. This could even have been a condition of the contest. That is, if we accept that the contest actually occurred, as I think we must, on the authority of Marsyas. Of course, when Philip lost his eye shortly afterwards (the dramatic and/or real date for the occasion must be in 355, if we accept Buckler's date, above, for the siege of Methone), the event would have taken on a new significance. It is even suspected (Riginos (1994): 110) that Philip got the nickname 'Kyklops' at court. At any rate, he seemed to be sensitive about the name ([Demetrios] *de Eloc.* 293).

Antigeneides . . . Oiniades: As both Foucart (1909: 139–41) and Riginos (1994: 110–11) correctly observe, Douris provided the names of three flute players, each of whom was performing the work of a different poet. Gibson (97) is quite wrong to interpret these as father and son teams, though he is followed in this by Cameron (2004: 146–7 and n. 128). The historical credibility of the anecdote rests upon the identification of these performers and poets. All six are known to have existed, but the dates for some of the flute players make it questionable whether they would have been still alive at the time. Date, of course, does not matter for the poets.

Antigeneides: The name is misspelled *ANTIΓENTHN* in the papyrus. A man of this name was a famous flute player from Thebes, who lived in the last half of the fifth century and into the fourth. For details of his career see the *Souda*, s.v. Antigeneides. Riginos (1994: 110 and n. 27) thinks he could 'still have been performing in 354'. Foucart (1909: 139–40), on the other hand, thought it unlikely that he was still alive and posits another flute player of the same name, mentioned by Plutarch (*Mor.* 410).

Philoxenos: The dithyrambic poet, Philoxenos of Kythera, was probably born in 445 and certainly died in 380. He was famous enough to merit an individual entry in the *Marmor Parium* (*FGrHist* 239) at epoch 69: 'From the time when Philoxenos the dithyrambic poet dies at age 65, 113 years, when Pytheas was archon at Athens' (380/79). He spent time at the court of Dionysios I, tyrant of Syracuse. It was there, according to tradition, that he composed his most famous work, the *Kyklops or Galateia,* maybe as an allegory on court life (see Page (1962): 815–24). It was apparently the first treatment of this subsequently popular theme, and may have been original in form (Sutton (1983): 37–43). It was so famous that Aristophanes parodied it in his *Ploutos* of 388 (lines 290 ff.). Cf. Foucart (1909): 140; Riginos (1994): 110 and n. 26.

Khrysogonos: Plutarch (*Alk.* 32) cites Douris of Samos for the detail that Khrysogonos, a flute player who had been victorious at the Pythian Games, played his flute at the homecoming to Athens of Alkibiades in 408/7, only to reject the idea as unlikely and uncorroborated by Theopompos, Ephoros, and Xenophon. Whilst this evidence confirms the celebrity of this performer, it locates him in the fifth century and makes it doubtful, once again, whether he could have been a realistic contender at Philip's contest. Furthermore, it raises the disquieting possibility that Douris had a penchant for embellishing fictitious anecdotes with specific names to add an air of verisimilitude.

[St]esikhoros: The *Marmor Parium* (*FGrHist* 239) at epoch 73 records the following: 'From the time when Stesikhoros of Himera took second prize (in a dithyrambic contest) at Athens and Megalopolis was founded [. . .].' The date must be 370/69. Nothing else is known about this poet (see Page (1962): 841), not even his relationship to the better known dithyrambist of the seventh century, also called Stesikhoros of Himera.

Timotheos and Oiniades: If the order is being maintained, we should expect Timotheos to be a flute player and Oiniades a poet. A suitable candidate for Timotheos the flute player does exist, a Theban *auletes* referred to by Khares of Mytilene (*FGrHist* 125 F4) as performing for Alexander at the royal weddings at Sousa in 324. Cf. Foucart (1909): 140; Riginos (1994): 110–11. Unfortunately, no poet of the name Oiniades is attested, though Page accepts Didymos' testimony and assigns him a *Kyklops* (1962: 840). By contrast, a Theban *auletes*, [Oi]niades, son of Pronomos, is known (*IG* ΙΙ² 3064) and Timotheos was the name of a dithyrambic poet, who was as famous as Philoxenos and is known to have written a *Kyklops* (see Page (1962): 777–804, especially 780–1 for the *Kyklops*). So, Foucart's suggestion (1909: 141) that the names have been reversed is not without merit, though it is rejected by Riginos (1994: 111 n. 33).

In sum, on balance, the evidence supports the view that there is no good reason to doubt that a contest of flute players actually took place at Philip's court at some time, and maybe even shortly before the siege of Methone, and that the participants could have been the ones named. On the other hand, the alternative view that, though Douris made some effort to add the appearance of factuality to his narrative (Riginos (1994): 111), he was more concerned with the sensational effect of the 'big name', cannot be entirely ruled out.

his right collarbone (was broken) in Illyria: The reading 'collarbone' (*KΛEIN*) is not universally agreed upon. The papyrus actually has *KNN*, which is meaningless. D-S took that to be an error for *KN⟨HMH⟩N* ('shin') and they have been followed by many (e.g. Ellis (1976): 136, 275 n. 35; Cawkwell (1978): 114; Griffith (1979): 471; Green (1982): 135 n. 16; Sealey (1993): 163), sometimes too categorically. P-S, on the other hand, following Crönert (1907: 387) and Foucart (1909: 142), cf. Heckel (1980: 456 n. 47), take the first *N* as *ΛI* and read *KΛIN*, which becomes *KΛEIN* by iotacism.

Palaeographically, in my opinion, this is the more straightforward interpretation and it has the additional advantage that it agrees with Demosthenes (Riginos (1994): 115, 116 n. 56). Gibson (97) also has 'collarbone'. The reference to 'right collarbone' must mean collarbone on the right-hand side.

This is the second of Philip's wounds in the order given by Demosthenes (18.67). That his list is in chronological order is apparent from the scholion to the passage, which distinguishes the different wounds by place and context: 'Philip had his eye struck (out) at Methone, his collarbone among Illyrians, and his leg and hand among Skythians.' The accepted dates are 355 (or 354) for Methone (see above), 345 for the Illyrian campaign (Cawkwell (1963): 126 f.; Ellis (1976): 136; Griffith (1979): 470; Sealey (1993): 162; contra, Diod. 16.69.7, who puts it under 344/3; cf. Wüst (1938): 54–8; Hammond (1966): 245; Heckel (1992): 8 and 339 for Skythia (see below). There is hardly any elaboration of this anecdote in the later tradition (see Riginos (1994): 115–16).

by a spear: I do not understand Gibson's translation 'in an ambush' here (97).

as he was pursuing the Illyrian Pleuratos: Riginos (1994: 115 n. 54) considers this clause 'admits some ambiguity as to who was charging whom' and, indeed, Gibson (97) translates 'they say that Pleuratus the Illyrian pursued him (and wounded) his right collarbone.' I follow those (e.g. Foucart (1909): 142; Hammond (1966): 245; Griffith (1979): 471) who believe that Philip was the pursuer. In the first place, it is hardly likely that any of Didymos' potential sources for this incident (probably Marsyas of Pella, or perhaps Theopompos; see below) would depict Philip in flight (the idea that this clause was added by an unknown third-century source to glorify the Illyrian royal house (Riginos (1994): 115 n. 54) is not persuasive). More importantly, Didymos is clearly following the structure and syntax of Demosthenes 18.67 here, which has Philip in the accusative as subject of passive verbs with the part of the body affected in the accusative of respect (i.e. 'knocked out as to his eye, broken as to his collarbone . . .'). Didymos' elliptical omission of the verb in the second limb confirms this. Thus, the accusative participle 'pursuing' must modify Philip.

Pleuratos, holder of 'a dynastic name in the royal house of the Ardiaei', (Hammond (1966): 245 and (1979): 22), was the king against whom Philip was waging this campaign (Ellis (1976): 136; Griffith (1979): 469–74), as part of a concerted assault upon Illyria in 345 (Cawkwell (1978): 42, 114) or 344 (Hammond (1994): 115–18 with map). He is not to be confused with the Pleurias, king of the Illyrians (probably the Autariatai, as argued by Hammond (1966): 243–5), against whom Philip was waging a separate campaign shortly before his assassination (Diod. 16.93.6).

one hundred and fifty of his Companions were wounded: This otherwise unrecorded detail is so specific that it must be assumed to come from a knowledgeable source, probably Marsyas of Pella (Foucart (1909): 142; Osborne: 207). I see no reason to believe that Douris was the intermediary, as is suggested by Stähelin (1905: 150); Heckel (1980: 456). Theopompos, who provides us with a vividly negative characterization (Shrimpton (1991): 165–6; Flower (1994): 218–19) of Philip's Companions (*ETAIPOI*), estimated their number at 800 (*FGrHist* 115 F225b). This was probably around the time of this campaign in Illyria (Griffith (1979): 408; Shrimpton (1991): 165), so the casualties were considerable. For a similar reporting of heavy Macedonian casualties see Arrian, 5.24. 5 (with Bosworth (1995): 334).

COLUMN THIRTEEN

Heading: The Heading looks ahead to the discussion of *On Organization*, the twelfth speech for Didymos, our thirteenth, which begins at col. 13. line 14 and continues to the end of the papyrus.

Hippostratos, son of Amyntas, died: That this man could be identified with the brother of Kleopatra, niece of Attalos, Philip's last wife, was recognized right away by Stähelin (1905: 151) and Foucart (1909: 143). Stähelin also saw that he could alternatively be the Hippostratos who was the father of Hegelokhos, one of Alexander's generals. He stated categorically, however, on the basis of Justin 11.5.1, that the two men could not be identical. This has been the accepted position (cf. Osborne: 209) until recently, when Heckel has argued that they were, in fact, the same (1992: 6–12).

his third wound in the assault on the Triballi: Philip was attacked by the Triballi in 339, on his way back to Macedon, laden with booty, from his expedition against the Skythian Ateas, who had been making incursions south of the Danube (see Ellis (1976): 185–6; Griffith (1979): 581–4; Archibald (1998): 237–9). Some ingratitude for his service by the Triballi, who walked off with all the booty! Our only narrative of the campaign in Skythia and its aftermath is Justin's *Epitome* of Pompeios Trogos' *Philippika*, 9.2.1– 9.3.3. The wound is recounted, much as it is in Didymos, in 9.3.2, though Justin adds the nice detail that the spear went through Philip's thigh and killed his horse, while Didymos' source reported that the weapon was a *sarissa* and was able to specify the 'right' thigh. The case has been made that Justin's source was Theopompos (Gardiner-Garden (1989): 29–40; see, however, Flower (1994): 6 n. 19). If this is near the mark, it might suggest that Didymos' source was different; maybe even Marsyas of Pella, again.

one of the men he was pursuing: I take the participle *ΔΙΩΚΟΜΕΝΩΝ* as passive. Others treat it as middle voice (see next note). In that case the translation would be 'one of his men who were in pursuit'.

thrust his sarissa into his right thigh: Didymos is the only authority for the detail that it was Philip's right thigh that was wounded. In fact, as Riginos has shown (1994: 117), there was so much doubt in antiquity about which leg was involved, that the question 'In which leg was Philip lame?' (Plut. *Mor.* 739b) could not be answered. The specification of the weapon as a *sarissa* (a long Macedonian pike) led Foucart (1909: 144–5) to propose that Philip was wounded by one of his own men (see above note). More likely, that detail of terminology gives away the origin of Didymos' source as a Macedonian one (cf. Osborne: 210).

it would seem that Alexander enjoyed better luck ... ten serious wounds: This casual note, comparing the fortunes of Philip and Alexander in relation to their wounds, is interesting for several reasons. First, the use of the formula with the potential optative ('it would seem') suggests that this was Didymos' own opinion (cf. Osborne: 210–11). This is quite likely. As the person who had collected the material on Philip's wounds he was well placed to make the comparison. On the other hand, he did not have to research Alexander's wounds. Clearly, a list of those already existed for him to use, as is indicated by his casual allusion ('he suffered ten serious wounds'). It is likely that that list had been produced by one of his predecessors, as is only to be expected from scholars working in Alexander's city (Alexandria), and it may have ultimately derived from Ptolemy (cf. Arrian, *Anab.* 6.9.10, 6.11.7). But, if Didymos can be credited with the observation that Alexander was 'luckier' in this regard than his father, it does not follow that he was responsible for the idea that he was 'lucky' (in absolute terms) in his wounds. This, I believe, would have been the conclusion advanced by the person(s) who had made a study of his injuries, and would have been part of the tradition that Didymos inherited.

This view may find some corroboration from the fact that, when Plutarch came to compose his two essays *On the Fortune or Virtue of*

Alexander (*Mor.* 326d–345b), in which he defends Alexander against the charge that he was Fortune's favourite, he uses Alexander's wounds, of which he provides a list (ten, in number) at *Mor.* 327a–b (cf. *Mor.* 341a–c; 344c–d), as proof that Fortune (*Tyche*) was his opponent not his ally. In other words, this casual allusion by Didymos shows that Plutarch was working in a well-established tradition rather than that he 'had made a special study of A's wounds' (Hamilton (1969): 156).

Some of Alexander's better attested wounds are: his thigh wound at the battle of Issos in 333 (Arrian, *Anab.* 2.12.1; Diod. 17.34.5; Plut. *Alex.* 20.8; Curt. 3.11.10; Justin 11.9.9); the wound to his shoulder from a catapult missile at the siege of Gaza in 332 (Arrian, *Anab.* 2.27.2; Plut. *Alex.* 35.5; Curt. 4.6.17); the arrow wound that smashed his shin (tibia or fibula?) at the River Jaxartes near Marakanda in 329 (Arrian, *Anab.* 3.30.11; Plut. *Alex.* 45.5; *Mor.* 341d; Curt. 7.6.3); the arrow wound to his ankle at the siege of Massaga in 327 (Arrian, *Anab.* 4.26.4; Plut. *Alex.* 28.3; *Mor.* 341b; Curt. 8.10.28); the arrow in his chest (perhaps accompanied before or after by a blow to the head) that nearly killed him at the town of the Malli in 326 (Arrian, *Anab.* 6.9.10, 6.11.7; Plut. *Alex.* 63.6–9; Diod. 17.99.3; Curt. 9.5.9).

Philip was damaged from head to toe: It was (and still can be), of course, a standard reality for most males, not only in antiquity, to be maimed in war, as several modern studies have emphasized (see e.g. Hanson (1989), Tritle (2000), and, on war and society in general, Raaflaub and Rosenstein (1999)). Often overlooked in these studies, however, are the young women who were married off to these mutilated bodies. Indeed, Philip must have been a most unattractive sight to Kleopatra on their wedding night, and Alexander can hardly have appeared more appealing to Rhoxane.

(Speech) 12: Didymos' text did not include the *Letter from Philip*, speech 12 in some of our manuscripts. In this respect, also, he sides with the tradition represented by S (Parisinus Graecus 2934). See notes to col. 1 at **had heard [the letter]**, p. 114) and col. 9 at **Ph[il]ip himself in his letter** (p. 200). For that reason, *On Organization* is, for him, the twelfth oration, whereas, for us, it is the thirteenth.

'Regarding the revenue at hand . . .': The *lemma* is Dem. 13.1.

And some people include . . . at any rate: As indicated by the Heading, Didymos begins his discussion of this speech by addressing the question whether it is, in fact, a *Philippic*. This is, of course, relevant to him, since this commentary is on the *Philippics*, as is revealed by the title in col. 15. It may seem contradictory, then, for him to include it, since he takes the position that it is not a *Philippic* (as does the author of the *hypothesis*). He has to do so, however, because some (or one) of his predecessors have classified it as such. See note to col. 11 at **culmination of the <u>Philippics</u>**, p. 216. Questions of authenticity, classification, and date were clearly fundamental concerns of Hellenistic scholarship and, consequently, of Didymos.

For there is not any mention . . . the Macedonian was involved in neither case: Didymos' criteria for definiton of a *Philippic*, whilst not the same as ours, are perfectly clear and logical. If a speech was not directed at Philip and his activities or if it failed to mention him, it was not a *Philippic*. It is rather hard to argue with that. Indeed, if this speech was delivered in 353/2 (Cawkwell (1969): 329) or the late 350s (Trevett (1994): 189), as has been maintained (see below), it belongs before the *First Philippic* and so at a time before Demosthenes had recognized the danger of Philip of Macedon. This is precisely the point made by the scholiast at 13.1: 'The date of the speech *On Organization* is not clear, but one could guess that it was spoken before the *Philippics*, since the allies had already revolted and Rhodes was under an oligarchic government, so that all those who classify it with the *Philippics* are entirely ignorant of the fact that it is earlier than the *Philippics*.'

Perinth[os, O]lynthos (and) Poteidaia: Didymos is working backwards: Perinthos was besieged in 341/0, Olynthos was attacked and destroyed in 349/8, Poteidaia was captured in 356/5.

freedom of (the) Rhodians and of (the) Mytilenians: The Rhodians and the Mytilenians were both founding members of the Second Athenian League (Cargill (1981): 25, 32; Harding (1985): no. 35). The Rhodians were part of the group (Khios, Kos, Rhodes) that seceded from the League and, together with Byzantion, fought Athens in the Social War (357–355). They were encouraged to do so by Mausolos of Karia, who subsequently put a garrison on the island (Hornblower (1982): 193 f.). When, in 351 (Ryder (2000): 52), some exiled democrats asked Athens to help 'free' Rhodes and put them back in power, Demosthenes spoke on their behalf (oration 15, *On the Freedom of the Rhodians*). Mytilene left the League sometime after 355 (Cargill (1981): 183), but renewed its alliance with Athens in 346 (*IG* II² 213; Harding (1985): no. 83). Thus, it should not be forgotten that Athens had other concerns in its foreign policy than the threat of Philip of Macedon (see Harding (1995): 105–25), though pursuit of 'the ghost of empire' was hardly one of them (*pace* Badian (1995): 79–105). Demosthenes only became a one-issue politician in 351 with the *First Philippic*.

And, perhaps, . . . Philip: As an elaboration of the argument about the classification of the speech, Didymos raises the issue of date (so, Osborne: 220). He does not discuss the authenticity of this speech, because he clearly did not doubt it ('Demosthenes *composed* this speech'); nor, for that matter, did any other ancient commentator (Trevett (1994): 179–80). Modern scholars have not been so confident. Debate on that issue began in the mid-nineteenth century (Schaefer (1858): iii. 2.89–94) and has been a perennial topic since. The arguments against authenticity were revived most recently by Sealey ((1967): 250–5; (1993): 235–7), who is followed with reservations by Badian (2000: 44 n. 70), but have been adequately refuted by Osborne (211–20) and Trevett (1994: 179–93).

As for the date, Didymos tentatively advances one theory (i.e. that it was after the Peace of Philokrates in 346), only to replace it with another (lines 40 ff.), seemingly without providing reasons for rejecting the first. At least, that is the way it appeared to West (1970: 292), who described the discussion here as 'extraordinarily confused and incoherent' (cf. Körte (1905): 397). Other, more sensitive, commentators have seen the matter in a different light, namely that Didymos was, in the first instance, reporting the theory of a predecessor ('And, perhaps . . .'), whose account also included the passage from 13.7 that belonged with it, and then put forward his own idea, beginning with the clause 'But one could detect . . .' with its give-away usage of the potential optative (Lossau (1964): 88–9). I prefer this approach to Foucart's (1909: 98–9), who thought that Didymos was responsible for both views, only that he felt more confident in the second. His interpretation still finds Didymos guilty of failing to give reasons for rejecting his first idea, whereas, if we follow Lossau, the worst he can be convicted of is deferential courtesy to a predecessor (maybe his teacher). His method is not so unusual; for example, Gibson (132–3) puts forward differing views on this question and leaves me, at any rate, in greater doubt about what he thinks than does Didymos. Osborne (222–3) is unhelpful here, since he misunderstands the meaning of *ΜΗΠΟΤΕ* ('perhaps').

***at a time when*:**   P-S, followed by Gibson (98). D-S's suggestion of 'since/because' is equally acceptable and is preferred by Wankel (1987: 222).

[things] *were* **quiet . . . Macedonian** *front***, but affairs in As[ia]** *kept them very* **busy:**   It is not a tenable hypothesis for anyone who was familiar with Athenian foreign policy after the Peace of Philokrates to maintain that 'things were quiet for the Athenians on the Macedonian front'. The Athenians had plenty of trouble with Philip, in Thrace and Euboia, over Halonnesos, and in the Peloponnese (cf. Griffith (1979): 450–584; Sealey (1993): 160–93). By contrast, Artaxerxes was busy elsewhere, especially in Egypt.

Didymos was well aware of these facts and had written about some of them in this commentary. So, unless we are artificially to create 'negligence', I believe we have to accept that he did not subscribe to this date. Conversely, we might get some insight into the quality of the scholarship he inherited. Unfortunately, his own suggestion is no better (see below). The true date was seen by the scholiast to 13.1 (translated above).

'For if it was sufficient . . . at Rhodes (also)':   The quotation is from 13.7–8. It belongs to the argument of the person who believed that the date of the speech was post-346, though, in fact, the references suit the circumstances of the late 350s better (Trevett (1994): 188). It contributes nothing helpful to the discourse with the manuscript tradition, though it looks as though it agrees with SA on the tense of 'is keeping watch' in line 36.

But one could detect . . . archonship of K[a]llimakhos: This same formula is probably correctly restored at col. 1.29. Kallimakhos of Pergase (*LGPN* p. 249 no. 76) was archon eponymous in 349/8 (*AO* 313). At the beginning of his year in office (to judge from the formula employed) the Athenians made an alliance with the Olynthians, who were under attack by Philip (Philokhoros, *FGrHist* 328 F49; Harding (1985): no.80). For that reason alone, Didymos' date is quite unacceptable, at least in terms of his own argument.

Apollodoros: This man was archon eponymous in 350/49 (*AO* 312). We know neither his patronymic nor his demotic, so that it is not possible to identify him more precisely. Apollodoros was a very popular name at Athens: there are 263 men with that name listed in *LGPN* (pp. 42–4). He is not to be identified with Apollodoros, son of

Pasion, even though he was politically active at this very time (see Trevett (1992): 124–54).

Why, do you suppose?:   A strangely conversational interjection. Osborne suggests that it 'reflects D's knowledge that he has not provided his reader with any foundation for expecting the precision of his dating' (225). It is just as likely that it reflects the fact that Didymos was dictating his commentary to his students, as Foucart envisaged (see Introduction under Didymos).

he mentions the actions . . . Sacred Orgas: At 13.32 Demosthenes points out the discrepancy between Athenian decrees and Athenian actions. As one example of this he refers to the case of the 'cursed Megarians', who were appropriating the Orgas. The Athenians had voted 'to march out, to stop (them), not to allow (it)', but had not followed through with action. For the history of this incident see Harding ((1985): no. 78; (1994): 125–7; Williams (2003): 89–124; Rhodes and Osborne (2003): 272–81). It probably took place over a period of three years from 352/1 to 350/49. The following quotation from Philokhoros narrates the concluding phase. It may well have been the only entry he had on this incident (see Harding (1994): 37–8). Didymos was alert enough to catch the reference and make the connection, which is accepted by all modern commentators. He deserves credit for that, but unfortunately, in making the deduction that the speech had to follow the event, was taken in by the date of the entry and completely failed to notice the disjunction between the historian's account of the *action* of Ephialtes and Demosthenes' point about Athens' failure to act (cf. Jacoby, *Notes*: 424).

recounted by Philokhoros: *FGrHist* 328 F155 (see Jacoby, *Text*:529–31; *Notes*: 424–6). Unusually, Didymos does not provide the precise reference. This fragment fits into the sixth book on Jacoby's reckoning (*Text*: 225–55). Philokhoros is cited for the date of the military action. That Ephialtes' campaign did not take place at the beginning of Apollodoros' year in office can be deduced from the absence of the formula ('in this man's archonship').

the Athenians had a dispute with the Megarians . . . Sacred [O]rgas: The territory involved was land consecrated to the two goddesses at Eleusis, Demeter and Persephone. Like all consecrated land it was not to be used and anyone who infringed upon it was 'cursed' (Williams (2003): 102–9). But, in this case, since it lay near the border between Athens and Megara, it was the subject of contention between them. The Athenians were not above invoking religion in territorial disputes, as they had already over this piece of land in the fifth century before the Peloponnesian War (Thuc. 1.139.2; cf. Williams (2003): 108). On this occasion they may also have managed to secure control of the borderlands (*EΣXATIAI*) which lay outside the Orgas, by fencing them around with *stelai*, after Delphi had declared that it was 'better if they left them un-tilled' (col. 13.54–8; 14.46–9). In fact, some believe that it was these borderlands that the dispute was about (Cawkwell (1969): 330–1; Williams (2003): 107–13; Rhodes and Osborne (2003): no. 58; contra, de Ste. Croix (1972): 388 n. 1).

Ephialtes, the general for the homeguard: This is not a common name at Athens. Only six are listed in *LGPN* (p. 191). Despite the absence of the demotic and patronymic, therefore, it is usual to identify him with the man who later went to Persia in 341/0 and came back with money to use against Philip (Plut. *Mor.* 847f, 848e; *AO* 335), who fought at Khaironeia and was one of those demanded by Alexander in 335 (Arrian, *Anab.* 1.10.4; cf. Bosworth (1980): 93–5; Deinarkhos 1.33; cf. Worthington (1992): 183–4) and who died fighting against Alexander at Halikarnassos (Diod. 17.27.3).

For the 'general for the homeguard' (*ΣTPATHΓOΣ EΠI THN XΩPAN*) see Arist. *Ath. Pol.* 61. 1). Though this position was likely created in the 370s as part of an overhaul of the ephebic system (cf. Harding (1995): 112), the first mention of it is in this very context, both in the fragment from Philokhoros and in *IG* II² 204. 16–20, where this general is one of those specifically detailed to take care of the Orgas (cf. Harding (1985): no. 78A; Rhodes and Osborne (2003):no. 58, p. 278).

Lakrateides the Hierophant and Hierok[l]eides the Dadoukhos: Lakrateides, whom we know from Isaios 7.9, was of the Eumolpidai, while his colleague Hierokleides was from the Kerykes. Both were old and distinguished clans in Attika, which controlled the most important priesthoods at the Eleusinian Mysteries throughout most of the classical period and traced their lineage back into Athens' mythical past (Harding (1994): 82–3). For the position of Hierophant ('revealer of the sacred rite'), the chief priest at Eleusis, see Clinton (1974: 10–46) and for the Dadoukhos ('torch-bearer') see Clinton (1974: 47–68).

sanctuary had responded . . . did not farm (them): For the elaborate process used by the Athenians to consult Apollo at Delphi on this matter, an amazing blend of cynicism and credulity, see *IG* II² 204. 23–54; Harding (1985: no. 78A); Williams (2003: 94–9); Rhodes and Osborne (2003: no. 58).

fenced it/them around with stelai . . . decree of Philokrates: According to Thucydides (1.139.2) this territory was 'not marked by boundary-stones' at the time of the fifth-century dispute that led to the Megarian Decrees. By the time of the decree in *IG* II² 204.65–75, however, markers had been put around the Orgas, as is clear from the reference to some of them being 'dug up'. The stelai referred to here may well have been concerned with enclosing the 'border-lands' (see Williams (2003): 100–13).

In *IG* II² 204. 54–5 there is reference to a 'previous decree, the one of Phi[l]o[k]rate[s regarding the] *holy places*'. Since *IG* II² 204 is dated by archon to 352/1, Philokrates' decree must pre-date that, but probably not by much. The temptation is to identify this Philokrates with Philokrates of Hagnous, the man after whom the Peace of Philokrates of 346 was named, and this may be correct (see below at col. 14. 57), but this was a common name at Athens (there are 195 people listed in *LGPN* 455–6).

it could be . . . speech was composed: For Didymos' mistaken deduction see above under **he mentions the actions** (p. 246). I think there is little question but that the author of the scholion on 13.1 (Dilts (1983–6): i. 163; cf. above under **For there is not any mention**, p. 243) is correct in dating this speech before the *Philippics*. It has all the hallmarks of an immature speech.

preparing in case there should, in fact, be (a war): In the context of the previous discussion, this suggestion is opaque and surprising.

there is found . . . in the (works) before this: Gibson's interpretation (134) of this awkward sentence is surely correct (against Osborne: 226). Didymos is explaining why his commentary on this speech will be so brief. It remains obscure whether he is saying that there is nothing in this speech that has not been mentioned in previous 'speeches' of Demosthenes or in previous 'commentaries' by himself. I think, with Gibson, that the latter is more likely, especially in light of the following sentence.

COLUMN FOURTEEN

Heading: Two issues are indicated in the Heading. One, on the Orgas, is really a continuation of the previous topic and, consequently, does not merit a *lemma*. The second looks ahead to lines 49–53, where the relevant passage from Dem. 13.32 is quoted.

Nevertheless, a brief clarification of the Orgas should be given: Both Gibson (134), for the reason given above, and Osborne (227), because this phrase reminds him of the one used at col. 12.42–3 where Didymos introduced his abbreviated version of his previous work on Philip's wounds, argue persuasively that Didymos is here summarizing his own research that he has presented elsewhere. Whether that is the case or whether he is rather presenting this research for the first time, there is no reason to believe that it is not entirely his own work. The specific citations and the range of authors referenced fit in with the character and scope of his known works (see Introduction under Didymos) and confirm his interest in etymology. Unfortunately, he must also accept responsibility for the lack of coherence in the organization of his thoughts.

Well, the term 'Orgas' . . . like a grove: Definitions of the area denoted by the word 'Orgas' were not lacking in antiquity nor are they today. The entry in LSJ (s.v. *OPΓAΣ*) describes it as a well-watered, fertile land or meadow, while the ancient lexicographers (Harpokration, the Souda, Photios, all with entries under *OPΓAΣ*) mention, together with its fertility, its overgrown and wooded aspect, resulting from the absence of cultivation. All this was, of course, known to Didymos, who begins his discussion of the 'common' usage of the term with a passing nod to this definition.

The word is formed on the basis of (the verb) . . . : Didymos attempts something more ambitious than definition, by trying to find the root meaning of the concept. His conclusion, that the word is derived from the verb signifying 'growing' or 'ripening', is accepted today (see e.g. Chantraine (1968–80): iii. 815–16 'être plein de suc'; Frisk (1955–72): ii. 411), though now the root is traced beyond the denominative verb to the noun $\dot{o}\rho\gamma\dot{\eta}$ and a number of associated words, involving ideas of passion. We might observe a felicitous combination of these ideas in Byzantine Greek, where the word $\dot{o}\rho\gamma\dot{a}s$ denoted a girl ripe for marriage (Chantraine (1968–80): iii. 816).

people are in the habit . . . impulse toward anything: The basic meaning is in this way generalized, in preparation for the discussion to follow.

for example, in everyday life we say . . . :   As a transition to the examples he will offer of the 'common' usage of the word, Didymos cites an everyday usage of a related word (ὀργάζω, 'knead', 'soften'). His example turns out to be 'as clear as mud', as we say. The first part of it is recognizable as the phrase for preparing mortar (clay) for making, joining, or plastering bricks, as in Aristophanes, *Birds* 839, 1140–7. But the concluding word (*ΑΛΟΙΦΑΣ*) most naturally translates as 'unguents' or 'ointment' (as in Gibson: 99). That does not seem the right sense here. My own translation adopts the meaning 'anointing' (LSJ s.v. *ΑΛΟΙΦΗ* II).

Lines 10–23:   Didymos illustrates the usage of the word (first the verb, then the noun, finally related parallels) with quotations from Sophokles, Aiskhylos, Homer, and an unnamed poet, who may be Euphorion. The passages are largely unknown and, quoted out of context, are difficult to interpret and even to translate.

Sophokles in [Sheph]erds: Radt (1977: F510). D-S, followed by P-S, restore the title as that of the known play *Shepherds*. Radt (ad loc.), whilst listing this with the fragments of that play, raises the question whether the title could actually be that of another known work by Sophokles, *Prophets*, which would fit the space just as well.
   Everything about the fragment is in doubt, from the punctuation to the text. My translation is based upon the punctuation in P-S, who have a comma after the first word, but it should be noted that neither D-S nor Radt have any punctuation in the line. The third word, which P-S read as the particle *ΔE* ('but' or 'and'), is restored as *ΔH* ('indeed', 'in fact') by Buecheler and Radt (rightly, I think), and as *ΔEI* ('it is necessary') by D-S. Amidst all this doubt enough of the first word is extant to make certain that it is a third person singular imperfect (Gibson's translation 'I have mixed' (99) cannot be correct) and the phrase 'softening (or 'kneading') mortar' is beyond question, which makes Osborne's assertion 'the line is clearly referring to the earth swelling (with moisture?) in preparation for bearing fruit' (228) unlikely.

And Aiskhy[l]os, over the corpses . . . :   This fragment is confidently assigned to Aiskhylos' *Eleusinians* by Mette (1959: F269), on the basis of Plut. *Theseus* 29.4–5. In its case the meaning is clear.

And people are in the habit . . . growth in length: One has to sympathize with Gibson, who elected to leave all the key words in this sentence untranslated (99) and restrict his commentary to identification of the author of the verse (134–5). Osborne (229) more boldly suggests that Didymos is now moving on to show that the term ὀργάς 'can signify that which grows on a given area of ground and not just the soil itself'. At the very least, we would have to say that Didymos is 'stretching things'. This is certainly true of the quotation, whose relevance to the argument is tenuous at best.

Nevertheless, there is unanimity in accepting Wilamowitz's identification (1926: 289–91) of the author as the abstruse, but influential, third-century poet, Euphorion of Khalkis (cf. Lloyd-Jones and Parsons (1983): 232, where this is fragment no. 453, not 454 as in P-S and Gibson: 99, 135). There is less agreement, however, about his restoration of the final word of the line as Mounippos, son of Killa (Hekabe's sister) by Priam. The papyrus reads *MYNEIT*[. . .], which could be Mounitos, son of Laodike, daughter of Priam and Hekabe (cf. Lloyd-Jones and Parsons (1983): 232).

Similar . . . in Homer: The quotation is from *Iliad* 18.56 (repeated at 18.437). Didymos has now moved beyond his immediate topic to parallel examples of other words exhibiting similar characteristics. So, Akhilleus' being likened to a young plant (i.e. growing thing) causes him to think of the word 'sapling', which was derived, so he believed, from the verb 'to begin to move'. Movement and growth are the connections.

the more common usage of the word 'orgas' . . . idiomatically as a name: Having dealt with the word as a 'common noun', Didymos extends his enquiry into its use as a 'proper noun', which is, of course, the usage that is pertinent to our context.

Lines 23–31:   Several instances are proffered of words that have both a general meaning and a specific application as a name. They require little comment, except to note that Didymos appears to have given a different account about Ida in his commentary on the *Iliad* (Schmidt (1854): 180–1; Osborne: 230–1; Gibson: 135) than he does here. There he provides the more obvious explanation that the name is derived from the act of 'seeing' (ἰδεῖν). The text of line 28 is corrupt, reading *E*(or*A*)*KTHΣATTIKHΣ*.

Gibson (99 n. 32) prefers to adopt the restoration of D-S (cf. Wankel (1987): 222), ⟨*AKTE*⟩ *H TE THΣ ATTIKHΣ*, because it

preserves the format of the series, but P-S's suggestion *H AKTH*
⟨TH⟩Σ ATTIKHΣ is palaeographically more satisfactory and,
in any case, the format is not strictly adhered to. Finally, Rhion
must be identified with the Molykrian Rhion of Thucydides 2.86.2,
which was situated on the northern shore of the Corinthian Gulf,
opposite another place of the same name in Akhaia. Mo[l]y[k]reion
is located hypothetically by the Barrington Atlas (55 B4) as a peak
on a spur of the Taphiassos mountain.

**And the speech of De[m]osthene[s] . . . about the Megar-
ian Orga[s]:**   Finally, Didymos brings the discussion back to the
point. In the case of the reference to 'Orgas' in oration 13, Demosthenes is using it as a proper noun.

even Kallimakhos has mentioned somewhere: As is obvious from the preceding, signs of haste are everywhere in this concluding section of the papyrus. Typical is this imprecise reference to
his famous predecessor. The carelessness must originate with Didymos (not our copyist), since it is embedded in the (dis-)organization
of the presentation. One has the feeling (see below on Androtion)
that Didymos was impatient to be done with this work, so that he
could get on to the next. But, the citation, which is listed as fragment 495 by Pfeiffer (1949: 367) and assigned tentatively to the *Hekale* (following Wilamowitz), is not 'merely decorative' (Gibson: 135).
It provides a specific example of the word 'Orgas' used as a proper
noun in a different context from the one under discussion and, incidentally, tells us something that we did not know, namely that there
was clearly a place with this designation on the Megarian side of the
border as well, though it could not have been consecrated, if it was
famous for its garlic.

And[r]otion, too . . . in the seventh (book) of the Atthides:
FGrHist 324 F30 (cf. Jacoby, *Text*: 142–3; *Notes*: 131; Harding (1994):
125–7; Williams (2003) 89–124). For the Atthidographer, Androtion,
see the Introduction under Sources. Didymos concludes his discussion of the Sacred Orgas, almost as though he were employing ring
composition, by recapitulating the information he had given before
from Philokhoros (col. 13.47–58) in almost precisely the same form
in this quotation from Androtion, who was himself the source of
Philokhoros' account (Jacoby, *Text*: 143, 530–1; Harding (1994):
37–8, 125). Why did he do this? Osborne (232–7) has attempted to
justify what seems to be a redundant citation by a close comparison

of the two texts, from which he concludes that Androtion's account emphasized the religious aspect of the incident, while Philokhoros was more interested in the military and political details. It was for this reason, he argues, that Didymos introduced this second quotation. Gibson (135) finds this 'ingenious', but not persuasive. I agree and would add that the absence of the military details is explained by the fact that the quotation begins at a later point in the narrative and that one would hardly expect Philokhoros, who was a seer and a diviner, to have downplayed the religious connotations. But Osborne is surely right on one point, that Jacoby's dictum that Didymos did not consult (or cite) Androtion directly, but took the quotation from a collection of material on the ὀργάς (Jacoby, *Text*: 142), is quite unfounded (Osborne: 233). There is no difference in the way this citation is introduced from the practice in other cases and, indeed, the reference here is more precise than for Philokhoros above.

But it does look as though Didymos has repeated himself. For his critics this is a sign of careless or clumsy redundancy, that he 'has evidently looked up his lexicographical files and reproduced the information which he found there without dovetailing it to its present context' (West (1970): 293). A more sympathetic view would consider it completeness, little different, for example, from a modern scholar adding a further reference under the rubric 'cf.'. And to talk of lexicographical files is probably anachronistic. Much of what Didymos produced was, I imagine, done from memory. And if, as he was dictating his text, he thought of a relevant reference too late, he could not scroll back the screen or cut and paste. Gibson is altogether more understanding of the process (135). Nevertheless, elsewhere Didymos was surprisingly competent at organizing his thoughts in a coherent fashion, so this last-minute addition must be taken as a further sign of haste and eagerness to finish.

Text: There are many signs of sloppiness in the transcription of this passage. These can hardly be blamed upon Didymos, but must be attributed to the scribe of the papyrus. In line 41 the papyrus has the participle *ΟΡΙΣΑΝΤΕΣ* and has 'the hierophant' in the genitive plural. In the next line Lakrateides' name is misspelled and *ΔΑΙΔΟΥΧΟΣ* has become *ΔΑΙΔΡΟΥΧΟΣ*. These small errors are simple to correct, not least from the text of Philokhoros. More importantly, from the first editors onward (i.e. both D-S and P-S), scholars have felt that there was something missing in line 39 and have been disconcerted by the use of the optative *ΒΟΥΛΟΙΝΤΟ*.

Recently, however, Wankel (1987: 222) has defended the text as it stands, and he has been followed by Gibson. My translation adopts his interpretation.

'Just like the motions . . . not to allow (it)': The *lemma* is from 13.32. Textually, in line 51 the papyrus has a reading *ΔΙΕΞΙΕΝΑΙ*, which is in disagreement with all the manuscripts.

He called the Megarians accursed . . . ill-disposed towards the Athenians: I find this the most disappointing note in the whole papyrus. It is disconcerting to think that a man who has just finished a lengthy discussion of the Sacred Orgas, in which he had included passages from both Philokhoros and Androtion that narrated the religious background to the conflict, should not have recognized the obvious reason why an Athenian at this time (cf. Dem. 23.212) would have called the Megarians 'accursed' (cf. Parker (1983): 160–6; Williams (2003): 105–11). It is true, as Osborne (237) points out, that Demosthenes was rather free in his usage of the word 'accursed' (κατάρατος), employing it of Aiskhines (at 18.209, 244, 290), of Timokrates (24.107, 198), of his attackers (18.322) or political opponents (23.201), and of Euboians (19.75), none of whom can be said to have incurred the wrath of the gods. But Didymos was not explicating those passages. The specificity of the *lemma* at this point calls for something more explicit than a generalized explanation that the Megarians and Boiotians were 'ill-disposed' to the Athenians. This, of course, is the term used in the quotation from Philokrates, given below, and one cannot escape the feeling that Didymos' memory was prompted, by the mention of Philokrates' name at the end of the passage from Androtion, to remember a speech attributed to him in Theopompos and that, when he only found this general charge of ill-will in it, he engineered the transition to justify including the inapposite quotation.

Theopompos attests in the 26th (book): *FGrHist* 115 F164. Jacoby assigns this fragment to the negotiations for the Peace of Philokrates of 346, as he does for F166 (discussed above at col. 8.60–4), which contains a supposed speech of Aristophon in reply. See Shrimpton (1991: 84–5) for a recreation of the relationship of the two speeches to each other. He sees them as a rhetorical *antilogia*, which provides 'a precious glimpse at Theopompos' summing up of Athens' desperate situation'.

the demagogue Philokrates: This man must be the Philokrates, son of Pythodoros of Hagnous, after whom is named the peace with Philip of Macedon of 346. Didymos assumes that he is the same as the Philokrates involved with delimitation of the Orgas. He may be correct. They are listed as two separate people by Kirchner (*PA* no. 14599, the ambassador; no. 14576, the proposer). They are tentatively identified as the same person by Develin (*AO* 296, xv, xvi; 310, i, ii; 317, ii; 320–1, v, xii, xiii, xvii, in all cases as a proposer). *LGPN* 455 no. 76 treats them as the same (cf. Whitehead (2000): 235). If this identification is correct, his political activity stretched from the Orgas incident in 353/2, via a prosecution for unconstitutional procedure (*graphe paranomon*) in 348/7, in which he was defended by Demosthenes (Aiskh. 2.13–15, 20, 109; 3.62; Dein. 1.28; cf. Hansen (1974): 34) to his self-imposed exile in 343, after he had been indicted by Hypereides through *eisangelia* for accepting bribes in the negotiations for the peace treaty (Dem. 19.114, 116, 119, 145–6, 245; Aiskh. 2.6; 3.79–81; Hypereides, *For Euxenippos* 29). Cf. Sealey (1993): 144–5, 147–9, 163, 175.

Col. 14.58–col. 15.10: 'So, consider . . . with Ph[i]lip': This speech was undoubtedly created by Theopompos (see above). In it he put into Philokrates' mouth words that he thought were appropriate. To what extent they represent what Philokrates actually said in the debate in the Assembly over the peace negotiations we cannot tell. Of course, this speech is quite unrelated to anything Philokrates said in proposing his decree for the Orgas. One presumes (hopes?) that Didymos knew that. He might have felt less uncomfortable about citing it out of context, because his date for *On Organization* (349/8) is closer to the Peace than has been argued here.

COLUMN FIFTEEN

Column 15 has no heading, because all it contains is the continuation of the speech of Philokrates.

DIDYMOS' ON DEMOSTHENES 28 OF THE PHILIPPICS

3: For the debate over the interpretation and significance of this subscript see the Introduction under The Papyrus and Commentary or Monograph?

9–12: The first words of the opening lines of each of the four speeches commented upon in this scroll of papyrus are given as a conclusion, to indicate to any future reader (or for the benefit of the person who was making this copy) what is contained. Gibson (103) maintains that the copyist added the numbers before the *lemmata*, because 'there is no evidence that Didymos himself ever referred to Demosthenes' speeches by number'. This is an argument from silence and I do not find it conclusive (see above at col. 1.26 **And because I consider**, p. 108).

REFERENCES

All texts of ancient authors are cited by standard editions, unless otherwise indicated.

ARCHIBALD, Z. H. (1998), *The Odrysian Kingdom of Thrace* (Oxford).

ARRIGHETTI, G. (1977), '*Hypomnemata* e *scholia*: Alcuni problemi', in *Museum Philologum Londiniense* (Uithoorn), 2: 49–67.

AUSTIN, C. (1973), *Comicorum Graecorum Fragmenta in Papyris reperta* (Berlin and New York).

BADIAN, E. (1961), 'Harpalus', *Journal of Hellenic Studies* 81: 16–43.

——(1991), 'The King's Peace', in M. A. Flower and M. Toher (eds.), *Georgica: Greek Studies in Honour of George Cawkwell* (*Institute of Classical Studies*, Bulletin Supplement 58, London): 25–48.

——(1995), 'The Ghost of Empire: Reflections on Athenian Foreign Policy in the Fourth Century BC', in W. Eder (ed.), *Die athenische Demokratie im 4. Jahrhundert v. Chr.* (Stuttgart): 79–105.

——(2000), 'The Road to Prominence', in I. Worthington (ed.), *Demosthenes: Statesman and Orator* (London and New York): 9–44.

BAKHUIZEN, S. C. (1989), 'The Ethnos of the Boeotians', in H. Beister and J. Buckler (eds.), *BOIOTIKA: Vorträge vom 5. internationalem Böotien-Koloquium* (Munich): 65–72.

BARBIERI, G. (1955), *Conone* (Rome).

BAUMAN, R. A. (1990), *Political Trials in Ancient Greece* (London and New York).

BEARZOT, C. (1985), *Focione tra storia e trasfigurazione ideale* (Milan).

BERTHOLD, R. M. (1984), *Rhodes in the Hellenistic Age* (Ithaca, NY).

BERVE, H. (1925–6), *Das Alexanderreich auf prosopographischer Grundlage*, 2 vols. (Munich).

BLASS, F. (1882), 'Neue Papyrusfragmente in Aegyptischen Museum zu Berlin. ii. Lexikon zu Demosthenes' *Aristokratea*', *Hermes* 17: 148–63.

——(1906), 'Literarische Texte mit Ausschluss der Christlichen', *Archiv für Papyrusforschung* 3: 284–92.

BLIQUEZ, L. (1969), 'Anthemocritus and the ὀργάς Disputes', *Greek, Roman and Byzantine Studies* 10: 157–61.

——(1972), 'A Note on the Didymus Papyrus XII. 35', *Classical Journal* 67: 356–7.

BOARDMAN, J. (1995), *Greek Sculpture: The Late Classical Period* (London and New York).

BOGAERT, R. (1968), *Banques et Banquiers dans les Cités grecques* (Leiden).

BOISACQ, E. (1938), *Dictionnaire étymologique de la langue grècque*, 3rd edn. (Heidelberg).

BOLLANSÉE, J. (1999), *Hermippos of Smyrna and his Biographical Writings (Studia Hellenistica* 35, Leiden).

—— (1996*b*), *Die Fragmente der griechischen Historiker*, IVa. 3: *Hermippos of Smyrna* (Leiden).

—— (2001), 'Aristotle and the Death of Hermias of Atarneus: Two Extracts from Hermippos' Monograph *On Aristotle*', *Simblos* 3: 67–98.

BÖMER, F. (1953), 'Der Commentarius', *Hermes* 81: 210–50.

BOSWORTH, A. B. (1980), *A Historical Commentary on Arrian's History of Alexander*, vol. 1 (Oxford).

—— (1995), *A Historical Commentary on Arrian's History of Alexander*, vol. 2 (Oxford).

—— (1997), 'The Emasculation of the Calchedonians: A Forgotten Episode of the Ionian War', *Chiron* 27: 297–313.

—— (2002), 'Vespasian and the Slave Trade', *Classical Quarterly* 52: 350–7.

BOUSQUET, J. (1991), 'Inscriptions de Delphes', *Bulletin de Correspondance Hellénique* 115: 167–81.

BOWRA, C. M. (1938), 'Aristotle's Hymn to Virtue', *Classical Quarterly* 32: 182–9.

BRIANT, P. (2002), *From Cyrus to Alexander: A History of the Persian Empire*, trans. P. T. Daniels (Winona Lake, Ind.).

—— (2003), *Darius dans l'ombre d'Alexandre* (Paris).

BRINGMANN, K. (1965), *Studien zu den politischen Ideen des Isokrates (Hypomnemata* 14, Göttingen).

BRUCE, I. A. F. (1966), 'Athenian Embassies in the Early Fourth Century BC', *Historia* 15: 272–81.

—— (1967), *An Historical Commentary on the Hellenica Oxyrhynchia* (Cambridge).

—— (2001), 'Philochoros on the King's Peace', in M. Joyal (ed.), *In Altum: Seventy-five Years of Classical Studies in Newfoundland* (St John's): 57–62.

BRUNT, P. A. (1969), 'Euboea in the Time of Philip II', *Classical Quarterly* 19: 245–65.

—— (1993), 'Plato's Academy and Politics', in P. A. Brunt, *Studies in Greek History and Thought* (Oxford): 282–342.

BUCHANAN, J. (1962), *Theorika* (New York).

BUCK, R. J. (1979), *A History of Boeotia* (Edmonton).

BUCKLER, J. (1980), *The Theban Hegemony* (Cambridge, Mass.).

—— (1989), *Philip II and the Sacred War (Mnemosyne* Suppl. 109, Leiden, New York, Copenhagen, Cologne).

—— (1994), 'Philip II, the Greeks, and the King 346–336 BC', *Illinois Classical Studies* 19: 99–122.

—— (1996), 'Philip II's Designs on Greece', in R. W. Wallace and E. M. Harris (eds.), *Transitions to Empire: Essays in Greco-Roman History, 360–146 BC, in honor of E. Badian* (Norman and London): 77–97.

BURKE, E. M. (1984), 'Eubulus, Olynthus, and Euboea', *Transactions of the American Philological Association* 114: 111–20.

BURKE, E. M. (1985), 'Lycurgan Finances', *Greek, Roman and Byzantine Studies* 26: 251– 64.

CAMERON, A. (2004), *Greek Mythography in the Roman World* (Oxford).

CANFORA, L. (1968), *Per la Chronologia di Demostene* (Bari).

CARGILL, J. (1981), *The Second Athenian League* (Berkeley and Los Angeles).

CARTLEDGE, P. (1987), *Agesilaos and the Crisis of Sparta* (London).

CAWKWELL, G. L. (1963), 'Demosthenes' Policy after the Peace of Philocrates', *Classical Quarterly* 13: 120–38 (Part I) and 200–13 (Part II).

——(1963*b*), 'Euboulos', *Journal of Hellenic Studies* 83: 47–67.

——(1969), 'Anthemocritus and the Megarians and the Decree of Charinus', *Revue des études grecques* 82: 327–35.

——(1976), 'The Imperialism of Thrasybulus', *Classical Quarterly* 26: 270–7.

——(1978), *Philip of Macedon* (London and Boston).

——(1978*b*), 'Euboea in the Late 340s', *Phoenix* 32: 42–67.

——(1981), 'The King's Peace', *Classical Quarterly* 31: 69–83.

——(1996), 'The End of Greek Liberty', in R. W. Wallace and E. H. Harris (eds.), *Transitions to Empire: Essays in Greco-Roman History, 360–146 BC, in honor of E. Badian* (Norman and London): 98–121.

CHANTRAINE, P. (1968–80), *Dictionnaire étymologique de la langue grecque: histoire des mots*, 4 vols. (Paris).

CHROUST, A.-H. (1972), 'Aristotle's Sojourn in Assos', *Historia* 21: 170–6.

CLARKE, J. T. (1882), *Report on the Excavations at Assos, 1881* (Boston).

——(1898), *Report on the Excavations at Assos, 1882, 1883*, Pt. I (New York).

——(1902–21), *Investigations at Assos: Drawings and Photographs of the Buildings and Objects Discovered during the Excavations of 1881–1882–1883* (Cambridge, Mass.).

CLINTON, K. (1974), *The Sacred Officials of the Eleusinian Mysteries* (Philadelphia).

CONOMIS, N. C. (1975), *Deinarchi Orationes cum Fragmentis* (Leipzig).

CONSTANTINIDES, E. (1969), 'Timokles' *Ikarioi Satyroi*: A Reconsideration', *Transactions of the American Philological Association* 100: 49–61.

COOK, J. M. (1973), *The Troad* (Oxford).

COOPER, C. (1992), 'The Development of the Biographical Tradition of the Athenian Orators during the Hellenistic Period' (Diss. Univ. of British Columbia, Vancouver).

CRÖNERT, W. (1907), 'Neue Lesungen des Didymospapyrus', *Rheinisches Museum* 62: 380–9.

——(1907*b*), Review of P. Wendland, *Anaximenes* in *Göttinische Gelehrte Anzeigen*: 267–76.

DAITZ, S. G. (1957), 'The Relationship of the *De Chersoneso* and the *Philippica Quarta* of Demosthenes', *Classical Philology* 52: 145–62.

DE STE. CROIX, G. E. M. (1972), *The Origins of the Peloponnesian War* (London).

DEVOTO, J. G. (1986), 'Agesilaus, Antalcidas and the Failed Peace of 392/91 BC', *Classical Philology* 81: 191–202.

DILKE, O. A. W. (1985), *Greek and Roman Maps* (Ithaca, NY).

DILTS, M. R. (1983–6), *Scholia Demosthenica*, 2 vols. (Leipzig).

——(1992), *Scholia in Aiskhinem* (Stuttgart and Leipzig).

DINDORF, W. (ed.) (1853), *Harpocrationis Lexicon in Decem Oratores Atticos*, 2 vols. (Oxford).

DOUGLAS, A. E. (1966), Review of M. Lossau, *Untersuchungen zur antiken Demosthenesexegese* in *Journal of Hellenic Studies* 86: 190–1.

DOVER, K. J. (1968), *Lysias and the* Corpus Lysiacum (Berkeley and Los Angeles).

——(1993), *Aristophanes Frogs* (Oxford).

DUNBAR, N. (1995), *Aristophanes Birds* (Oxford).

DÜRING, I. (1957), *Aristotle in the Ancient Biographical Tradition* (Göteburg).

DUSANIC, S. (1999), 'Isocrates and the Political Context of the *Euthydemus*', *Journal of Hellenic Studies* 119: 1–16.

EDMONDS, J. M. (1957–61), *The Fragments of Attic Comedy after Meineke, Bergk, and Köck*, 3 vols. (Leiden).

ELLIS, J. R. (1976), *Philip II and Macedonian Imperialism* (London).

ENGELMANN, H. and MERKELBACH, R. (1972), *Die Inschriften von Erythrai und Klazomenai* (Bonn).

ERRINGTON, R. M. (1981), 'Review-Discussion: Four Interpretations of Philip II', *American Journal of Ancient History* 6: 69–88.

ESCHBACH, N. (1986), *Statuen auf panathenäischen Preisamphoren des 4. Jhrs. v. Chr.* (Mainz).

FLORIAN, W. (1908), *Studia Didymea Historica ad Saeculum quartum pertinentia* (Diss. Leipzig).

FLOWER, M. (1994), *Theopompus of Chios* (Oxford).

FORNARA, C. W. (1982), *Archaic Times to the End of the Peloponnesian War*, 2nd edn. (Cambridge).

——(1983), *The Nature of History in Ancient Greece and Rome* (Berkeley, Los Angeles, and London).

FOUCART, M. P. (1909), 'Étude sur Didymos d' après un papyrus de Berlin', *Mémoires de L' Institut National de France. Académie des Inscriptions et Belles-Lettres* 38: 27–218.

FRISK, H. (1955–72), *Griechisches etymologisches Wörterbuch*, 3 vols. (Heidelberg).

FUHR, K. (1904), Review of H. Diels and W. Schubart (eds.), *Didymos: Kommentar zu Demosthenes* (*Berliner Klassikertexte* I, Berlin) and *Didymi de Demosthene commenta* (*Volumina Aegyptiaca* IV, Leipzig) in *Berliner philologische Wochenschrift* 24: 1123–31.

——(1910), 'Demosthenica I', *Berliner philologische Wochenschrift* 30: 1142–3.

GAISER, K. (1985), *Theophrast in Assos* (Heidelberg).

——(1988), *Philodems Academica* (*Supplementum Platonicum* I, Stuttgart-Bad Cannstatt).

GARDINER-GARDEN, J. (1989), 'Ateas and Theopompus', *Journal of Hellenic Studies* 109: 29–40.

GEHRKE, H.-J. (1976), *Phokion* (*Zetemata* 64, Munich).

GIBSON, C. A. (1997), 'P. Berol. inv. 5008, Didymus, and Harpocration Reconsidered', *Classical Philology* 92: 375–81.

——(2000), 'The Critical Note above Col. 12 of the Didymus Papyrus (P. Berol. Inv. 9780)', *Zeitschrift für Papyrologie und Epigraphik* 132: 148.

——(2001), 'An Amphictyonic Decree, Aristotle, and the Scythians: A Crux in Didymus' Commentary on Demosthenes', *Greek, Roman and Byzantine Studies* 42: 43–56.

GIGNAC, F. T. (1976), *A Grammar of the Greek Papyri of the Roman and Byzantine Periods*, 2 vols. (Milan).

GIGON, O. (ed.) (1987), *Aristotelis Opera: Volumen Tertium, Librorum deperditorum Fragmenta* (Berlin and New York).

GOLDEN, M. (1998), *Sport and Society in Ancient Greece* (Cambridge).

GOW, A. S. F. and PAGE, D. L. (1965), *The Greek Anthology*, 2 vols. (Cambridge).

GREEN, P. (1982), 'The Royal Tombs at Vergina: A Historical Analysis', in W. L. Adams and E. N. Borza (eds.), *Philip II, Alexander the Great and the Macedonian Heritage* (Washington, DC).

GRIFFITH, G. T. (1979), 'The Reign of Philip the Second', in N. G. L. Hammond and G. T. Griffith, *A History of Macedonia*, vol. II (Oxford).

GROTE, G. (1862), *A History of Greece*, rev. edn., 8 vols. (London).

GUTHRIE, W. K. C. (1975), *A History of Greek Philosophy*, vol. 4 (Cambridge).

——(1978), *A History of Greek Philosophy*, vol. 5 (Cambridge).

——(1981), *A History of Greek Philosophy*, vol. 6 (Cambridge).

HABICHT, C. (1999), *Athens from Alexander to Antony*, trans. D. Schneider (Cambridge, Mass. and London).

HAJDU, I. (2002), *Kommentar zur 4. Philippischen Rede des Demosthenes* (Berlin and New York).

HAMILTON, C. D. (1979), *Sparta's Bitter Victories* (Ithaca, NY).

——(1991), *Agesilaus and the Failure of the Spartan Hegemony* (Ithaca, NY).

HAMILTON, J. R. (1969), *Plutarch, Alexander: A Commentary* (Oxford).

HAMMOND, N. G. L. (1966), 'The Kingdoms in Illyria *circa* 400–167 BC', *Annual of the British School at Athens* 61: 239–53.

——(1979), 'The Development of the Macedonian State and the Struggle for Survival', in N. G. L. Hammond and G. T. Griffith, *A History of Macedonia*, vol. 2 (Oxford).

——(1993), 'Philip's *Letter* to Athens in 340 BC', *Antichthon* 27: 13–20.

——(1994), *Philip of Macedon* (London).

HANSEN, M. H. (1974), *The Sovereignty of the People's Court in Athens in the Fourth Century BC and the Public Action against Unconstitutional Proposals* (*Odense University Classical Studies* 4, Odense).

HANSEN, M. H. (1976), 'The Theoric Fund and the *Graphe Paranomon* against Apollodorus', *Greek, Roman and Byzantine Studies* 17: 235–46.

HANSON, V. D. (1989), *The Western Way of War: Infantry Battle in Classical Greece* (New York).

HARDING, P. (1974), 'Androtion's View of Solon's *Seisachtheia*', *Phoenix* 28: 282–9.

——(1976), 'Androtion's Political Career', *Historia* 25: 186–200.

——(1985), *From the End of the Peloponnesian War to the Battle of Ipsus* (Cambridge).

——(1987), 'Rhetoric and Politics in Fourth-Century Athens', *Phoenix* 41: 25–39.

——(1988), 'Athenian Defensive Strategy in the Fourth Century', *Phoenix* 42: 61–71.

——(1994), *Androtion and the* Atthis (Oxford).

——(1994*b*), 'Comedy and Rhetoric', in I. Worthington (ed.), *Persuasion* (London), 196–221.

——(1995), 'Athenian Foreign Policy in the Fourth Century', *Klio* 77: 105–25.

——(2000), 'Demosthenes in the Underworld: A Chapter in the *Nachleben* of a *rhetor*', in I. Worthington (ed.), *Demosthenes: Statesman and Orator* (London and New York), 246–71.

HARRIS, E. M. (1989), 'More Chalcenteric Negligence', *Classical Philology* 84: 36–44.

——(1995), *Aiskhines and Athenian Politics* (Oxford and New York).

——(1996), 'Demosthenes and the Theoric Fund', in R. W. Wallace and E. M. Harris (eds.), *Transitions to Empire: Essays in Greco-Roman History, 360–146 BC, in honor of E. Badian* (Norman and London): 57–76.

HAUSMANN, B. ([1921], 1978), *Demosthenis fragmenta in papyris et membranis servata* (diss. Leipzig, 1921), reproduced, with an appendix of new discoveries by P. Mertens, by R. Pintaudi (ed.) in *Papyrologica Florentina* 4 (Florence, 1978).

HECKEL, W. (1980), 'Marsyas of Pella, Historian of Macedon', *Hermes* 108, 444–62.

——(1984), *Quintus Curtius Rufus: The History of Alexander*, trans. J. Yardley, with Introduction and Notes by W. Heckel (Harmondsworth).

——(1992), *The Marshals of Alexander's Empire* (London and New York).

HENRY, A. (1983), *Honours and Privileges in Athenian Decrees: The Principal Formulae of Athenian Honorary Decrees* (Hildesheim).

HERMAN, G. (1987), *Ritualised Friendship and the Greek City* (Cambridge).

HOFSTETTER, J. (1978), *Die Griechen in Persien: Prosopographie der Griechen im persischen Reich vor Alexander* (Berlin).

HORNBLOWER, S. (1982), *Mausolus* (Oxford).

HUBBELL, H. M. (1957), 'A Papyrus Commentary on Demosthenes', *Yale Classical Studies* 15, 181–93.

IRMER, D. (1961), *Zum Primat des Codex S in der Demostheneskritik* (Diss. Hamburg).

——(1968), 'Beobachtungen zur Demosthenesüberlieferung', *Philologus* 112: 43–62.

IRMER, D. (1972), *Zur Genealogie der jungeren Demostheneshandschriften* (*Hamburger philologische Studien* 20, Hamburg).

JAEGER, W. (1948), *Aristotle: Fundamentals of the History of his Development*, trans. R. Robinson, 2nd edn. (Oxford).

JEHNE, M. (1994), *Koine Eirene: Untersuchungen zu den Befriedungs-und Stabilisierungsbemühungen in der griechischen Poliswelt des 4. Jahrhunderts v. Chr.* (*Hermes*, Einzelschriften 63, Stuttgart).

JUDEICH, W. (1892), *Kleinasiatische Studien: Untersuchungen zur griechisch-persischen Geschichte des IV Jahrhunderts v. Chr.* (Marburg).

KASSEL, R. and AUSTIN, C. (eds.) (1983–), *Poetae Comici Graecae*, 9 vols. (Berlin and New York).

KEBRIC, R. B. (1977), *In the Shadow of Macedon: Duris of Samos* (*Historia*, Einzelschriften 29, Wiesbaden).

KEEN, A. G. (1995), 'A 'Confused' Passage of Philochoros (F149a) and the Peace of 392/1', *Historia* 44: 1–10.

——(1998), 'Philochoros F149A and B: A Further Note', *Historia* 47: 375–8.

KEIL, B. (1902), *Anonymus Argentinensis: Fragmente zur Geschichte des perikleischen Athen aus einem Strassburger Papyrus* (Strassburg).

KIENAST, D. (1973), *Philipp II. von Macedonien und das Reich der Achamieniden* (Munich).

KNELL, H. (2000), *Athen im 4. Jahrhundert v. Chr.—Eine Stadt verändert ihr Gesicht* (Darmstadt).

KÖRTE, A. (1905), 'Zu Didymos' Demosthenes-Commentar', *Rheinisches Museum* 60: 388–416.

——(1906), 'Anaximenes von Lampsakos als Alexanderhistoriker', *Rheinisches Museum* 61: 476–80.

KUNZ, K. (1923), *Rhetorische Papyri* (*Berliner Klassikertexte*, Heft 7, Berlin).

LAMBRIANIDES, K., SPENCER, N., VARDAR, S. and GÜMÜS, H. (1996), 'The Madra Çay Delta Archaeological Project: First Preliminary Report', *Anatolian Studies* 46: 167–200.

LANE FOX, R. (1973), *Alexander the Great* (London).

——(1986), 'Theopompus of Chios and the Greek World, 411–322 BC', in J. Boardman and C. E. Vaphopoulou-Richardson (eds.), *CHIOS: A Conference at the Homereion in Chios, 1984* (Oxford).

——(1997), 'Demosthenes, Dionysius and the Dating of Six Early Speeches', *Classica et Mediaevalia* 48: 167–203.

LEAF, W. (1923), *Strabo on the Troad* (Cambridge).

LEFÈVRE, F. (1998), *L'Amphictionie pyléo-delphique: Histoire et Institutions* (Paris).

LELAND, T. (trans.) (1806), *The Orations of Demosthenes, Pronounced to Excite the Athenians against Philip, King of Macedon*, 2nd edn., 2 vols. (London).

LENCHANTIN DE GUBERNATIS, M. (1921), 'Frammenti didimei di Filocoro', *Aegyptus* 2: 23–32.

LEO, F. (1904), 'Didymos *ΠΕΡΙ ΔΗΜΟΣΘΕΝΟΥΣ*', *Nachrichten von der Königlichen Gesellschaft der Wissenschaften zu Göttingen, philologisch-historische*

Klasse, 254–61 in *Ausgewählte kleine Schriften*, II (Rome, 1960): 387–94.

LEUTSCH, E. L. and SCHNEIDEWIN, F. G. (eds.) (1839–51), *Paroemiographi Graeci*, 2 vols. (Göttingen), with a suppl. by L. Cohn (Breslau, 1887).

LEWIS, D. M. (1977), *Sparta and Persia* (Leiden).

——(1997), 'On the Dating of Demosthenes' Speeches', in P. J. Rhodes (ed.), *Selected Papers in Greek and Near Eastern History by David M. Lewis* (Cambridge): 230–51.

LLOYD-JONES, H. and PARSONS, P. (1983), *Supplementum Hellenisticum* (Berlin and New York).

LONDEY, P. (1990), 'The Outbreak of the 4th Sacred War', *Chiron* 20: 239–60.

LOSSAU, M. (1964), *Untersuchungen zur antiken Demosthenesexegese* (*Palingenesia* II, Bad Homburg).

MACDOWELL, D. M. (1962), *Andocides: On the Mysteries* (Oxford).

——(2000), *Demosthenes: On the False Embassy (Oration 19)* (Oxford).

MACHER, E. (1914), *Der Hermiasepisode im Demostheneskommentar des Didymos* (Lundenburg).

McNAMEE, K. (1992), *Sigla and Select Marginalia in Greek Literary Papyri* (*Papyrologica Bruxellensia* 26, Brussels).

MAEHLER, H. (1992), 'Der Streit um den Schatten des Esels', in A. H. S. El-Mosalamy (ed.), *Proceedings of the XIXth International Congress of Papyrology*, vol. 1 (Cairo): 625–33

MARKLE, M. M. (1976), 'Support of Athenian Intellectuals for Philip: A Study of Isocrates' *Philippus* and Speusippos' *Letter to Philip*', *Journal of Hellenic Studies* 96: 80–99.

MARSDEN, E. W. (1969), *Greek and Roman Artillery: Historical Development* (Oxford).

MATTHIEU, G. (1947), *Démosthène: Plaidoyers politiques*, vol. 4 (Paris).

MAYSER, E. (1906–70), *Grammatik der griechischen Papyri aus der Ptolemäerzeit*, 2 vols. (Leipzig and Berlin).

METTE, H. I. (1959), *Die Fragmente der Tragödien des Aischylos* (Berlin).

MILLETT, P. (1991), *Lending and Borrowing in Ancient Athens* (Cambridge, New York, Melbourne, Sydney, and Port Chester).

MILNS, R. D. (1987), 'Hermias of Atarneus and the Fourth Philippic Speech', in C. Questa (ed.), *Filologia e forme letterarie: Studi offerti a Francesco Della Corte*, vol. 1: 287–302.

——(1994), 'Didymea', in I. Worthington (ed.), *Ventures into Greek History* (Oxford): 70–88.

MISSIOU-LADI, A. (1992), *The Subversive Oratory of Andokides* (Cambridge, New York, and Melbourne)

MITFORD, W. (1838), *A History of Greece*, 3rd edn. rev., 8 vols. (London).

MOSCATI CASTELNUOVO, L. (1980), 'La carriera politica dell' Attidografo Androzione', *Acme* 33: 251–78.

MOSLEY, D. J. (1973), *Envoys and Diplomacy in Ancient Greece* (*Historia*, Einzelschriften 22, Wiesbaden).

MRAS, K. (ed.) (1983), *Eusebius Werke*, vol. 8: *Die Praeparatio Evangelica* (Berlin).

MULVANY, C. M. (1926), 'Notes on the Legend of Aristotle', *Classical Quarterly* 20: 153–67.

NAOUMIDES, M. (1969), 'The Fragments of Greek Lexicography in the Papyri', in *Classical Studies presented to Ben Edwin Perry* (Urbana, Chicago, and London): 181–202.

OWEN, G. E. L. (1983), 'Philosophical Invective', *Oxford Studies in Ancient Philosophy* 1: 1–25.

PACK, R. A. (1965), *The Greek and Latin Literary Texts from Greco-Roman Egypt*, 2nd edn. (Ann Arbor).

PAGE, D. L. (1941), *Select Papyri*, vol. 3 (London and Cambridge, Mass.).

—— (1962), *Poetae Melici Graeci* (Oxford).

—— (1968), *Lyrica Graeca Selecta* (Oxford).

—— (1975), *Epigrammata Graeca* (Oxford).

PARKE, H. W. (1933), *Greek Mercenary Soldiers* (Oxford).

PARKER, R. (1983), *Miasma: Pollution and Purification in Early Greek Religion* (Oxford).

—— (1986), 'Khares Angelethen' (Diss. Univ. of British Columbia, Vancouver).

PEARSON, L. (1960), *The Lost Histories of Alexander the Great* (Philadelphia and New York).

—— (1976), *The Art of Demosthenes* (Meisenheim am Glan).

PERETTI, A. (1979), *Il Periplo di Scilace* (Pisa).

PFEIFFER, R. (ed.) (1949), *Callimachus*, vol. I, *Fragmenta* (Oxford).

—— (1968), *A History of Classical Scholarship: From the Beginnings to the End of the Hellenistic Age* (Oxford).

POHLENZ, M. (1929), 'Philipps Schreiben an Athen', *Hermes* 64: 41–62.

PORALLA, P. ([1913], 1985), *Prosopographie der Lakedaimonier bis auf die Zeit Alexanders des Grossen* (Breslau, 1913), rev. edn. by A. S. Bradford (Chicago, 1985).

POTTER, D. S. (1999), *Literary Texts and the Roman Historian* (London and New York).

POWNALL, F. S. (1995), '*Presbeis Autokratores*: Andocides' *De Pace*', *Phoenix* 49: 140–9.

PRITCHETT, W. K. P. (1971), *Ancient Greek Military Practices: Part I* (Berkeley, Los Angeles, and London).

RAAFLAUB, K. and ROSENSTEIN, N. (eds.) (1999), *War and Society in the Ancient and Medieval Worlds* (Cambridge, Mass. and London).

RADT, S. L. (ed.) (1977), *Tragicorum Graecorum Fragmenta*, vol. 4, *Sophoclis Fragmenta* (Göttingen).

RENEHAN, R. (1982), 'Aristotle as Lyric Poet: The Hermias Poem', *Greek, Roman and Byzantine Studies* 23: 251–74.

RHODES, P. J. (1981), *A Commentary on the Aristotelian* Athenaion Politeia (Oxford).

RHODES, P. J. with Lewis, D. M. (1997), *The Decrees of the Greek States* (Oxford).

——and OSBORNE, R. (eds.) (2003), *Greek Historical Inscriptions 404–323 BC* (Oxford).

RIDGWAY, B. S. (1997), *Fourth-Century Styles in Greek Sculpture* (Madison).

RIGINOS, A. S. (1994), 'The Wounding of Philip II of Macedon: Fact and Fabrication', *Journal of Hellenic Studies* 114: 103–19.

RIGSBY, K. (1998), 'Geographical Readings', *Epigraphica Anatolica* 30: 137–41.

ROUGEMONT, C. (1977), *Corpus des Inscriptions de Delphes*, vol. 1: *Lois sacrées et Règlements religieux* (Paris).

RUNIA, D. T. (1986), 'Theocritus of Chios' Epigram against Aristotle', *Classical Quarterly* 36: 531–4.

RUSTEN, J. (1987), Review of L. Pearson and S. Stephens, *Didymi in Demosthenem Commenta* (Stuttgart, 1983) in *Classical Philology* 82: 265–9.

RUTHERFORD, I. (2001), *Pindar's Paeans: A Reading of the Fragments with a Survey of the Genre* (Oxford).

RYDER, T. T. B. (1965), *Koine Eirene* (London, New York, and Toronto).

——(2000), 'Demosthenes and Philip II', in I. Worthington (ed.), *Demosthenes: Statesman and Orator* (London and New York): 45–89.

SCHACHTER, A. (1985), 'Kadmos and the Implications of the Tradition for Boiotian History', in G. Argoud and P. Roesch (eds.), *La Béotie antique* (Paris).

SCHAEFER, A. (1885–7), *Demosthenes und seine Zeit*, 2nd edn., 3 vols. but vol. 3.2 only in 1st edn. (1858) (Leipzig).

SCHMIDT, M. (ed.) (1854), *Didymi Chalcenteri Grammatici Alexandrini Fragmenta* (Leipzig).

SCHNEIDER, C. (1967–9), *Kultur-Geschichte des Hellenismus*, 2 vols. (Munich).

SCHUBART, W. (1911), *Papyri Graecae Berolinenses* (Bonn).

——(1918), *Einführung in die Papyruskunde* (Berlin).

——(1925), *Griechische Palaeographie* in *Handbuch der Altertumswissenschaft*, vol. 1. 4 (Munich).

SEAGER, R. (1967), 'Thrasybulus, Conon and Athenian Imperialism, 396–386 BC', *Journal of Hellenic Studies* 87: 95–115.

SEAGER, R. and TUPLIN, C. J. (1980), 'The Freedom of the Greeks in Asia', *Journal of Hellenic Studies* 100: 141–54.

SEALEY, R. (1955), 'Dionysius of Halicarnassus and some Demosthenic Dates', *Revue des études grecques* 68: 77–120.

——(1955*b*), 'Athens after the Social War', *Journal of Hellenic Studies* 75: 74–81.

——(1956), 'Callistratus of Aphidna and his Contemporaries', *Historia* 5: 178–203.

——(1967), *Essays in Greek Politics* (New York).

——(1978), 'Philipp II. und Athen, 334/3 und 339', *Historia* 27: 295–316.

——(1993), *Demosthenes and his Time* (Oxford).

SEIDLER, R. (1970), *Paläographie der griechischen Papyri*, vol. 2 (Stuttgart).

SHRIMPTON, G. (1991), *Theopompus the Historian* (Montreal, Kingston, London, and Buffalo).

SKYDSGAARD, J. E. (1968), *Varro the Scholar: Studies in the First Book of Varro's 'De Re Rustica'* (Hafniae).

SMITH, R. M. (1995), 'A New Look at the Canon of the Ten Attic Orators', *Mnemosyne* 48: 66–79.

SMYTH, H. W. (1956), *Greek Grammar*, rev. G. Lessing (Cambridge, Mass.).

STÄHELIN, F. (1905), 'Die griechischen Historiker-Fragmente bei Didymos', *Klio* 5: 141–54.

STAUBER, J. (1996), *Die Bucht von Adramytteion*, 2 vols. (Bonn).

STRAUSS, B. (1986), *Athens after the Peloponnesian War* (Ithaca, NY).

STROUD, R. S. (1998), *The Athenian Grain-Tax Law of 374/3 BC* (*Hesperia* Supplement 29, Princeton).

STYLIANOU, P. J. (1998), *A Historical Commentary on Diodorus Siculus, Book 15* (Oxford).

SUTTON, D. F. (1983), 'Dithyramb as δρᾶμα: Philoxenus of Cythera's *Cyclops or Galatea*', *Quaderni Urbinati di Cultura Classica* 13: 37–41.

THOMPSON, W. E. (1974), 'Tot Atheniensibus idem nomen erat . . .', in D. W. Bradeen and M. F. McGregor (eds.), *Phoros: Tribute to Benjamin Dean Meritt* (New York): 144–9.

——(1978), 'The Athenian Investor', *Rivista di Storia Classica* 26: 403–23.

TRAMPEDACH, K. (1994), *Platon, die Akademie und die Zeitgenössische Politik* (*Hermes*, Einzelschriften 66, Stuttgart).

TREVETT, J. (1992), *Apollodorus the Son of Pasion* (Oxford).

——(1994), 'Demosthenes' Speech *On Organization*', *Greek, Roman and Byzantine Studies* 35: 179–93.

——(1999), 'Demosthenes and Thebes', *Historia* 48: 184–202.

TRITLE, L. (1981), 'Phokion Phokou Potamios?', *American Journal of Ancient History* 6: 118–32.

——(1988), *Phokion the Good* (London, New York, and Sydney).

——(2000), *From Melos to My Lai: Violence, Culture, and Survival* (London and New York).

TURNER, E. G. (1968), *Greek Papyri* (Oxford).

URBAN, R. (1991), *Der Königsfrieden von 387/86 v. Chr.* (*Historia*, Einzelschriften 68, Wiesbaden).

VARINLUOGLU, E. (1981), 'Inscriptions from Erythrai', *Zeitschrift für Papyrologie und Epigraphik* 44: 45–50

WADE-GERY, H. T. and MERITT, B. D. (1957), 'Athenian Resources in 449 and 431 BC', *Hesperia* 26: 163–97.

WAGNER, J. T. (1905), *Symbolarum ad Comicorum Graecorum Historiam criticam capita quattuor* (Diss. Leipzig).

WALBANK, F. W. (1960), 'History and Tragedy', *Historia* 9: 216–34.

WANKEL, H. (1976), *Demosthenes: Rede für Ktesiphon über den Kranz*, 2 vols. (Heidelberg).

WANKEL, H. (1987), Review of L. Pearson and S. Stephens (eds.), *Didymi in Demosthenem Commenta* (Stuttgart, 1983), in *Gnomon* 59: 213–23.

WEHRLI, F. (1974), *Hermippos der Kallimacheer* (Basel and Stuttgart).

WEIL, H. (1883–6), *Les Plaidoyers politiques de Démosthène*, 2nd edn., 2 vols. (Paris).

——(1912), *Les Harangues de Démosthène* (Paris).

WEISKOPF, M. (1989), *The So-called 'Great Satraps' Revolt, 366–360 BC*, (*Historia*, Einzelschriften 63, Wiesbaden).

WENDLAND, P. (1904), 'Die Schriftstellerei des Anaximenes', *Hermes* 39: 419–43, 499–542.

——((1905), *Anaximenes von Lampsakos* (Berlin).

WEST, S. (1970), 'Chalcenteric Negligence', *Classical Quarterly* 20: 288–96.

WHITEHEAD, D. (1979), 'Ant⟨i⟩alkidas, or, the Case of the Intrusive Iota', *Liverpool Classical Monthly* 4: 191–3.

——(1983), 'Competitive Outlay and Community Profit: Φιλοτιμία in Democratic Athens', *Classica et Mediaevalia* 34: 55–74.

——(1986). 'The Political Career of Aristophon', *Classical Philology* 81: 313–19.

——(2000), *Hypereides: The Forensic Speeches* (Oxford).

WILAMOWITZ-MOELLENDORFF, U. VON (1893), *Aristoteles und Athen* (Berlin).

——(1926), 'Lesefrüchte', *Hermes* 61: 289–91.

WILCKEN, U. (1907), 'Der Anonymus Argentinensis', *Hermes* 42: 374–418.

——(1920), 'Die Subskription des Didymus-Papyrus', *Hermes* 55: 324–5.

WILSON, C. H. (1970), 'Athenian Military Finances, 378/7 to the Peace of 375', *Athenaeum* 58: 302–26.

WILLIAMS, A. L. (2003), 'Sacred Land in Classical Athens' (Diss. Univ. of British Columbia, Vancouver).

WORMELL, D. E. (1935), 'The Literary Tradition concerning Hermias of Atarneus', *Yale Classical Studies* 5: 57–92.

WORTHINGTON, I. (1991), 'The Authenticity of Demosthenes' Fourth *Philippic*', *Mnemosyne* 44: 425–8.

——(1992), *A Historical Commentary on Dinarchus: Rhetoric and Conspiracy in Later Fourth-Century Athens* (Ann Arbor).

WÜST, F. R. (1938), *Philipp II von Makedonien und Griechenland in den Jahren von 346 bis 338* (Munich).

YUNIS, H. (1997), 'What Kind of Commentary is the περὶ Δημοσθένους of Didymus?', *Archiv für Papyrusforschung* 3: 1049–55.

INDEX OF PASSAGES CITED

Sections of the papyrus have not been indexed

GENERAL INDEX

The following words have not been indexed, because they are so pervasive: Didymos, Demosthenes, Philip II of Macedon. In addition, note that no attempt has been made in the index to indicate restored or partly restored words or names.